GEORGE WOODCOCK

The Century That Made Us

CANADA 1814–1914

Toronto
Oxford University Press
1989

Oxford University Press, 70 Wynford Drive, Don Mills, Ontario, M3C 1J9

Toronto Oxford New York Delhi Bombay Calcutta Madras Karachi
Petaling Jaya Singapore Hong Kong Tokyo Nairobi Dar es Salaam
Cape Town Melbourne Auckland

and associated companies in
Berlin Ibadan

FOR SARAH McALPINE

CANADIAN CATALOGUING IN PUBLICATION DATA
Woodcock, George, 1912-
The century that made us
Bibliography: p.
Includes index.
ISBN 0-19-540703-2
1. Canada—Social conditions—19th century.
2. Canada—Social conditions—1867-1918.*
3. Nationalism—Canada—History.   I. Title.
HN103.W66 1989   971.05   C89-093334-0

Contents

Illustrations iv

Introduction v

1. The War of 1812: Actuality and Myth 1

2. Canada in 1814 16

3. Gentlemen and Others: Class in Canada 26

4. The Radical Thesis: Rebellion and Reform 57

5. The Tory Antithesis: Nationalism and Imperialism 88

6. Pioneers! O, Pioneers! The Roles of Women 114

7. The Noble Chieftain: Myth and Reality 138

8. Neighbours and Strangers 168

9. Entering the Land 196

10. The Visual Imagination and the Mystique of the Land 220

11. The Liberation of the Literary Imagination 242

Epilogue 266

A List of Sources 267

Index 275

Illustrations

HEADPIECES

Page 1. Sir James Dennis (engraved by Thomas Sutherland), *The Battle of Queenston, October 13th, 1812*, 1836. Metropolitan Toronto Library, T 14987.

Page 16. George Williams, *Plan of Town of York, 1813*. National Map Collection, National Archives of Canada, 22819 (H2/440).

Page 26. *King Street East, 1834, Toronto, showing the Jail, the Court House, and St James' Church* (though the spire was not erected until 1836). Engraving after the drawing by Thomas Young.

Page 57. *The Shooting of Colonel Moodie in front of Montgomery's Tavern, December 1837*. From Charles Lindsey, *The Life and Times of Wm. Lyon Mackenzie*, 1863.

Page 88. Lucius O'Brien, *A Division Court at Mono Mills, Simcoe County, Ontario*, 1855. John Ross Robertson Collection (3345), Metropolitan Toronto Library.

Page 114. W.T. Smedley, *Interior of a Settler's Cabin*. From *Picturesque Canada*, p. 296.

Page 138. Peter Rindisbacher, *A War Party at Fort Douglas discharging their Guns in the Air as a token of their peaceable Intentions*. Watercolour and ink, 1825. Royal Ontario Museum, 1466 (951.87.3).

Page 168. W.J. Topley, *Immigrants Arriving at Quebec*, c. 1911. National Archives of Canada, C-5655.

Page 196. R.A. Sproule, *View of Montreal from St Helen's Island, 1830*, showing different types of travel by water. National Archives of Canada.

Page 220. W.G.R. Hind, *The Leather Pass, Rocky Mountains*, 1862. Watercolour. McCord Museum of Canadian History, Montreal. M472.

Page 242. F.B. Schell, *Grand Pré, and Basin of Minas, from Wolfville*. From *Picturesque Canada*, facing page 789.

ILLUSTRATIONS IN CHAPTER 10

Page 222. James Pattison Cockburn, *The Lower City of Quebec from the Parapet of the Upper City*, 1833. Colour aquatint. Metropolitan Toronto Library, John Ross Robertson Collection (88).

Page 224. Paul Kane, *Boat Encampment*. Watercolour on paper. Courtesy Stark Museum of Art, Orange, Texas.

B.F. Baltzly, *Making Portage of Canoes over the bluff at the Upper Gate of Murchison's Rapids, in the North Thompson River, B.C., 7 November 1871*. National Archives of Canada, 22618.

Page 230. James Wilson Morrice, *Winter Street with Horses and Sleighs*, c. 1905. Oil on panel. Art Gallery of Ontario, 55/21.

Page 233. Lucius O'Brien, *Wagon Road on the Fraser*, 1887. Watercolour. National Gallery of Canada, 14580.

Page 238. Homer Watson, *Log-cutting in the Woods*, 1894. Oil on canvas. The Montreal Museum of Fine Arts, 927.427.

Page 241. Tom Thomson, *Parry Sound Harbour*, 1914. Oil on board. National Gallery of Canada, 4664.

Introduction

The century this book addresses is the period of exactly a hundred years that is bracketed by two of the three wars of prime importance to Canadians. The first was the War of 1812 to 1814 that Britain and the United States fought largely on Canadian soil. In world terms, and in the broader context of the Napoleonic wars, it was a small localized affair, but to Canadians it was of great and real importance in preserving the integrity of their territory and the survival of their embryonic culture, and it acquired an added mythic importance to many Canadians, since in a successful defence they perceived the first manifestation of their identity as a nation.

The century that followed was abruptly and dramatically terminated by the Great War in 1914, which began three months less than a century after the Treaty of Ghent brought an end to North American hostilities in December 1814. It was the century of what has sometimes been called the Pax Britannica, when wars—if not abolished—were at least restricted, so that the Crimean War and the Franco-Prussian War did not spread into world conflicts or even continental conflicts like the wars of the French Revolution and the Napoleonic Empire. During that period Canada was involved in four small insurrections, and a few Canadians fought abroad in the little wars of the British Empire. But these events had none of the cataclysmic quality of major wars or revolutions. They merely contributed in various ways to the evolutionary pattern of reform and steady change that characterized Canadian society, like many other societies, during the long Victorian era and the briefer Edwardian reign that together occupied more than three quarters of the century that is discussed.

Yet evolutionary processes can in the long run have revolutionary effects; gradual change can result over a century in shifts as dramatic as those achieved in a shorter time by brief but intense periods of international or national conflict. Compared with the two thinly populated provinces, with their settlements along the St Lawrence and Lake Ontario, that Canada comprised in 1814, the Canada of 1914 was in area one of the largest countries in the world, stretching over a continent and united by an immense network of transport and communication. It had moved through political changes that by the Great War had taken it far on the road towards independence. Its original, relatively simple racial mixture of native people, French, and British had become so variegated that a multicultural and pluralist society already existed in fact, even if these terms were unknown. It was an actively changing society, in which both women and working people showed a growing militancy, and in which literature and the arts were emerging from the cocoon of colonialism and developing new ways of observing and reflecting society and the land. Technological changes had been vast, from the birchbark canoe to the first aeroplanes, from water power to electrical power, from the mail coach to wireless telegraphy.

This book is a study of the changing attitudes among Canadians that underlay and accompanied such political, social, and technological changes. It is not a chronological history but a series of essays, related though discontinuous, that study changing viewpoints, and changing concepts of the Canadian world and of human society within it. I have concentrated on a number of specific aspects of Canadian society and culture. The first two chapters discuss the importance of the War of 1812-14 in actual and mythic terms as an opening to the period, and describe the state of Canadian society at the end of the war. The next three chapters are closely related, discussing the changing nature of class relations in Canada, and relating them to the dual political trends of the century: the radical trend leading through rebellion to reform, and the Tory trend that in the nineteenth century took on the peculiar form of a nationalism that sought its fulfilment through a broadened imperialism. In the next three chapters I discuss the evolution of attitudes towards submerged groups in Canadian society, notably women and native peoples, and the relationship between the numerically dominant British and French, and the other ethnic elements that later entered the Canadian population. In the final three chapters I turn towards more narrowly cultural concerns by showing how, with the geographical extension of the Dominion and the building of the great railways, a mystique of the land developed that led Canadian writers and painters towards a genuine Canadian tradition based on the recognition of the special nature of the northern environment and of human experience within it.

These essays do not of course claim to provide a complete survey of Canadian society and culture during the century that made them. Religion and education; the press and performing arts; popular culture, including entertainment, sports, work patterns, and domestic life; and the voluntary institutions of mutual aid that were so important before the rise of the welfare state—our century offers a rich field for discussion in all these areas that await, and deserve, treatment in a second volume (which has already taken shape in my mind).

In view of the recent battles in Canada between academic and 'popular' historians, I should make my own attitude clear. I regard what I write as serious non-academic history. Much that passes in Canada these days for 'popular' history is spoilt by a pseudo-epic manner and an attempt to isolate certain individuals in the historic process and give them a hollow appearance of heroic quality. Even academic historians occasionally fail in this way, as Donald Creighton did in his adulatory life of Sir John A. Macdonald. Sharing Tolstoy's view of the negative role of 'Great Men' in history, I have no desire to emulate writing of this kind, which in my view gives a false, even if a gratifying, view of our past. This is not to say, however, that I have neglected to take account of the individual, or of his or her voice. I have drawn heavily from contemporary writings, the many quotations from which give first-hand experiences and observations, and imaginative interpretations of them, a significant place in these discussions.

Yet, having served time in the academies, I have learnt how far, in the vain pursuit of a narrow literalism, history as an art has been betrayed by *soi-disant* scholars in the foolish hope of turning it into a science. History depends on the imagination to make sense of the formless chaos of the past; and on the crafts of literature to communicate its truths to people outside the learned societies. The ancients understood this when they gave history a muse, Clio, and we can say with justification that any writing not acceptable as literature is also not in the full sense history, since it has lost the power of speech. Academic writers who cultivate obscurity by writing a jargon-ridden patois, thus hiding their insights in forests of statistics and fact—blinding themselves to symbols and larger meanings—may be chroniclers of a kind, but they are not, in the sense of Herodotus or Thucydides, of Gibbon or Buckhardt or Toynbee, the kind of true historian whose perceptions far outlive their time.

One final word about my approach. In this work intended mainly for the general reader I have chosen not to include the footnotes or bibliographical apparatus—save a long list of sources at the end—that in the world of scholarly publishing documents and draws attention to the minutiae of research. Wishing to engage interest in my ideas and impressions rather than in my research, I have preferred instead to encourage the reader to make a personal exploration of my sources.

1

The War of 1812:
Actuality and Myth

The War of 1812 was a small conflict that started with a sea quarrel between two nations—the United Kingdom and the United States—in whose histories it plays a distinctly minor role. For the most part it took place away from their soils in a territory one of them claimed to possess and the other coveted. It was fought largely by the people of the two Canadas themselves, serving beside the British regulars commanded by General Isaac Brock and the Indian tribesmen led by the great Shawnee chief Tecumseh. In Canadian history the war is therefore a major event. The beginning of a sense of Canada as a living community, united in sentiment and experience, is often traced to it.

That war has in fact moved out of military history to become one of the great myths of Canada as a nation, and its metamorphosis runs parallel to the development of Canadian nationalist sentiments. With one exception it did not become a subject of literature or serious historical study until at least a generation after it had been brought to an end with the acceptance of the *status quo ante*. Apart from Robert Christie's *The Military and Naval Operations in the Late War with the United States*, which appeared in 1818, the main literary by-products of the war in the early years were ballads that largely celebrated General Brock. Brock soon became a popular hero whose exploits were surrounded by a growing body of legend, and the ballads had a notable anti-American flavour:

> There was a bold commander, brave General Brock by name,
> Took shipping at Niagara and down to York he came,
> He says, 'My gallant heroes, if you'll come along with me,
> We'll fight those proud Yankees in the West of Canadee.'

The sole example of genuine literature relating to the War before the 1840s was John Richardson's Byronic poem, *Tecumseh; or, The Warrior of the West* (1828), which was less an expression of the patriotic implications of 1812 than a bathetic celebration of Tecumseh as the noble savage. The poem was thus a counterpart to Richardson's study of the variant forms of the white man's baseness in his novel *Wacousta; or The Prophecy*, which appeared four years later. In the 1840s and 1850s, after the 1837 rebellions had caused a patriotic reaction, Canadian writers all at once became interested in the events of 1812-14. Some who had taken part began to write about them. Others began to see in those events—and in their participants—the makings of a national myth.

John Richardson returned to the days of his youth, when he had fought and been taken prisoner as a teenager, for his sequel to *Wacousta* about the war, *The Canadian Brothers; or, The Prophecy Fulfilled*, which appeared in 1840. He followed this with a serialized and idiosyncratic history, *The War of 1812*, published between 1841 and 1842 in his own paper, *The New Era: or the Canadian Chronicle*, and in 1842 in book form; and between 1843 and 1844 he published a new weekly that he called *The Canadian Loyalist and Spirit of 1812*. Shortly afterwards, in the *Literary Garland* between June and November 1847, William ('Tiger') Dunlop published his 'Recollections of the American War, 1812-14'.

In the next decade the war became the subject of deepening patriotic sentiment as events began to move towards Confederation. The idea of a nation from ocean to ocean was emerging even in the minds of journalists on distant Vancouver Island, where in 1860 Amor de Cosmos was calling for 'a British American policy to put an end to disjointed provinces'. A typical literary expression of national ideas afoot at the time is the poem—'Brock: October 13th, 1859'—Charles Sangster wrote in 1859 to celebrate the dedication of a monument on Queenston Heights to Sir Isaac Brock, which replaced the original one that had been defaced by the rebels in 1837. The idea of the war as a uniting event in Canadian history, and the sense of a continuity with those who fought it, emerges from the first resonant verse:

> One voice, one people, one in heart
> And soul, and feeling, and desire!
> Re-light the smouldering martial fire,
> Sound the mute trumpet, strike the lyre,

> The hero deed can not expire.
> The dead still play their part.

A later verse selects Brock from among those who died at Queenston Heights as the particular hero of the war:

> No tongue need blazon forth their fame—
> The cheers that stir the sacred hill
> And but mere promptings of the will
> That conquered then, that conquers still;
> And generations yet shall thrill
> At Brock's remembered name.

And at the end Brock enters fully into myth as one of 'the Hesperides' (here mysteriously changed in sex) who are sent by heaven to 'guard the golden age' and are described in a final absurdly Sangsterian stanza.

> Each in his lofty sphere sublime
> Sits crowned above the common throng,
> Wrestling with some Pythonic wrong,
> In prayer, in thunder, thought or song;
> Briareus-limbed, they sweep along,
> The Typhons of the time.

The myth of 1812 as the true birth-time of the Canadian nation gained its sanctification and perhaps its most ambitious literary expression in the hands of the proto-nationalists of Canada First, and especially of Charles Mair, whose flawed but often eloquent drama, *Tecumseh*, appeared in 1886. *Tecumseh* was the final result of many years' thought about the loose and insecure assemblage of colonial territories that had been put together under the British North America Act of 1867, and about its ultimate destiny. Like all his associates among the original Canada First group of the 1860s, Mair had long looked back on the War of 1812 as a crucial time in Canadian history. Following John Richardson, and anticipating later generations, he found in Tecumseh and Brock Canadian heroes of mythical dimensions.

As early as 1868, around the time of his meeting with George Denison and the other Canada Firsters, Mair had published in *Dreamland* a poem entitled 'Prologue to Tecumseh' in which he talked of the Indian chief as one of the 'brave of yore' whose 'mem'ries haunt adown the wid'ning years,/ Still teazing us from quiet into tears'. Apart from showing Mair's special preoccupation with the period of the 1812 war, it also suggests that in 1868, long before *Tecumseh*'s completion and publication in 1886, he was already thinking of giving the story of the Indian leader the form of a closet drama, as opposed to the mock-epic form previously adopted by Richardson.

A decade after that, in the very year of 1878 when Sir John A. Macdonald launched the National Policy and much that Canada First had fought for seemed on the edge of fulfilment, Mair confided to Denison: 'I dream of taking up the character of Tecumseh and making something of it; it is a noble subject.' The drama itself, on which he worked intermittently from 1878, played a role in the development of national myth that took its origins from the War of 1812.

In January 1884, writing one of many letters encouraging Mair in his efforts, Denison described the war as 'the grandest period of our national history' and went on to assert that:

> . . . the capture of Detroit saved us as a people, made us what we are today, and years hence when we are both gone, if it pleases God to give our Native Land a position among the great nations of the earth and free from the United States—even if in connection with our mother country— the people of Canada will look back to Brock and Tecumseh and the capture of Detroit as being inseparably linked with our birth as a nation.

Mair himself, writing a preface to a later edition of *Tecumseh* (*Tecumseh and Other Poems*, 1901), talked of the war as 'the turning point of Canada's destiny', and wrote as if 'the courage and vigor of the Canadian people of both races' were among the main reasons why 'the invaders were at last everywhere discomfited, and at its close had been driven to a man from Canadian soil', though he also said that it was the 'transcendent ability and the self-sacrifice' of Tecumseh and his great counterpart Brock that reflected 'in the clearest light the spirit and springs of action which have made Canada what she is.'

Here we have a salutary myth whose relevance to our view of Canada as a developing nation cannot be denied. At the same time it is helpful to look back at the actual circumstances of the time—an exercise that provides an alternative view no less historically valid: that in fact the war did not give the scattered populations of the British North American territories the sense of being a nation or even, for the most part, the sense of being Canadian. Rather, as A.R. Lower once remarked, 'it furnished them with an enemy and ever afterward they were quick to detect hostility in his glance.'

Certainly the war was not a Canadian national effort, since no Canadian nation yet existed. Only native-born inhabitants of the two Canadas at that time thought of themselves as Canadians, and in practice this meant a majority of the inhabitants of Lower Canada but only a tiny minority of the population of Upper Canada, where in 1812 almost every adult was an immigrant or a British soldier or official on temporary assignment. Michael Smith, a contemporary geographer writing at the midpoint of the war (1813), estimated that while about a fifth of the hundred thousand or so inhabitants of the upper province were British by origin, no less than four-fifths were American, of whom only a quarter were Loyalists. As for the people of the Maritime provinces, their attitude was summed up by Northrop Frye, who remarked of Thomas Chandler Haliburton that he 'would never have called himself a Canadian. He was a Nova Scotian, a Bluenose.' Nova Scotians and New Brunswickers, both largely originating in New England, remembered the cruel and primitive warfare carried into their territories by the militia of New France and their Indian allies, and distrusted the people of Quebec even after the Conquest. To them Upper Canada must have seemed a distant collection of puny upstart communities.

What all these colonies shared, in greater or lesser degree, was the common enemy, and history has shown that a shared danger is much more effective in creating an awareness of common interest than any constructive incentive.

It is interesting to compare the attitudes of British North Americans to the situation in 1812-14 with those they held at the time of the American War of Independence, when Upper Canada did not exist. In Nova Scotia the former New Englanders who formed such a large proportion of its inhabitants chose not to join the colonies to the south unless forced to do so by successful invaders, who never came. But in Quebec some of the Canadians did give aid in various ways to the Americans who captured Montreal and besieged the town of Quebec during 1775.

There was no *Canadien* support for the American invaders in 1812; the *habitants* had evidently decided in the half-century since the Conquest that they would have more chance to follow their own ways under the British than they would under the Americans, whose numbers would have overwhelmed them and whose Protestantism was aggressive. Even after the little reign of terror that the governor Sir John Craig set on foot in 1810, closing down newspapers and imprisoning his critics in the town of Quebec, the French Canadians rallied under the more sympathetic rule of the next governor, Sir George Prevost, and soldiers from Quebec—under officers from the seigneurial class, such as Colonel de Salaberry—helped defeat the American invasion.

In Upper Canada there may have been in the beginning a great deal of passive sympathy for the invaders, owing to the preponderance of settlers of American origin, though direct evidence of this is scarce. But surprisingly little active support was given, and as the war dragged on, the tactics of the Americans, and especially their indiscriminate pillaging and destruction of farms and villages in Upper Canada, turned passive sympathy into passive hostility. Almost nobody in Upper Canada, whatever his or her origins, regretted seeing the last of the American soldiers when the war ended in 1814. The Americans had by their own acts transformed their collective image into that of the Enemy; the various populations of the Canadas were united in hating and fearing them.

Such hostile feelings ran especially strong for the rest of the century in Upper Canada (later Ontario), the province that had endured most of their depredations.

Resistance to the Americans in 1812-14 was spread surprisingly widely over the whole span of British North America, from the Atlantic to the Pacific. Though Newfoundland was as yet not even a Crown colony, still ranking merely as a fishing station, a Royal Newfoundland Regiment was recruited there in 1812-14 and served beside the British regulars in Upper Canada. Nova Scotia played its part and made its profits by issuing letters of marque to no less than 44 privateers that harassed and plundered shipping down the Atlantic coast, bringing more than 200 captured American ships into Halifax as prizes. Even in the Far West a motley company of fur traders and *voyageurs* belonging to the North West Company seized the American-owned Fort Astoria at the mouth of the Columbia River, thus establishing a British claim to the territory (now Washington and part of Oregon) that was not liquidated until the Oregon Boundary Treaty of 1846. Other Northwesters assisted in the capture of Michilimackinac. The only places where British North Americans did not become actively engaged against Americans were the Red River country—where the North West Company and Lord Selkirk's settlers were involved in an internecine struggle of their own—and New Brunswick, where a brisk illicit trade was carried on with the people of Maine across the border who had little zest for the war, even though the very persistence of the British presence on the American continent was being fought over the Canadas.

But in 1812-14 fear and resentment of—and shared action against—a common enemy did not amount to even the beginnings of a Canadian nation or a national sentiment. In spite of the legends that have since grown up about Canadian settlers marching gallantly to the salvation of their unborn nation, their active participation and their show of patriotism were minimal. The most active defenders of Canada were in fact those who had the least direct interest in its survival.

Even more important than the militia as an effective fighting force, at least during the earlier part of the war, were the Indian warriors under Tecumseh who contributed notably to the capture of Detroit. But certainly neither Tecumseh nor his warriors were concerned about the fate of Canada; they were fighting to retain their own lands and to protect their way of life in the regions west of the settlement frontier—regions that were still in the dubious borderland between Royal and Republican territory and that, thanks to Captain Charles Roberts' capture of Michilimackinac at the beginning of hostilities, had been placed in the hands of the British for the duration of the war.

As for General Brock and his regiments, and even the regular provincial corps like de Salaberry's Canadian Voltigeurs and the Glengarry

Fencibles, they were all officially British troops paid by Britain. They were waging a British war to hold on to the remaining North American colonies. The aim was to sustain the continental balance of power and to provide space for Britain's superfluous men and women to find homes, which they began to do in large numbers shortly after the end of the war in the Americas and of the Napoleonic wars in Europe. The eventual emergence of a Canadian nation was far from General Brock's thought, and had he foreseen it he would likely have recoiled in imperial horror, considering it a repetition of the débâcle of the thirteen colonies to the south.

Perhaps the greatest factor in the defeat of the Americans was a lack of concerted will on the part of the invaders. There was great internal opposition to the war, particularly in New England, where the people of Vermont and Maine avoided hostilities and continued trading—profitably for both sides—with their neighbours to the north. American militia regiments often refused to fight beyond the border of the Union. American commanders turned out to be catastrophic incompetents. But for these shortcomings on the part of the invaders, the 100,000 people of Upper Canada, along with a handful of second-rate regular regiments and a few thousand Indians who melted away after Tecumseh's death, could not possibly have held their own against a nation of eight million. And yet the strange small alliance of redcoats, native warriors, provincial lawyers, and men from the plough stood their ground; and so to the combination of hatred and fear in the minds of British North Americans were added a pride in having survived the ordeal, and a sense of shared endurance. These would be important uniting factors in the years to come.

If a study of our changing perceptions of the War of 1812 can show how actual situations from the past are gradually transformed into myth and in this form move into the centre of our cultural history—uniting myth and history in the process—a study of historians' clichés about the period can reveal more than their mechanical repetition often suggests. One often-repeated cliché—that Canadian history differs so sharply from that of the United States because the American nation sprang from a revolution and Canada evolved slowly as a political, social, and cultural entity from traditional forms—has a particular bearing on the War of 1812 and its aftermath.

Historical clichés always require cautious handling. They are usually frozen truths whose apparent meanings may have sometimes become obsolete and therefore false, but whose origins are important in a consideration of the ways in which the past illuminates the present. The cliché about revolutionary America and non-revolutionary Canada has a great deal of relevance when we look at Canadian society as it emerged—

more self-assured because of its survival and more prosperous because of the war—after the end of fighting in 1814.

It is true that Canada has never experienced a revolution similar to the one that took place between 1775 and 1783 when the colonies to the south fought for and gained their freedom, a revolution involving the complete rejection of external authority and the creation of a radical democratic order. There has never been a Canadian Declaration of Independence; there has never been a revolutionary Canadian constitution that divided powers, created checks and balances, and involved the individual citizen in the processes of election and government to the extent that the various American constitutions, federal and state, have done. At no time in Canada has there been a sense of beginning anew as there was in the United States, and in France and Russia after their revolutions, and even in England after the series of radical changes that took place there between 1640 and 1688 and led one king to the scaffold and another into exile.

Because Canada has no revolutionary tradition, it is often assumed that this is a conservative country. But Canada does have a history of rebellion and rebellious thought; rebellion of one kind or another has been an important element in the nation's evolutionary process. During the century between 1814 and 1914 there were no less than four armed rebellions: those in Upper and Lower Canada in 1837-8, and those on the Prairies in 1870 and 1885. All these insurrections failed, for short-run failure is in the nature of rebellions, which merely challenge power, unlike revolutions, which transfer it. But none of the rebellions were in vain. Out of their failures changes eventually came.

As Albert Camus pointed out in his classic essay *The Rebel*, the distinction between revolution and rebellion is fundamental. Revolution tends to be absolute, and to subordinate the interests of individuals and minorities to those of the majority, as in the United States, or, as in later revolutionary régimes, to those of the state represented by the ruling party; it tends to be totalitarian and all-embracing. Rebellion, on the other hand, is libertarian and limited in its aims. The idea of rebellion implies the idea of restraint.

So unrevolutionary has Canada been from the beginning that the British North American colonies that eventually became its provinces all chose without hesitation to develop local versions of the English political system, with its representative democracy, its responsible government, and power undivided and vested in Parliament. In this system, authority is more firmly entrenched than liberty, since it lends itself not only to the creation of parties that stifle the play of individual opinion and conscience, but to the concentration of power in caucuses and cabinets that reign without consulting the people for the four or five years of a government's term. After the enactment of the Canadian Constitution in 1982, the Charter of Rights for the first time introduced a division of powers: the courts can to an extent restrain and modify the acts of government. Otherwise Canadians have no recourse between elections other than protest, legal and extra-legal. And extra-legal protest, however passive, amounts to rebellion.

Protest and rebellion—political, social, cultural—have constantly countered and modified the static and authoritarian tendencies in Canadian society. The other two modifying elements have arisen from the regional differentiation imposed on Canadian development by the country's geography and its variety of ancestral strains, and from ethnic and intellectual incursions.

Physical incursion has taken two forms: invasion and immigration. The main effect of the American invasion in 1812 was to create a sense of fearful enmity and to ensure that the political development of Canada diverged permanently from the American model, despite the social and cultural effects of proximity to the United States. The British conquest of New France, however—as unwanted an intrusion in the beginning as that of the Americans half-a-century later—changed French-Canadian society radically and permanently. By introducing British forms of government, with an elected assembly for both Lower and Upper Canada under the Constitutional Act of 1791, the British brought an end to the power of the seigneurial class and encouraged the appearance of a new and politically active middle class. Paradoxically, an alliance of convenience guaranteed the continuing power of the Church in Quebec, where the bishops and the parish priests were to wield great political and moral power for a century and a half, long after the authority of their counterparts had withered away in metropolitan France. At the same time, by allowing printing presses to operate for the first time in Quebec, and by tolerating the earliest newspapers, even if they occasionally suppressed them, the British occupiers were responsible before the end of the century not only for the introduction of English ideas of constitutional government, which radical Québécois politicians would soon learn to use against their governors, but also for the first dawning of the Enlightenment in a colony where the writings of Voltaire had hitherto gone unread and the performance of Molière's *Tartuffe* had been forbidden.

Already by 1812 the effect of the Conquest in terms of immigration had resulted in a dilution of the hitherto exceptionally homogeneous society of New France, which had not allowed room even for Frenchmen of the wrong beliefs, like the Huguenots, let alone foreign residents. The number of British officers who married the daughters of seigneurs, and of privates in Scottish regiments who fathered French-speaking québécois families, has doubtless been romantically exaggerated. It is possible that, but for the American Revolution, the British presence in Canada might for long have remained like the British presence in India:

a Raj of transient officers and administrators, few of whom would have stayed long enough to set down roots and establish lineages, and a small merchant class more closely immersed in colonial life. But once the fortunes of the war in the American colonies began to turn against the British and it was evident that their supporters would be forced into flight, Quebec and Acadia became not merely conquered provinces but settlement territories, and the whole character of the British presence in the northern half of the sub-continent was transformed.

The Loyalists arrived in 1783—some of them before. A few thousand of them went into the Eastern Townships of Quebec, where for generations afterwards a local British preponderance combined with the Anglo-Scottish mercantile dominance in Montreal to break up the traditional homogeneity of French-Canadian society even in its Quebec heartland. But the majority of the Loyalists were settled east and west of Quebec, in what one can see in hindsight as a kind of pincer movement sealing off the French within their original territory. The part of Nova Scotia where the Loyalists settled, alongside the French-speaking remnants of the Acadian people, was carved out and turned into a separate colony (New Brunswick) in 1784. The western wilderness north of the Great Lakes, which the people of New France had called the *pays d'en haut*, was transformed into another Loyalist refuge under the name of Upper Canada in 1791, with a separate Assembly, so that the British settlers would not be subordinated to a majority of French voters. In the creation of the Upper and Lower provinces under the Constitution Act, the name of Canada first came into official use in British North America, though the native-born inhabitants of New France had long described themselves as *Canadiens*.

The tiny settlements and scattered farms the Loyalists established along the lakeshores and in the great forests of Upper Canada constituted only the rudimentary beginnings of a community. It is not surprising that to swell the population the British authorities tolerated, even if they did not exactly welcome, the considerable influx during the 1790s and the early 1800s of American settlers, who were attracted not by loyalty but by land. The result was that by 1812 the population of the two Canadas and the maritime colonies were divided roughly, two to one, between French-speakers and English-speakers, with small enclaves of Germans at Lunenburg in Nova Scotia and in Upper Canada, where there were also a few Loyalist Dutch from New York.

The Indians in this part of the British domain were already a dwindling and powerless minority. A large area had been granted to the Six Nations Confederacy, led by Chief Joseph Brant, in recognition of their loyalty during the War of Independence. But Brant's efforts, preceding those of Tecumseh, to create a native confederacy to counter the westward spread of American power were discouraged by the British, so that when the clash with the Americans eventually came, the Indian allies who fought under Tecumseh beside the British soldiers and the Canadians were mostly from other, more westerly tribes.

West of Upper Canada, however, where the great sweep of plains and mountains and tundra stretching to the Pacific and the Arctic Oceans had only recently been explored (David Thompson did not complete his great map of it until 1814), the Indian peoples still carried on their lives in apparent independence. For the most part they were unaware that King George III claimed sovereignty over them. They were lords of the land for the present and were sustained by its abundant wild life, though the fur traders—first agents of white incursion—had already begun their economic enslavement by making them dependent on trade goods, and especially on firearms and ammunition.

The traders themselves, vanguard of a great invasion before the end of the century, consisted of a small number of Scottish and English employees of the Hudson's Bay and North West Companies, and a rather larger number of *voyageurs* and other servants, among whom the traditional preponderance of Québécois was diminishing as Orkneymen and Métis took their places. Resulting from the inter-breeding of Indians and Europeans, a manifestation of the early effects of white incursion, the Métis were rapidly acquiring a strong sense of their identity as they pursued their nomadic life centred on the buffalo hunt. As for the fur companies, they sustained their trading forts and the routes of their fur brigades, defended themselves sturdily against hostile Indians, and competed bitterly and sometimes violently with each other. But they made no attempt to govern the country; they were there for profit, not for power. In the whole vast area of the West, the only settlement at this time was Lord Selkirk's Red River Colony, founded in 1812 and populated by displaced crofters from the Scottish highlands. In 1814 its future was still problematical because of the hostility of the North West Company's traders and their Métis employees.

These varied patterns of incursion from the eastern seaboard to the middle west of the continent combined with geographical contrasts to make inevitable both the discord and the vitality that strong regional tendencies eventually bring to a nation. When Lord Durham came as Governor of British North America in 1838—after the rebellions in Lower and Upper Canada had subsided—to investigate the British North American possessions and the causes for their unrest, he was surprised to find in the maritime colonies a clear hostility towards the idea of a union of the British possessions on the sub-continent. Thirty years later, in 1868, the year after Confederation, the voters of both New Brunswick and Nova Scotia showed their displeasure at being linked to the original Canadian provinces; it was only the imperial government's firm resolution not to repeal the British North America Act that prevented these provinces at this late date from asserting their autonomy. Prince Edward Island entered Confederation unwillingly and late, in 1873, only to gain relief from the intolerable burden of a railway-building debt, while Newfoundland stood aloof until 1949, at times displaying a hostility to Canada and things Canadian expressed in a well-known song that is occasionally heard even now:

> Men, hurrah for our own native land, Newfoundland,
> Not a stranger shall hold one inch of her strand;
> Her face turns to Britain, her back to the Gulf.
> Come near at your peril, Canadian Wolf!

And indeed, in 1814 not only Newfoundland but Nova Scotia turned more to Britain than to the interior provinces of Canada. Where the latter were landlocked and obliged to find their earliest economic base in agriculture (mainly subsistence), followed later by lumber, both Newfoundland and Nova Scotia were maritime in more than name, since Newfoundland depended on the sea for its great industries of fishing and sealing, and Nova Scotia was nearing its peak as a centre for the building of wooden ships. Not only did Nova Scotians build the ships, they sailed them. Despite the presence of a certain amount of small farming, the province's flourishing pre-Confederation economy depended on a seaborne trade oriented not only eastward to Britain but also southward to New England and the West Indies. In 1814 Newfoundland's and Nova Scotia's trade with Canada was minimal, and to the merchants of St John's or Halifax the idea of a kind of British North American economic union, with all the colonies taking in each other's products, would have seemed chimerical.

It was only the economic changes of the 1850s, when their wooden sailing ships were being challenged by iron steamships and their traditional markets began to seem less certain, that Nova Scotians began to think of closer links (rather than ties) with the Province of Canada, and even then they showed a characteristic British North American preoccupation: they thought in terms of communication rather than union. Some of the first suggestions of a transcontinental railway came from Haligonians like Joseph Howe, who in a remarkable speech in 1851 made the surprisingly exact prophecy that 'many in this room will live to hear the whistle of the steam engine in the passes of the Rocky Mountains, and to make the journey from Halifax to the Pacific in five or six days'. But his attitude towards the 'boundless and prolific region' of British North America was really that of a trader contemplating a promising commercial hinterland, and he saw the maritime provinces as 'the wharves upon which its business will be transacted and beside which its rich argosies are to lie'. For Howe, as much as for Thomas Chandler Haliburton, 'my country' was always Nova Scotia.

Regionalism has always been a matter of culture even more than of politics or economics, and in any culture—if we regard it in the broader sense of the sum of the features and functions that give a society or a people its special characteristics—the factors of tradition and environment (or history and geography) are always dominant. Where we come from and where we live are the elements of *becoming* that merge into our consciousness of *being* as a group. It is in the process of transition from *becoming* (the pioneer society) to *being* (the settled society) that culture in its narrower sense of the arts begins to perform its interpretive and defining role.

But the community must emerge and take its shape before art—in word, form, or sound—can define it, and that is why societies struggling to take shape are societies without art, or with art only in a rudimentary 'folk' form. And the shaping geographical and historical elements that culturally separate the regions of Canada to this day were already present in 1814.

Newfoundland, with its treacherous seas, its dour land hostile to the plough, its minute merchant-dominated capital, and its scattered outports inhabited by the descendants of Devon fishermen and southern Irish peasants, was a different society—almost a different world—from Nova Scotia. In Nova Scotia the British military and naval traditions of the garrison city of Halifax contrasted with the craft- and commerce-dominated lives of smaller seacoast towns that had busy shipyards and harbours, and with a rural pattern of small landholding where farming and fishing and lumbering supported each other, and where the apple orchards of the Annapolis Valley reflected a softer and more traditionally rustic life than was possible in Newfoundland or even, as early as 1814, in Upper Canada. With its pattern of early Yankee settlement already being diluted by German, Scottish, and Yorkshire immigration, Nova Scotia offered a different mixture of traditions not only from Newfoundland but from New Brunswick, where the somewhat hierarchically minded Loyalists—refugees of all classes who came from many rebel states—mingled with the remnants of the Acadians, mostly simple peasants.

In Upper Canada the real mixture of peoples had hardly begun, so quickly did the war follow on first settlement. Its rudimentary garrison and settler society was to change radically in the decades after 1814 as it passed through the maelstrom of conflict in the Rebellion of 1837 and congealed into the white Anglo-Saxon Protestant culture of Ontario. The American-born majority that was so uncomfortably evident there in 1812 had been replaced through heavy transatlantic migration by a British-born majority: Scots and Irish Protestants were dominant and Irish Catholics a significant minority. The former and future Quebec was the one region in Canada whose culture was already shaped and defined and defended—by religion and by language, by the rural traditions of northern France that the *habitants* had brought with them, by half a century of cruel Indian warfare, by half-willing submission to French kings and British conquerors, and by adaptation to a climate far harsher than that of the temperate Norman and Breton farmlands of their ancestors.

In the rest of what would later be Canada, the plains of the West and the great mountain ranges that stepped down to the Pacific—regions dwarfing in their immensity all the settled and half-settled eastern provinces—the dominant cultures were still the doomed ones of the native peoples. These were most sophisticated among the buffalo-hunting democracies of the plains Indians and the ceremonially oriented and hierarchically inclined tribes on the Pacific coast, who were about to experience the last exuberant flowering of their visual and dramatic arts, thanks to the increased wealth and the metal tools brought by the fur traders.

Apart from the troubled Red River Settlement, with its few hundred insecure inhabitants, the white men of the West in 1814 were traders and their servants, who came and went, rarely staying long in a single post. There were hardly more than two thousand of them at any given time, spread over the whole great area from Fort William at the head of Lake Superior to Fort Vancouver on the Pacific Coast. The fur-trading culture they established was fragile and fleeting, yet their achievements were of enduring importance. It was they who explored the wilderness, established the routes on which later communications would be based and that oriented the development of Canada westward rather than southward; and it was they who, first on the South Saskatchewan River and by 1814 in New Caledonia (later British Columbia), practised the earliest farming in the West, in small fields and plots around their forts.

The differences between the regions of British North America that existed in 1814 were to persist throughout the century that is our period, and indeed they still continue—however their immediate manifestations may have changed—seventy years after the Great War that marked the period's end.

The islands that form the extremities of Canada—Newfoundland, Prince Edward Island, and Cape Breton on the east and Vancouver Island and the Queen Charlottes on the west—still remain peculiar enclaves, small worlds of their own, separated from the mainland as much by cultural idiosyncrasy as by marine barriers. Nova Scotia, the quintessential maritime province in the sense that its fortunes and misfortunes have always been linked to the sea, still differs as much in its values and interests from Protestant and anglophone Ontario as it does from Catholic and francophone Quebec. If a shared discontent with the political and economic domination of Canada seems to unite the maritime provinces with those of the West, the bond is illusory, for the historical traditions of the two areas are as remote from each other as endless Prairies are from seacoasts bitten into tiny harbours. Even the West has never been a homogeneous region, for the Cordillera does not merely divide the plains from the mountains that bring the traveller down to a different ocean; it separates peoples who came at different times from different places by different routes. British Columbia's name (and the retention of it) is no mere historical accident; it represents a population mainly British by descent. But the great immigrations of the 1890s and the 1900s from Central and Eastern Europe turned the prairie provinces into the reservoir of Canadians who were neither French nor British by descent or by mother tongue.

These regional differences may not have been created between 1814 and 1914—in the relations between the Atlantic provinces and the Canadas and also between the Canadas themselves they were already present by the War of 1812—but they were ultimately defined and reconciled during that long and difficult century of penetrating and settling the land, when the lineaments of a nation gradually took form, and found expression and definition in the arts of life.

So the Canadian nation, which took so long to coalesce out of so many traditions and circumstances, apparently did not emerge fully developed, as the myth implies, out of the preservation of Canada in 1814 by a strange loose alliance of British regulars, Indian bands, and Loyalist militiamen. It evolved instead during the long century of development we shall be discussing. Yet throughout much of that century the War of 1812 remained, in the minds of Canadians, as the memory of disaster avoided, and as an evocation of the enemy whose memory kept them united.

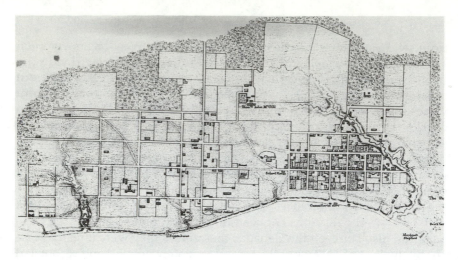

Plan of York, 1813

2

Canada in 1814

The two Canadas that emerged from the War of 1812, and the other communities of British North America, were colonial territories small in population and for the most part large in area. Politically they were impoverished, for they had entered merely on the first stages of their progression towards real democracy. All of them—except for Newfoundland, which had to wait until 1832, and the territories of Rupert's Land and New Caledonia administered by the Hudson's Bay Company—had representative assemblies; but with few exceptions these were based on franchises limited, as in Britain at the time, to adult males who were property owners. Moreover, though the assemblies had certain powers over the raising and spending of revenue, their scope was limited by the existence of appointed Legislative Councils that acted as restraining mechanisms on the actions of the elected houses. The Legislative Councils overlapped the Executive Councils, composed of office-holders who carried on the real administration of the colonies, presided over by the Governor or Lieutenant-Governor. Though he acted as the King's representative, the Governor in an early nineteenth-century colony enjoyed far more power than the monarch in his own country, where royal action was already limited by the existence, if not of universal suffrage, at least of responsible government. The first third of the century after the War of 1812 would be dominated by the process of bringing the British North American colonies to the same level of political maturity as Britain itself.

The ideas that inspired such developments take their place in a consideration of the complex of myths and ideals, of images and forms—an ever-changing manifestation of the collective imagination—that constitutes the culture as distinct from the *polis*. The same applies to economic life, and especially to technological advancement, which first affect our material existence, but then modify the ways we conceive our collective and even our personal lives.

The men and women who emerged from the War of 1812 were poised unknowingly on the edge of an era of continuous and radical technological change. The war had been fought, and the fighters had been supplied, almost entirely by the means of a pre-mechanical age. The navies that skirmished on the Great Lakes were propelled by sail, and the only instances of mechanized transport in the colonies at that time were John Molson's steamboats. In 1809, more than twenty years before the first steamship crossed the Atlantic, Molson—better remembered as a brewer and banker—had started to operate his paddle boat, the *Accommodation*, between Montreal and Quebec. During the war his second ship, the *Swiftsure*, was chartered by the Quarter-master's Department and profitably transported 5,000 troops between the two cities. This affected the progress of the war, but also advertised the advantages of steam navigation, thus promoting its development in a country where water transport had traditionally been dominant because rivers and lakes formed the only clear thoroughfares through the forests.

In every other direction the old techniques still held sway. Such industrial plants as existed—mainly grist and sawmills, breweries, and a few primitive foundries—were operated by the capricious elements, wind and mostly water. Land transport was still dependent on animal power, and in most colonies the means of making and moving had not progressed beyond those current in the late middle ages, while in the vast areas of the wilderness there had actually been a regression to the stone age in the use by the native peoples of birchbark canoes, snowshoes, and dogsleighs, which were so well adapted to the terrain that they were also used by the fur-traders.

It is hard now to guess how people who had emerged in 1814 from two years of warfare grasped the extraordinary potentialities of the century that lay before them. There were no futurists among them, and pioneer societies are by and large too closely involved in dealing with day-to-day necessities to have much time for utopian speculation, which in any case has never been very much in the Canadian grain. But it must have been evident to them that, in material terms at least, the provinces had already moved a long way forward since the earliest years of the century.

In the east Halifax had prospered on the traffic generated by carrying troops and supplies from Britain for the defence of the Canadas; the foundations of great shipping enterprises like that of the Cunards were laid at this period. Both Nova Scotia and New Brunswick had benefited from the general blockade of American ports by the British fleet; goods imported into Halifax were traded clandestinely over the border into Maine. Liverpool, Nova Scotia, grew fat on privateering.

Montreal merchants had done a brisk trade with Vermont, importing the food needed for British regulars and Canadian militiamen operating in Lower Canada, and supplying the Vermonters with manufactured goods from Britain. Even in Upper Canada, where trade with the enemy was less extensive, the funds sent from Britain to pay and maintain the troops engaged there and to build ships in the Kingston dockyard had not only provided employment (1,200 labourers worked in the dockyard when the never-launched 104-gun *St Lawrence* was being built by hand), but also put cash in the pockets of farmers, millers, and suppliers of lumber. A shipbuilding industry developed far from the ocean. Not long after the war, in 1817, the *Frontenac* was launched on Lake Ontario, becoming the first steamboat to operate on the Great Lakes.

As well as enjoying material benefits from the war, people in all the colonies emerged from the conflict with a new sense of confidence. Having played their parts in driving off a much stronger enemy, they now saw the need to deal with the challenges of peace—though their views of how to do this differed widely. They must put their political arrangements in order. They needed to provide communications between the various parts of their provinces, and the provinces themselves, that would improve their defences and their internal trade. In the construction of canals and later of railways, what we now recognize as a characteristic Canadian pattern and obsession emerged: providing national systems through combining state and private investment, and, where private investment was not generated, undertaking projects entirely at public expense. The Welland Canal, started in 1824, would fall into the first category, and the Rideau Canal, started in 1826, into the second; they were the first examples of a Canadian compromise with socialism that has continued ever since.

Yet in general appearance the country that, looking backward, we see poised for a century of often chaotic growth, may have seemed to the contemporary visitor little changed by the experience of war. When Francis Hall visited the capital of Upper Canada in 1816, two years after the end of hostilities, he found it merely contemptible.

York being the seat of government for the upper province, is a place of considerable importance in the eyes of its inhabitants; to a stranger, however, it presents little more than about 100 wooden houses, several of them conveniently and even elegantly built, and I think one, or perhaps two, of brick. The public buildings were destroyed by the Americans, but as no ruins of them are visible, we must conclude, either, that the destruction exceeded that of Jerusalem, or that the loss to the arts is not quite irreparable. I believe they did not leave one stone upon another, for they did not find one. Before the city, a long flat tongue of land runs into the lake, called Gibraltar Point, probably from being very *unlike* Gibraltar. York, wholly useless either as a port, or military post, would sink into a village, and the seat of government be transferred to Kingston, but for the influence of those, whose property in the place would be depreciated by the change.

Mary Gapper arrived twelve years later, in 1828; she eventually became Mary O'Brien and the mother of the notable Canadian landscape painter, Lucius O'Brien. York, in her eyes still seemed unimpressive. Taking her first sight of the town from the water, she remarked that 'It did not cut so gay an appearance as the Yankee towns from the absence of the spires that always abounded there. At York there are but two . . .' And even after she had lived a winter in the locality, she was still disturbed by its difference from the tightly knit English towns.

It seems to be all suburb. The streets are laid out parallel and at right angles to each other, and are formed by low, scattered houses. The shops are numerous but do not make much show. There is a neat church and a Catholic chapel. In addition there are two high and not very elegant buildings, both on the same plan, one of which is the jail, the other the court house. They stand side by side in the central part, though the town is so scattered that I hardly know where the centre may be.

York's main rivals—Quebec, Montreal, and Halifax—all made a more emphatic impression on the visitor, Quebec for its touch of European feudal grandeur and the other two for their commercial activity. Montreal's dominant role in the fur trade would shortly come to an end with the consolidation of the rival fur companies in 1821 into an enlarged Hudson's Bay Company, but in 1814 the North West Company's operations in the city on the St Lawrence were still in full swing, and other staples were already beginning to take fur's place, as timber floated down in great rafts from the Ottawa valley and wheat came from the farms of Upper Canada that by the 1820s were beginning to emerge from the elementary subsistence pattern. The increase in steamboat traffic and the introduction of tugs to pull sailing ships upriver were already allowing Montreal to replace Quebec as the principal port on the St Lawrence.

Still, Montreal was not a town that appealed to all its visitors. John MacGregor, who spent five years mostly in the colonies of the Atlantic seaboard during the early 1820s, was unimpressed:

> There are no wharfs at Montreal, and the ships and steamers lie quietly in pretty deep water, close to the clayey and generally filthy bank of the city. The whole of the lower town is covered with gloomy-looking houses, having dark iron shutters, and although it may be a little cleaner than Quebec, it is still very dirty; and the streets are not only narrow and ill-paved, but the footpaths are interrupted by slanting cellar doors and other projections.

John Howison, however—whose *Sketches of Upper Canada* was published in 1821—spoke well of the city's prospects.

> Montreal improves with great rapidity, and will soon contain some very pretty streets. Its suburbs and outskirts are embellished by numerous villas, built in the English style, and many of these are surrounded by pleasure grounds, the variety and beauty of which prove the wealth and taste of their owners.

The iron shutters and iron outer doors of the Montreal houses were adopted to minimize the spread of fires, and Edward Allen Talbot, who arrived in 1818 and published his *Five Years' Residence* in Canada in 1824, declared that on Sunday and holidays, when the doors and shutters were all closed, 'the whole city seems one vast prison.' Even a decade afterwards, when Susanna Moodie and Catharine Parr Traill arrived on separate ships in 1832, the city did not seem any more attractive to European eyes and particularly to European noses, for Susanna complained of the 'intolerable effluvia' and Catharine of the 'noisome vapour' arising from the open sewers.

As for Halifax, what struck most visitors at the time was the haphazard appearance of this comparatively new colonial capital, a mere eighty years old when Captain William Moorsom arrived and wrote from there his *Letters from Nova Scotia* (1830), describing it as a place of 'roads garnished with buildings mostly of wood, some of brick, and others of stone, of all sizes, shapes and dimensions, from one storey to three; some neatly painted, others setting the ingenuity of the colourist at naught.' Still, he was impressed by the business of the little provincial seaport, and remarked that:

> The wharfs are . . . crowded with vessels of all kinds discharging their cargoes or taking in the returns. Signals are constantly flying at the citadel for vessels coming in; merchants are running about, in anticipation of their freights; officers of the garrison are seen striding down with a determined pace to welcome a detachment from the depot, or a pipe of Sneyd's claret for the mess, and ladies, tripping along on the tiptoe of expectation, flock into two or three *soi-disant* bazaars for the latest *à-la-mode* bonnets.

When these outsiders' observations of the cities of British North America were written, the great post-Napoleonic migration from Britain was getting under way, mingling the genteel and working-class poor. But it was the people who had experienced the War of 1812, and who did not look upon their world with the critical eyes of newcomers from a more stable world, who played such important roles in the beginnings of nineteenth-century Canada. They included Tories and Reformers: members of the élites that history remembers as the Family Compact in Upper Canada and the Château Clique in Lower Canada, and opponents who contended against them bitterly, even to the point of armed rebellion.

John Strachan—rector of York and later Bishop of Toronto—did not fight in the war, but he played his own courageous part at York in 1813 when the Americans invaded the city and, in the absence of any military or political authority, took it upon himself, like a medieval princely ecclesiastic, to negotiate with the American commanders and save as much as possible of the little capital from destruction. He was the personification of everything conservative in matters political, educational, and ecclesiastical, fighting to preserve the ascendancy in government of a small, self-perpetuating oligarchy of rank and intellect, and to sustain the dominance of the Anglican church both in religion and in education. Also present, fighting in the Upper Canadian militia, were Colonel Joseph Ryerson and his three older sons, of whom George, the eldest, was badly wounded at Lundy's Lane. Even though Joseph Ryerson was to remain an Anglican and a mild Tory, his sons came to represent and to work for everything that Strachan detested: Methodism, with all its enthusiasms, democratic politics, and the secularization and universalization of education. It was Egerton Ryerson, the son too young to fight in 1812, who in act and argument became Strachan's most formidable— and not wholly unesteemed—adversary.

In the rebellions that shook the Canadas in 1837, veterans of 1812 would be seen on both sides, representing opposing concepts of political justice and political arrangements. Allan MacNab, an early Upper Canadian lawyer who in 1812, at the age of fourteen, had served as ensign, not only became the leading enemy in the Upper Canada legislative assembly of the radical leader William Lyon Mackenzie, but also, as lieutenant-colonel of the Gore militia from Hamilton, helped to lead the hastily assembled little loyalist army that marched off up Yonge Street to disperse the badly armed and ragged little company of farmer rebels that Mackenzie had assembled at Montgomery's tavern. Another veteran of 1812, John Beverley Robinson, had taken part in the capture of Detroit and fought at Queenston Heights on the day Brock was killed; eventually, in his role of Chief Justice, he was responsible for the hanging of two of the rebel leaders of 1837, Samuel Lount and Peter Mathews, who had let themselves be caught when Mackenzie bolted for the border.

At least three 1812ers were among the leaders of the rebellion in Lower Canada. One was Louis-Joseph Papineau, who served as a militia officer from the beginning of the War of 1812 and, like John Beverley Robinson, was present at the capture of Detroit. Two years later he was elected to the Legislative Assembly of Lower Canada and began his career of opposition to the British ruling clique and their mercantile allies that would eventually take him to the point of leading the *patriotes* at least nominally in their revolt. There was a bizarre consistency in Papineau's actions. As a land-owning seigneur who continued to the end to enjoy his estate at Montebello, he logically supported the British in 1812 against American invaders whose respect for traditional *canadien* privileges could not be relied on. Then, fearing British commercial and land-speculating interests would gain the ascendancy in the rest of Quebec as they had in Montreal, he was carried along on the stream of a movement of resistance that steadily became more radical, until—though temperamentally as well as theoretically opposed to violent means—he found himself heading an insurrection. Having accepted the rank of command-in-chief of the *patriote* forces, he then slipped over the border even more nimbly than his Upper Canadian counterpart, Mackenzie.

Among those who drove the *patriote* movement on its extreme course, and stayed behind to fight, were the brothers Wolfred and Robert Nelson, who had also served in 1812 as regimental surgeons. Less ambiguous than Papineau in their political radicalism, they joined the *patriote* movement, with its predominantly French-speaking membership, because at the time it was the only effective opposition to the ruling oligarchy in Lower Canada.

That oligarchy itself was by no means racially homogenous, since it included many *Canadien* landowners and office-holders. Among them was yet another 1812er, Charles Michel d'Irumberry de Salaberry, commander of the small army that defeated the American invaders at Châteauguay. The Salaberry clan were assiduous supporters of the established government, and at one time both Charles and his father Ignace served in the appointed Legislative Council of Lower Canada.

The two main political inclinations of nineteenth-century Canadians—Reformism and Toryism, with its imperial implications—were already being projected by the men who stepped out of their uniforms to remake their country after the wars had ended. But politics was only one area into which the 1812ers moved with energy and influence. Strachan's insistence on traditional values in education—which he followed both in the school at Cornwall where, before 1812, he had educated many of Canada's future rulers, and later in the creation of Anglican institutions of higher education in Toronto, King's College and Trinity College—stood in opposition to the democratic values developed by his rival Egerton Ryerson, who created for Ontario the first universal educational system in Canada. Yet Strachan and Ryerson complemented each other as well, and educational philosophies and practices in Canada have owed a great deal to both of them.

In different ways from the fur trade, even before the railways, the war had made Canadians aware of the importance of communications, and canals began to open up the Canadian countryside and the outlook of its people. Here one of the leaders was yet another 1812er, William Hamilton Merritt, who commanded a troop of cavalry and was captured by the Americans at Lundy's Lane. Merritt became the promoter of the Welland Canal, which crossed the Niagara Peninsula from Lake Ontario to Lake Erie and helped develop the inland communities of Upper Canada. After the Lachine Canal of 1825, the Welland Canal—which was opened to boats in 1829—was the second important inland waterway constructed in the Canadas. The cost of building it led to a series of loans and stock purchases by the Upper Canadian administration that established the peculiar symbiosis between transport and government that has continued in Canada to the present day. Colonel William By, the creator of the other great early Canadian canal, served in Canada from 1802 to 1811. Though he just missed being an 1812er, he shared the attitudes of the men of his time, and when he started work on the Rideau Canal in 1826 he gave material form to a strategic concept that had developed out of the war.

Transport went hand in hand with land development, and in the popular mind in nineteenth-century Canada the acquisition of land often assumed an importance far beyond its material significance. Though land rushes were never as spectacular in their suddenness and brevity as gold rushes, they were more lasting in their transformation of the country and in their creation of local populations and local societies. While gold was eventually worked out, the land remained.

Here also the men of 1812 were active. They aspired to become Canadian versions of English country squires or, like William Dunlop, served as officials of land companies. The famous Colonel Thomas Talbot, who was commander of the lst Middlesex Militia in 1812, and whose mill at Port Talbot was burnt down by the Americans in 1814, eventually amassed some 65,000 acres of land fronting on Lake Erie, much of which he gave in 50- and 100-acre lots to settlers he approved. Despite his autocracy and his drunken eccentricity, Talbot was a good administrator, encouraging sound farming methods among the settlers and making them build a better road system than then existed in most of the primitive backwoods of Upper Canada.

William Dunlop, nicknamed 'Tiger', had served as a surgeon in the 89th regiment during the War of 1812. He then went on with his regiment to India, earning his sobriquet because of his predilection for tiger hunting, and returned to Upper Canada in 1826 with the Scottish novelist John Galt to take part in one of the greatest land-speculation schemes, that of the Canada Company, which acquired two and a half million acres for $295,000, or less than twelve cents an acre. The Company set about attracting settlers from Britain. Whether it brought in many more people than would have come of their own accord is uncertain, since it was soon suffering well-publicized attacks in the Upper Canadian Assembly for the cavalier attitude it was said to adopt towards those who purchased land. Dunlop, a kind of Red Tory before his time, complained about the Company's neglect of the settlers' interests. When he resigned from its employment in 1838 he openly attacked its practices and was elected to the Assembly of the united Province of Canada in 1841 as a Reformer. The Company, despite its difficulties, stubbornly survived for well over a century, dissolving itself unobtrusively when the last of its holdings had been sold off in the 1950s.

But Dunlop—and here again the many-sidedness of the 1812ers emerged—was much more than a land-company official with a conscience. Like John Richardson, Dunlop became one of the few early Canadian writers whose name still means something in the late twentieth century, even though little that he wrote is read today. Dunlop's most considerable book, the inappropriately named *Statistical Sketches of Upper Canada, for the Use of Emigrants* (1832), which he published under the *nom-de-plume* of 'A Backwoodsman', is opinionated and inaccurate, filled with jibes at the Methodists and other groups that his Toryism led him to discountenance, and garnished with such sallies as this:

> The climate is infinitely more healthy than that of England. Indeed, it may be pronounced the most healthy country under the sun, considering that whiskey can be procured for about one shilling sterling per gallon.

Yet Dunlop has a special importance for the active role he played—along with a few others, of whom Susanna Moodie and Catharine Parr Traill were the most prominent—in establishing a kind of rudimentary literary society in Canada. He founded the Toronto Literary Club in 1836; he contributed—for scanty payment, if any—to some of the earliest cultural journals, like the *Canadian Literary Magazine* and the *Literary Garland*. Dunlop and his associates show Canadian writers for the first time gathering together with a feeling of common interest to discuss and propagate their works.

Unlike Dunlop, Richardson was a prolific, committed, and even obsessed writer, and though his dull panegyric on Tecumseh is no longer read except by specialists, and his later pot-boilers—*The Monk Knight of St. John: A Tale of the Crusaders* (New York, 1950) and *Hardscrabble; or the Fall of Chicago. A Tale of Indian Warfare* (New York, 1950)—are generally ignored, *Wacousta; or The Prophecy: A Tale of the Canadas* (3 vols, Edinburgh, 1832) and its sequel, *The Canadian Brothers: or, The Prophecy Fulfilled* (Montreal, 1840), which deals with the War of 1812 and is clearly autobiographical, have found a considerable modern readership. They owe this less to their intrinsic literary merits, which have been exaggerated by romantically minded critics, than to their presentation of archetypal anxieties that lie deep in the Canadian consciousness: the fear of being absorbed, rather than annihilated, by the wilderness; the unavoidable ambivalences of white-Indian relationships; the fragility of civilized values in the face of natural forces; the alarming presence of the Other within and beside us; the fascination and the terror of the unknown. We read *Wacousta* as we might chant a spell, not for what it says but for what it calls up.

Richardson revitalized the worn conventions of European gothicism by using them to demonstrate the difference of the New World and life there from the Old. His other claim to our attention—more prosaic perhaps, but still laudable—is that he was perhaps the first Canadian writer who set out deliberately to be a professional, to earn his living by writing. The fact that he failed in Canada showed more than anything else how far he was ahead of his time, but it also made him a pioneer in another, sadder way. He was one of the great company of Canadian writers who, realizing that their country had not enough readers to support them, set out to make their names and their fortunes elsewhere. Richardson did achieve greater repute among Americans than among Canadians, but fortune eluded him and he died (in 1852) in great poverty a few years after he made his residence in New York. Yet in him had stirred the impulses that would lead writers to create out of Canadian experience a native literature.

3

Gentlemen and Others:
Class in Canada

In the nineteenth century, as in our own day, views about the role of class in Canadian society differed widely. Was it a free and mobile society in which class pretensions had little real meaning? Or was it a society where, despite the appearance of a growing democracy and despite all appearances of upward mobility, élites still controlled the nerve-centres of a nation visibly divided between the rich and the poor, the powerful and the weak?

One of the most eloquent defenders during the Victorian era of the view of Canada as an open society was that most genial of tragic enthusiasts, Thomas D'Arcy McGee, who told the Canadian Legislative Assembly:

> We have here no traditions and ancient venerable institutions; here, there are no aristocratic elements hallowed by time or bright deeds; here, every man is the first settler of the land, or removed from the first settler one or two generations at the furtherest; here, we have no architectural monuments calling up old associations; here, we have none of those popular legends and stories which in other countries have exercised a powerful share in the government; here, every man is the son of his own works.

Canon John Burgon Bickersteth, who as a young man travelled the Prairies just before the Great War, was so impressed by the appearance of social flexibility he encountered there that he called his narrative *The Land of Open Doors* (1914). He remarked:

> One is now in a country where it is no shame to work with one's hands. Manual work is not necessarily menial work. The possession of wealth may give some kind of social pre-eminence, but the absence of it certainly does not imply social inferiority. It is a case of every man playing for his own hand, and the weakest go to the wall.

The young men Bickersteth saw, who shortly afterwards went to fight in the Great War, gave such an appearance of independence that book after book on that conflict—the most recent of them is Pierre Berton's *Vimy* (1986)—has remarked on how impressed observers were at the time by the absence of class distinction in the Canadian armed forces as compared with the strictly hierarchical British Army.

Yet in 1892 we find the poet Wilfred Campbell writing in the first issue of the column 'At the Mermaid Inn'—which he shared in the Toronto *Globe* with his fellow poets Duncan Campbell Scott and Archibald Lampman—a bitter indictment of class attitudes:

> The class distinction on the continent of America has developed further than we have realized. The concentration of wealth into the control of a few, and the gradually growing poverty of the working classes, is becoming more apparent every day. Here in Canada as in the States the so-called middle class is dying out as the result of the absorption of capital. The liberty and safety of the State has so far mainly depended on the influence of this class. When it goes, then may come the long-prophesied struggle of the rich and poor. For selfish ends of their own men deny this state of things, but it is heart-rending to go into some of our large cities and see the immense amount of wealth squandered on personal aggrandizement and selfish luxuries and then to note the corresponding destitution, degradation, and misery both within the shadow of the same church spire or within the sound of the same Sabbath bell. Religionists may cry out about the hopelessness of mere humanity as a religion, but it would be better did they put a little more hope into the anguish of this world by putting more of the humanities into their religion.

What is most striking about Campbell's statement is that he was in no sense a social revolutionary; nor was he even, like Agnes Maule Machar, a socially concerned Christian. He was a Tory imperialist, but he expressed a view that was widespread among writers of his time—from the ironic observation of the blind callousness of the well-to-do that Stephen Leacock (a pupil of Thorstein Veblen) projected in *Arcadian Adventures with the Idle Rich* (1914), to the romantic socialism of Campbell's associate, Archibald Lampman. In an unpublished essay, 'On Socialism', Lampman declared:

There is a wrong and inhuman principle at the bottom of our whole industrial system; the principle that the private individual may take possession of the common earth and use it in any way he will for his own advantage.

And in some of his later sonnets, like 'The Modern Politician' and 'To a Millionaire', Lampman, rather like William Morris, combined a romantic vision of a better past, 'the world's iron youth', with the present 'transit age, the age of brass', which his millionaire, battening on the unfortunate, seems to personify:

> The world in gloom and splendour passes by,
> And thou in the midst of it with brows that gleam,
> A creature of the old distorted dream
> That makes the sound of life an evil cry.
> Good men perform just deeds, and brave men die,
> And win not honour such as gold can give,
> While the vain multitudes plod on, and live,
> And serve the curse that pins them down: But I
> Think only of the unnumbered broken hearts,
> The hunger and the mortal strife for bread,
> Old age and youth alike mistaught, misfed,
> By want and rags and homelessness made vile,
> The griefs and hates, and all the meaner parts
> That balance thy one grim misgotten pile.

In one sense both viewpoints are true. With regard to birth and manners, or the tightly graded Victorian English class system that was very near to a caste system, Canada did develop during the nineteenth century in the direction of an open and classless society. The only class accents in Canada are imported ones that fade in the second generation; variations in speech patterns are mostly regional, with an extended vocabulary rather than a different accent distinguishing the educated. Though writers like John Porter in his *Vertical Mosaic* (1965) have pointed out that hereditary élites in politics and business have been persistent in Canada, there has always been room to move upwards, so that a former stonemason, builder, and contractor like Alexander Mackenzie could become Prime Minister in 1872, an event unthinkable in Britain then or for long afterwards.

But in terms of power and privilege, as distinct from manners, class exists, and has always existed, in Canada. In this sense it was frankly defended in 1839 by Sir Francis Bond Head:

The 'family compact' of Upper Canada is composed of those members of its society who, either by their abilities and character, have been honoured by the confidence of the executive government, or who, by their industry and intelligence, have amassed wealth. The party, I own, is a comparatively small one; but to put the multitude at the top and the few at the

bottom is a radical reversion of the pyramid of society which every reflecting man must foresee can end only in its downfall.

In these remarks Head tacitly recognized that the ruling class in Canada had become differentiated from the traditional English ruling class.
It was not based only on hereditary title, which would have pleased the
Tories, or on land holding, which would have pleased the Whigs. It
allowed, in its emphasis on the amassing of wealth, for the self-made
man. The power of the merchants—especially in Montreal, but increasingly in Toronto and the other Upper Canadian towns—emphasized this
inclination.

In fact the first successful ranked and graded society in British North
America was a mercantile one. There had been early attempts in the
seventeenth century to create gentry-based settlements in Newfoundland and Nova Scotia. These failed. Even the attempt to replicate the
French *ancien régime* in New France was incompletely successful, owing
to the divergence between landed and fur-trading interests. But the
hierarchical structure established by the Hudson's Bay Company in its
far-flung posts did not fail.

Like similar enterprises, such as the East India Company, the Hudson's Bay Company imitated the grandees of Venice and the Hanse
towns of medieval Germany by establishing a mercantile patriciate that
endured unchanged well into the nineteenth century. After the Conquest and the coming of the Loyalists, the rival Scottish and American
merchants who took over from the French established the same kind of
hierarchy in the North West Company. In 1821, when the two companies
were united, a carefully built structure of power and prestige emerged.

Those who worked for the Company were divided into two groups:
the gentlemen and the *engagés*, each with their own ranking order defined by rates of pay. Lowest of the *engagés* were the labourers around
the forts, who earned £14 a year; above them, the *voyageurs* earned
between £17 and £22 according to their positions in the canoes, the
steersmen ranking highest. Yet higher were guides, interpreters, and
skilled workmen who earned about £25. An able *engagé* might eventually
become postmaster, in charge of some outlying establishment. He would
earn perhaps £40, but he remained an *engagé* and could not rise into the
ranks of gentlemen traders; in the Hudson's Bay Company the chances
of promotion from the ranks were even slighter than in the British Army.

A gentleman officer began as a youth signing his indentures and
shipping to Hudson Bay to start as an apprentice clerk at £20 a year.
After eight years he was regarded as 'finished', and might become an
accountant in one of the Company's forts or even command a minor
post at £100 a year. There were 150 clerks, and by no means all of them
were able to rise to the commissioned rank of Chief Trader, which meant

control of an establishment of some importance and brought a share in the profits of the trade as well as a salary. The highest rank was that of Chief Factor, who controlled a district centring on a major fort, where he was in direct charge. The Chief Factor was a man of truly baronial consequence. As an old Company man, Joseph William McKay, recollected:

> This exalted functionary was lord paramount; his word was law; he was necessarily surrounded by a halo of dignity, and his person was sacred, so to speak. He was dressed every day in a suit of black or dark blue, white shirt, collars to his ears, frock coat, velvet stock, and straps to the bottom of his trousers. When he went out of doors he wore a black beaver hat worth forty shillings. When travelling in a canoe or boat he was lifted in or out of the craft by the crew; he still wore his beaver hat, but it was protected by an oiled silk cover, and over his black frock coat he wore a long cloak made of the Royal Stuart tartan, lined with scarlet or dark blue coating. The cloak had a soft Genoa velvet collar which was fastened across by mosaic gold clasps and chain . . . Salutes were fired on his departure from the fort and his return.

At the pinnacle of the structure, responsible only to the directing Committee in London, was the Governor. That post was held by George Simpson for almost forty years, from 1821 to 1860. Nicknamed 'the Little Emperor', Simpson ruled the whole expanse of the Company's domain, from Lake Superior to the Pacific, as an intermittently enlightened despot. Gentlemen and *engagés* alike quaked when Simpson, eventually Sir George, swept through their territories on his inspection trips. His picked crew of Iroquois paddlers often propelled the Governor—seated in the centre of the canoe with his personal piper behind him—through the wilderness at an average of a hundred miles a day. A sense of the pomp, as well as the perils that attended his progress, is given in Chief Trader Archibald Macdonald's account of Simpson's arrival at Fort St James in New Caledonia, the territory that later became British Columbia. The section of the journey they were completing had been made on horseback.

> The day, as yet, being fine, the flag was put up; the pipe in full Highland costume; and every arrangement was made to arrive in FORT ST. JAMES in the most imposing manner we could, for the sake of the establishment, descending a gentle hill, a gun was fired, the bugle sounded, and soon after, the piper commenced the celebrated march of the clans . . . . The guide, with the British ensign, led the van, followed by the band; then the Governor, on horseback, supported by Doctor Hamlyn and myself on our chargers, two deep; twenty men, with their burdens, next formed the line; then one loaded horse, and lastly Mr. McGillivray (with his wife and light infantry) closed the rear. During a brisk discharge of small arms and wall pieces from the Fort, Mr. Douglas . . . met us a short distance in advance, and in this order we made our entree into the capital of Western Caledonia.

Nowhere else in Canada, except among the rank-conscious Indian tribes of the Pacific coast, was there such a rigidly graded society as that of Rupert's Land and New Caledonia, a society that survived more or less intact until the end of the Company's domination of the territory. It did so for two reasons. It was composed of no more than two thousand people of closely interlocking interests, gentlemen and *engagés*; such a small number, in such a vast area, required rigid cohesion for their dominance to survive. John McLean, a disaffected fur-trader writing of the Company in the 1820s, described it as 'an authority combining the despotism of military rule with the strict surveillance and mean parsimony of the avaricious trader'.

Elsewhere in British North America the original garrison societies of Quebec and Halifax, where during the eighteenth century a similar kind of cohesion existed, had by 1814 been greatly diluted by civilians, and a diffuse society with many elements and layers now emerged: officials, merchants, lawyers, clergymen, artisans, settlers, and the indeterminate proletariat, largely poor Irish, that began to sift into the town as soon as large-scale emigrations from the British Isles began in the 1820s.

Apart from the officers temporarily stationed in the country, the élite groups consisted of the officials, the clergy, the English officers and other gentry who obtained land grants in Upper Canada and in parts of the Lower province, notably the Eastern Townships, together with the remnants of the old French gentry in their seigneuries along the St Lawrence and the rising and increasingly politicized class of lawyers and notaries in the towns and villages.

There were in fact considerable differences between the ruling cliques in the towns of Lower and Upper Canada, partly because in the lower province the structures of power and social influence were divided between Quebec, the administrative, ecclesiastical, and garrison centre, and Montreal, the mercantile centre. From the beginning, as a result of the fur trade, Montreal developed a society dominated by merchants; the Scots of the North West Company quickly replaced their French predecessors after 1760, and shipping interests came in at a later period—after the advent of steam navigation—when overseas trade began to shift upriver from Quebec.

In Upper Canada, Governor Simcoe's new capital of York (Toronto) quickly took precedence over the earlier Loyalist centres like Niagara and Kingston, and it was only later in the nineteenth century that anything in the nature of an extensive mercantile class developed in Toronto (and then it was largely infiltrated by officials and lawyers who had become entrepreneurs). The original urban élite of Upper Canada, which the political radicals of the 1830s—including William Lyon Mackenzie—would dub the 'Family Compact', was basically an official and professional one.

The political aspects of the Family Compact will be discussed in a later chapter. As a social phenomenon it came into being partly owing to Governor Simcoe's desire to establish a gentry-based society, and partly from the natural mutual interests of those who benefited from that effort. The nucleus consisted of imperially appointed officers of state and local officials chosen by Simcoe from Loyalists of his acquaintance. The formally aristocratic society Simcoe had envisaged never came into being, largely because the British government feared it might provoke rebellion. Nevertheless the officials favoured by Simcoe formed the nucleus of the quasi-aristocratic élite that did spring up and that left power in the hands of a number of families—like the Jarvises and Ridouts, the Robinsons and Boultons—who remained influential in Toronto for many generations. In the first four decades of the nineteenth century they consolidated social prestige as well as political influence in their hands and dominated the emerging legal profession. Since Toronto was never a major garrison town, politics and the law dominated society until mid-century; the one great exception was John Strachan, the leading clergyman of Upper Canada, who, through his pastoral influence and his domination of upper-class education, became the kingpin of the élite.

Positions were assured, virtually by right of descent, to members of the official families. In this way a system of patronage by holders of political power in Canada was initiated that would continue long after the Family Compact came to an end and responsible government was achieved—although later in our era, especially under the governments of Sir John A. Macdonald and Sir Wilfrid Laurier, political services rather than descent in the approved line would bring reward.

In early nineteenth-century York the official families often intermarried (who else, locally, was of befitting status?). The social life that was developing there by the end of the 1820s seemed like a gallant imitation of contemporary Mayfair in London, if one can judge from a letter written by the young élitist John Elmsley—son of an early judge of the colony and himself a future Executive Councillor—to his mother Mary Elmsley in 1827:

> The winter has set in with all its rigours, and the gay season has commenced in unusual style for York. His Exy. ye. Lt. Govr. gave a most splendid Ball on Friday 30 ulto his good example was followed by the Lady of one of the puisne judges on the Friday following. His Honor the Chief Just: has issued cards for a Ball Tomorrow. The Attorney Genl. Ditto for Thursday. H.M.R. Genl. [His Majesty's Receiver General] Ditto for Friday, and the Lady of the other Puisne Judge is just now sending round his invites for Ditto on Monday next. Six most magnificent Balls in the space of little more than a fortnight besides official Dinners Parties Routes and conversaziones on the intervening days.

The importance of the officials began to decline from 1848 onwards after responsible government came into being, since now they had to share the power they had formerly enjoyed uncontested with a new élite of elected politicians. More stable was the position of the merchants, who prospered and spread their influence over the country regardless of political changes. It was in this period that they established the strong position that commercial and industrial interests have sustained among the Canadian upper class ever since—largely (but not entirely) replacing the criterion of birth by that of wealth.

In the cities of Lower Canada, and especially in Montreal, the English-speaking merchants were the most powerful class, socially and financially; their communities seemed like alien enclaves set in a countryside where the majority of the people were detached from them in class and culture alike. There was as much truth as condescension in the portrait of the *Canadien* farmer at the end of the nineteenth century that Goldwin Smith offered in *Canada and the Canadian Question (1891)*.

> The habitant is a French peasant of the Bourbon day. The 'Angelus' would be his picture, only that in the 'Angelus' the devotion of the men seems less thorough than that of the women, whereas the *habitant* and his wife are alike devout. He is simple, ignorant, submissive, credulous, unprogressive, but kindly, courteous, and probably, as his wants are few, not unhappy . . . He tills in the most primitive manner his paternal lot, reduced by subdivision, executed lengthways, to a riband-like strip with, if possible, a water-front; the river having been the only highway of an unprosperous colony when the lots were first laid out. His food is home-raised, and includes a good deal of pea soup, which affords jokes for the mockers. His raiment is homespun, and beneath his roof the hum of the spinning-wheel is still heard. His wife is the robust and active partner of his toil. Their cabin, though very humble, is clean. Such decorations as it has are religious. The Church services are to the pair the poetry and pageantry of life. If either reads anything, it is the prayer-book.

Out of this peasant class, as traditional as any in Europe, a new middle class was beginning to emerge through the seminaries and colleges that the Roman Catholic Church had begun to create shortly after the establishment of New France. Lord Durham, in his *Report* of 1840, attached great importance to these institutions and to their effect on the class structure of Lower Canada.

> The number of pupils in these establishments is estimated altogether at about a thousand; and they turn out every year, as far as I could ascertain, between two and three hundred young men thus educated. Almost all of these are members of the family of some habitant, whom the possession of greater quickness than his brothers has induced the father or the curate of the parish to select and send to the seminary. These young men possessing a degree of information immeasurably superior to that of the fam-

ilies, are naturally averse to what they regard as descending to the humble occupations of their parents. A few become priests; but as the military and naval professions are closed against the colonist, the greater part can only find a position suited to their notions of their own qualifications in the learned professions of advocate, notary and surgeon. As from this cause these professions are greatly overstocked, we find every village in Lower Canada filled with notaries and surgeons, with little practice to occupy their attention, and living among their families, or at any rate among the same class . . . . The most perfect equality always marks their intercourse, and the superior in education is separated by no barrier of manners, or pride, or distinct interests, from the singularly ignorant peasantry by which he is surrounded. He combines, therefore, the influences of superior knowledge and social equality and wields a power over the mass, which I do not believe that the educated class of any other portion of the world possess. To this singular state of things I attribute the extraordinary influence of the Canadian demagogue.

A different kind of symbiosis emerged in the rural districts of Upper Canada. There the immigrant English gentlemen were at first anxious to create a class society similar to that in the rural areas of England, from which many of them came, but they were singularly unsuccessful in establishing an ascendancy. The first of the would-be squires appeared during the 1790s under the governorship of John Graves Simcoe, when an early wavelet of officers obtained land grants on resigning their commissions after the Peace of Amiens in 1802, and a few of them, like the famous Colonel Talbot, were temporarily successful in creating something resembling the traditional relationship between an English lord of the manor and his tenants.

After the Napoleonic wars, when officers were gradually let go on half-pay, the second and much greater wave of British gentry arrived in the Canadas during the 1820s and the early 1830s. They came at the same time as the poverty-stricken labourerers—victims of the Agricultural Revolution whom the English parishes (to William Cobbett's great annoyance) were busily exporting—and the growing numbers of the famine-driven Irish poor. But if the gentry imagined that in the kaleidoscope of immigration the raw materials of the society they had left behind would shake down into the pattern as before, they were mistaken.

The English farm labourers and Irish peasants who arrived in the British North American colonies found that they had come, as Joseph Howe said of Nova Scotia, to 'an excellent poor man's country, because almost any man, in any walk of industry, by perseverence and economy, can secure the comforts of life.' Those who arrived early found a society in which the egalitarian manners of the New World had already established a certain ascendancy. An 1820 pamphlet 'By an English farmer', entitled 'A Few Plain Directions to Persons intending to Proceed as Settlers to His Majesty's province of Upper Canada', remarked:

The inhabitants of Upper Canada consist of British and Americans, with several families of Germans, and some of French extraction. From this mixture arises a great diversity of manners, and customs in the province, but as the emigrants from the United States form by far the greater moiety of the people, the rest are, in some measure, compelled to conform to their habits and usages.

And, although the Loyalist and other American components of the population were quickly diluted by the flood of immigration in the 1830s, their influence on social relations continued, as the astonished British immigrant gentry quickly discovered. Susanna Moodie, in *Roughing it in the Bush* (1852), remarked on the influence of the 'low-born Yankee' even on the 'British peasantry and mechanics', who became rapidly 'Yankeefied'.

They no sooner set foot upon the Canadian shores than they become possessed with this ultra-republican spirit . . . They demand to eat at your table, and to sit in your company, and if you refuse to listen to their dishonest and extravagent claims, they tell you that 'they are free; that no contract signed in the old country is binding in "Meriky"; that you may look for another person to fill their place as soon as you like . . .'

But the most important difference between Britain and Canada probably lay in the availability of land. The land in England was already owned; it was hard for a non-owner, unless he had made a fortune in trade, to change his status. But in Upper Canada, during the first three decades after Waterloo, there was enough land for everyone, gentlemen and others, to get their share. The former labourer was no longer dependent on the gentleman who owned the land. With land came independence, and with independence came dignity—at least for those who succeeded in hacking a farm out of the wilderness. All this is suggested in an often-quoted letter, written in the early 1850s to a friend remaining in England by the former day-labourer Philip Annett, who seems to have been one of the men assisted by his English parish to immigrate to Canada so that he would not be a burden on the poor rate.

I think you was better sell your house and get a little of the parish and come to Canada whilst you have a chance. If you don't come soon it is likely you will starve, and if you don't your children will; whilst if you was to come hither with your family, any one would be glad to take one or two of them and keep them as their own children until of age, and then give them 100 acres of land and stock besides. I was agreeably surprised when I came here to see what a fine country it was. It being excellent land, bearing crops of wheat and other corn for twenty or thirty years without any dung. Here you have no rent to pay, no poor-rates, and scarcely any taxes. No game-keepers or lords over you. Here you can go and shoot wild deer, Turkeys, Pheasants, Quails, Pigeons, any other sort of game and catch plenty of fish without molestation whatever; here you can raise anything of your own that you want to make use of in your family. You can make your own soap, candles, sugar, treacle and vinegar without paying any duty . . . I am satisfied with this country, and so is Luesa, for we are as much respected here as any of our neighbours, and so would you if you come.

Such men believed, with justification, that it was they—as free men wrestling their own farms out of the wilderness on land they would never have possessed at home—who were the real creators of Upper Canada, as the *habitants* had been of New France. Their feelings were projected in the writings of Robert Sellar, who wrote admiringly of the achievements of Anglo-Celtic settlers (though he was not so fair to those of their French-speaking counterparts). In *Gleaner Tales* (1886) he reflected the antagonisms that flourished in areas like the Eastern Townships where Scottish immigrants came into contact early in the nineteenth century with people of another language and religion. In his most interesting book Sellar used his extensive research into the past of his own people two generations before to write a narrative of Defoe-like verisimilitude: *The True Makers of Canada: The Narrative of Gordon Sellar, Who Emigrated to Canada in 1825* (1915). So authentic did this novel of life in York County, Upper Canada, seem that it was long taken for autobiography; perhaps most authentic of all was the passion with which Sellar exalted the role of the common man in the creation of Canada.

> But no suppression of fact, no titles the crown is minded to confer, no Windsor uniforms, no strutting in swords and cocked hats, no declarations and resolutions of Parliament, no blare of party conventions, no lies graven on marble, no statues of bronze can change the truth, that the true makers of Canada were those who, in obscurity and poverty, made it with axe and spade, with plough and scythe, with sweat of face and strength of arm.

Sellar, an old man writing in 1915, was looking back to the period of his father's generation, but Catharine Parr Traill wrote *The Backwoods of Canada* (1836) at the very time of the great immigrations of the 1830s, and though her standpoint was that of the gentlewoman, she looked with exemplary objectivity on the fortunes of the various classes of people who were involved in the opening of Upper Canada.

> It is a good country for the honest, industrious artisan. It is a fine country for the poor labourer who, after a few years of hard toil, can sit down in his own log-house and look abroad on his own land and see his children settled in life as independent freeholders. It is a grand country for the rich speculator who can afford to lay out a large sum in purchasing land in eligible situations; for if he have any judgment he will make a hundred per cent as interest for his money after waiting a few years. But it is a hard country for the poor gentlemen whose habits have rendered him unfit for manual labour.

This 'gentlemen' class was one that Traill and her sister Susanne Moodie knew best, because they belonged to it. Some of the officers who came from England were men of high rank, like the farming admiral Anna Jameson encountered in 1836, but most were marginal gentlemen, in wealth and antecedents alike. One of their sharper critics, Robert Davis, in *The Canadian Farmer's Travels* (1837), written on the eve of the rebellion in Upper Canada, remarked that their

> pretensions of superiority over other settlers, would disgust a dog . . . . Many of these have been Ensigns in the old country, but when they arrived in Canada they called themselves *Captains*.

Both Thomas Traill and Dunbar Moodie were mere Lieutenants of the 21st Fusiliers. Their wives were daughters of Thomas Strickland, a merchant who had used the money earned by trade to buy land and gain a place in the squirearchy—a place so insecure that when he had business failures his literary daughters had to use their pens to earn money in a ladylike manner. Nevertheless they had all acquired the attitudes of the squirearchy, and they sought as far as possible to recreate in the backwoods of Canada a life as refined as the one they had left behind in England.

Their efforts were often subjected to contempt and suspicion. During the 1890s a pair of spirited sisters of Loyalist descent, Robina and Kathleen M. Lizars, produced two lively 'histories': *In the Days of the Canada Company* (1896) and *Humours of '37, Grave, Gay and Grim: Rebellion Times in the Canadas* (1897). They wrote with some style, and with a jocular vigour reminiscent more of Tiger Dunlop then of any 'lady' writer of the era; though they plagiarized freely and frankly without naming their sources, it is obvious that they had access to reminiscences of people active in the times they wrote about. And despite their own genteel ancestry, they did not mince words when talking about the snobbery of Upper Canadian society in the 1830s.

> There was an ominous smoke from the fire in Canadian hearts over this question of class prejudices. Those were the days when a barrister would not shake hands with a solicitor, nor would a 'dissenting' minister be allowed within the pale of society . . . . A store-keeping officer refused a challenge because the second who brought it was a saddler. The honourable profession of teaching was looked at so askance that to become a teacher was an avowal of poverty and hopelessness. Yet joined to this Old World nonsense, transplanted to a world so new that the crops sprang out of untilled ground, was the fact that many of the noblesse, indigenous as the burdock and thistle, drew their rent rolls from the village stores, and with the rearing of the head of what was called 'the Hydra-headed democracy', Froissart's fear was shared 'that all gentility was about to perish'.

In fact, circumstances made it impossible to maintain a class society in the backwoods without great concessions to the ways of the New World. The 'bush-ladies', as Catharine Parr Traill ironically described herself and her kind, and their agriculturally inept menfolk were hampered by lack of capital and experience, and by the absence of a docile labouring class such as existed in England. While Traill was insistent in *The Backwoods of Canada* that 'our society', which was 'mostly military and naval', was too attached to 'good breeding and polite life' to 'allow any deviation from those laws that good taste, good sense and good feeling have established', she also declared that

> here it is considered by no means derogatory for the wife of an officer or gentleman to assist in the work of the house, or to perform its entire duties, if occasion requires it; to understand the mystery of soap, candle, and sugar-making; to make bread, butter and cheese, and even to milk her own cows, to knit and spin, and prepare the wool for the loom. In these matters we bush-ladies have a wholesome disregard for what Mr. or Mrs. So-and-so thinks or says.

Traill further exhorts the emigrant to 'discard everything exclusively pertaining to the artificial refinement of fashionable life in England', which did not mean the abandonment of the real standards of civilization and culture learnt at home. 'It is education and manners that must distinguish the gentleman in this country.'

There is a certain gentle desperation in such exhortations, and in fact the gentleman seeking to establish himself in the Upper Canadian bush, unless he had great wealth, soon found himself forced to accommodate to the 'hydra-headed democracy' of the backwoods. Labourers and servants were not easy to find, particularly by the gentleman who was trying to eke out his capital until his land became productive, and they expected not only to be well paid, but also to be treated as equals. Moreover, every settler found it convenient and necessary, particularly in a new and uncleared area, to fit into the network of mutual activities that were known collectively as bees. A bee was a gathering of neighbours called together to help a settler in some task difficult to perform alone. There were raising bees, to construct the walls and roofs of a house or a barn; logging bees to clear and burn fallen timber before a field could be cultivated; and among the women there were bees to husk corn, to prepare apples for drying, and to make quilts. Bees were occasions for socializing as well as for work, and a man's and a woman's prestige in the district would depend largely on the amount of food and whisky they provided. At these times the gentleman farmer, unless he could afford to do without voluntary help, was at one with his neighbour. As Catharine Parr Traill remarked, while praising 'this laudable practice', which 'has grown out of necessity':

In no situation, and under no other circumstance, does the equalizing system of America appear to such advantage as in meetings of this sort. All distinctions of rank, education and wealth are for the time temporarily laid aside. You will see the son of the educated gentleman and that of the poor artisan, the officer and the private soldier, the independent settler and the labourer who works out for hire, cheerfully uniting in one common cause. Each individual is actuated by the benevolent desire of affording help to the helpless, and exerting himself to raise a home for the homeless.

Yet in spite of the levelling influence of life in the bush, the gentry did strive to perpetuate the manners of their class and to sustain its educational standards, as the multitude of English-style private schools in Canada attests to this day. And we owe to the early gentlemen in Canada, and even more to the early gentlewomen, the beginnings of a literature that was not merely utilitarian, not merely didactic and descriptive (as will be shown in greater detail in Chapter 11).

Since the gentry who came to Upper Canada never succeeded in establishing the landed power that would have enabled them to take on the functions as well as the pretensions of an aristocracy, it was the merchants who came to form the real patrician class. Not only in the earlier mercantile centres like Montreal and Quebec, but also in the smaller towns of Upper Canada as the century went on, stratified societies emerged in which class was associated with trading patterns— as Sara Jeannette Duncan suggested in *The Imperialist* (1904) when she described the small manufacturing town of Elgin, which was based on her hometown of Brantford:

> Dry goods were held in respect and chemists in comparative esteem; house furnishings and hardware made an appreciable claim, and quite a leading family was occupied with seed grains. Groceries, on the other hand, were harder to swallow . . . smaller trades made smaller pretensions; Mrs. Milbourn could tell you where to draw the line . . . Anything 'wholesale' or manufacturing stood, of course, on its own feet; there was nothing ridiculous in molasses; nothing objectionable in a tannery; nothing amusing in soap.

When the power of the appointed officials of the 'Family Compact' period dwindled halfway through the century with the advent of responsible government, it was the merchants and their allies, the lawyers, who slipped into the places of power. Some Victorian Canadians, like Goldwin Smith, saw this as a development that robbed Canada of the benefits of an enlightened Toryism.

> There are in Canada no social materials for a House of Lords, nor is there anything like that independent gentry which has furnished the conservative element in the House of Commons. The leading men in Canada are commercial, and cannot leave their business offices for Ottawa, or if they do, it is on business of their own.

If, seen from this point of view, the Canadian Senate was a travesty of the House of Lords and the House of Commons a parody of its Westminster counterpart, there was also a certain risible quality in the earnest efforts of successive governors-general and their entourages to provide Canada with the ceremonial and social attributes of a monarchy. Sometimes their attempts to take regality to the people were arduous in the extreme. Anticipating a Maritime tour in the 1870s, Lady Dufferin, the wife of the Governor-General of Canada, somewhat wryly noted in her diary:

> Next week we have four balls, three monster picnics, three dinners, a concert, a cricket-match and a review. Is it not fearfully kind? 'What I must wear,' is a question I must decide seriously every day.

One high-spirited young woman, Frances (Feo) Monck—a daughter-in-law of the Governor-General of British North America—gave some vivid accounts in her diary of one such vice-regal event: the 'duty ball' given in Quebec City on the occasion of the gathering at which the basis of Confederation was worked out; it took place on 15 October 1864.

> It was arranged that I was to follow the G.-G. with the Prime Minister, Sir E. Taché, and to dance the first quadrille with him, but Sir E. is so very old that he can't dance, and he would not take me in for fear of having to dance with me, so he walked in first alone. Then came the G.G., then John A. with me, and then Cartier and Mrs. Godley. 'God save the Queen' was played, and we marched up to the throne in procession. Sir R. Macdonnell (Governor of Nova Scotia) and his wife chose to come very late—I believe they thought it grand to do so. Between their being late, and old Sir Etienne hiding behind a screen to escape from me, the first quadrille was spoilt. The G.-G. danced with Madame Cartier, and I with some New Brunswick minister, Colonel Grey by name. The ministers were very angry about my being left without my proper partner, and made apologies, but poor Sir Etienne is about seventy, so I think he was right to hide! . . . . The G.-G. then introduced me to Sir Robert Macdonnell. He asked me to walk about with him and have some refreshments, so off we went. He is supposed to be handsome, but I don't admire him; he wore a red riband and order, but otherwise looked nothing much. Well, this old king and I wandered on and on for a long time, he being too grand to ask the way . . . . With difficulty I at last got an ice, and then we lost ourselves quite, and found at last that we were seated under the wrong throne, in the wrong room! This all took up some time, and when we at last found the right room, I danced with Dr. Tupper, Prime Minister of Nova Scotia, who trembled with nervousness as I whirled him through the lancers . . . .

Feo went home early, tired of the provincial politicians whom 'wigs, spectacles and grey hair don't . . . hinder from dancing.' The next day she added a comment that reflected curiously on the behaviour of mid-century politicians gathering to create a nation:

F. Burrowes' account of the end of the ball was most amusing; such drunkenness, pushing, kicking, and tearing, he says he never saw; his own coat tails were nearly torn off; the supper room floor was covered with meat, drink, and broken bottles.

A few months later Feo described a different kind of gathering, the Stadacona Ball, also in Quebec.

The crowd was very great, and at first I could not see anyone I knew. At last my partners found me, and I danced a great deal. There were only quadrilles and galops, and but *one* valse, whilst I was there . . . . I never could describe to you the dresses; everyone almost had a bow hanging at the back with long ends, like a cow's tail. One woman had a pink, dirty, old silk, with the body of it made like a corset *over* a dirty loose white silk low Garibaldi!—her hair short and not done at all! She looked as if she were undressing to go to bed. Another had an old black silk trimmed with deep red—the body made like a corset with a deep red *net* puffed above the corset . . . . One woman wore a long dishevelled white feather, which reached from the front of her large head to her shoulders at the back. You could imagine some had dressed up to make others laugh . . . . You know these balls are very mixed; all the shop-keepers attend them. When I first came to the ball, I remarked several paper bags flying about the room, and I verily believe that people bring refreshments in these bags, as you can only get tea, ice, etc, there. Captain King said, 'Yes they all bring their nose bags with them.'

Such occasions reinforce one's impression that even in the towns, while a fairly rigid class system existed in terms of privilege and power, in terms of manners and mingling it was far more open and informal than English society at the time.

As settlement spread from Upper Canada across the continent, the English gentry accompanied it. The nineteenth century, with its large families, was a difficult time for younger sons. Thanks to the long Pax Britannica of the Victorian age, wars were small, senior officers survived, and service in the Indian army, the main garrison force in the Empire, was not to everybody's taste. The Indian and the colonial civil services, now selected by examinations, were no longer wholly class preserves. Even the clergy was being invaded by the lower classes. An anonymous publication in 1887 devoted to the potentialities of British Columbia remarked:

Our object in exploring this little known country was to test its capabilities as a home for some of the public-school and university men, who in this overcrowded old England of ours, every year find themselves more *de trop* . . . . They cannot dig, . . . their soul is distinctly unfettered to an office stool; the Arts, the Professions and the Services are all 'Full inside' . . . . Emigration is the one help left.

The first gentleman settler in the Far West reached the Pacific coast in 1849, the very year the colony of Vancouver Island was founded: he was Captain Walter Colquhoun Grant, a twenty-six-year-old ex-officer in the Scots Greys. Grant took the precaution of taking eight English labourers with him to work the land he took up at Sooke, thirty miles west of Victoria, but they immediately deserted him for the goldfields of California. In 1853 Grant sold out to John Muir, a mining foreman who had been working at Fort Rupert in the north-east of the island and who was much more suited to the task of clearing and cultivating the land than Grant, whose 'flightingness', as one Hudson's Bay man remarked, 'amounts almost to lunacy'. In his memoirs Dr J.A.S. Helmcken, who had recently arrived as the young surgeon attached to Fort Victoria, left a vivid vignette of Grant, who arrived at the Fort on a visit.

> There were a good many in Bachelor's Hall—all young men. After a while Capt. Grant began 'to entertain the company'. He showed how to use the sword. He stuck a candle on the back of a chair, and snuffed it therewith, but I am bound to confess he took a good bit of the candle with it, and down it went. Again the candle was stuck up. Then he split it longitudinally and this time splendidly. He wanted to 'cut' a button off Benson's coat (he had none too many). But Benson said—Oh! Oh! cut a button—no, no—split or spit one too! ho! ho! After a while he wanted to escort Her Majesty to Windsor Castle. All were to be cavalry. So down everybody went Kangaroo fashion. Grant being in command, took the lead, and so we hopped in this style round the room, and made considerable of a racket.

Grant devoted much of his time, which he should have spent on his land, around Victoria, where a fellow officer, Captain Edward Edwards Langford, had become bailiff for the Puget Sound Agricultural Company, the Hudson's Bay Company's farming wing. Langford's sister started up a Young Ladies' Academy that was attended by, among others, the daughters of Governor Douglas and his mixed-blood wife, and Langford himself provided a centre for social life by his constant entertaining. In this he was encouraged by the naval officers at Esquimalt: in one year, 1853, he spent four times his salary on riding parties, picnics, and evening gatherings and was reprimanded for charging it all up to the Company's account. As for Grant, flighty or not, he had the foresight to build the first independent sawmill on Vancouver Island, thus starting a great industry.

Less than a decade later the discovery of gold in the Fraser Canyon opened up the mainland of British Columbia, and gentleman settlers began to arrive along with the miners. One of the first was Thomas Glennie, who pre-empted land near Fort Hope, the transhipping point for furs brought by packhorse brigades from the interior of New Caledonia. Like Langford, Glennie did everything extravagantly. He booked first-class passages for himself, his wife, the former Susan Moir, and her two daughters by her first marriage, and sent round the Horn a choice of elegant possessions: a rosewood piano, a historic silver candelabrum, specially painted portraits of the two girls; wardrobes for the wilderness included riding habits. It was clear that Glennie intended to replicate the life of an English squire in the spacious log house, 'Hopelands', that he built. Not till his extravagent entertainments threatened him with bankruptcy did he take to farming, with a disastrous lack of success. He was sold up, and shortly afterwards, in 1864, he disappeared. The two girls married men who played a great part in developing British Columbia. Jane's husband was Edward Dewdney, later Lieutenant-Governor of the Northwest Territories, and Susan's was John Fall Allison, after whom the Allison Pass through the Cascades is named.

Susan Allison showed another side of the English gentry. Stoical, energetic, competent, she accompanied Allison when he went to the still-wild Okanagan Valley to rear cattle, and became an excellent ranch wife. Remembering those days, she wrote in her memoirs:

It has been a busy life, too; no day spent in idleness.
My children were good and obedient. I had taught the four older ones to read and write, and as I had few books fitted for children, I had made stories from English History and Grecian and Roman History, too. I don't think they ever forgot what they learnt in the Okanagan, though they learned little enough after. I myself had learnt patience, to fish and cure the fish, and dry Venison. Dumby taught me to gather straw and grass and make hats for the children; even my husband did not scorn the hats I made. I now could mend the little boots, make mocassins, cut rawhide into strands and make a braid for lariats to lasso the horses.

She lassoed the horses as well, and milked the cows. Yet she was disturbed when her husband's American partner mocked her for dressing for dinner, a habit she retained throughout her ranching years.

The second great British migration to Canada took place in the years after the Canadian Pacific Railway was completed, and peaked in 1911-13, when 150,000 emigrants arrived from the British Isles. They were mostly working people, but gentry were among them, including the famous remittance men—young men of 'good families' who had been wastrels or failures at home and were sent to Canada with a regular monthly allowance to keep them from public view. (The same treatment does not seem to have been meted out to the other sex; I have never heard of a remittance woman.)

The remittance men never became a lasting element in Canadian life because their loyalties were always towards the world that rejected them; their underlying desire to prove themselves worthy of reacceptance was demonstrated in two world wars when almost all of them went to fight for the England that had expelled them, and few returned. The individual remittance men were not the only ephemerae in the summer of

Canada's turn-of-the century expansion. There were more resplendent but equally transient manifestations: several groups in the West imitated Governor Simcoe's long-past efforts to recreate in a Canadian ambience the microcosm of an English society.

One of these curious archaic experiments was Cannington Manor. In 1882 Captain Edward Michell Pierce gained title to an area forty miles south of Moosomin (in what would become Saskatchewan) that he would describe to prospective settlers as 'all the land as far as the eye can see'. His idea was to create a self-contained community that would sustain near-feudal values at a safe distance from the corroding influences of a changing England, and he attracted a dozen British families who came with their grooms and servants and racehorses. He built a 26-room stone house, a stable, flour mill, smithy, carpenter shop, general store, and hotel, and established an energetic social life, which included a hunt with a pack of fox hounds. Pierce also undertook to train young gentlemen in Canadian farming, for a hundred pounds 'all found'. The Scottish farmer he had engaged to train them remarked: 'I was glad when the young gentlemen took to tennis, so that I could get on with the work.' His remark sets the tone for the history of Cannington Manor. The grooms went off to become homesteaders; the housemaids found Canadian husbands; the hunters became bored with pursuing the coyote, so much more resourceful than the English fox. And when neither of the trans-Canadian railways came near Cannington Manor, its precarious economy collapsed, and the gentry departed, leaving their stone houses to the weather and the wildlife. The Anglican church alone remained, with Captain Pierce reposing in its graveyard. (The site is now a provincial historic park and some of the buildings have been reconstructed.)

A similar vision inspired the Marquis of Anglesey's plan to create a colony for English gentry in British Columbia. He chose an area of benchland overlooking the Thompson River, not far west of Kamloops—arid land that needed only water to transform it into flourishing orchards. The settlement was named Walhachin, which in the local Salish dialect meant Land of Plenty. The orchards were owned individually, but the structure of flumes to bring water to the orchards was owned communally. A hundred and fifty people settled at Walhachin and created orchards with the help of Chinese labourers. But in the week when war was declared in 1914 the forty-three Englishmen, all of military age, departed. None returned. For a while the women, with the help of the Chinese, tried to keep things going, but torrential rains destroyed the flumes, and in a couple of years Walhachin was deserted, the land returned to desert, and the fruit trees died.

Ventures like Cannington Manor and Walhachin failed because they were colonies in the strict sense, seeking to hive off fragments of English society into an alien environment. They had no relation to the present or future of Canadian society, or even to the class system as it developed in Canada, for they were the domains of a class that had no place there.

The other famous western colony of British stock during this period was the Barr colony in present-day Saskatchewan. It was much more strident and less gentlemanly in its intentions than either Cannington Manor or Walhachin. Its founder, the Rev. Isaac Moses Barr, and its chaplain, the Rev. Exton Lloyd, both Englishmen with a previous experience of Canada, were appalled by Clifford Sifton's turn-of-the-century policies of filling the vacant Prairies with peasants from Eastern and Central Europe. Canada, they felt, was fast slipping away from its destiny. (Like most of their kind, they conveniently forgot the French past.) The solution, Barr declared in a prospectus he boldly entitled *CANADA FOR THE BRITISH*, was to establish settlements by people devoted to the imperial allegiance, rather than to gentlemanly traditions, and so he called for settlers willing to risk their futures in establishing a series of completely British colonies on the prairie. He received a surprising response. Almost 2,000 people were willing to set off in the spring of 1903 in a former troopship of the South African war, the *Lake Manitoba*, which was designed to carry 800 people. Early in April they arrived in Montreal and the *Gazette* duly reported their departure westward.

> Four special trains carrying the Barr colonists, numbering 1,960, left here today for the Saskatoon district, where the new Canadians will establish homes and cities. The party, which is declared to be the greatest emigration from England since the departure of William Penn, arrived Saturday morning on the steamship *Lake Manitoba* whose cargo of humanity was packed like fish in a box. The colonists bring with them 1/2 million pounds sterling. They are probably the finest body of men, women and children that ever landed here. Lawyers, doctors, clergymen, merchants, aristocrats, artisans, domestics, tradesmen and labourers are included, besides babies by the score . . . . Rev. I.M. Barr, the organizer of the party, is a brisk businesslike man, who is full of enthusiasm over the prospects of his scheme. He says 1,500 more colonists are to follow, and that 10,000 more will come next year.

The report, based on Barr's statements, may have exaggerated the inclusion of aristocrats (on another occasion he boasted of being accompanied by 'five earls' nephews') and professional men, but it seems to have portrayed fairly accurately the social heterogeneity of the colonists, who included people from all classes, united only in their desire to save Canada for Britain, and doomed to be divided by the way they used their aitches. After irksome weeks reaching their future home on the bare prairie, many of the settlers drifted away in discouragement. The rest, feeling their confidence betrayed and their money mishandled, deposed Barr from the leadership and elected Lloyd in his place. By now the snobbish, the frivolous, and the incompetent had left, and the remnant that Lloyd salvaged consisted of hard-working people who farmed the prairie like any other immigrants, and whose ultimate contribution was not to preserve the dominance of the British strain, but to pioneer in the environs of Lloydminister (named after Exton Lloyd) the settlement of the North Saskatchewan area. It was their variety of classes and the unusual social flexibility of those who stayed, after the snobs in droves had fled, that enabled them to carry on and succeed.

A special area in which the British gentleman and his imitators long predominated in Canada was the military life. For more than half our period, Canada virtually depended for the defence of its borders on British regiments, and for almost the whole of the period it depended on the Royal Navy to cast an umbrella of defence over its shores. Canadians came very slowly and reluctantly to the conclusion that they must accept the expense and inconvenience of defending themselves. This was at least partly because by its nature Canadian society from the beginning was generally peaceable, lacking the military cults of European societies and, despite its occasional rebellions, also lacking the sustained republican violences of the American frontier. This does not mean that Canadians did not fight, bravely and skilfully, when they felt they must. But out of wartime they have not generally been eager soldiers; they have always been anxious, as soon as wars were ended, to finish with conscription and to dismantle large armies. In other words, they can be seen as citizen-soldiers—part of the long tradition stretching back to the Athenians marching out to Marathon and Cincinnatus leaving the plough.

In the aftermath of the War of 1812 there was a rapid demilitarization in the British North American territories. The local regiments of fencibles, recruited as regulars for colonial defence, had been disbanded by 1816, and in 1819 the British garrison itself had been reduced to seven regiments. Many of the militia formations that had been mustered for the war retained a paper existence, and produced a multitude of military titles for worthy citizens, but they quickly lapsed from training.

Anna Jameson described one occasion, just prior to the Rebellion of 1837, when she went to Erindale to visit her friends, the M——'s, and found the sons of the house preparing for the annual parade of the district militia—'one in the pretty green costume of a rifleman, the other all covered with embroidery as a captain of lancers.'

> On a rising ground above the river which ran gurgling and sparkling through the green ravine beneath, the motley troops, about three or four hundred men, were marshalled—no, not marshalled, but scattered in a far more picturesque fashion hither and thither: a few log-houses and a saw-mill on the river-bank, and a little wooden church crowning the opposite height, formed the chief features of the scene. The boundless forest

spread all around us. A few men, well mounted, and dressed as lancers, in uniforms which were, however, anything but uniform, flourished backwards and forwards on the green sward, to the manifest peril of the spectators, themselves and their horses, equally wild, disorderly, spirited, undisciplined; but this was perfection compared with the infantry. Here there was no uniformity attempted of dress, of appearance, of movement; a few had coats, others jackets; a greater number had neither coats nor jackets, but appeared in their shirt-sleeves, white or checked, or clean or dirty, in edifying variety! Some wore hats, others caps, others their own shaggy heads of hair. Some had firelocks; some had old swords, suspended in belts, or stuck in their waistbands; but the greater number shouldered sticks or umbrellas . . . . Now they ran after each other, elbowed and kicked each other, straddled, stooped, chattered; and if the commanding officer turned his back for a moment, very coolly sat down to rest on the bank. Charles M. made himself hoarse with shouting out orders which no one obeyed, except, perhaps, two or three men in the front; and James, with his horsemen, flourished their lances, and galloped, and capered, and curveted to admiration. James is the popular storekeeper and postmaster of the village, and when, after the show, we went into his warehouse to rest, I was not a little amused to see our captain of lancers come in, and, taking off his plumed helmet, jump over the counter to serve one customer to a 'pennyworth of tobacco', and another to 'a yard of check' . . . .

The parade day ended in a drunken bout and a riot, in which, as I was afterwards informed, the colonel had been knocked down.

Jameson's account may seem exaggerated for effect, yet the fact is that during the Rebellions of 1837-8 many men on both sides marched off to war without firearms and even without training.

The rebellions themselves led to a doubling of the British garrison, and the fluctuations of military personnel in British North America continued until the 1860s and reached a crescendo in 1861 when an American naval vessel stopped the British steamer *Trent* and precipitated an international crisis by seizing two Confederate agents who were on board. Fourteen thousand troops, including artillery and engineers and regiments of the Guards, were rushed to Canada in case of war. It was the largest contingent of British troops to cross the Atlantic since 1814. At the same time, a British naval presence built up on the Pacific coast, reacting first to the American threat during the Oregon Boundary dispute of 1846, and later to the Russian threat during the Crimean War, and warships eventually found an established calling-place at the naval depot of Esquimalt, close to Victoria.

The continued presence of the garrisons in Halifax and Quebec and of British detachments in other urban centres was socially influential in two respects. It meant that a kind of protocol was retained in the British North American colonies such as no longer existed in cities south of the border, with a corresponding ordering of social life. And it provided something of a cultural veneer since, as we will see, some of the officers were among the best of early Canadian artists, regimental bands made music familiar in public places, and the Canadian theatre of those early days was largely the creation of soldier amateurs. Feo Monck, in her diary, conjured up many charming and light-hearted social occasions created by the military in Quebec in the 1860s.

> In the evening there was a very large dinner party here—all the colonels of the regiments, also Colonel Neville and Colonel Peel. Captain Eliot took me in to dinner; he is so pleasant and amusing. After dinner the string band played out on the verandah. It was like a scene in a play—the moon made a silver path across the water, a ship standing out so clearly on the water that the rigging could be seen quite plain, and the band 'discoursing sweet music' the while. The K.O.B.'s play so exquisitely. The red coats of the officers formed a very good foreground to the picture. The servants had dancing at one end of the verandah and at our end could be seen the *very* tall Captain Eliot and Captain Pip-tin valsing together!

Because most of the officers were members of the British gentry, and some of the nobility, their very presence encouraged the local growth of snobbery. Quebec was protected to some extent by the duality of its culture, but the social life of Halifax was virtually shaped by the military presence, as one traveller in 1830 remarked:

> The garrison forms about one-eighth of this population, and of course materially influences the tone of society. A young officer . . . finds himself raised at once to a level above that accorded to the scarlet cloth at home— his society generally sought, frequently courted, and himself esteemed.

All this led, at least in the early Regency days, to much freedom and frivolity, as one Governor, Lord Dalhousie, remarked when he noted in his journal the effects of a fire in the officers' quarters in June 1817.

> As is generally the case, the cause of the fire cannot be ascertained, but I do not think it in any way surprising that such an accident should happen in a large wooden building, 3 stories high, and full of officers lodged in pigeon holes with their swords near them. All descriptions of ill-behaved people going in and out. The morning scene I am told was most ludicrous, Gentlemen and Ladies, bolting in the utmost consternation, little or no cloaths on them, one saving a box of money, another a bundle of cloaths, Ladies flying but blushing at their dilemma, trying still to hide; rain pouring fortunately in torrents, and affording abundant supply for the Pipes, helped at once to check the flames and start them flying from their lurking places, not unlike rabbits in a warren when a ferret is first among them. With such a swarm I was not surprised at the accident.

Men like Joseph Howe were less amused than the alien Governor at the effect the presence of the garrison was having on their city and its people; in 1834 he wrote:

We by no means wish to undervalue the benefits which Halifax derives from the expenditures of the British and local governments . . . but the whole tendency of military society in a town like this is towards habits of idleness, dissipation and expense. We have colonels, majors, captains, and subalterns—all having fixed incomes provided by the crown—many of them gentlemen of fortune, and polished manners. If our population would be content to borrow only what is estimable, to copy only what was worthy of imitation, we might derive from it a great deal of good and but very little harm. But unfortunately we are all prone to copy each other's vices and virtues, and too many of our young men, without acquiring the grace and polish of their Garrison associates, have learned their disregard of time, their habits of expense, and their contempt for the low pursuits of business.

By the mid-Victorian age the shades of evangelical Christianity had lengthened over the streets of Halifax. The military were still very much in evidence, but pomposity rather than libertinism had become the prevailing tone. The American visitor Frederick S. Cozzens remarked in 1859:

The city hill of Halifax rises proudly from its wharves and shipping in a multitude of mouse-coloured wooden houses, until it is crowned by the citadel. As it is a garrison town, as well as a naval station you meet in the streets red-coats and blue-jackets without number; yonder, with a brilliant staff, the Governor, Sir John Gaspard le Marchant, and here, in a carriage, is Admiral Fanshawe, C.B., of the *Boscawen* Flag-ship. Everything is suggestive of impending hostilities; war, in burnished trappings, encounters you at the street corners, and the air vibrates from time to time with bugles, fifes and drums. But oh! What a slow place it is! Even two Crimean regiments with medals and decorations could not wake it up.

Far away in Victoria, where there was no army establishment, the regular visits of men-of-war still contributed notably to the social life of the young colony of Vancouver Island. In 1859, Lieutenant Charles Wilson helped to organize a typical west-coast social occasion, and the underlying condescension in his account provides an ironic comment on the social pretensions of the islanders.

We gave a ball to the fair ladies here; two of the men of war, the 'Satellite' and 'Plumper', determined to join together and give a grand ball to the ladies of Vancouver Island. I was appointed one of the ball committee with some others and we set our heads together to do the best we could in this part of the world. The first thing was to find a place large enough for the occasion & the only house we could find was the marketplace, a most dismal-looking place, enough to drive all thoughts of dancing out of one's head, however we got all the flags we could from the ships & turned in 30 or 40 sailors, & in a short time a fair palace of flags was erected, so that not a particle of the building was visible; we then rigged up some large chandeliers & sconces of bayonets and ramrods wreathed with evergreens which when lighted up produced a regular blaze of light & made it quite a fair scene. We also got a large supper room in the same style & managed to provide a first rate supper. Every body came to the ball from the governor downwards nearly 200 in all & we kept dancing up with great spirit until 1/2 past three in the morning. Every body was quite delighted & it goes by the name of 'the Party par excellence'; nobody says ball in this part of the world, it is always party. The ladies were very nicely dressed, & some of them danced very well, though they would look much better if they would only learn to wear their crinolines properly, it is most lamentable to see the objects they make of themselves, some of the hoops being quite oval, while others had only one hoop rather high up, the remainder of the dress hanging down perpendicularly.

Because Confederation was a military as well as a political event, it had considerable effect on Canadian social attitudes. As part of the price of unity and autonomy, Canada had to accept the burden of self-protection, on land at least—for the Royal Navy continued to operate in Canadian waters and to sustain its naval depots at Halifax and Esquimalt until they were handed over in 1905. British regiments were rapidly withdrawn after the end of the American Civil War. The last task in which they took part on British soil occurred when the lst battalion of the lst Royal Rifles and some detachments of the Royal Artillery and Royal Engineers joined with militia battalions from Quebec and Ontario to form Colonel Garnet Wolseley's combined British and Canadian expeditionary force to Red River in 1870; this seemed justified to demonstrate the transfer of authority from Britain to Canada after the Red River Rebellion. The force arrived on 24 August; but the British soldiers left five days later. When they boarded the troopships in September and sailed down the St Lawrence and out to sea, the long British presence in North America was, in physical terms at least, almost at an end.

The Canadian militia, as it continued to be called until the end of our period, became the new country's only land defence. There had been militia in Canada ever since the days of New France, and the concept of the *levée en masse* (general mobilization) had been continued after the Conquest in the legal obligation for every man between sixteen and sixty (except for members of sects—Quakers, Mennonites and Tunkers—exempted for their religious pacifism) to serve in the militia when called. But, as Goldwin Smith remarked in 1891:

> The enrolled Militia, comprising all men of military age, exists only on paper, though by Canadian politicians, speaking to the British public and anxious to please their hearers, it has been represented as an organized force ready at any moment to spring to arms.

There were times, a generation before Confederation, when there had been grave doubts as to whether the militia was either loyal or well equipped to be of much practical use. Lord Durham remarked that in 1839 in Lower Canada:

The militia, on which the main defence of the Province against external enemies, and the discharge of many of the functions of internal police have hitherto depended, is completely disorganised. A muster of the force would, in some districts, be the occasion for quarrels between the races, and in the greater part of the country [Lower Canada] the attempting to arm or employ it would be merely arming the enemies of the country.

Even when the militia seemed to be loyal they often did not have the means with which to fight. After Sir Francis Bond Head made his unregretted departure from Upper Canada in 1838, the acting Administrator of the colony, John Beverley Robinson, fearing a further rebellion, wrote desperately to Sir John Colborne in Lower Canada: 'Muskets and ball cartridges are our chief want. You would be delighted to see the fine forward spirit of the people—but there are not the means of arming one twentieth of those who are eager to turn out for duty.'

Canadians shared with the British their traditional distrust of a standing army, and the professional soldiers of the militia—the so-called Permanent Force—was limited by law to a thousand men, growing to this size only slowly. It began with the staff of the Royal Military College, which was founded in 1876 to train militia officers, and was augmented later by those of the nine artillery, cavalry, and infantry schools. The volunteer regiments of the embodied militia consisted mainly of young men from the middle and lower middle classes who trained in camp for two weeks every year and in the case of the city regiments had weekly or fortnightly drills. There were about 40,000 of them just after Confederation, and by 1914 there were about 60,000 of these partially trained men to form the nucleus of the Canadian Corps that fought in the Great War.

The effect of this situation was that the British officer caste, which did so much to set the Canadian social tone before Confederation, was not replaced by a parallel Canadian caste of professional soldiers. In many ways British military influence continued for a long time. The command of the militia was in the hands of a British general, and there were also British officers in the Permanent Force who automatically took precedence over Canadians of the same rank; promising Canadian officers were sent for special training to England, where the best of them got commissions in the British Army and were lost to Canada. The British general, Frederick Middleton, blimpishly led the unwieldy expeditionary force, consisting of several thousand militia, against a few hundred Métis rebels during the North West Rebellion of 1885. This was the first time an actual Canadian army—with all its ancillary services of artillery, engineers, and baggage train—went into action on its own. Inevitably there were clashes between the British generals, who were trying to turn the militia into an effective fighting force, and the politicians, who were more concerned with its political aspects and with having units, however inefficient, in their constituencies so that they could exploit the patronage involved in conferring ranks on amateur majors and colonels. Eventually, in 1908, a Canadian officer was appointed chief of the militia general staff. He was Brigadier-General William Otter, who had lost to the Cree the battle of Cut Knife Hill in 1885.

Like the British garrisons, the militia had its social aspects; for many of its members the snobbish pleasure of belonging to a fashionable unit was a more compelling motive than mere patriotism, and in this sense the militia helped to perpetuate a class system in Canada. Many units, apart from their period of training under canvas, tended to function as fraternities that were as exclusive as social clubs in their choice of members. The units picked their own uniforms, for which the volunteers were expected to pay, and since these were often elaborate and expensive, this fact alone helped to keep out the plebeians. Appearance took precedence over efficiency, and in 1868 Colonel MacDougall, the Adjutant General of Militia, complained that the volunteers

> take a pride in turning out on parade smart and clean and soldierlike as regards the outer appearance; but it is too often the case . . . that their rifles are so foul that they cannot be fired. Yet it is upon the serviceable condition of his weapon at any moment that the value of a volunteer depends. Unless it is kept constantly in use the volunteer is only a sham soldier, and his external trappings are but a useless expense to the country.

A rank in the militia had automatic social standing, and many of the city units sought to imitate the British regiments by organizing social events, like balls or the amateur theatricals in which the Queen's Own in Toronto, which had a whole company of university students, excelled. Most of the officers were well-connected young men, for whose benefit the lists were padded with commissions, and by the 1890s the militia began to take on the appearance of a contemporary South American army; in 1894 it was revealed that the ratio of officers, and NCO's and bandsmen, to privates was 1 : 2 : 2.4.

Rural units seem to have been much less well-organized than the city units, and the mobilization in 1885 on the occasion of the North West Rebellion showed how ill-prepared many of them were. Joseph Crowe, whose recollections of his experiences are preserved in the National Archives, was a private in the Midland Regiment, centred on Kingston, which consisted mainly of rural units. He described the difficult introduction of these ill-trained or untrained men to military life. Apparently not much had changed since Anna Jameson's time:

> Some of the men had never drilled or soldiered before, and knew nothing of order or discipline. Most of us had been 'smelling the cork', and as a result there were quite a few that had to be put in the guard room for the night. The next day we were furnished with brand new uniforms from

head to foot . . . . One mistake was to issue Glengarry caps for a trip of this kind as they were of little use so far as being protection from the weather. The barracks at Kingston reminded us of a large prison. We were placed in large rooms to sleep on a hard dry floor . . . . The men were hard to control since a great number of them had never been under any military rule, and an order was never obeyed without question. I remember an officer going on his rounds at lights out, and he received a severe blow from a boot which someone threw in the dark at him.

Yet, despite the trivial pursuit of titles, the social frivolities, and the rustic inadequacies, the militia developed a mystique. It reflected not only the national feeling that began to develop somewhat fitfully after Confederation, but also a broader patriotism aware of imperial traditions. Even after the breaking of political ties with Britain, that patriotism survived in the minds of ardent militia leaders like Colonel George Denison and his relatives (known collectively as 'The Fighting Denisons'), who had passed from nationalism into imperialism and never doubted that both might best be sustained by the cultivation of military virtues. During the Edwardian decade patriotism found a response among the English-speaking middle classes, and increased steadily during the years immediately preceding the First World War. By 1913, 55,000 militiamen were turning out for annual training, and the burden on the taxpayer grew accordingly, from $1.6 million as a militia appropriation in 1897 to $7 million in 1911, and $11 million budgeted for 1914 even before war was declared.

A special manifestation of the entry into Canadian life of the military spirit, with its class implications, was the creation in 1873 of the Northwest Mounted Police and the peculiar mythology that developed around it, largely because it was the NWMP (in 1919 it became the Royal Canadian Mounted Police) rather than the army that provided a show of defence for Canadian territorial integrity on critical occasions.

During the interlude between the acquisition of the Hudson's Bay Company's rights over Rupert's Land in 1869 and the creation of Manitoba in 1870, the federal politicians had already been considering the creation of a miniature frontier force of 250 all-round soldiers. Macdonald remarked at this time:

It seems to me that the best force would be Mounted Riflemen, trained to act as cavalry, but also instructed in the rifle exercises. They should also be instructed, as some of the line are, in the use of artillery.

After the Red River Rebellion a short-lived garrison of 300 men called the Manitoba Force was created in Winnipeg, and the idea of a body to protect the whole of Rupert's Land faded into the background until Canadians were provoked into action by the infiltration of American wolfers and whisky traders over the border from Montana, and their insolent creation of establishments like the notorious Fort Whoop-up, which flew the American flag on Canadian territory. But by now Macdonald and his associates had second thoughts about creating an actual military force; they feared the Americans might regard that as provocative, and when he introduced the legislation founding the Northwest Mounted Police he said:

> They are to be purely a civil, not a military body, with as little gold lace, fuss and fine feathers as possible, not a crack cavalry regiment, but an efficient police force for the rough and ready—particularly ready—enforcement of law and justice.

Nevertheless, when the North West Mounted Police came into being it wore the red uniform of British regulars. Its men were armed not only with carbines, pistols, and lances like cavalrymen, but also with field artillery pieces; its drill and discipline were military; and in the beginning at least its officers were usually addressed by the military equivalent—colonel or major—of their police ranks. Two-thirds of the first 300, irrespective of rank, were former soldiers, and often—like the first commissioner, Colonel John French—they had started off in the British Army or, like the famous Sam Steele, came of British naval or military families. As Steele himself remarked: 'the force . . . in every respect had more the characteristics of a first-class cavalry regiment than those of an ordinary police force.'

Right from the beginning there was a duality of role about the force that struck participants even when it set out in June 1874 on its first great march to show the flag along the frontier. Not counting the scouts who preceded it, the procession straggled $2^1/_2$ miles over the prairie. In the words of Colonel French:

> To a stranger it would have appeared an astonishing cavalcade. Armed men and guns looked as if fighting had to be done. What could ploughs, harrows, mowing machines, cows, calves, etc., be for? But that little force had a double duty to perform, to fight if necessary, but in any case to establish posts in the far west.

Because in the beginning it was the only agency representing Canada in the West, the NWMP was in fact forced into roles that distinguished it from both ordinary military units and ordinary police forces. It established relationships with the natives on the prairie that made treaties with them feasible in 1876 and 1877. Ironically, the one occasion when the NWMP became involved in a purely military action—the battle of Duck Lake, where Gabriel Dumont and his Métis sharpshooters defeated them at the beginning of the North West Rebellion in 1885—was its most dramatic failure. On the other hand it provided an effective semblance of a civil service in the new territories until a regular one could be established.

In 1897-8, during the Klondike Gold Rush, the NWMP was once again called upon to act as a frontier force, and showed the flag at the passes of the Yukon under the hard conditions that Sam Steele later described:

> It would be difficult to describe the hardships gone through by the Mounted Police stationed on the passes. The camp on the Chilkoot, under Inspector Belcher, was pitched on the summit, where it is bounded by high mountains. A wooden cabin was erected in a couple of days; the place where it was in the pass was only about 100 yards wide. Below the summit, on the Canadian side, was Crater Lake, named after an extinct volcano. On its icy surface the men were forced to encamp when they arrived. On the night of February 18 the water rose in the lake to the depth of six inches. Blankets and bedding were wet, the temperature below zero in the blizzard. The tents could not be moved and the sleds had to be taken into them to enable the men to keep above the water at night. The storm blew for days with great violence, but on the 21st had abated sufficiently to admit of the tents being moved to the top of the hill, where, although the cold was intense, it was better than the water-covered ice of Crater Lake.
>
> The nearest firewood was 7 miles away, and the man sent for it often returned badly frost-bitten. Belcher, collecting customs, performing military as well as police duty on the summits, lived in the shack, which had all the discomforts of a shower bath. Snow fell so thickly and constantly that everything was damp, and paper became mildewed. From February 25 to March 3 the weather was dry and cold, but on that date another terrific storm began and continued almost uninterrupted until May 1! This storm reached its height on Saturday, the 3rd, when the snow buried the cabin and all the tents on the summit, the snowfall for the day being 6 feet on the level.

Yet even among these hardships the military traditions of rank and class prevailed. Steele went to take charge of Lake Bennett, where thousands of people were awaiting the spring break-up to sail the makeshift boats they had built over winter down the Yukon River to Dawson. He and his men were quartered in a small building and he relates that when 'the N.C.O's and men . . . finished their meals and [had] gone to work I had mine cooked and served at the same table. Captain Rant, late of a British cavalry regiment, and Mr. Godson, a customs officer on my staff, messed with me . . .' Captain Rant was the local stipendiary magistrate. Among the Mounties, as elsewhere, the Gentlemen kept apart form the Others.

In later years the NWMP would continue the same roles in the Far North, manning the frontiers and establishing civil authority. They sustained this role largely because there were never challenges on Canada's far borders serious enough to require any other force. It was this accidental fact of their being a mainly symbolic presence that led to the

Mounties' becoming a national myth—which the militia never did. During the Klondike rush the Yukon Field Force, a unit consisting of 203 men and officers from the militia's Permanent Force, made an epic march to the goldfields to take over obviously military duties from the NWMP. Yet it was the Mounties who entered the myth of the Klondike, while the Yukon Field Force was ignored in the literature of the Gold Rush; today it is so little remembered that Pierre Berton devoted only 13 lines to it in his 472-page popular history, *Klondike*, in which the Mounted Police are given lengthy treatment and heroic stature.

The presence of the NWMP has often been treated by Canadian historians, especially popular ones, as the main reason why the Canadian frontier was opened out in a less chaotic and more law-abiding way than its American counterpart. Yet so far as this is true, the Mounted Police were assisted by circumstances that had already distinguished the western parts of British North America from the American plains. Despite their internecine feuds during the years preceding the union of the North West Company and the Hudson's Bay Company, the fur traders had prudently avoided the pattern of confrontation with the native peoples that marked the surge of settlement into the Ohio country and the American mid-west. The Canadian fur traders in their day were alive to the dangers of American penetration, and it was a Hudson's Bay man, James Douglas, who—long before the formation of the Mounted Police—capably closed the frontier to Californian lawlessness at the time of the Fraser Valley gold rush in 1858. Moreover, unlike the American cavalry, the British Army had never adopted the role of an exterminative force dedicated to the destruction of native societies and to the establishment of white supremacy. The Mounted Police, with their red coats, inherited the goodwill of these predecessors.

I suggest that the Mounted Police had another influential role in the West that was a social one. It was under their protection that Ontarians and English moved into the Prairies and established there—before the arrival of the eastern-European peasant immigrants—the kind of class system that had developed in Upper Canada in which, as men of the military élite, the officers of the force took their due place. A social structure was created—headed by officials, politicians, lawyers, and entrepreneurs—that did not merely survive the strong currents of western social radicalism but resulted in an even more extreme polarization of classes and interests than existed in eastern and central Canada.

4

The Radical Thesis:

Rebellion and Reform

'Wherever there is authority, there is a natural inclination to disobedience,' wrote Thomas Chandler Haliburton in one of his later books, *Sam
Slick's Wise Saws* (1853). The old Tory judge was looking back over a
turbulent period in British North American history that had seen armed
rebellions in Upper and Lower Canada, bitter election riots in Newfoundland, and disobedient juries remaking the laws according to their
own conception of justice—like that which in Haliburton's own Nova
Scotia acquitted the reformer Joseph Howe in 1835 on a charge of criminal
libel when, technically, he was undoubtedly guilty. Haliburton was not
advocating disobedience. He was merely noting that in conservative
communities like the North American colonies, where the monarchist
principle presupposed an authoritarian hierarchy gradually adapting
itself to a changing world, disobedience was the necessary alternative
to revolution; rebellion, of course, is the transfer of disobedience from
the moral to the physical plane.

In 1849 Lord Elgin, Governor-General of the united Province of Canada, had every right to feel that the fragile barrier between rebellion and
revolution was almost breached. His approval of the Rebellion Losses
Act, which the legislative assembly had passed on 25 April, resulted in

riots; a mob of English-speaking Montrealers attacked him personally and burned down the parliament buildings. A few days later Elgin wrote to Earl Grey, the incumbent Colonial Secretary in Westminster:

> Excesses correct themselves, and I have no doubt that the violence of the disaffected will elicit a great counter-demonstration. At the same time I confess I did not before know how thin is the crust of order that covers the anarchical elements that boil and toss beneath our feet.

Preventing the crust of order from breaking is what distinguishes a reformist from a revolutionary society. This does not mean that a reformist society is calm and undisturbed; on the contrary it can tolerate more disturbance than a revolutionary society, once established, could allow. But in the reformist society changes emerge, not from the revolutionary dialectic of tyranny and overthrow that leave the absolutism of authority untouched, but from the dialectic of rebellion and moderation that leads to genuine changes in the nature of authority rather than merely in its tenure. Revolutions do not eliminate privilege; they merely institutionalize élites through the transfer, rather than the elimination of, power and therefore of privilege. Reformist societies modify and erode privilege, and it was at a crucial point in this process that Lord Elgin wrote his querulous note to Lord Grey in 1849. The riots over the Rebellion Losses Bill were the final dramatic episode in a cycle of rebellion and reform that had lasted for the best part of two decades. Through unsuccessful rebellions rather than through a successful revolution, the character of Canadian political life was changed. The popular image we have acquired as a cautious, reasonable people has never entirely accorded with reality.

The rebellions of 1837-8 were so close together that in hindsight they give the appearance of a concerted and more or less homogeneous movement spreading over both Lower and Upper Canada. The first fighting in the Lower Canada rebellion took place on 23 November when the *patriotes* effected a temporary defeat of Colonel Gore's troops at St Denis. The only fighting in the Upper Canadian rebellion took place north of Toronto on 5 December, when William Lyon Mackenzie's rebel force dissolved on the approach of three columns of loyalist militia and Tory volunteers. Some grievances were shared by rebels in both provinces. A meeting of Friends of Reform at Doel's Brewery in Toronto on 28 July called for a convention of Upper Canadian delegates and proposed that this convention should send 'seven persons of approved judgment, discretion and patriotism, to proceed to Lower Canada', there to meet representatives of the *patriotes* 'and deliberate on matters of mutual interest to these Colonies.' Mackenzie, who proposed the resolution, said later on, in May 1838 when the uprisings had flared and failed:

Let it suffice to say, that we kept up a good understanding with the reformers in Lower Canada; and concluding that arbitrary imprisonments and a declaration of military execution would follow on the anticipated outbreak at Montreal, we resolved to second the Lower Canada movements by others equally prompt and decisive.

He also claimed at the same time that 'an executive in the city was named' to keep in touch with Papineau and the other *patriote* leaders. But the lack of real co-ordination at the time of the rebellions, and the equal lack of effective preparedness on the part of the rebels in both provinces, suggests a minimum of joint planning and co-ordination.

Certainly those who witnessed the events of that time tended to see the rebellions as quite separate events, and to be preoccupied with insurrection in their respective provinces. Some of the most insightful comments on the events of that period were made by women, perhaps because they did not have to mount a horse to defend the status quo or shoulder a gun or a pike to overthrow it, and they could therefore be more objective and even compassionate. An example was Susanna Moodie's recollection of the times, which she included—a third of a century after the events—in the essay entitled 'Canada: A Contrast' that prefaced the first Canadian edition of *Roughing It in the Bush* in 1871.

When we first came to the country it was a mere struggle for bread to the many, while all the offices of emolument and power were held by a favoured few. The country was rent to pieces by political factions, and a fierce hostility existed between the native born Canadians—the first pioneers of the forest—and the British emigrants, who looked upon each other as mutual enemies who were seeking to appropriate the larger share of the new country.

Those who settled down in the woods were happily unconscious that these quarrels threatened to destroy the peace of the colony.

The insurrection of 1837 came upon them like a thunder clap; they could hardly believe such an incredible tale. Intensely loyal, the emigrant officers rose to a man to defend the British flag and chastise the rebels and their rash leader.

In their zeal to uphold British authority, they made no excuse for the wrongs that the dominant party had heaped upon a clever and high-spirited man. *To them he was a traitor*, and, as such, a public enemy. Yet the blow struck by that injured man, weak as it was, without money, arms or the necessary munitions of war, and defeated and broken in its first effort, gave freedom to Canada, and laid the foundations of the excellent constitution that we now enjoy.

It is a passage of great understanding and fairness, in which Susanna, justifying her husband Dunbar, who served in the provincial militia, but honouring the defeated enemy—William Lyon Mackenzie—against whom he fought, showed her comprehension of the process by which rebellion, failing to produce revolution, can lead to positive reform.

In Upper Canada there was resistance not only to the privileged network of officials and their cronies who administered the colony without any responsibility to the electorate, but also to the policy of granting large areas of land to officers and gentlemen and of favouring the Church of England through the Clergy Reserves, which were denied to the dissenting Protestant churches that represented the majority of the Upper Canadians. Many of the grievances were more basic, related to Susanna's 'struggle for bread'. A poignant passage in an early issue of Mackenzie's newspaper, *The Colonial Advocate* (29 July 1824), illustrates them:

> In Chinguacousy . . . not one tenth of the settlers have got deeds. It is really bad policy to deprive those industrious settlers, who have left their homes in Britain, to seek an asylum in the woods of North America, of their birthright, because they cannot pay £15, £10, or £20 of fees; yet such is the case. Not one of these people who have done settlement duty, and built houses on their farms, can obtain deeds, without first paying as much for one deed, as would furnish parchment, printing, sealing-wax, and slender clerks, to fill up blanks to half a township . . . . Many families in the woods have fared very hard this season for want of the necessaries of life. The opinion of several farmers in the New Survey is, that the present crop in the ground will scarcely be an average one, on account of the cold in the early part of the year, the ground retaining the water in many places being new . . . .
>
> The poverty of the people in this back country can be inferred from the following statement, which may be relied on: 'that not one fifth of all the people in the new townships, settled for two to five years, raise their own provisions.'

From among such people would come many of Mackenzie's supporters in his desperate venture of 1837.

A Reform movement began as early as the 1820s, led largely by immigrants from Britain. Mackenzie and John Rolph, Dr William Warren Baldwin and his son Robert, were all influenced by the reform movement and Chartism in Britain. They were joined by liberal Loyalists, notably the Methodist Egerton Ryerson, and by other immigrants from the United States like Barnabas Bidwell and his son Marshall Spring Bidwell, both of whom suffered from the widespread distrust of non-Loyalist Americans after the War of 1812. When the Bidwells were elected to the Legislative Assembly in 1821 and 1822 respectively they were declared ineligible, as aliens, for membership. (Marshall Spring Bidwell was re-elected in 1825 and allowed to take his seat under a new electoral law.) Lawyers, doctors, shopkeepers—these men were members of a middle-class that was growing in prosperity and social aspirations; they therefore represented a group especially aggrieved by the unequal sharing of authority under the existing system.

Popular opinion was originally on the side of the Reformers. They gained a majority in the Assembly in 1828, and spent their time in office mainly formulating grievances, since they had little power to initiate positive measures. In 1836 two of their leaders, Baldwin and Rolph, were appointed to the Executive Council, but resigned because the Lieutenant-Governor, Sir Francis Bond Head, refused to consult them in the matter of appointments. An election followed and the Tories won.

The years when the Reformers dominated the Assembly had revealed broad rifts in their ranks, which were observed and noted in 1836 by Anna Jameson when, after describing the Tories of Upper Canada, she added:

> Another party, professing the same boundless loyalty to the mother country, and the same dislike for the principles and institutions of their Yankee neighbours, may be called the Whigs of Upper Canada; these look with jealousy and scorn on the power and prejudices of the Tory families, and insist on the necessity of many reforms in the colonial government. Many of these are young men of talent, and professional men, who find themselves shut out from what they regard as their fair proportion of social consideration and influence, such as, in a small society like this, their superior education and character ought to command for them.
>
> Another set are the Radicals, whom I generally hear mentioned as 'those scoundrels', or 'those rascals', or with some epithet expressive of the utmost contempt or disgust. They are those who wish to see this country erected into a republic, like the United States. A few among them are men of talent and education, but at present they are neither influential nor formidable.

In fact, by this time a third group had emerged. Egerton Ryerson, in a series of letters by 'A Canadian', published in the London *Times* between June 1826 and January 1837, dissociated himself from the radical cause in a way that also offended those whom Jameson described as 'Whigs'. His influence over the Methodists is thought to have turned the election of 1836 against the Reformers, just as that of the Methodist leaders helped prevent the English reform movement from taking a violent course at the time of the French Revolution.

William Lyon Mackenzie represented the extreme wing of the radicals. Writing in his paper the *Colonial Advocate* (1824-34), and as a troublesome member of the Assembly (first elected in 1828, he was expelled in 1831 for calling it a 'sycophantic office'; several re-elections and expulsions were to follow), Mackenzie had no systematic ideology and was more effective as a critic than as a planner. He could probably be classed as an agrarian populist, with the distrust of large corporations that had traditionally accompanied such a stance, and with an illusion—of which experience would rid him—that because the elective principle was carried further there, the United States harboured a freer society than the British system. His own policy, as he 'restated' it in his *Colonial Advocate* on 8 December 1825, was neither very original nor very radical in the sense of suggesting social as distinct from political change.

> I think the British empire the greatest and the wisest that ever has been; but am of opinion that we colonists *do not enjoy* our just privileges as members of that empire—I think that taxation and representation ought to go hand in hand; that the best and safest substitute for *nobility here* is a general election, widely diffused; that, as the colonies *cannot* be represented in England, they ought to be allowed more freedom from oppressive and arbitrary enactments; that there is no danger either to the interests of religion, or to civil rights, likely to arise from our putting down that black and dark shadow to a free country, a political church establishment; that all religious denominations ought to be, for every political purpose, in the eye of the law *equal;* . . . that the contest between the court party in this colony and the representatives of the people is, on the one hand, a struggle for political power, and on the other for political existence— might against right.

The sharpness and the persistence of his attacks on the governing clique earned Mackenzie many enemies, which seemed to please him. John Beverley Robinson, whom he had indeed slandered to the edge of libel, referred to him as 'that mean little creature who among honourable men and in an honourable age, would be *spurned* as a thing whose touch must calumniate,' while Sir Francis Bond Head affected to look upon him with amused contempt, as in his description of a visit Mackenzie paid him to present the case of the malcontents in the Assembly.

> Afraid to look me in the face, he sat, with his feet not reaching to the ground, and with his countenance averted from me, at an angle of about 70 degrees; while, with the eccentricity, the volubility, and indeed the appearance of a madman, the tiny creature raved in all directions about grievances here, and grievances there.

Mackenzie, of course, saw himself somewhat differently, and we can fairly assume that the following passage in an issue of the *Colonial Advocate* in 4 May 1826 was intended as a self-portrait.

> A Patriot is none of your raving, railing, canting, enquiring, accusing radicals—nor is he one of your idle, stall-fed, greasy good for nothing sinecurists or pluralists—he is in deed and in truth a friend to his country. He studies the laws and institutions of his nation, that he may improve others, endeavours rather to cultivate the acquaintance of, and shew a correct example to the better informed classes; he associates only with those whose private conduct is in unison with their public professions. Is not a mob hunter, nor a lecturer of the multitude; desires rather the secret

approbation of the enlightened few than the ephemeral popularity of the many.

Though Mackenzie's instability and anger, and his occasional irrepressible desire to injure others, tended to spoil the picture, there was enough truth in it for even Susanna Moodie to see him, in the end, as an essentially good man who, though misguided, had been wronged.

Under the pressure of events after the election of 1836, the reform movement was rapidly polarized and Mackenzie became increasingly isolated. Except for a few radical idealists like the physicians John Rolfe and Charles Duncombe, who organized a separate uprising in western Upper Canada in December 1837, he was left to find his following among the poorer farmers, whose grievances he inflamed as he toured the province during the summer of 1837, arguing that constitutional means had failed and armed rebellion offered the only hope for change. In the Broadside he issued at the end of November 1837, a few days before he led his followers in rebellion, he made the promises of an extravagant agrarian reformer:

> CANADIANS! It is the design of the Friends of Liberty to give several hundred acres to every Volunteer—to root out the unlawful Canada Company, and give *free deeds* to all settlers who live on their lands—to give free gifts of the Clergy Reserve lots, to good citizens who have settled on them—and the like to settlers on Church of England Glebe Lots, so that the yeomanry may feel independent, and be able to improve the country instead of sending the fruit of their labour to foreign lands. The fifty-seven Rectories will be at once given to the people, and all public lands used for Education, Internal Improvements and the public good.

He duly threatened his enemies:

> Mark all those who join our enemies—act as spies for them—fight for them—or aid them—these men's properties shall pay the expense of the struggle—they are traitors to Canadian Freedom, and as such we will deal with them.

And he ended with a resounding call to arms, like a Messianic Jacobin:

> Up then, brave Canadians! Get ready your rifles, and make short work of it; a connection with England would involve us in all her wars, undertaken for her own advantage, never for ours; with governors from England, we will have bribery at elections, corruption, villainy and perpetual discord in every township, but Independence would give us the means of enjoying many blessings. Our enemies in Toronto are in terror and dismay—they know their wickedness and dread our vengeance . . . . Aye, and now's the day and the hour! Woe be to those who oppose us, for 'In God is our trust.'

Thus it was essentially a latter-day peasant's revolt that Mackenzie led when his 800 followers (many of them armed only with pitchforks, like Wat Tyler's men in 1381) assembled at the head of Yonge Street with the ill-defined intent of throwing over the Family Compact and establishing a populist republic.

In Lower Canada the *patriotes* shared with their Upper Canadian counterparts the political grievances over the concentration of power in the executive branch of government, which represented a restricted and privileged caste. But they were also engaged in a kind of racial civil war on behalf of the subject French-speakers against the merchant-led militant Tory British group in Montreal. They had broader support, resisted more obstinately, and under Robert Nelson even launched a second rebellion in 1838, which showed that they reflected the feelings of the ordinary people in Lower Canada more faithfully than Mackenzie in Upper Canada. In 1839 Lord Durham, in a famous passage of his *Report*, presented hostility between British and French as the real clue to the situation in Lower Canada.

> I expected to find a contest between a government and a people: I found two nations warring in the bosom of a single state; I found a struggle, not of principles, but of races; and I perceived that it would be idle to attempt any amelioration of laws or institutions until we could first succeed in terminating the deadly animosity that now separates the inhabitants of Lower Canada into the hostile divisions of French and English.

It has often been said that Durham was influenced by the Anglo-Celtic merchants from whom he and his subordinates obtained much of their information about Lower Canada, yet the impression he conveys is remarkably similar to that conveyed in 1906 by André Siegfried, the astute observer, visiting from France, who had no need to go to Westmount for his opinions.

> When the French of Canada speak of the English, they think chiefly of the English in the provinces of Quebec and Ontario, side by side with whom they have had to pass their existence. After a hundred and fifty years of life in common as neighbours, under the same laws and the same flag, they remain foreigners, and in most cases adversaries. The two races have no more love for each other now than they had at the beginning, and it is easy to see we are face to face with one of those deep and lasting antipathies against which all efforts of conciliators are in vain.

'However,' as Siegfried adds, 'like brothers that hate each other, French and English have to dwell under one roof', and much of Canadian history is affected by the compromises occasioned by that necessity, which began shortly after the rebellions.

How reform reaped the harvest that eluded rebellion is a story told too often to need more at this point than the briefest summary. Lord

Durham came and made his *Report*, which sought a way by which the French minority might be led to merge by osmosis into the larger British society of North America. He envisaged this by proposing a legislative union of all the North American colonies that would ensure the numerical preponderance of the English speakers and would achieve what the British prime minister, Lord Melbourne, enunciated as the 'fundamental principle that the French must not be reinstated in power in Lower Canada.' But having put forward this Tory proposal, Durham in his persona as Radical Jack then offered the proposals for immediate responsible government that had been urged on him by the Upper Canadian Reformers. The British government, in the Act of Union of 1840, decreed a limited legislative union of Upper and Lower Canada, leaving the other colonies apart, and rejected the proposal for responsible government.

Nevertheless the union, intended to prevent the repetition of rebellion, promoted the cause of reform, since within the same legislative body the two opposition movements that in the past had followed their separate courses in Upper and Lower Canada found enough in common to work together, and under Robert Baldwin and Hippolyte Lafontaine a strong Reform party came into being in which English and French moderates reached a degree of harmony that would have astonished Durham, had he lived to witness it; in the meantime, a similar party emerged in Nova Scotia under Joseph Howe's leadership. In all the colonies assemblies pressed for responsible government, and administrations in Britain more sympathetic than Lord Melbourne's reacted favourably. Thus responsible government—achieved quietly through administrative fiat by governors acting under the instruction of the Colonial Office rather than by statute—came into being just over a decade after the rebellions had failed. Durham's son-in-law, Lord Elgin, as Governor, acknowledged the principle by calling on the reform leaders to form a government in the Province of Canada in 1848, the very year when peoples in Europe were trying vainly to solve their political problems by revolution. Responsible government came to Nova Scotia later in 1848, to Prince Edward Island in 1851, to New Brunswick in 1854, and to Newfoundland in 1855. The colonies had taken their first step towards the independence they would achieve collectively in later decades.

From a cultural point of view, one of the era's most interesting aspects is the change of Canadian attitudes towards the rebellions and especially towards the rebels of 1837. Only a small minority in either Lower or Upper Canada actively engaged in the insurrections. In each province there was a large inert group, discontented with the political status quo but unwilling and discouraged by their church leaders (by John Strachan and Egerton Ryerson in the Upper as much as by the Catholic bishops in the Lower province) from joining a movement that might result in prolonged civil war or, worse, in American intervention. Most Canadians were content to accept the British monarchy and the imperial connection if the alternative might be embarkation on revolutionary adventure.

Yet, as Susanna Moodie so clearly recognized, the rebellions played a crucial role in the process of Canadian reform in the dawning Victorian age. For the most part the rebels were received back into Canadian society without great difficulty and found their eventual places among the heroes of the national myth, in a way that seems remarkable when one compares it with the vindictiveness the Americans showed in an essentially parallel situation, when they persecuted the Loyalists, their own rebels against the accepted system.

Even in the immediate aftermath of the rebellions, the vindictiveness of the Tory establishment, which led to Chief Justice John Beverley Robinson's sentencing to death two minor leaders of the Upper Canadian rebellion, Samuel Lount and Peter Mathews, resulted in a great wave of sympathy for the condemned men. John Ryerson wrote to his brother Egerton of their execution on 12 April 1838:

> Very few persons present except the military & the ruff scruff of the city. The general feeling is in total opposition to the execution of these men. At their execution they manifested *very good* composure. Sheriff Jarvis burst into tears when he entered the room to prepare them for execution. They said to him very calmly, 'Mr. Jarvis, do your duty; we are prepared to meet death and our Judge.' They then, both of them put their arms around his neck and kissed him. They were then prepared for execution. They walked to the gallows with entire composure and firmness of step. Rev. J. Richardson walked alongside of Lount, and Dr. Beatty alongside of Mathews. They ascended the scaffold & knelt down on the *drop*, the rope was fastened to their necks while they were on their knees. Mr. Richardson engaged in prayer & when he came to the part of the Lord's Prayer, *Forgive us our trespasses as we forgive them that trespass against us*, the drop fell.

Another account, published in the United States in 1839, and probably written by Mackenzie, talked of petitions, 'signed by upwards of 30,000 persons', that had asked for the lives of Lount and Mathews to be spared, but 'in vain'.

In Lower Canada, where the influence of Lord Durham as Radical Jack was stronger, clemency at first prevailed. Wolfred Nelson and seven other captured leaders were exiled to the salubrious island of Bermuda (an illegal if good-natured act that led to Melbourne's reprimand and Durham's resignation), and for the rest there was an early amnesty. Only after the second rebellion in November 1838—led by Robert Nelson, who proclaimed Canada a republic and himself its president—was Upper Canadian severity repeated in the Lower province. Like Mackenzie and Papineau, Nelson evaded capture; he lived out his life in New

York and California. Twelve of his followers were executed and fifty-eight transported to Australia. Even more than in Upper Canada, this harshness resulted in an upsurge of sympathy for the victims. It is said that the transportees were more greatly mourned than the hanged men. Not for the last time in history, death was thought to be less alarming than Australia.

Of the rebels who were regarded as redeemed and therefore acceptable, perhaps the most striking were Hippolyte Lafontaine, whom we have already noticed as Robert Baldwin's associate, and George-Étienne Cartier.

John Charles Dent, one of the most important early Canadian historians, wrote a great deal in the 1880s, the last decade of his short life (he died in 1888 at the age of 46 after a career that combined law, journalism, and historiography) about the men who were important in Canada during the decades between the rebellions and Confederation. His *The Last Forty Years: The Union of 1841 to Confederation* (1881), one of the most important books written on that period by a contemporary, is filled with vignettes of the leading figures of the time. Of Lafontaine, Dent tells us that he

> was essentially a man of the world; a man of high ambitions; a man brilliant and showy, fully capable of asserting and maintaining all that of right belonged to him. He early took rank among his contemporaries as a leader of men. In 1830, when he was twenty-three years old, he was returned to the Lower Canadian Assembly, where he advocated the rights of his compatriots with much fervour and eloquence until the breaking out of the rebellion. That Mr. Lafontaine would have been glad enough to see that movement succeed may safely enough be taken for granted, but he was too prudent to identify himself with it. After the engagements at St. Denis and St. Charles he found himself placed in an embarrassing position. The rebels looked to him for active support; but he knew the hopelessness of the insurrection, and had no idea of imperilling his liberty or his life in a lost cause. On the other hand, he found himself an object of suspicion to the Government.

Lafontaine fled to England and thence to France, where he stayed until Durham's amnesty in 1838. But then, at the time of Robert Nelson's second Lower Canadian insurrection, he was arrested under suspicion, and released almost immediately for lack of evidence against him. That brief imprisonment, and a rather remarkable physical resemblance to Napoleon I, assured him the support of his fellow Québécois, while by 1841 he had won the respect of the English moderate reformers to such an extent that when he was defeated in his old constituency of Terrebonne in Canada East, Robert Baldwin found a seat for him in one of the York ridings in Canada West. From this point Lafontaine and Baldwin instituted their joint leadership of the Reform group in the Canadian

Legislative Assembly, and the man who had only shortly before been under arrest on suspicion of treason became attorney-general of Canada East and in 1842 *de facto* joint prime minister of the Province of Canada.

Cartier was much more closely and dangerously involved in the rebellion than Lafontaine, for he actually carried a musket in the insurrectionary ranks. Dent says of him:

> Being a clever young *avocat* he of course turned his attention to politics and—equally of course—he soon came under the influence of Mr. Papineau. He joined the Sons of Liberty, and in 1837 took an active part in the rebellion. He fought bravely at St. Denis under Dr. Nelson, and was compelled to fly the country and seek refuge in the United States. After a time he secretly returned, and remained in hiding until an unofficial intimation from the authorities assured him that no attempt would be made to arrest him if he conducted himself with discretion. He accordingly resumed his practice in Montreal, and did not come conspicuously before the public until about ten years afterwards, though he continued to take a keen interest in the political events of the time.

Finally, in 1848, Cartier became a member of the Assembly of the Province of Canada; by 1856 he was a cabinet minister. In 1867 the man who had fought in the ranks as a rebel was one of the architects of Confederation.

Other rebels, even more active, found forgiveness and reacceptance in a surprisingly short time. Both John Rolph from Upper Canada and Wolfred Nelson from the Lower province returned unmolested in 1843. Nelson was at once elected to the Legislative Assembly and later withdrew from political life to become a prison inspector and eventually chairman of the board of prison inspection. Immediately on his return from exile Rolph founded the Toronto School of Medicine, one of the first of its kind in the country, which eventually became incorporated into Victoria University. He returned to politics, entering the Assembly and gaining ministerial rank as Commissioner of Crown Lands and later as President of the Council in the administration of Francis Hincks, whose fall he precipitated by voting against his colleagues in 1854. His radical inclinations remained with him; he was one of the founders of the 'Clear Grit' movement, which extended the aims of the rebels of 1837 by demanding universal male suffrage.

The principal leaders of the rebellion also found a welcome on returning to their homeland after unhappy years abroad. Papineau came back in 1844, and from 1848 to 1854, when he retired from politics to preside like a seigneurial Jefferson over his estate at Montebello, he served in the Legislative Assembly. He was shortly joined there by William Lyon Mackenzie, who came back in 1849 and two years later demonstrated that he could still command a following in rural Ontario by defeating the formidable George Brown in the county of Haldimand.

But neither of the former leaders played a significant role in his second political career. Events had passed them by; much they had fought for had been won by peaceful means, and their radicalism seemed to inspire a later generation than their own. Papineau's influence, for example, was strongest on the young *rouges* of the 1860s, like the Dorion brothers and Laurent-Olivier David, while through his grandson, Henri Bourassa, he left the heritage of a Quebec nationalism that saw its place within a broader and independent Canadian nation.

Yet, given the dramatic roles they played on the small stage of Canadian public life, the eventual political beatification of Mackenzie and Papineau was inevitable, once the vision of an independent Canada, treating on terms of equality with Britain and other established nations, became popular. By the end of the nineteenth century they were incorporated into the emergent national mythography. *The Life and Times of Wm. Lyon Mackenzie* (1862), an early adulatory biography by Mackenzie's son-in-law Charles Lindsey, provided a basis for a series of favourable studies of the Upper Canadian leader. When W.D. LeSueur, in the Edwardian era, wrote a more critical work, Mackenzie's descendants successfully prevented its publication by legal action; it did not finally appear until 1979. (Among those most active in the suppression of the book was Mackenzie's grandson William Lyon Mackenzie King, an ardent admirer of the old rebel and a striking personification of the symbiotic relationship between reformism and rebellion in the Canadian tradition.) An admiring biography of Papineau by Laurent-Olivier David appeared in 1896. But the final acceptance of both rebels as key figures in the transition from colony to nation was evidenced by their inclusion in the *Makers of Canada* series, in which A.-D. DeCelles published a book on Papineau and Cartier in 1904, and G.G.S. Lindsey, son of his original biographer, published one on Mackenzie in 1908.

Seen in hindsight, the reconciliation between the rebels and their society, and their adoption into the mythology of Canada, seems a necessary episode in our history. Truly revolutionary societies have no place for reconciliation because they have no place for dissent; emigrés from them remain emigrés, as did American loyalists, French aristocrats, and Russian tsarists. But a non-revolutionary society like that of Canada did not impose the distinction between the faithful and the infidel; our instinct for compromise appeared early. The pressures that rebellion had revealed were quickly relieved by reformist measures. The reconciliation of the rebels and their neutralization by absorption into the national myth was the final stage in an arrangement that, apart from being morally laudable, was imperative in a society as young and fragile as that of the Canadas in the 1830s. The rebellions betokened grave fissures in both Canadian societies, and the fissures had to be knit as soon as possible if British America were to survive as a distinct community. The willingness of Canadians to forgive, and to do so quickly, was one of the first true signs of national solidarity in our history.

The classic rebellions of 1837-8 were not Canada's only ones. They were followed by two armed insurrections in 1870 and 1885 of the Métis—a term that commonly refers to the French-speaking half-breeds, though at Red River in 1870 English-speaking half-breeds were passive supporters of rebellion—and by movements, not entirely without violence, in the direction of socialism in the late nineteenth and early twentieth centuries.

The Métis rebellions offered situations quite different from those of 1837 and 1838, where the rebels were mainly Upper and Lower Canadian farmers and the leaders were in their own way ornaments of the establishment, a former Mayor of Toronto and a Speaker of the Lower Canadian Legislative Assembly. And the results were also different in the West, for though reform came out of rebellions in 1870 and 1885—on the Red River and in present-day Saskatchewan respectively—it came more slowly and reconciliation was reluctant. This was because the rebels stood outside the general stream of Canadian life, outside the compact masses of French-speakers and English-speakers established in their respective societies. Rebels like Mackenzie, Papineau, and their followers had challenged the society in terms of its own democratic pretensions, and the disputes to which their followers gave physical expression could be solved by modifications within the society. But the challenging of dominant values by the Métis, even liberal ones as understood at the time, introduced an element that Canadian society has always found difficult to cope with: the fact that its own inherent pluralism incessantly casts up minorities whose interests cannot be satisfied by some easy formula within the general society.

The Métis had developed a free nomadic life on the prairie that depended on the survival of the buffalo herds and on the existence of open hunting grounds. Their very social organization was the loose democracy of the buffalo hunt, with leaders chosen for specific roles but without enduring power. In his book *The Red River Settlement*, published in 1856, the fur-trader Alexander Ross remembered the vigour of their libertarian semi-nomadic society.

> Like the American peasantry, these people are all politicians, but of a peculiar creed, favouring a barbarous state of society and self-will; for they cordially detest all the laws and restraints of civilized life, believing all men were born to be free. In their own estimation they are all great men, and wonderfully wise; and so long as they wander about in these wild and lawless expeditions, they will never become a thoroughly civilized people, nor orderly subjects in a civilized community. Feeling their own strength, from being constantly armed, and free from control, they despise

all others; but above all, they are marvellously tenacious of their own original habits....They are all republicans in principle, and a licentious freedom is their besetting sin.

When the buffalo dwindled, the Métis attempted reluctantly to settle down, and followed the example of their Québécois ancestors on the paternal side by establishing strip farms beside the Red River and the Saskatchewan like those along the St Lawrence. Their attitude to life, their concept of land-holding, were opposed to those of the agrarian Upper Canadians who began to settle in the West during the 1860s, and there was a symbolic appropriateness in the fact that the first Métis rebellion began in 1870 when Louis Riel and his associates interfered with a group of surveyors trying to impose the quadrilateral division of the land, which became the rule on the prairie, on the straggling strip farms of the Red River Métis. It was the rebellion of free form against geometry.

The moral issue, as the Métis saw it, was expounded with great clarity by Louis Riel in his remarkable speech of self-defence as he was being tried for his life in Regina in 1885.

> I suppose the Half-Breeds in Manitoba, in 1870, did not fight for two hundred and forty acres of land, but it is to be understood that there were two societies who treated together. One was small, but in its smallness it had its rights. The other was great, but in its greatness it had no greater rights than the rights of the small, because the right is the same for everyone, and when they began treating the leaders of that small community as bandits, as outlaws, leaving them without protection, they disorganized that community.

The second uprising of the Métis, the North West Rebellion of 1885, also concerned surveyors and land. Settlement had moved over the prairie, with speculators in the van, and the Métis feared they would be treated as squatters and swept away from the plots that gave them a precarious foothold in the great prairie where they had once ranged far and wide, challenged only by those other free nomads, the Plains Indians. As they themselves put it in the peroration to one of the many petitions they sent in vain to the Dominion government during the 1880s:

> Having been so long regarded as the masters of this country, having defended it against the Indians at the cost of our blood, we do not consider that we are asking too much when we call on the government to allow us to occupy our lands in peace and to exempt us from the regulations by making free grants of land to the Métis of the North-west.

Of course there were other reasons for the clash between the Métis and the Anglo-Celtic Protestants who came uninvited into their country, not least the collective pride of the Métis themselves. By 1870 they had seen themselves for a couple of generations as a 'nation', equivalent to the other powers of the West: the Hudson's Bay Company and the great Indian confederations of the plains. When they learned that obscure negotiations between the imperial government, the Hudson's Bay Company, and the new Dominion were selling Rupert's Land without their voices being heard, the Métis saw no alternative, as direct-minded men of action who in the past had taken up arms against the Indian nations as well as the Hudson's Bay Company, but to do so again and to form their own provisional government.

In 1869 the few Canadians who had already settled on the Red River, and those who agitated in Ontario for an immediate takeover of the West, saw the Métis as rebels, which technically they were not, since Canadian law did not yet operate in Rupert's Land and the representatives at Red River of the Hudson's Bay Company, the *de facto* authority there, offered no resistance to Riel's formation of a provisional government in November. This idea was supported not only by most of the Métis, but also by the other groups, the English-speaking mixed bloods and the descendants of Lord Selkirk's Scottish settlers. Only a small group of Canadians, led by Dr Schultz and supported by the Canada Firsters, strongly opposed them. Riel's one mistake in an otherwise well-planned uprising was the execution of Thomas Scott, which gave a justification to the Anglo-Celtic Protestants of Ontario for seeing the Métis as an irritating vestige of the past, a tiny group of nomads of inferior race barring the way to progress.

The Orange Order of Ontario and its allies could not prevent the legal compromise by which, once again, reform followed rebellion. Though Riel suffered banishment, the Red River Settlement became in 1870 the nucleus of Canada's fifth province, Manitoba. But in this case, unlike that of the rebellions of 1837, the third phase of the process was missing: reform was not followed by reconciliation.

In the aftermath of the Red River Rebellion the new province was quickly flooded with settlers, mostly Protestant, mostly English-speaking, and the Métis were treated as an inferior and alien group. Shrewd speculators persuaded many of them to give up for derisory payments the lands they had acquired under the Manitoba Act of 1870 (under which Hudson's Bay Company lands in the Northwest were transferred to Canada), and these dispossessed people resumed the nomadic existence of the past, following the dwindling buffalo to the far plains of the Saskatchewan region. In 1890 the government of Manitoba, dominated by Anglo-Celtic Protestants, breached the agreement that had ended the Red River uprising by withdrawing financial support for Catholic schools, thus violating the clauses of the Manitoba Act that provided for a dual system of Catholic and Protestant schools.

The fact that the agreement that ended the Red River Rebellion in 1869-70 was broken five years after the defeat of the North West Rebellion of 1885 is not accidental; the minority that challenged accepted social values had been rendered powerless and now could be safely ignored. The North West Rebellion also had been provoked by disputes over land and by the refusal of the Dominion government to allow for the divergent viewpoint of the Métis. When the situation first emerged, the Métis leaders enjoyed the support of white settlers and English-speaking mixed bloods. But once they decided to take up arms they were left without support. This time they were in actual rebellion against the constituted government of Canada, as Mackenzie and Papineau had been, and their uprising was ruthlessly crushed. The oral account by Gabriel Dumont— the 'adjutant-general' of the Métis leader, Louis Riel—of the last hours of the fall of the rebel hamlet-capital of Batoche, gives a vivid sense not only of the chaos of warfare but also of a lost cause finally disintegrating into the hopeless actions of individuals.

> When the troops entered Batoche . . . our men first withdrew half a mile. I myself stayed on the higher ground with six of my brave comrades. I held up the enemy's progress there for a whole hour. What kept me there, I should say, was the courage of old Ouelette. Several times I said to him, 'Come on, Father, we must pull back!' And the good old man always replied: 'Just a minute! I want to kill another Englishman!' Then I said to him, 'Very well, let us die here.' When he was hit, I thanked him for his courage, but I could not stay any longer, and I drew back to my other companions . . . Then I went down to the riverside, where I ran into seven or eight men who, like plenty of others were in flight. I asked them to come with me so that we could ambush the enemy. When they refused, I threatened to kill the first man who made off. They then came with me, and we kept the English at bay for another half-hour.

At the end, with the village in the hands of General Middleton's troops, Dumont came upon Riel in a wood on the outskirts; it was the last time they met, for Riel was shortly to surrender and Dumont to become a fugitive.

> 'What are we going to do?' he said, as he saw me: 'We are defeated,' I said to him: 'We shall perish. But you must have known, when we took up arms, that we would be beaten. So, they will destroy us!'

And indeed, as the 'nation' they had once thought themselves, the Métis ceased to exist. Once again there was a measure of reform, in that the system of land grants was reorganized and humanized. But there was no real reconciliation, no acceptance of the Métis as an acknowledged group into the larger society. They remained a defeated, marginal people, retreating into the fringes of settlement, where Marcel Giraud would find them in the 1930s when he came from France to gather the material for his monumental and elegiac work, *Le Métis canadien*.

Even today, when native peoples' claims to recognition are being heard, and Métis leaders like Louis Riel and Gabriel Dumont have been given heroic status within the national myth, the way of life they sought to preserve, with its remarkable system of direct democracy, is little understood. The Métis rebellions never led to a real reconciliation because reconciliation with an archaistic minority was not seen as necessary for the survival of the community as a whole, as it had been in the case of the rebels of 1837.

Socialism in Canada, I believe, fits into the pattern of reform and rebellion that I have outlined in relation to the various armed uprisings during the nineteenth century. It too, however, has had its impulses of rebellion, represented mostly by industrial disputes that led sometimes to violence and culminated not long after the end of our period in the act of mass defiance known as the Winnipeg General Strike in 1919. But though it has had its extreme and revolutionary sects, Canadian socialism has in general pursued the gradualist direction, offering usually an evolutionary approach to an alternative pattern of social relations rather than the revolutionary vision of a world transformed.

The first Canadian socialist was a follower of Robert Owen, a purser of the Royal Navy on half-pay named Henry Jones. He had become interested during the 1820s in Owen's proposals for 'villages of unity and co-operation', self-sufficient communities in which he saw a solution to the problem of acute unemployment among the hand-weavers who were being replaced by machinery. Jones had already been involved in one unsuccessful community venture before he set out in 1827 to seek land in Upper Canada for an experiment of his own. He obtained the land near Sarnia on Lake Huron, and there in 1829 he established his community, importing about eighty people, almost all of them Lowland Scots and unemployed handloom weavers. He called the community Maxwell, after Robert Owen's residence in Scotland, and built a single large log building to house the members in individual apartments for families, with common kitchens and dining-rooms. He also opened a school and a store run on Owenite principles. Cultivation of the land was begun and a fishery established on the lake. But soon the community members began to leave, perhaps attracted by the possibility of obtaining land of their own elsewhere in Upper Canada. By 1834, when the central building burnt down, Maxwell was already in a state of advanced disintegration; it virtually came to an end in 1835 when Jones returned to England.

Jones was essentially a utopian socialist. He believed that by creating miniatures of a working society here and now, one could begin the process of social transformation without waiting for revolutionary events or social convulsion. He was virtually alone in Canada, whereas in the revolutionary atmosphere that pervaded the expanding United States during the early and mid-nineteenth century, hundreds of utopian colonies of various kinds were founded in the American Atlantic states, the mid-West, and Texas. Utopians south of the border largely attempted to put into practice proposals for ideal communities formulated by European socialists like Owen (who himself spent a period in the United States attempting to further the cause), by the French social philosopher Charles Fourier, with his idea for a social and economic organization in which groups of about 150 people would live in community buildings called *phalanstères* (of which a leading American example was Brook Farm with its links to the New England Transcendentalists), and by another French utopian socialist, Étienne Cabet, whose romance of an ideal village, *Voyage en Icarie* (1840), inspired many settlements, particularly in Texas. There were also communities inspired by native thinkers: John Humphrey Noyes, for example, and his Oneida Community with its experiments in free love, and Josiah Warren with his anarchist ventures, The Village of Equity and Modern Times. Such communities played an important role in the westward extension of the American frontier, and also in the development of American intellectual life.

But none of them hived off into Canada, for Jones's Maxwell was a product of Owenism in its earlier British phase. Canada, in fact, has been remarkably resistant to utopian thinking, and has essayed few ideal commonwealths either in literary or in practical form. In a century that in Europe and the United States produced dozens of utopian romances and proposals of ideally organized and regulated societies, the sole Canadian example is James De Mille's *A Strange Manuscript Found in a Copper Cylinder* (1888). But even that is a dubious one, since in presenting the strange Antarctic world of his imaginary people, the Kosekin, De Mille seemed—like Samuel Butler in *Erewhon*—to be satirizing the world he belonged to rather than offering a desirable new model for society.

Henry Jones had no successors. The most ambitious Canadian secular community appeared long after the American movement had gone into decline. It was founded on Malcolm Island off the coast of British Columbia by Finns employed in the Vancouver Island collieries who wished to establish a setting in which both their socialist principles and their native culture would be sustained. They invited a well-known Finnish writer, Matti Kurikka, to lead them. In December 1901 the first settlers reached the island, which they named Sointula, meaning Harmony. They set out to operate their colony according to the principle of utopian communism, with everything shared. Plenty of people arrived, including Finns from the United States and even Finland itself. Two thousand people lived for short or long periods on Sointula between 1901 and 1905, when the community was dissolved, though there appear to have been no more than 300 there at any one time.

This alarming degree of transience was undoubtedly connected with Kurikka's poor leadership. He had already been involved in an unsuccessful community experiment in Australia, and on Sointula he allowed the community to sink into debt in spite of the hard work its members put into the farming, fishing, and logging that the island's rich resources encouraged. After the community disintegrated, some of the original members remained to fish and cultivate the land as individuals, and they retained their socialist ideals. On Sointula in 1909 British Columbia's first co-operative was established; in 1917, on receiving news of the Russian Revolution, the Sointulans raised the red flag and a boatload of RCMP was sent from the mainland to haul it down. A West Coast legend was created, but the experiment in utopian living was never repeated.

Most efforts at community living in Canada have in fact been inspired by religious aims rather than by ideas of secular socialism. Monastic communities existed in New France almost from the beginning. The largest of all Canadian community experiments was the Doukhobor Christian Community of Universal Brotherhood, with its six thousand members and its quite complicated industrial and agricultural economy. It survived—with interludes of very Spartan living—for almost thirty years, from 1909 until its economic base was weakened by a combination of bad management and Depression conditions and the banks foreclosed on it in 1938. Some nineteenth-century Protestant missionaries, precursors of the Social Gospel, created settlements with strong communitarian elements, like William Duncan's famous model village of Metlakalta among the Tsimshian Indians of British Columbia.

Almost all of these community experiments, whether utopian or religious, were initiated by immigrants rather than by native Canadians, and this adds emphasis to one's impression that Canadians resist seeing life in terms of the absolute solutions utopias offer.

When a continuous socialist tradition did emerge in Canada, beginning in the 1870s, it was linked with the broader labour movement and remained so, even though it attracted intellectuals and, at times, sympathetic capitalists. There was labour action of a kind in the Canadas as early as the 1820s, when the largely Irish labourers working on the Welland and Rideau Canals conducted a series of often violent strikes that were virtually unorganized outbursts of collective anger. The first real organization began among the craft-workers of Montreal in the 1830s. The craft-union concept, which really derived from the medieval guilds and presupposed skilled workers maintaining both their standards of living and their standards of workmanship within a stable society, continued to dominate Canadian unionism until the 1880s. Sometimes an English union would be transplanted to Canada, as happened with the Amalgamated Society of Carpenters and Joiners; more often American craft unions found their way north over the border, and five of them are said to have been in operation at the time of Confederation, along with a few local Canadian unions.

Craft unions, which maintained a kind of class structure among the workers, elevating the skilled above the unskilled, tended to be cautious and conservative; but until the 1870s even they existed under the shadow of illegality, since in all the provinces they were liable to charges of conspiracy under the English common law. In Britain, Gladstone had introduced legislation in 1871 allowing for collective bargaining, but under the British North America Act new British laws no longer applied in Canada after 1867. In 1872 workers in Ontario and Montreal began to agitate for a nine-hour day. The Toronto printers initiated a strike aimed mainly at the *Globe* and its proprietor George Brown, who was an enemy of labour organization; the law was invoked against them and they were charged with conspiracy. Sir John A. Macdonald saw a fine chance of scoring against an old rival. On 12 July he addressed a gathering of workmen and with jocular condescension identified himself with them:

> I ought to have a special interest in this subject because I am a working man myself. I know that I work more than nine hours every day, and then I think I am a practical mechanic. If you look at the Confederation Act, in the framing of which I had some hand, you will admit that I am a pretty good joiner; and as for cabinet making I have as much experience as Jacques and Hay themselves.*

Macdonald passed legislation exempting labour unions from the laws against conspiracy, and thus implicitly recognized collective bargaining. His action won him two Toronto seats in the next election and an appreciative address from the local Trades Council.

In fact right to the end of the nineteenth century Canadian workers, except in a few areas like British Columbia where militancy ran high, were inclined to vote for one of the two main parties, and, as in Britain, the Tory working-man was by no means unknown. The first artisan elected to the House of Commons, in 1872, obtained his seat on the Liberal Conservative ticket. He was Henry Buckingham Whitton, the member for Hamilton, a self-educated man with a considerable autodidactic erudition who worked as a foreman in the shops of the Great Western Railway. Lady Dufferin, in her diary, recorded meeting him on 29 April 1873:

> In the evening we had a large parliamentary dinner. One of my neighbours was very interesting. He is a 'working man' member; we had met him

---

*Jacques and Hay were well-known Toronto furniture-makers.

soon after his election when he dined in a rough coat, but now he wears evening clothes.

When another working-man, John Burns, was nominated in 1886 by the Conservative convention in Hamilton, the local newspaper, the *Hamilton Spectator*, pointed out what it regarded as the advantage to the workers of having their representatives within the Tory ranks:

> Mr. Burns is neither more nor less a working man than before his nomination by the conservative convention—neither more nor less now a conservative than then. He was a working man before his nomination; he is a conservative still. He can do just as much for the working man as if elected to the legislature by the votes of working men alone. The only difference in his position is this; he could not be elected by the votes of working men alone; he can and will be elected by the votes of working men and conservatives.

Even labour newspapers, at least as early as the 1870s, tended to ignore class rhetoric. On occasion they might even have a word of praise for capitalists, as in the case of the *Ontario Workman*, which in 1872 not only accepted advertisements from Timothy Eaton, but even editorialized:

> When Mr. Eaton placards the city that he has goods and cheap dresses, shawls, blankets or anything else in his line of business, you will invariably, on visiting his store, find him ready and prepared to sell just as he has advertized to do. Mechanics and their families in want of drygoods are recommended to make Mr. Eaton an early call and we can assure them that they will be well repaid for so doing.

Until the Great War labour unions were actually small and for the most part weak, so that the thought of independent working-class political action required a certain daring. Canadians were still predominantly rural people. At the time of the first census after 1871 four out of five of them lived on their farms or in villages or small towns; not until the 1920s did the balance tip decisively in favour of the cities and the larger towns. Most people still made their living by farming; the craftsmen and shopkeepers in little communities were either self-employed or belonged to small groups in workshops and stores. Only on canal and railway construction, in the earlier days, did men work in large numbers together. Manufacturing, in Ontario and Quebec, did not involve large factories until after Confederation; in 1851 there were only 37 establishments in Canada East that employed more than 25 men. In the West concentrated employment came even later, first in the construction of the Canadian Pacific Railway in the 1880s, then in logging, and, after the end of the individualism of the placer era, in mining.

The first general organization of trade unionists, founded in 1873, immediately after Macdonald's legalization of association, was a particularly fragile plant. This was the Canadian Labour Union. It consisted only of Ontario workers; and of the 15 organizations whose 59 branches sent delegates to its founding convention, twelve were restricted—so far as their Canadian membership went—to Toronto, though six were international unions. The uncertainty pervading the gathering found expression in the inaugural address of the first President, John Carter, which ended by reminding the delegates of

> . . . the necessity of being wise and moderate in your deliberations and enactments, and let those who are watching your movements at this, the first Canadian labour congress, be compelled to admit that we are honest, earnest and prudent workers.

The Canadian Labour Union rapidly declined. At its third convention in 1875 hardly a quorum of delegates appeared, and nothing was heard of it afterwards.

Then in 1883 a more durable organization appeared in the Trades and Labour Congress. It eventually included workers from all parts of Canada and continued until 1956, when it combined with the Canadian Congress of Labour to form the present-day Canadian Labour Congress. The Trades and Labour Congress owed its survival, and whatever progress it made in the 1880s and early 1890s, to the activities of the Knights of Labour, an American industrial union willing to gather in workers of all crafts and races—though, like many unions of the period, it drew the line at Chinese! The Knights of Labour believed that labour unions should handle the great social issues beyond 'mere unionism', and their attitude was reflected in labour journals like *The Palladium of Labour*, whose editor, Arthur H. Rowe, wrote on 5 January 1884:

> While embodying Trade Unionism we have striven to take a broader and more comprehensive view of the entire subject of Labor Reform than is embodied in mere unionism, and to grasp and apply those great underlying principles of equity and justice between men which alone can permanently and satisfactorily solve the issues between Labor and Capital. We have in season and out of season striven to impress upon workers that great truth that men are in reality born free and equal so far as rights are concerned and that all wrong and injustice of the social system arise out of the denial to the many of the opportunities and joys monopolized by the privileged few. We have endeavoured to enforce the doctrine that as labor is the source of all wealth no man is of right entitled to what he does not earn in the sense of giving positive value to it, and that the plea of acquiring something for nothing, by which so many speculators, usurers, landgrabbers and other classes of idlers live on the labour of other classes is a fraud and a wrong to those by whose toil they subsist.

Thanks to the Knights' energetic recruiting, union membership in Canada rose by the end of the century to about 20,000, still a minute proportion even of the industrial workers. Everything else in the movement was proportionately modest. In 1896 the total revenue of the Trades and Labour Congress was $255.66, and not until 1902 did it have an office with a one-person full-time staff: 'a stenographer, and a typewriter and two desks and a chair.'

The very early years of the twentieth century were a time of comparatively rapid expansion. The Knights of Labour were in rapid decline, and the American Federation of Labour, a crafts-oriented organization, moved into the vacuum to recruit members for the international unions. By the end of 1902 the number of unionists in Canada had tripled to more than 60,000. By 1914 there were probably 100,000 union members in Canada.

But in spite of Macdonald's politically astute legalization of union activities, the attitude of the state towards workers' organizations remained ambivalent. A federal Royal Commission on the Relations of Capital and Labour recognized in its 1889 report that Canada was undergoing a belated industrial revolution in which the interests of the workers were threatened and that in the circumstances unions were needed as bargaining agencies. 'The man who sells labour', it concluded, 'should, in selling it, be on an equality with the man who buys it.'

Yet unions still had few rights beyond the right to exist. The state might look with qualified benevolence on the presence of workers' organizations, but no law obliged an employer to negotiate with, or even recognize, a union that represented his workers, and no law prevented him from sacking a union member. Employers could request the protection of the militia or even the regular military forces if their striking employees even appeared to threaten violence, and they often invoked this protection. One of the first operations of the new Royal Canadian Navy was the suppression in 1911, with the help of sailors from HMCS *Rainbow*, of a violent labourers' strike in Prince Rupert.

It was in these circumstances that labour militants began to consider various means of asserting their wishes independently of the established political parties. Many of the pioneer labour militants were Englishmen who had brought with them traditions of radicalism that stemmed from the days of Robert Owen, from the Grand National Consolidated Trades Union, and from the Chartists, and who had kept in touch with the development in Britain of groups like the Social Democratic Federation and the Socialist League. Some workers from Europe were influenced by the socialist doctrines of various kinds that had been spreading there since the foundation of the International Workingmen's Association in the 1860s. And a later group, connected with the Western Miners' Federation and the Industrial Workers of the World, founded in Chicago in 1905, introduced the direct-action methods of revolutionary syndicalism into the labour scene in the western provinces. In this connection a curious ghostly presence appeared in 1907, for in that year a certain Honoré J. Jaxon appeared as a fraternal delegate for the Western School

of Miners. Honoré Jaxon was none other than W.H. Jackson, the young
English settler who was Riel's secretary during the 1885 rebellion, who
had been converted to anarchism in New York, and who had become
a kind of wandering proselytizer. In a flamboyant and eccentric speech
he compared the natives resisting the encroachment of white civilization
with the miners resisting the onslaught of capitalism.

> The spirit of freedom was engendered in the men who came in contact
> with the Indians. The descendants of these pioneers are now in the ma-
> jority in the Western Federation of Miners . . . . Our western people have
> had a different function to those of the east. They saw, as the Indians
> before them saw, that there was no more west for them to be driven to;
> it was for them to make the stand against the hitherto overwhelming power
> of capital.

The Industrial Workers of the World (better known as the IWW or
the Wobblies) quickly gained influence in British Columbia among migratory workers, loggers, hardrock miners, fishermen, and railway
workers. By 1912 they had a membership there of 10,000; they were
great fighters for free speech and in that year successfully defied an
attempt by the Vancouver City Council to ban street demonstrations.
They also organized a strike of 7,000 labourers laying the Canadian
Northern Railway through the Fraser Canyon. The famous American
worker-poet, Joe Hill, came north to give his support. One of his best-
remembered songs, 'Where the Fraser River Flows', was written about
this strike:

> Where the Fraser River flows, each fellow worker knows,
> They have bullied and oppressed us, but still our Union grows,
> And we're going to find a way, boys, for shorter hours and
>   better pay, boys,
> And we're going to win the day, boys, where the River Fraser flows.

The boys did not win on the Fraser River, but the next year, 1913, the
Wobblies and their associates in the United Mine Workers of America
created a virtual insurrection in the coal-mining town of Nanaimo. A
strike had begun over bad working conditions. The Dunsmuir family,
who owned the mines, kept them working by employing Chinese and
Japanese strike-breakers, and this provoked the miners to open rebellion.
In August 1918 a thousand miners rioted and seized control of Nanaimo,
burning buildings, destroying property, and attacking strike-breakers
and special police. It was a genuine rebellion, and the provisional government replied as governments do. On 13 August the acting premier,
Bill Bowser, announced:

> When day broke this morning there were nearly 1,000 men in the strike
> zone wearing the uniform of His Majesty and prepared to quell the dis-
> turbances. This is my answer to the proposition of the strikers that they

> will preserve the peace if they are left unmolested by the special Police.
> If the men will not obey the Police, they must have the military, and now
> that we are in the field, we intend to stay to the bitter end.

And indeed the thousand militia stayed. Nanaimo was an occupied town
for the whole year, with the militia escorting the strike-breakers to work
and protecting the mines, until the First World War began.

Behind this kind of violent direct action loomed the revolutionary
syndicalist philosophy of the Wobbly leaders, who saw their struggle
as preparation for a final struggle in which capitalism would be over-
thrown and the free organization of the workers would take its place.
But in practice their actions were rebellions rather than revolutionary
acts, and the goals they did achieve, like winning free-speech rights in
many communities, were essentially reformist ones.

Another point of view, that of the gradualists, advocated proceeding
through the parliamentary system and using it for the benefit of the
workers. One of the most active advocates of this approach was the
Toronto labour journalist Thomas Phillips Thompson, who suggested
that a small group of labour members should be elected in the principal
cities to act as an independent faction in Parliament, rather like the Irish
nationalists who, under the leadership of Charles Stewart Parnell, were
at this time giving an example of successful filibustering in the British
House of Commons. Writing in the *Paladium of Labour* in March 1885
under the *nom-de-plume* of Enjolras, Thompson argued for the election
of six labour members from the larger cities who would form an independent group that might on occasion hold the balance of power between the larger older parties.

> So long as the Irish representatives ranged themselves in the rank and file
> of the old British parties and were counted in as Whigs and Tories they
> got nothing. When they abandoned their former party affiliation and bent
> all their energies to the single object of securing justice in Ireland, they
> were able to hold the balance of power and force a concession that would
> otherwise have been refused. There is no reason why a balance of power
> party of labour reformers should not emulate their example.

Though in the late nineteenth century many people were beginning
to talk like socialists, and to emphasize the contrast between the growing
power and wealth of the capitalist and the growing distress of the poor,
neither a labour reform party nor a socialist party existed in Canada.
Writing in 1891 in the *Labour Advocate*, one of the many papers that
appeared in the later years of the century in response to the growing
labour-radical movement, Phillips Thompson, who was perhaps the most
eloquent and certainly one of the most prolific radical journalists of the
time, declared:

We have made great progress of late years—great strides in the direction of material development and national prosperity. And as a natural, inevitable consequence under the system of monopoly and land and capital and competition among the workers, we have chronic pauperism, soup kitchens and the bitter cry of the unemployed and disinherited who, though they may not know it, are poor because they have been robbed.

Thompson's reference to the 'monopoly of land and capital' is indicative of a transition in his radical thinking that reflected a general shift in labour-radical circles in his time. During the 1880s, and even the early 1890s, when the Canadian labour movement was still dominated by the Knights of Labour, the great radical prophet had been neither Karl Marx nor his great rival Michael Bakunin, but the American shaman Henry George, a populist rather than a socialist, who argued that increased land values were the main reason for economic inequality. He proposed a single tax on increases in land value that would pay all the costs of government, including the increased social services that George advocated. Such a teaching had a natural appeal in an agrarian period when the settlement of the West was still a high priority, when men were eagerly seeking land, when land booms and land speculation flourished; its influence would naturally decline as an industrial economy developed, and the balance shifted from a land-oriented to a city-oriented society. In that intermediate period, late in the nineteenth century, even many industrial workers were attracted by the arguments George had offered so persuasively in *Progress and Poverty* in 1879, and his teachings were especially popular among the Knights of Labour, of which he was a member. In 1884 the Canadian Knights brought George across the border, and he led a procession through Hamilton—riding a horse like King Billy and surrounded by bands and union banners—to the Crystal Palace, where an estimated ten thousand people heard him deliver his message of salvation through a 'single tax' on land, the source of all wealth. As late as 1893, when the influence of the Knights had dwindled, the Trades and Labour Congress was still passing resolutions couched in Georgeite phrases. 'The earth, with its lands, forests, and other natural opportunities, is the gift of nature not to a part, but to the whole of humanity.'

The sentiments of Georgism spread far into the intellectual world of Canada in the last years of the nineteenth century. It is true that George Monro Grant attacked both Henry George and Father J.O.S. Huntington, the American Episcopalian priest who set out to give George's single-tax teachings a Christian application, and that Goldwin Smith looked skeptically on all radical doctrines, including single-taxism. Yet it was in the columns of Smith's periodical, *The Week* (13 Feb. 1891), that the novelist Agnes Maule Machar, writing as 'Fidelis', defended Huntington and by implication Henry George, on the grounds that they were sustaining the essential teachings of the Sermon on the Mount. From a point of view that anticipated later social Gospellers like J.S. Woodsworth and Salem Bland, she denounced capitalism in terms as uncompromising as those of any secular radical of her time:

> Had this been kept in the foreground as the integral, human side of the Christian religion, had the Christian church been steadily faithful in this part of the message to 'all sorts and conditions of men', should we have today, the spectacle of capital endeavouring everywhere to screw down the receipts of a labourer to a minimum for which men otherwise starving can be induced to work? Should we have the complementary spectacle of labour everywhere striving to free from the reluctant grasp of capital a fairer share of its profits that labour toils to gain? Is there not everywhere the assumption that the employing classes have a prescriptive right to live in spacious and generally luxurious houses, to wear 'purple and fine linen' and to 'live sumptuously every day'; while the unemployed must consider themselves fortunate if they can 'make both ends meet' in a bare subsistance; if their cramped bodies have a roof to keep out the rain, walls that will afford some adequate protection from the winter's frost, and a floor not charged with hidden germs of disease; an ideal not frequently realized even in this Canada of ours?

It was not until the flames of Georgism began to die down towards the end of the century that Marxism—or even socialism in a more general sense—had more than a little success in Canada, though some, like Thompson, seemed to veer towards it. As early as 1894 a labour weekly, *The Voice*, began to appear in Winnipeg, under the editorship of A.W. Puttee, and working-class candidates in provincial and federal elections, when they were not attached to the older parties, ran as labour representatives. Under such auspices the Ottawa printer P.J. O'Donohue was elected to the Ontario legislature as early as 1874, and in 1888 one of the leading Knights of Labour in Montreal, L.A. Lépine, was elected to the House of Commons. Ralph Smith, President of the Trades and Labour Congress, who had represented the mining constituency of Nanaimo in British Columbia for several years, fought a Dominion election successfully.

But apart from the fact that they were elected to represent the interests of the workers in industrial matters, the labour representatives of this period had no clear political philosophies, and—like Ralph Smith, who drifted into the Liberal orbit—were easily co-opted. Things began to change when the Winnipeg Trades and Labour Council in 1900 decided to support Puttee, now publisher of *The Voice*, as a labour candidate in the Manitoba provincial elections. Puttee concocted a platform that seemed to represent most of the populist strains of the time. He called for direct legislation by referendum and popular initiative for the Georgite single tax, and, in a more orthodox socialist sense, for public ownership of all natural resources. He won by eight votes, and, if *The Voice* is to be believed, he manifested his independence in a whimsical way:

> The new member in advancing to salute the speaker passed upon the opposition side of the mace, which caused the gentlemen on that side of the house to applaud prodigiously. After 'shaking' the new member retraced his steps, turned to the right and sought a seat in the 'independent' corner, which caused the government side to take up applause amid a general laugh.

The first Canadian socialist organization, founded in 1894, was a Toronto branch of the American Daniel De Leon's Socialist Labour Party, a Marxist organization so doctrinaire that it separated itself from the real labour movement by refusing all co-operation with the trade unions. In 1899 a Canadian Socialist League appeared, with branches in Ontario, Quebec, and British Columbia. Christian and populist in orientation, distinguishing 'public' ownership from both private and government ownership of the means of production, it was first organized by George Wrigley, the Toronto radical journalist and editor of *Citizen and Country*, who in 1902 renamed his paper the *Canadian Socialist*.

> Having aided in the establishment of an organization whose members do not fear to be known as socialists and having, by persistent denial of the untruthful charges hurled against socialists and by timely explanation concerning the purpose of socialism created a more friendly sentiment towards our movement to lessen the burden of those who toil and suffer under unjust conditions, we now adopt the name of *Canadian Socialist* for our publication.

The next development came in British Columbia, whose volatile population of migratory workers in the great primary industries like mining, logging, and fishing produced an inclination towards radical initiatives. By the beginning of the twentieth century B.C. harboured a number of socialist sects, none of which were strong enough to emerge as a real party. In 1901 these groups came together and formed the Socialist Party of British Columbia. For a while a dissident group, centred in Nanaimo, held aloof, rejecting gradualism and calling for the immediate emancipation of the workers. In its publication, *The Independent*, it declared:

> The Revolutionary Socialist Party of Canada proclaims itself the political exponent of the working class interests. It will deviate neither to the right nor to the left of the line laid down in its platform. It will neither endorse nor accept endorsement. It has no compromise to make.

At that time in British Columbia the extreme line of the Nanaimo Revolutionary Socialists seemed irresistibly attractive, so that by 1902 the two groups united under an uncompromising socialist program. Phillips Thompson, now the organizer of the Canadian Socialist League in Ontario and still striving to keep in the vanguard of Canadian radicalism as it evolved, sent an enthusiastic message of support.

> There is no question that the example you have set us of what can be accomplished by a rigid adherence to the principles of international socialism and eschewing all ideas of fusion or compromise have wonderfully stiffened the backbone of Ontario socialism and brought many waverers into line.

In the same year two avowed socialists, J.H. Hawthornthwaite and Parker Williams, were elected to the provincial legislature, the first successful candidates in Canada to stand on an uncompromising socialist platform. In 1904 the Socialist Party of British Columbia and the Canadian Socialist League, which had now moved leftward, combined to form the Socialist Party of Canada, which until the appearance of the Communist Party after the Great War remained the custodian of doctrinaire Marxism. Rejecting all types of reform, since they believed the capitalist system could not be improved and was doomed in any case to collapse, its members envisaged a revolutionary change in the political and social order that would lead to the abolition of the wage system and to public ownership of the means of production. Just what form that public ownership would take they left undecided.

Undoubtedly the members of the Socialist Party of Canada saw themselves as representing the future. But it was not a Canadian future: other Canadians could make no room for their extreme views. Their policies found little support in the labour movement, which they continued to antagonize and deride. About this time Samuel Gompers, the head of the American Federation of Labour, visited Vancouver, the spiritual headquarters of the Socialist Party of Canada, to preach his doctrine of reformist trade unionism. Hecklers from the Party tried to break up his meeting, and then held an open-air meeting attacking Gompers and the labour unions; as he recollected:

> They denounced me in the vilest language I have ever heard. They gathered about them a mob of 50 and when I came into the street all joined in the howling and booing after me. I lit my cigar and with the committee slowly walked forward to the hotel. Others joined the howling mob that followed me. I walked more slowly.

But the times were on the side of Samuel Gompers. Given the tendency of Canadians towards reform and compromise, no matter how much rebellion goes into achieving them, it was inevitable that a more moderate, less dogmatic, and less revolutionary type of socialism should emerge. This was represented by the Social Democratic Party, which was founded in Vancouver in 1909 and quickly established branches in all the provinces. A.W. Puttee had by this time abandoned socialism and begun his drift towards progressivism, but his paper, *The Voice*, maintained its allegiance, supporting the new Social Democratic trend, and on 30 April 1909 issued a manifesto that explained the reasons for the rift in the socialist movement and foreshadowed a return to gradualism:

> We realize that socialism will come, if it comes at all, as an evolutionary process as all changes in the past have come; and the more of the public utilities we can get into our hands while this system lasts the easier will be the transformation when the time is ripe for the final overthrow of capitalism. It is absurd to argue, as some of the leaders of the Socialist Party of Canada do, that there is no value at all in 'immediate demands'.

Because they took a revolutionary standpoint and denied the possibility that Canadian society and its economic system could be reformed, the Marxists in the Socialist Party of Canada were described in the jargon of the period as Impossibilists. By 1910 their party was in decline.

The Social Democrats were 'Possibilists'. They believed that through a proper mingling of rebellion and reform, meaningful progress could be made in changing the existing order without revolution. Their view survived as the majority tradition in both the industrial and the political streams of the Canadian labour movement. In recent times the CCF (Co-operative Commonwealth Federation) and its successor the NDP (New Democratic Party) have been heirs of the Social Democratic Party rather than of the Socialist Party of Canada—because, in the last resort, Canadians are Possibilists. The whole of our history has been based on the imaginative recognition of the possible even in the heart of improbability. The acceptance of challenges, and the refusal to be denied, are factors that made possible our unwieldy and unlikely country and have allowed it to survive.

5

The Tory Antithesis:
Nationalism and Imperialism

A good Canadian nationalist must *be a good British Imperialist.*
—Charles G.D. Roberts.

A myth accepted by the authoritarian Left is that non-revolutionary societies are static and conservative, and revolutionary societies are fluid and progressive. History shows something different. Revolutionary societies, having established the ascendancy of their guiding 'truth', tend to become static; change, where it occurs in them, is slow and reluctantly accepted. Russia, in the enduring grip of a ruling party ridden by nineteenth-century political dogmas, is an example repeatedly held up, and until recently with justification, by critics in the West.

   In comparison, non-revolutionary societies with genuine traditions of personal freedom are flexible and changeable, and tend to move generally forward—though not without reactionary oscillations—by a kind of Proudhonian rather than a Marxian dialectic; thesis (reformism) and antithesis (toryism) push each other on without ever reaching that revolutionary dead-end called, by the Marxists, synthesis. Here appearances are often confusing: a society that to the outsider seems static may be undergoing a deep-seated process of change. Though formally conservative, it may in fact be evolving steadily behind its rigid façade.

Canada has been, and still is, such a society. Henry David Thoreau—an observant man on his own lakeside, but not always so perceptive away from Walden—wandered to Canada in 1851 and noted in his journal:

> Why should Canada, wild and unsettled, impress one as an older country than the States, except that her institutions are old. All things seem to contend there with a certain rust of antiquity, such as forms on old armour and iron guns, the rust of convention and formalities. If the rust was not on the tinned roofs and spires, it was on the inhabitants.

Thoreau was judging from appearances in Quebec, where he saw the British military presence that 'parades itself before you' and the ostentatious authority of the Catholic Church. He did not take into account that the country he regarded as coated with 'the rust of convention and formalities' had been involved in two insurrections a little more than a decade before, that its parliament house in Montreal had been burnt down by an aggrieved mob a mere two years before, and that after long reform agitations the colonies of British North America were in the process of achieving responsible government. The red-coated troops might parade on the Champ de Mars; the judges might wear their traditional wigs (and black caps for murderers); the Usher of the Black Rod might still—as he does to this day—knock on the door of the elected assembly to summon its members into the presence of the Queen's representative; and the Queen's head might appear on coins and postage stamps. But the Canadians and Nova Scotians and New Brunswickers had made a step forward in democracy that the American Constitution, with its revolutionary rigidity, denied to Thoreau and his fellow Americans: Canadian governments henceforward remained in office only so long as they retained the confidence of the people's representatives. The situation in which a President, the executive head of a country, could still hold office in opposition to a Congress that did not support his policies could not exist in Canada, now that the old system of administration by a governor and his executive council had come to an end. Ironically the 'revolutionary' American system had remained nearer to the old colonial governments of the eighteenth century than the reformist Canadian system had now become.

The striking fact about the Canadian situation was that the triumph of reformism did not mean the end of Toryism. Toryism is a view of social relations and obligations, a philosophy of inter-related functions, as much as it is a system of political dogma. Archdeacon (later Bishop) John Strachan, by virtue of his double roles as leader of the established church and the teacher of the sons of officials, was perhaps more than anyone else the spokesman for Canadian Toryism in the decades after the War of 1812, and in a sermon he preached in September 1824 he gave expression to the Tory ideal of a society graded and harmonized.

> One is formed to rule, another to obey . . . . Subordination in the Moral World is manifest and this appearance of nature indicates the intention of its Author. The beauty and advantages of this arrangement are obvious and universally acknowledged . . . . The various relations of Individuals and Societies require a mutual exchange of good offices . . . . Hence it would appear that they who labour in the inferior departments of life are not on that account the slaves of their superiors . . . . The lowest order enjoys its peculiar comforts and privileges, and contributes equally with the highest to the support and dignity of Society.

Toryism changes with times and circumstances, but the kind of organic view of society it projects survives and reappears in various guises. Even in the century we are considering it passed through a number of transformations.

Perhaps the earliest epitome of Toryism in Canada at its best was Isaac Brock, who became a Tory hero. He was not a Canadian but a British career officer, and when the Americans started the war in 1812 he happened to be both commander of the armed forces and administrator of Upper Canada in the absence of the governor. He found himself in charge of a province largely settled by Americans of dubious loyalty, facing an initially obstructive Assembly, and dependent on a demoralized and unreliable militia to support his small force of British regulars. 'Most of the people have lost all confidence,' he remarked as the war began. 'I however speak loud and look big.' He not only looked big; he acted decisively. Supported by Tecumseh's Indians and by some of the more efficient militia formations dominated by Loyalists, he drove out the Americans who had crossed into Upper Canada and occupied Amherstburg, and followed them over the border to capture Detroit, an action that immediately changed the look of the situation and rallied the waverers. Brock's stance was clearly revealed in his speech to the Assembly on 27 July 1812, a few weeks before the capture of Detroit:

> We are engaged in an awful and eventful contest. By unanimity and despatch in our councils and vigour in our operations, we will teach the enemy this lesson, that a country defended by their King and constitution, can never be conquered.

Brock was posing the British system of government against the American, but he was also posing the Tory argument that men are most free in a hierarchical situation where roles are understood. 'King and constitution', in this period, meant King, Lords, and Commons.

Brock's reliable supporters were the Loyalists and their descendants, and those few British who had come to Canada before 1812 as officers or office-holders and had been encouraged to settle by grants of lands. This policy, as we have seen, had been instituted by Governor Simcoe in the 1790s, with the idea of creating a Tory replica of the British social order in the form of a powerful squirearchy, if not a titled aristocracy, and a state church funded by the Clergy Reserves: a seventh of the public lands in both Upper and Lower Canada was set aside, under the Constitutional Act of 1791, for the benefit of 'Protestant Clergy', i.e. of the Church of England, a system that persisted into the 1840s.

The advocates of Canadian Toryism took as their ideal the England of the pre-democratic days before the Reform Bill of 1832 started the country on its way towards universal suffrage. When Bishop Jacob Mountain of Quebec died in 1825, John Strachan preached a memorial sermon in York, in which he made clear the link between good laws, wise politics, and a religious establishment, which at that time was central to the Tory view of society. Of England, he said:

> To the able administration of her excellent laws, and the wisdom of her political institutions, all nations turn their eyes not only to admire, but to imitate. She stands aloft like the sun in the heavens, dispensing her charities wherever distress is to be found, without regard to difference of language, climate or complexion. Not satisfied with shewing the way, she compels, by entreaties and donations, other nations to pursue her virtuous course . . . . Never without a religious establishment could she have soared so high above other nations—it is this that diffuses through her whole population, the most sublime and disinterested principles . . . .

After the War of 1812 this Tory ideal was sustained by the loosely knotted groups known as the Family Compact in Upper Canada and the Château Clique in Lower Canada, composed of men of some education and administrative skills—many of them friends, often further linked by marriage—who became members of the Executive and Legislative Councils and on whom the Governors depended to sustain their authority. They did not see themselves as belonging to a clique, however. The collective epithets that have clung to them in history books derive from an early example of the power of the press. Thomas Dalton, the editor of the Kingston *Patriot*, wrote in 1824 of the 'family compacted junto' that governed his city, and the term was quickly adopted by the Reformers in York, and especially by William Lyon Mackenzie, in the *Colonial Advocate* and in his *Sketches of Canada and the United States* (New York, 1833), in which he talked of the Compact as a great conspiracy of people largely related by blood (i.e. family): 'This family compact surround the Lieutenant-Governor, and mould him, like wax, to their will.'

That a privileged group existed in the years before the rebellions is confirmed by witnesses who may have had sympathies with reform but in many ways were attached to the ruling system. One of them was the patronizing but very astute Anna Jameson. Unhappily married to Robert

Jameson, who had been made attorney general of Upper Canada in 1833, she visited her husband in Toronto in 1836, mingling with members of the 'family compact', and exploring neighbouring regions; she left in 1837. 'I am not one of those who opine sagely', she once remarked, 'that women have nothing to do with politics.' She could hardly be called a reformer, however, still less a radical; yet, writing in the year before the rebellions, she was strongly aware of the presence of a cohesive right-wing ruling group.

> You must recollect that the first settlers in Upper Canada were those who were obliged to fly from the United States during the revolutionary war, in consequence of their attachment to the British government, and the soldiers and non-commissioned officers who had fought during the war. These were recompensed for their losses, sufferings, and services, by grants of land in Upper Canada. Thus the very first elements out of which our social system was framed, were repugnance and contempt for the new institutions of the United States, and a dislike of the people of that country,— a very natural result of foregone causes; and thus it has happened that the slightest tinge of democratic, or even liberal principles in politics, were for a long time a sufficient impeachment of the loyalty, a stain upon the personal character, of those who held them. The Tories have been hitherto the influential party; in their hands we find the sales and grants of land, for a long series of years.

To this 'influential party' belonged the office-holders and the professional men (with the exception of a few radical country doctors), plus a few town merchants, and some of the half-pay officers who had become gentlemen-farmers in the hinterland. It was a tight, if not entirely closed, circle, but it could at times draw on the loyalty of wider sections of the population, as it did in the elections of 1836, when the Reformers were thrown out of power in the Assembly—an event that led the radicals to their disastrous adventure in 1837. The Lieutenant-Governor, Sir Francis Bond Head, was so sure that the 'outbreak' of William Lyon Mackenzie and his followers, of which he had been warned, would inevitably fail that he sent all regular soldiers to the aid of Sir John Colborne to meet the uprising in Quebec. In the event, Head was certainly right when he said later: 'The little outbreak in this province has been completely put down by the people themselves, for I had no other assistance.'

Yet the rebellions were opposed less out of loyalty to the ruling group than to the British connection by people who feared that a successful rebellion might turn into a revolution that would make Canada an appendage of the United States. In the years following the Rebellions of 1837-8 the kind of Tory political structure imagined by Governor Simcoe and defended with obvious sincerity by men like Strachan, and Chief Justice John Beverley Robinson (Strachan's former pupil), could withstand neither the growing strength of the dissenting Methodist and

Baptist churches, nor the mass migrations in the second third of the nineteenth century, when tens of thousands of working people from England, dispossessed crofters from Scotland, and famished peasants from Ireland reached the North American colonies and settled mostly in Upper Canada.

Throughout these changes and incursions, however, Toryism survived. Its advocates were often men of considerable brilliance, like John Beverley Robinson, who was remembered with reluctant admiration even by his ardent reformist opponent Marshall Spring Bidwell:

> His features were classically and singularly beautiful, his countenance was luminous with intelligence and animation; his whole appearance that of a man of genius and a polished gentleman, equally dignified and graceful . . . . He was a consummate advocate, as well as a profound and accurate lawyer.

And the élitist attitude, which is part of Toryism, did not die away quickly in a society where many people still believed the sentiments expressed in a hymn then widely sung:

> The rich man in his castle,
>   The poor man at his gate,
> God made them high and lowly
>   And ordered their estate.

Such an attitude seemed natural even to Tiger Dunlop and the Moodies, who—though they actively opposed the rebellion—considered themselves political reformers. Susanna Moodie may have thought that the Canadian backwoods was no place for gentlemen, but she still believed gentleman had their place and their duties. Her husband Dunbar Moodie accepted a post as sheriff in 1839, when Responsible Government was still almost a decade away, and he probably saw no inconsistency between reformist attitudes and a society in which gentlemen would live by *noblesse oblige* and be suitably rewarded.

Even when the rule of the Family Compact came to an end with the establishment of Responsible Government in the united provinces of Canada, Bishop Strachan still unrepentingly praised the old Tory system, and denounced the emergence of a party system, as when he wrote to a Scottish friend in 1848:

> I am still the same Tory that you knew me to be forty years ago, and am of opinion that till we had responsible government in the colony we knew nothing of the corruption of government. Now the ministry, as they call it, whether conservative or reform, seem to have no other object than to get good places. All is party and, I may say, all is corruption; and it matters not which faction is in power.

Under the resurgent Toryism of the 1870s Strachan's complaints of partisanship would be revived by the Canada First movement, which declared in its journal, the *Nation*, that 'our main object is to look at all public questions not from the party but from the national point of view.'

Toryism, of course, is not identical with Conservative political parties. Variants of Tory attitudes appear in surprising places: among the Lower Canadian *Patriotes* of 1837, for example, who—despite rebellious actions—defended the old semi-feudal seigneurial system against the intrusion of a freehold system that would favour Anglo-Saxon land speculators. And among Canadian literary Tories there was a tendency to distrust professional politicians of all parties because of the compromising of principles that even Sir Wilfrid Laurier recognized sadly in a letter written near the end of his career:

> Remember this, that in politics the question seldom arises to do the ideal right. The best that can generally be done is to attain a certain object and for the accomplishment of this object, many things have to be done which are questionable, and many things have to be submitted to which, if vigorously investigated, could not be approved of.

Writers who concerned themselves with the polity often restricted themselves to admonition and criticism, largely because they realized the dangers involved in trying to fit principles to action. Thomas Chandler Haliburton—a temperamental Tory who was at the same time a splendid social critic and who once lamented that 'colonists have no nationality'— expressed his misgivings in the 1830s through the mouth of Sam Slick:

> Politics makes a man as crooked as a pack does a pedlar, not that they are so awful heavy either, but it teaches a man to stoop in the long run.

And in Toronto in the 1860s the gentlemanly and fastidious Goldwin Smith, with more than half an eye on his perennial political enemy, John A. Macdonald, remarked: 'If public life is the noblest of all callings, it is the vilest of all trades.' Here again a Tory hierarchy is implied: patricians can afford to make public life a calling, but plebeians are forced by necessity to make it a trade.

The notion that idealism and practical politics cannot live together has perhaps its most striking Canadian literary expression during this period in Sara Jeannette Duncan's novel *The Imperialist* (1904), especially the scene at the end when Lorne Murchison—having taken to heart the teachings of Imperial federation and run for Parliament, using them in all sincerity as his platform—is cast aside by the political professionals when a new election is held in their constituency. Murchison's dedication to the Imperialist ideal had become politically embarrassing:

> They had dedicated what Horace Williams called 'the job' to Mr. Farquharson, and he was actually struggling with the preliminaries of it, when

Bingham, uncomfortable under the curious quietude of the young fellow's attention, burst out with the whole thing.

'The fact is, Murchison, you can't poll the vote. There's no man in the Riding we'd be better pleased to send to the House; but we've got to win this election and we can't win it with you.'

'You think you can't?' said Lorne.

'You see, old man,' Horace Williams put in, 'you didn't get rid of that save-the-Empire-or-die scheme of yours soon enough. People got to think you mean something by it.'

'I shall never get rid of it,' Lorne returned simply, and the others looked at one another.

'The popular idea seems to be,' said Mr. Farguharson judicially, 'that you would not hesitate to put Canada to some material loss, or at least to postpone her development in various important directions, for the sake of the imperial connection.'

'Wasn't that,' Lorne asked him, 'what, six months ago, you were all prepared to do?'

'Oh, no,' said Bingham, with an air of repudiating for everybody concerned. 'Not for a cent. We were willing at one time to work it for what it was worth, but it never was worth that, and if you'd had a little more experience, Murchison, you'd have realised it.'

'That's right, Lorne,' contributed Horace Williams. 'Experience—that's what you want. You've got everything else, and a darn sight more. We'll get you there, all in good time. But this time—'

'You want me to step down and out,' said Lorne.

And step out he does, with dignity and with none of the difficulty the professionals had expected. He left them with a brief excuse, and they stood together in a moment's silence, three practical politicians who had delivered themselves from a dangerous network involving higher things.

This scene clearly implies that practical politics—in Canada certainly, and probably elsewhere—was a matter of sordid calculation, and that those who were searching for 'higher things' in it did so at their peril. It is in keeping with Duncan's evident views that the two nineteenth-century Canadian movements one can most easily define as manifestations of Tory idealism—the nationalism of the 1860s and the imperialism of the 1880s and later—were developed largely by men who never ran for office. The one exception of a practising politician who became involved in these movements at the time and almost proved the rule was Edward Blake (1833-1912), the brilliant Liberal who never fitted into any machine, who never followed a course to any end but his own, and who was an ultimate failure as a politician because of his moral fastidiousness.

But an important distinction must be made. There was a movement towards autonomy that was based on the mutual convenience of imperial rulers and colonial politicians and that also reflected a simple desire on the part of many inhabitants of the colonies to arrange their own local affairs. This led to the pragmatic arrangement known as Confederation. And there was the movement of young intellectuals, aging with the century, that called itself Canada First and that developed the conceptual basis and the guiding myths of a nationalism that stressed the need for political and cultural independence from the United States and for a unification of the British North American territories. It differed from late twentieth-century varieties of Canadian nationalism by stressing the British connection, to the degree that nationalism merged eventually into a new imperialism in which Canada would cease to be a grouping of colonies and become an equal partner in a revived empire.

The thought that Canada—which for a long time meant the two Upper and Lower colonies that in 1840 became united into the single Province of Canada—might become an entity quite separate from the United Kingdom had of course been part of the radical philosophy that inspired Mackenzie and his followers in Upper Canada, and Papineau and the *Patriotes* in Lower Canada. And the idea of a self-reliant community deserving a patriotism of its own recurred persistently in newspaper editorials in the 1850s, without the insurrectionary implications of the years of rebellion. For example, in its issue of 16 April 1850 the Montreal *Pilot* linked ideas of Canadian self-sufficiency to the inclination towards shedding colonial responsibilities shown by imperial politicians of the period:

> It cannot be too strongly impressed upon every mind that it is on Canadian energy, Canadian ambition, Canadian self-reliance, skill and enterprise, in a word, on Canadian patriotism, that depends Canadian prosperity, elevation and happiness . . . . In agricultural productiveness, Canada is superior to New York; . . . its mineral resources are ample to supply its own implements and industry, as its cattle and flocks are equal to its wants for labor, food and clothing. Its sky is as clear as that of Italy, and its climate as healthy as that of Germany; its institutions are even freer than those of England, and its administration of justice confessedly more independent and impartial than that of the United States.

Similar ideas emerge even among early Tories of the Family Compact period. John Beverley Robinson seems to have invented the concept of a 'Kingdom of Canada', which would parallel rather than defer to the parent monarchy, whose hierarchical forms Robinson and his associates hoped might be duplicated with transatlantic modifications. The idea of equality within the Empire also found rudimentary expression in the thoughts of Thomas Chandler Haliburton, whose early experiences as a Nova Scotian in England in the late 1850s had led him to the conclusion that 'colonists are the pariahs of the Empire', whereas they should stand on the same footing as the citizens of England and Scotland.

Another Nova Scotian, plain William Alexander Smith—metamorphosed into the British Columbian editor and maverick politician Amor de Cosmos—was among the early advocates not merely of the autonomy of the North American colonies, but also of their union into a single nation, which he saw as a prerequisite for real independence. When the Prince of Wales toured Canada in 1860, de Cosmos celebrated the occasion with an editorial in Victoria's *British Colonist* that expressed his hope that 'provincial and imperial statesmen' would

> take advantage of the Prince's visit to initiate a British North American policy to put an end to disjointed provinces. Call them petty monarchies or petty republics, or what you please, so long as there is no union of the North American provinces, there will be few subjects of common interest to bind them together. They will lead a humdrum life as subordinates to the Colonial office. They will possess no field for the expansion of their intellect.

More than twenty years later, in 1882, de Cosmos brought his political career to an abrupt end by offending the loyal voters of Victoria with a remarkable statement on colonialism and national destiny. The occasion was a debate in the House of Commons on 21 April 1882 on the question of commercial treaties. De Cosmos argued that the imperial government, away in Westminster, did not have the local knowledge that would make it competent to conduct Canada's foreign affairs. 'I am one of those', he said, 'who believe that this country should have the right to negotiate its commercial treaties. I go a step further. I believe this country should have the right to negotiate every treaty.' He then went on to make the statement that so offended the people of Queen Victoria's namesake city:

> I see no reason why the people of Canada should not look forward to Canada becoming a sovereign and independent State. The right hon. gentleman states that he was born a British subject and hopes to die one. Sir, I was born a British colonist, but do not wish to die a tadpole British colonist. I do not wish to die without having all the rights, privileges and immunities of the citizen of a nation.

Amor de Cosmos was ahead of most Canadians. But he was not ahead of Canada First, though there is no evidence that he had any links with them. Canada First sprang out of the discontent of young idealistic Canadians with the political realities of Confederation. It came into being in the spring of 1868, the year after the Dominion of Canada became a reality.

The accidental pivot of the movement was Henry J. Morgan, who has a small fame as the creator of the first companion to Canadian writing, the *Bibliotheca Canadensis*, which he published in 1867. In 1868 Morgan was a clerk in the Secretary of State's Office, and in that year he was visited in Ottawa's Revere Hotel by the young poet Charles Mair, whom he had already met in Montreal.

Morgan was a man of many acquaintances, and three of them were in Ottawa at the same time as Mair. There was a brilliant young lawyer who practised in the city, William A. Foster, and another lawyer from Halifax, Robert Grant Haliburton, son of the creator of Sam Slick. The third man, George Taylor Denison, also a lawyer, came of a military tradition and fancied himself as a soldier; his father, Colonel George Taylor Denison, had served in the War of 1812, and in 1837 commanded a troop of volunteer dragoons he later reorganized as Denison's Horse. Young George Denison began his military career as a cornet in the family regiment, and now he was lieutenant-colonel commanding the unit, renamed the Governor-General's Body Guard; in this capacity he had seen service during the Fenian raids of 1866, so that his patriotism had been at least metaphorically blooded. He considered himself a military tactician of the first order, and was encouraged in this opinion in 1877 when his *History of Cavalry, from the Earliest Times, with Lessons for the Future*, received the prize offered by the Czar of Russia for the best work on mounted warfare.

Except for Haliburton, all these young men were still in their twenties. Like many others of their age, particularly in Ontario, they were filled with what Denison later called 'visions of a great and powerful country stretching from ocean to ocean and destined to be one of the dominant powers of the world.' A year after the establishment of the Dominion they were disappointed with the progress their country had made. They saw, correctly, that Confederation had been less the materialization of a political vision than an expedient arrangement between colonial and imperial leaders. For the former it provided a way out of the perennial deadlocks that had arisen in the united province of Canada through the effort to bring together the English and the French in a single political entity; for the latter it offered a federation of hitherto disparate provinces that would have a prospect of surviving the resurgence of American hostility after the Civil War and might eventually relieve the imperial government of the burden of its defence.

A union based so clearly on mundane political considerations aroused little patriotic feeling, and that mainly in Ontario. In Quebec a large and growing minority regarded the new dispensation as a threat to the French-speaking culture. Two of the Maritime colonies, Prince Edward Island and Newfoundland, held aloof. (Prince Edward Island joined Canada six years later to save itself from bankruptcy, but Newfoundland would keep separate for eighty years.) Both Nova Scotia and New Brunswick tried to withdraw from the Dominion even before it came into existence; they were retained only after some rather sordid political manoeuvres. Armed resistance to incorporation into Canada would shortly flare up on the Red River in 1869-70, while British Columbia was divided to the last minute about whether to join the Dominion, and did so in 1871 with a profound mistrust, to which Amor de Cosmos gave expression when he told his fellow Victorians in early 1870:

> I would not object to a little revolution now and again in British Columbia, if we were treated unfairly; for I am one of those who believe that political hatreds attest the vitality of the state.

Even in the Canadian heartland of the Dominion, with provincial constitutions recognizing their respective linguistic and religious rights, the English and French remained restive partners; and many in Ontario, and even in Montreal, sustained the belief expressed in Lord Durham's famous report of 1839, that the only solution to the clash of cultures must be the anglicization of the French. Durham had hoped this would be achieved by the fusion of Lower and Upper Canada into a single political unit; but after this was done in 1840 events proved him wrong. By the late nineteenth century many pessimists shared the view that Goldwin Smith, then in his continentalist phase, expressed in the *Bystander* in 1889:

> To make a nation there must be a common life, common sentiments, common aims, and common hopes. Of these, in the case of Quebec and Ontario, there is none.

The young men of Canada First who met in the Revere Hotel in 1868 never shared Goldwin Smith's eventual loss of hope in Canada, though (as we shall see later) this academic Vicar of Bray associated with them for a period of his changeable life. But like most later Canadian nationalists, the members of Canada First saw provincialism as the great enemy of the new political community they were setting out to create, and this meant in practice that Canada First remained an Anglo-Canadian movement in its own rather narrow way. The idea of a partnership between two cultures never entered the minds of these impetuous and ardent young men, and the concept of a French nationality within Canada would have been anathema to them. They wanted a society in which the English language would be dominant and English political and social norms would prevail. Indeed, to make the English Canadians appear as equals with the English on English terms was one of the main hidden aims of Canada First, and eventually it would lead these passionate nationalists back full-circle to a renewed imperialism.

It also gave the movement more than a tinge of racialism, which emerged in connection with events at Red River in 1869-70. There Charles Mair became involved in the Canadian party led by Dr John Christian Schultz, whose goal was to turn the West into a virtual colony of Ontario, and whose contempt for the local Métis population was shared by Mair. After Riel established his provisional government and resorted to extreme measures, largely because of the provocations of the Canadian party, and Mair and Schultz had fled back to Canada, the most discreditable phase of Canada First began: its members formed a tacit alliance with the Orange Lodges in Ontario to stir up feeling against Riel and against a settlement that would respect the demands of the Métis.

Despite this early excursion into reactionary populism, Canada First never became a mass movement. A profound distrust of professional politicians was one of its enduring characteristics, and a fear of being corrupted by holding office prevented its members from forming themselves into one of those third and fourth parties whose presence and persistence have distinguished the pluralist Canadian political pattern from the rigid American republican one.

Instead, Canada First remained a group of gentlemanly propagandists whose cause generated much emotion but little originality of thought. Its first real manifesto did not appear until 1871, when W.A. Foster's pamphlet, *Canada First: Or Our New Nationality*, was published. Nowadays it impresses us with its rhetorical emptiness. Even Foster seemed aware that he was appealing less to intelligence than to feeling when he admitted:

> We may lay ourselves open to the charge of sentimentalism, but men die for sentiment and often sacrifice everything for an idea. There is a national heart that can be stirred to its depths; a national imagination that can be aroused to a fervent glow; and when noble deeds are to be done, and great thoughts of progress and reform to be achieved, we appeal in vain to reason to lead the forlorn hope or mount to the imminent breach, but at the first trumpet-blast, passion, enthusiasm, youth, step proudly to the front and press forward with restless eager pace.

The publication of *Canada First* more or less coincided with the arrival in Canada of Goldwin Smith in 1871. A historian, he had been Regius Professor of History at Oxford and had taught at Cornell before finally choosing Canada as a home. His real interests lay in the present rather than the past, and when his private means were considerably increased by his marriage to a rich Toronto widow, he settled down to a career of high-level journalism. His contribution was notable; he used his wealth to found and support intelligent periodicals and spent much of his time writing for them, so that he had a broad influence on Canadian journalism at a crucial period. Within a year of his arrival he was helping to found the excellent magazine of affairs, the *Canadian Monthly and National Review*, and in 1874 he moved into more popular journalism by establishing the *Evening Telegram* with John Ross Robertson. Smith gave himself a more personal organ of expression in the *Bystander*, much of which he wrote himself, starting it as a weekly in 1889, and then, as demands on his time became more compelling, changing it to a quarterly. He founded *The Week* in 1883, and some of the best Canadian writers of the time, including Sara Jeannette Duncan and Charles G.D. Roberts, contributed; Roberts was even briefly its editor. When Smith closed down *The Week* in 1896, he salvaged from bankruptcy the *Weekly Sun*, the organ of the Farmers' Movement, and kept it going until 1909, the year before his death.

Smith was a man of agile and inquiring mind, with no great profundity of thought, but he had a gift of eloquence and a magnetic personality. Frances Monck, the Governor-General's daughter-in-law who kept a racy diary in Canada during the 1860s, met him during one of his early visits to Canada in 1864 and made him the subject of one of her sharp vignettes: ' . . . he has a very sneering face and manner, but is very clever and agreeable to talk to. I am glad to have met him. I told him before I crossed the Atlantic I agreed with him about giving up the Colonies, and wished then that I knew him. He is a democrat. He certainly has wonderful violet eyes, with all his faults.' Inconsistency was one of those faults: for each of the eventually conflicting causes he embraced, Smith showed an equal ardour.

Perhaps the most important vestige of Smith's career as a historian was his deep interest in the fate of North America. This led him, in the early 1860s while he was still at Oxford, to write the series of letters to the London *Daily News* to which Frances Monck referred, in which he elaborated on the Cobdenite belief that England should divest itself of colonial possessions, not only for its own benefit but also for that of the colonial inhabitants. He not only posed a clear distinction between colonial dependence and independence; he introduced a third element when he commented that some Canadians seemed to be convinced that the United States wielded a political and cultural attraction that constituted 'a centripetal force beyond their control'.

Once he had arrived in Canada, Smith set about seeking a cause that would provide a forum for his journalistic abilities and in which he could also play the role of grey eminence, which he enjoyed and which the existing conformation of Canadian politics denied him in regular party groupings. He found it in Canada First, with whose members he came into contact shortly after his arrival in Canada. He offered them money, advice, and eloquence at the very time when they were debating whether to proceed into serious political activity. He subsidized their first and only journal, the *Nation*, and when they hesitated to declare themselves a political party, he helped them found the Canadian National Association as a halfway organization, and the National Club (of which he became first president) as its headquarters. At the inaugural meeting of the National Club, Smith declared in his keynote address: 'A principle, if it is sound, a sentiment, if it is genuine and strong, will in due time find an organization and if necessary a leader.'

Smith did not see himself as a leader. His nature was that of the hidden kingmaker, and he had already made his choice in Edward Blake. One of the most gifted figures Canadian Liberalism ever produced, Blake was wandering in the political wilderness after leaving the government of Alexander Mackenzie in 1874. Encouraged by Smith, he drifted towards the Canada Firsters. On 3 October 1874, at a Liberal rally in Aurora, Ontario, he made a fervently nationalist speech, published as *A National Sentiment* (1874). More than a century later it seems full of redundant eloquence in the spirit of the period, with much vague and undefined talk of 'national spirit' and 'national attributes' and sundry ringing calls, as when Blake declared:

> The time will come when that national spirit which has been spoken of will be truly felt among us, when we shall realize that we are four million Britons who are not free, when we shall be ready to take up that freedom, and ask what the late prime minister of England assured us we should not be denied—our share of national rights.

By 1875 Blake returned to the Liberal fold. The last issue of the *Nation* appeared in 1876, but not before being editorially condemned by George Brown's paper, the *Globe*, as 'disloyal to England'. Goldwin Smith drifted away to follow the course that would eventually lead him to a fatalistic acceptance of absorption into the United States as Canada's destiny. Even the original group of Canada Firsters had by this time moved apart, for Foster withdrew after the termination of *The Nation*, Haliburton's interests turned towards anthropology and ethnology, and Mair went to Prince Albert in the North West Territories. Mair, however, kept in touch with Denison, who would personify the transition from Canada First to an Imperial federation.

Ironically, it was shortly after the *Nation* had ceased to appear and Canada First had withered away that nationalism began to spread more widely. Edward Blake's much-reprinted Aurora speech had introduced nationalism into the political thought and parlance of the day, and within a very short time it was regarded as seductive enough to win votes. When Sir John A. Macdonald in 1878 created a platform on which to emerge in 1873 from the humiliating defeat of the Pacific Scandal, he called it the National Policy and rode it to victory. For Macdonald the Policy was a matter of expediency rather than principle. But the fact that it was accepted enthusiastically by the forgiving electorate showed not only that the national idea had found a place in the Canadian consciousness that it certainly had not held at the time of Confederation, but also that it was well on the way to becoming a guiding myth. The proposals of the National Policy were pragmatic ones for strengthening the weak edifice of the Dominion: a variety of tariffs to encourage industries in central Canada; the completion of the transcontinental railway to placate

British Columbians; the encouragement of immigration to fill the spaces the railway would open in the West.

There have always been two aspects to nationalism in Canada. It seeks to strengthen and unify the nation, which is why it tends to be hostile to provincial and regional aims, and it seeks to define the nation against the world. Except indirectly, in so far as the CPR and the peopling of the West would provide an insurance against further American adventures, the National Policy was not concerned with Canada's external relations; until the Great War, these tended to be relations within the Empire. In the eyes of most people at that time, politicians and voters alike, the establishment of a condition of equality within the Empire was more urgent than any other aspect of external relations, apart from those with the United States.

But even relations with America were closely intertwined with relations with Britain. The Dominion, after all, had come into existence at least partly from a desire on the part of the Imperial government to diminish the British presence in North America so as to minimize potential areas of difference with the United States and ultimately to abandon the responsibility to defend the northern part of the subcontinent. After Confederation, Britain retained control over Canada's external relations, and made treaties relating to them. The desire of successive British governments to retain American goodwill resulted in repeated neglect of Canadian interests, a process that started with the negotiations for the Treaty of Washington of 1871, which settled outstanding differences relating to the Civil War period. As a sop to the Canadians, Sir John A. Macdonald was included in the British delegation, and he found his role entirely frustrating. While Britain agreed to pay damages over the depredations of the Confederate privateer *Alabama*, which had sailed from British ports, the Americans refused to make corresponding redress for the Fenian raids on Canadian soil from American territory; and far from Macdonald's obtaining a satisfactory trading arrangement with the United States, he saw his British fellow-delegates opening the inshore fisheries of the Atlantic provinces to American fisherman. When he protested, the British Prime Minister, William Ewart Gladstone, declared that Macdonald was being 'rampantly unreasonable', and his views were ignored. No wonder he wrote to his friend and colleague Alexander Morris (then Minister of Inland Revenue) in April 1871: 'Never in the whole course of my public life have I been in so disagreeable a position and had such an unpleasant duty to perform as the one upon which I am now engaged here.'

Thirty years later another Canadian Prime Minster would be expressing similar discontent at the British handling of Canadian interests in negotiations with the United States. The reason for this was the Alaska Boundary Award of 1903, in which the British delegate joined with

Theodore Roosevelt's three hand-picked American representatives against the two Canadians in reaching a decision that gave away not only land but also navigational rights that would have facilitated the development of northern British Columbia. Wilfrid Laurier gave expression to the resentment of many Canadians when he blamed the Americans directly for their greed, and the British implicitly for failing in the act of stewardship on behalf of the colonies that was implied in the imperial relationship:

> I have often regretted . . . and never more than on the present occasion, that we are living beside a great neighbour who I believe I can say without being deemed unfriendly to them, are very grasping in their national actions, and who are determined on every occasion to get the best in any agreement that they make. I have often regretted also that we have not in our hands the treaty-making powers which would enable us to dispose of our own affairs . . . . It is important that we should ask the British Parliament for more extensive powers so that if we ever have to deal with similar matters again, we shall deal with them in our own way, in our own fashion, according to the best light we have.

Meanwhile a profound change in British attitudes had taken place, and by the latter part of Victoria's reign the neglect of imperial goals that had marked British policies as late as the 1870s was dramatically reversed. The Raj in India, the daughter dominions, and the far-flung colonies became matters of national pride. Nationalistic English-speaking Canadians were caught up in the euphoria of the times, and it seemed to men like Colonel Denison, the old Canada Firster, that Canada might preserve the British heritage and at the same time achieve a full national status by transforming the imperial relationship of colonial dependence to a federation of national states. Laurier, fêted and dubbed Sir Wilfrid when he attended the Diamond Jubilee celebrations in 1897, toyed with the paradox of 'A colony—yet a nation—words never before in the history of the world associated together.'

The merging of Canadian nationalism into imperialism arose during the 1880s in reaction against the continentalist trends that found expression in the Commercial Union movement of the same decade, which advocated a virtual *zollverein* (customs union) with the United States. Swinging half-circle from his Canada First days, Goldwin Smith became one of Commercial Union's main advocates, supported for a while at least by Grit papers like the *Globe*. He justified his position in the eloquent but specious book, *Canada and the Canadian Question*, which infuriated nationalists in 1891; it declared that the facts of geography, history, and race called for a single Anglo-Saxon nation inhabiting the North American continent, and that the separation of Canada from the United States would always work to its economic disadvantage and create unnecessary suffering for its people.

How far Goldwin Smith was running against the currents of his time was shown by the extent to which other leading Canadian intellectuals were being attracted towards the new Imperialism. These included not only Denison, but also leading academic figures like George Parkin, who gave up the headmastership of the Collegiate School in Fredericton to tour the Empire and lecture on the idea of imperial federation, and George Monro Grant, principal of Queen's University and polymorphic popularizer. Grant declared that the British Empire was 'the highest secular instrument the world has ever known' for bringing about the universal reign of 'freedom, of justice and of peace', and Parkin presented an elevated version of Kipling's concept of the 'white man's burden' when he declared that

> Three hundred millions of mankind who do not share British blood, of various races in various climes, acknowledge British sway, and look to it for guidance and protection; their hopes of civilization and social elevation depend upon the justice with which it is exercised, while anarchy awaits them should the role be reversed.

The plea for closer involvement by British North Americans in the affairs of the Empire was not a new one; Joseph Howe had even used it as an argument against Confederation. In the 1860s he suggested that an imperial union with an imperial parliament, to which the North American provinces sent their representatives, would offer a better guarantee of local freedoms and interests than a North American union dominated by the more populous provinces of Ontario and Quebec. But now the emphasis had shifted from the idea of colonials being equals in an imperial parliament to the idea of former colonies becoming equal nations in a union conceived on much the same lines as the later Commonwealth.

Even when imperialism waned in Britain it waxed in Canada during the last years of the nineteenth century; the Canadian branch of the Imperial Federation in fact became stronger than its metropolitan parent organization. Imperial and nationalist fervours began to spread within the middle class as well as among the intellectuals.

In 1893 the first Canadian Club, intended to discuss national affairs and promote national feeling, was founded in Hamilton; it was quickly replicated in other Ontario cities. In 1898, May 23—the day preceding the Queen's Birthday—was declared Empire Day in the schools of Ontario and Nova Scotia and in the Protestant schools of Quebec. In 1900 the Imperial Order Daughters of the Empire was founded, with the aim of 'directing women's influence to the bettering of all things connected with our great Empire'. And shortly after the turn of the century a hundred writers began work on that monument of popular and patriotic scholarship, the twenty-three volumes of *Canada and Its Provinces: A*

History of the Canadian People and Its Institutions (1913-19), said by its editors, Adam Shortt and Arthur G. Doughty, to be devoted to promoting 'an enlightened patriotism which vibrates with the sentiment of nationality.' Only slightly less ambitious, and equally indicative of the spirit of the times, was the *Makers of Canada* series (1903-11), biographies of men important in the development of the country. Its twenty volumes stretched from Champlain to Macdonald, and it was edited by the poet Duncan Campbell Scott, the university professor and literary critic Pelham Edgar, and the positivist civil servant and essayist, William Dawson LeSueur.

At the same time a kind of nationalism clearly opposed to imperialism had begun to emerge with the dawn of the new century, represented by John Skirving Ewart, a lawyer who made a name for himself advocating separate Catholic schools in Manitoba and who published a series of books that called for the complete constitutional independence of Canada; mostly collections of essays, they included *The Kingdom of Canada* (1908), *Canadian Independence* (1911), and *The Kingdom Papers* (1911-14). In the same period, in a series of polemical pamphlets, the French-Canadian nationalist Henri Bourassa began to explore the potentialities of a Canadian nation in which those of British and French descents could come together in a North American nation, independent of European links and European obligations.

Both imperialism and nationalism now moved out of the intellectual coverts of men who scorned the idea of taking office and became important factors in the political arena, with rather strange consequences. As the Conservative party fell into decay under the succession of brief administrations that followed Macdonald's death in 1891, the nationalist-imperialists, for all their innate Toryism, turned towards the Liberals. Laurier had recognized that the consolidation of national autonomy and the retention of power by his party were interdependent. He gained the support of men like Denison and Grant in the difficult task of retaining a significant role for Canada within the Empire, and in the process he brought their idealism down to the level of political expediency. He had to reconcile conflicting needs: to win approval in Ontario and western Canada he must appear as the friend of Britain, but to retain support in Quebec, which he needed to remain in power, he must assert independence of Britain. And so, in 1897, Laurier figured prominently in the Diamond Jubilee celebrations as Prime Minister of the leading Dominion. But when he later represented Canada at imperial policy conferences, he so successfully evaded binding commitments that the notorious Dr Jameson, then prime minister of Cape Colony, complained bitterly of 'the damned dancing master' who had frustrated all the imperial plans of the Colonial Secretary, Joseph Chamberlain.

The conflict that emerged in practice between nationalism and imperialism haunted Laurier. The initial time of reckoning came with the
South African War, the first foreign conflict in which units of Canadians
fought. The socially and politically influential officers of the militia, together with the members of the Imperial Federation League, formed the
spearhead of the English-speaking Canadians who pressured him to
send Canadian volunteers to support the British against the Boers. Two
thousand Canadians were sent officially; the British were allowed to
recruit several thousand more. They were mostly either imperial patriots,
or men with a *Boy's Own Paper* sense of adventure—or both, like George
Taylor Denison's brother, Septimus Julius Augustus: 'I heard the first
gun,' he recalled, 'and thanked God I had found at last what I had been
searching for for years, an enemy.' The actions of the Canadians at the
battle of Paardeburg in February 1900 became the subject of patriotic
verse, celebrated by Alexander Muir, the author of 'The Maple Leaf
Forever', in a new song entitled 'Young Canada Was There':

> Go, ask the hard won battle field
> Where heroes fought and fell,
> Where Cronje's Boers by British pluck
> Were backward hurled pell-mell,
>
> Whose valiant deeds and iron nerve
> Deserve the palm to bear?
> The answer comes with ringing cheers,
> 'Young Canada was there'

Henri Bourassa, Laurier's former friend, insisted that in becoming
involved in South Africa Canada was creating a precedent in involvement in Britain's wars, and this may partly have influenced Laurier and
have led him—when Canada was asked to contribute to an expanded
British navy that might counter the German threat at sea—to create
instead an autonomous Canadian Navy under the Naval Service Act of
1910. But there could be no final evasion of the incompatability of Canada's nationalist aims and its imperial ties. When Britain went to war
against Germany in 1914, Canada joined her, but it was not with a single
mind. The great majority of British-born men of military age volunteered
with enthusiasm. But Canadian-born farmers and industrial workers,
even of British descent, were not so enthusiastic, and non-British immigrants were even less eager. But it was among French-speaking Canadians that opposition to the war and to participation in it was strongest.
It was from this point—when English-Canadian nationalism, dominated
by its imperialist inclinations, took the path of involvement in distant
wars—that French-Canadian nationalism began to move forward from
sentiment into action.

The element of racial conflict had always been present when Canadians turned to nationalism. It is true that Henri Bourassa dreamed of a Canada where French and British would live together in brotherhood (though he roughly rejected the East-European immigrants of the late nineteenth century), and there were writers who tried to prove that the Norman French in Quebec and the English were not merely linked historically, but were also of the same Nordic race. But a strong undercurrent of racial rivalry appeared in the propaganda of Canada First, especially in the writings of Charles Mair and his associates at the time of the Red River Rebellion, when Mair made clear in a letter he wrote in 1870 to the *Toronto Telegraph*—though he talked of 'a young and vigorous race coming to the front . . . which is no longer English, Scotch or Irish, but thoroughly and distinctly Canadian'—that the French were to be kept apart, and the North West 'shall be British and not French and shall not be governed by the nominee of either priests or proletarians.'

Nationalism and imperialism alike were stimulated by the republic south of the border, which represented both a threat and an attraction. Foreigners visiting the two countries almost habitually pointed to the contrast between the rich and energetic American states and the poor and backward provinces of Canada. In one of the most eloquent passages of Lord Durham's *Report on the Affairs of British North America*, perhaps because it presented what he had seen with his own eyes rather than what he had been told by self-interested informants, he compared the impressions the two countries made on the traveller crossing the border.

> On the American side, all is activity and bustle. The forest has been widely cleared; every year numerous settlements are formed, and thousands of farms created out of the waste; the country is intersected by common roads; canals and railroads are finished, or in the course of formation; the ways of communication and transport are crowded with people, and enlivened by numerous carriages and large steam-boats . . . . Every village has its schoolhouse and place of public worship. Every town has many of both, with its township buildings, its book stores, and probably one or two banks and newspapers; and the cities, with their fine churches, their great hotels, their exchanges, courthouses and municipal halls, of stone or marble, so new and fresh as to mark the recent existence of the forest where they now stand, would be admired in any part of the Old World. On the British side of the line, with the exception of a few favoured spots, where some approach to American prosperity is apparent, all seems waste and desolate. There is but one railroad in all British America, and that, running between the St. Lawrence and Lake Champlain, is only fifteen miles long. The ancient city of Montreal, which is naturally the commercial capital of the Canadas, will not bear the least comparison, in any respect, with Buffalo, which is a creation of yesterday. But it is not in the difference between the larger towns on the two sides that we shall find the best evidence of our own inferiority. That painful but undeniable truth is most manifest in the country districts through which the line of national sep-

aration passes for 1,000 miles. There, on the side of both the Canadas, and also of New Brunswick and Nova Scotia, a widely scattered population, poor, and apparently unenterprising, though hardy and industrious, separated from each other by tracts of intervening forest, without towns and markets, almost without roads, living in mean houses, drawing little more than a rude subsistence from ill-cultivated land, and seemingly incapable of improving their condition, present the most instructive contrast to their enterprising and thriving neighbours on the American side.

More than twenty years later, the English novelist Anthony Trollope reached similarly melancholy conclusions and noted in his *North America* (1862):

I must confess that in going from the States into Canada, an Englishman is struck by the feeling that he is going from a richer country into one that is poorer, and from a greater country into one that is less.

And a quarter of a century farther on, twenty years after Confederation, Friedrich Engels, in a letter he wrote to Marx's New York disciple Victor Sorge on 10 September 1888, not only made the same comparisons, but also threw doubt on Canada's ability to resist the magnetic attraction of the vigorous country to the south.

It is a strange transition from the States to Canada. First one imagines that one is in Europe again, and then one thinks one is in a positively retrogressing and decaying country. Here one sees how necessary the feverish speculative spirit of the Americans is for the rapid development of a new country (presupposing capitalist production as a basis); and in ten years this sleepy Canada will be ripe for annexation—the farmers in Manitoba, etc., will demand it for themselves. Besides, the country is half-annexed already socially—hotels, newspapers, advertising, etc., all on the American pattern. And they may tug and resist as much as they like; the economic necessity of an infusion of Yankee blood will have its way and abolish this ridiculous boundary line, and when that time comes, John Bull will say 'Yes and Amen' to it.

Engels was right to the extent that throughout the nineteenth century the United States held a powerful attraction for Canadians. Culturally there is no doubt that at this period, while the old influences of Britain and France remained strong, the new cultural trends tended to be influenced by fashions and tendencies in the United States. Literally hundreds of thousands of people were sucked out of Canada by the material possibilities below the border. Many of the immigrants who reached Canada paused only briefly to survey the scene and almost immediately proceeded into the states to the south that were voracious for labour and still had land to offer. Canadians also were tempted and many voted with their feet; between 1850 and 1890 around three quarters of a million of them left for the United States. Whether they were English-speaking or French-speaking did not matter greatly; work opportunities and the dream of wealth attracted people from both groups, and hundreds of thousands of emigrants from Quebec and the Acadian areas of New Brunswick created the Franco-American population of New England.

Such inclinations were not restricted to the working class or the potential farmer. Paradoxically, the late-Victorian period, when a nationalism metamorphosing into imperialism became one of the strongest political urges in Canada, was also a time when the fascination of American cultural developments made it seem for the time being as though New York would become the artistic and literary capital of Canada. The ambivalence of those times was reflected in some of the era's most consciously Canadian individuals. Sara Jeannette Duncan, as imperialist in political sympathies as the protagonist of her best-known novel—which she actually entitled *The Imperialist*—nevertheless accepted Henry James and William Dean Howells as her literary masters because there were no Canadian masters at the time; she concluded in *The Week* (July 1887) that there was no alternative but for Canadian writers to look to America for their readers even if they found their inspiration at home:

> The market for Canadian literary wares of all sorts is self-evidently New York, where the intellectual life of the continent is rapidly centralizing. It is true that it will never become a great or profitable market until some original process of development is applied to the transplanted romance of our North-west, to the somewhat squat and uninteresting life of Ontario, to our treasure-trove, Quebec; but when this is done, we may be sure that it will be with an eye upon immediate American appreciation, and in the spirit and methods of American literary productions.

Whether or not she could find publishers in Canada, Duncan always liked her novels to appear in New York, though instead of going there to write she married an Englishman whom she had met in India and settled there, becoming a brilliant novelist of the Raj. Numerous Canadian writers in our period were successfully published in the United States, among them James De Mille, Marshall Saunders, Ralph Connor (Charles W. Gordon), May Agnes Fleming, Norman Duncan, Basil King, and Ernest Thompson Seton; the last four lived much of their life and died there. Bliss Carman lived the last two decades of his life in Connecticut and died there, though he was buried in Fredericton. John Richardson, whose move to New York in 1849 was tragically disappointing, though he published several novels there, even adapted *The Canadian Brothers* (so anti-American in its original form) to suit American tastes as *Maud Montgomerie* (New York, 1851).

Charles G.D. Roberts lived in New York from 1897 to 1907, adapting his writing to the requirements of American editors, without seeming to find that inconsistent with his fervent patriotism and his impatience with Canada's failure to stand on its own that emerges in the ranting chauvinism of his poem 'Canada' (1886):

> O Child of nations, giant-limbed,
>   Who stand'st among the nations now
> Unheeded, unadorned, unhymned,
>   With unanointed brow,—
>
> How long the ignoble sloth, how long
>   The trust in greatness not thine own?
> Surely the lion's breed is strong
>   To front the world alone! . . .

Time proved Engels wrong, though the century was not lacking in its American-related alarms and excursions. The fear inspired by 1812 remained strong. (As late as the early 1930s the leading war-plan of the Canadian General Staff was one providing for appropriate action in the event of another invasion from the south.) Occasionally groups of aggrieved citizens would demand annexation to the United States: in Montreal in 1849; in Victoria in 1870, just before British Columbia entered Confederation; in Newfoundland during the 'Join America' campaign of the 1890s. And Goldwin Smith, game to the end, declared in 1910, the last year of his life: 'The ultimate Union of this Northern Continent seems to me as certain as the rising of tomorrow's sun.'

He also was wrong. Canada survived, and the reasons are political, but social and cultural as well. Nationalism, which extended from the political expediency of Macdonald's National Policy to Denison's idealistic marriage of nation and empire, provided the ideological counterpart to such practical achievements as the completion of the Canadian Pacific Railway and the settling of the West. The very migrations to the United States tended to strengthen the sense of a Canadian identity distinct from an American one. Those who were less enterprising remained, but so also did the hardier; and the departure of those with frail loyalties meant that the men and women who stayed were most attached to traditional British or French values and therefore more likely to reject American republican ones. Those who stayed tended to make a virtue out of the necessity of their circumstances. Beyond the rhetoric of Tennyson's much-used phrase 'that True North', there grew up a whole mythos of the Canadians as being, in Robert Grant Haliburton's phrase, the 'Northmen of the New World', for whom 'the cold north wind that rocked the cradle of our race, still blows through our forests, and breathes the spirit of liberty into our hearts.' In 1884 an obscure pamphleteer declared, 'Northern nations always excel southern ones in energy and stamina, which accounts for their prevailing power,' and similar sentiments were expressed by almost all the Canada Firsters.

Captain Frederick Marryat, the popular Victorian boys' novelist, seems to have looked more closely than Trollope and Engels when he remarked in his 1839 *Diary in America:*

> You are at once struck with the difference between the English and the American population, system and ideas. On the other side of the lake, you have much more apparent prosperity, but much less real solidarity and security. The houses and stores of Toronto are not to be compared with those of the American towns opposite. But the Englishman has built according to his means—the American according to his expectations.

Canadians might read cheap American books, might dress like their neighbours, and, with modifications, might speak according to Webster rather than according to Samuel Johnson or—later—the *Oxford English Dictionary*; but they still preferred a restricted and orderly life to an expansive disorderly one, and in opening their hinterland they established the infrastructure of an ordered society before the settlers arrived, so that, except for the two Métis rebellions, there was never a Canadian Wild West.

In manners and methods Canadians were certainly influenced by the Americans; the Americans, after all, had been the first pioneers, and their experience counted. But imitation, or even emulation, and liking are two different things, and the resentments inherited from 1812 helped to shape Canadian attitudes for the rest of the century. Lord Minto, when he was Governor General, observed in 1899:

> There is a general dislike of the Yankee here and I do not wonder at it . . . . What the Canadian sees and hears is constant Yankee bluff and swagger & that eventually he means to possess Canada for himself. And he reads with wonder of the so-called reapprochement of the old country with a people with which he, the Canadian, has no sympathy and whom he thoroughly distrusts.

One of the last important outside observers of Canada during our period was the French writer André Siegfried, whose Protestantism enabled him to look rather objectively at Quebec and not unsympathetically at English Canada. In *The Race Question in Canada*, which appeared in 1907, Siegfried shrewdly separated the cultural from the political factors, and, while distinguishing the American from the Canadian, he also distinguished the Canadian from the British. He saw no threat to Canada from 'the American nation'. In this he was right, since by the early twentieth century few American politicians thought of annexation. They had experienced enough difficulty reassimilating their own Southern states. To bring in Canada, with its large French-speaking population, would have been an even more uncertain task. 'Rather,' Siegfried said, 'it is the American civilization that threatens to supplant the British.' And he continued with a great deal of prophetic insight:

It is safe now to predict that Canada will become less and less British and more and more American. The best we can wish for—a wish that may well be realized, is that she may become Canadian first and foremost.

In the generations that have followed, Canada has become, in cultural terms at least, 'Canadian first and foremost'. The imperial impulse within Canadian Toryism died away; the national impulse triumphed.

6

Pioneers! O, Pioneers!

The Roles of Women

As this book continues, the reader will observe that I perceive Canadian attitudes as being dominated by divisions brought about largely by the country's special history. I see it following patterns that involve conflict and reconciliation, but that always end with the survival in some adapted form of the original binary relationship: gentlemen and others, aborigines and white men, French and English, founding peoples and latecomers. It seems to be in the nature of our culture that we are held together as much by original differences as by acquired similarities. The aim of a homogenized Canada—speaking one language and maintaining a single culture—that emerged occasionally during the nineteenth century and has since been sporadically revived, seems as unattainable as it would be undesirable.

There is another division too fundamental to be merely Canadian: the division between the genders. Nineteenth-century popular writers like Ralph Connor and Gilbert Parker tried to establish the image of Canada as that of a male and muscular Christian society. But much earlier, that percipient and detached observer, Anna Jameson, saw the cruel reality in such a society of the woman's becoming either a drudge, like some of the Indians she had encountered, or a victim disguised as an idol.

> We may assume as a general principle, that the true importance and real dignity of woman is everywhere, in savage and civilized communities, regulated by her capacity of being useful; or, in other words, that her condition is decided by the share she takes in providing for her own subsistence and the well-being of society as a productive labourer. Where she is idle and useless by privilege of sex, a divinity and an idol, a victim and a toy, is not her position quite as lamentable, as false, as injurious to herself and all social progress, as where she is the drudge, slave and possession of man?

Much of the history of women in Canada is in fact embraced in the struggle to be productive but also free, neither a drudge nor a goddess.

The matter of women's role in the development of a Canadian culture during our period can be related to some recent speculations that have been made on the gender of the Canadian psyche. In her cultural history, *The Wacousta Syndrome*, Gaile McGregor notes the strange symptoms of effeminacy that John Richardson in his novel *Wacousta* attributed to the officers of the Detroit garrison, as opposed to Wacousta's 'exaggerated masculinity'. She remarks: 'Instead of Mother Nature versus a paternalistic military establishment, therefore, *Wacousta* seems to pit a feminine garrison against a masculine gothic landscape.' She draws from this and other literary evidence the conclusion that 'the Canadian symbolic ego . . . whatever the sex of its various literary personae' becomes 'feminine in temperament and function; emotional, passive and vulnerable.' As Otto Rank points out, women's psychology—like, it would appear, the representative Canadian's—"can be designated as insideness, in contradiction to man's centrifugal outsideness".'

Such conclusions may seem to contradict much in early Canadian history that suggests a paternalistic society with macho values. Yet as a collectivity Canada has always been vulnerable in its relations with imperial powers, forced often into the subordination that characterizes the feminine role in a paternalistic order; hence it developed its passivity and inwardness in relation to the outside world. Canada's great achievements, in which the 'masculine' virtues of daring and endurance shine forth, have always occurred within its own territory. Even the imperial urge that Canadians may at times have appeared to share with other Anglo-Saxon peoples has been internalized in its concrete expression; until 1905 the centre colonized the West while it was administered as a territory, and subsequently did so in the northern territories until they began to attain some degree of autonomy in the 1980s.

Thus McGregor's argument has its portion of truth. Even if it over-simplifies the complex phenomena of collective psychology, it provides a useful beginning for considering relations between men and women in Canada prior to the First World War. Basically, this means nineteenth-century Canada, and the nineteenth century, in the minds of Canadians even more than of the British, means the Victorian era, the matriarchal reign that spanned generations and saw the development of Canada from a precarious group of scantily populated colonies into something near a nation.

Anna Jameson heard the news of Victoria's accession while sailing through a dark dawn on Lake Huron in the early summer of 1837 and thought with 'compassionate awe' of this young girl ascending the throne. Sixty years later Wilfred Campbell composed an 'Ode', a classic piece of Canadian bad verse, to celebrate her Jubilee:

> Let the cannon thunder out, and the miles of voices shout—Victoria!
> Let the bells peal out afar, till the rocket tells the star,
> And the ocean shouts its paean to the thunder-answering bar;
> England's glory, Britain's pride,
> Revered of half a world beside,
> O good grey queen, Victoria!

And on 20 January 1901, a few weeks into the new century, young Lucy Maud Montgomery noted in her journal the end of an era.

> Today when the mail came I pounced on the *Daily Patriot*—published yesterday—and the first thing I saw, blazoned in great black letters across the page, was 'The Queen died today.'
> The news was expected for she had been very ill and little hope was held of her recovery. Still, it was a very decided shock. One felt as if the foundations of all existing things were crumbling and every trustworthy landmark swept away. Who ever thought that Queen Victoria *could* die? 'The queen' seemed a fact as enduring and unchangeable as the everlasting hills. The sense of loss seemed almost personal.

Victoria was Canada's one significant monarch. Mad George III and his undignified sons left little mark on the popular imagination. Though Edward VII aroused enthusiasm when he came to Canada as a beardless Prince of Wales in 1860, neither he nor any later ruler made such an impression on the Canadian consciousness as the great old queen who reigned longer than many people then lived. Ruling as an impeccably constitutional monarch, though not without her friends in office, she acquired the skills of influencing rather than directing, and the influence on manners and morals that emanated from Buckingham Palace and Windsor Castle during these years penetrated the farthest corners of the Empire and helped to shape its small remote societies. Under her ex-ample respect for family virtues—and hence respect for woman as the centre of the family—was enhanced, and cities like Toronto projected in their staid ways of life the sturdy Protestant respectability she represented. By practising her eminently middle-class virtues, she removed from the monarchy the associations of aristocratic irresponsibility and autocratic caprice that the Hanoverian princes had lodged in people's minds when she came to the throne in 1837. If the Reform movements, in Britain and Canada alike, escaped being taken over by radical republicans, that was in some part the result of the trust she slowly built up among her subjects.

Victoria took a close interest in Canada, and if she never visited it—or any other of the colonies or dominions, including India, from which she took the title of Empress—she sent her children: Edward, Prince of Wales, on a visit in 1861; Alice, wife of the Marquis of Lorne, who was Governor General from 1878 to 1883; and Arthur, Duke of Connaught, who was Governor General from 1911 to 1916. She picked the site of the capital. Cities were named after her—Victoria, Regina, and Victoriaville, Que.,—and Alberta and Prince Albert commemorated her unfortunate consort, whose marriage to her was celebrated by the people of the young city of Toronto on 2 April 1840 by the proclamation of a general holiday and the roasting of an ox in the market-place.

To this day the symbolic vestiges of that long and crucial reign linger among us. Victoria Day is still a public holiday in Canada, which it is not in Britain. All over the land, outside provincial parliament buildings and city halls, her statues stand, green with the verdigris of generations. They trace her life, from the slim and erect young woman who stares over the harbour of her own city, Victoria, to the ample matriarch, grandmother of the tribe, who formidably presides outside the legislature in Winnipeg.

Such enduring reverence for the great old Queen, the mother of her peoples, suggests the memory of a matriarchy. So, in feeling, Victorian Canada was, though in fact the men ruled in the Queen's name and the women had to struggle for their rights, as has happened under all the notable female rulers from Elizabeth I down to Indira Gandhi.

In every part of Canada women were scarce at the beginning of settlement, in comparison with the men who arrived to establish the fur trade, the fisheries, the logging operations, the bush farms. From the beginning, in the settled areas at least, rulers and philanthropists would send out batches of young women as potential wives. Les Filles du Roi were shipped out for this purpose to New France as early as the reign of Louis XIV, and they seem to have turned out well and to have had daughters who were a credit to their sex, for the eighteenth-century Intendant Gilles Hocquart remarked that the *habitant* women were intelligent and sharp-witted. 'The peasants never undertake any matter of importance without their advice and approval.'

The problem of shortage of women continued as settlement moved farther west. At the time of the Cariboo gold rush, Hudson's Bay Company official Alexander Grant Dallas wrote to the London *Times* on 1 January 1862:

> Permit me to draw attention to a crying evil—the want of women. I believe there is not one to every hundred men at the mines; without them the male population will never settle in this country and innumerable evils are the consequence. A large number of the weaker sex could obtain wages, with the certainty of marriage in the background.
>
> The miner is not very particular—'plain, fat and 50' even would not be objected to; while good-looking girls would be the nuggets and prized accordingly. An immigration of such character would be a great boon to the colony as I am sure it would be to many under-paid and over-worked women who drag out a weary existence in the dismal streets and alleys of the metropolis.

Partly, perhaps, as a result of Dallas's letter, Baroness Burdett-Coutts and the London Emigration Society set about recruiting young English women and in the same year of 1862 the 'Brideship' (the *Tynemouth*) was sent out with a load of eligible young women who were snapped up on the wharfside at Victoria by men hungry for marriage; few of these women reached the goldfields, where many of the miners had to be content for female company with the 'hurdy-gurdy girls'.

> Hurdy-Gurdy damsels [said the *Cariboo Sentinel* on 6 September 1866] are unsophisticated maidens of Dutch extraction, from 'poor but honest parents' and, morally speaking, they are really not what they are generally put down for. They are generally brought to America by some speculating, conscienceless scoundrel of a being commonly called a 'Boss Hurdy'. This man binds them in his service until he has received about a thousand per cent on his outlay. The girls receive a few lessons in the terpsichorean art, are put into a kind of uniform, generally consisting of a red waist, cotton print skirt, and a half-mourning headdress resembling somewhat in shape the top-knot of a male turkey . . . .
>
> The hurdy style of dancing differs from all other schools. If you ever saw a ring of bells in motion, you have seen the exact positions these young ladies are put through during the dance. The more muscular the dancer, the nearer the approximation of the lady's pedal extremities to the ceiling; and the gent who can 'hoist' his girl the highest is considered the best dancer. The poor girls as a general thing earn their money very hardly.

As settlement moved into British Columbia, the first of the farmers found a more regular solution by taking Indian women for companionship and Chinese men to do the domestic work. George Monro Grant, when he travelled with Sandford Fleming to Kamloops in 1872, found the ranchers of this area already prospering.

As there are very few women most of the settlers live with squaws—or Klootchmen as they are called on the Pacific; and little agricultural progress or advance of any kind can be expedited until immigration brings in women accustomed to dairy and regular farm-work, to be wives for the white men.

. . . It seems wonderful that these prosperous farmers should not have white wives; but the remoteness of the place must be remembered, and they say, too, that the Victoria girls are unwilling to give up the picnics and gaieties of the capital for farm life and hard work in the interior. Of course there are no servant girls at Kamloops. A young Chinaman, answering the common name of John, was cook and maid of all work at the fort.

The farmers of Kamloops were perpetuating an established British North American tradition. For among the first of the many generations of women who in Canada made their special contributions to the necessary tasks involved in creating a new home and a new society in the wilderness were the native peoples and Métisses whom the fur-traders would marry in accordance with the custom of the country (à la façon du pays). Very often chosen for their links with important native clans, they had a special role to play as intermediaries or interpreters. But even when this was not the case, their specialized skills in preparing the food, clothes, and equipment necessary for travel made them important members of the fur-trading community. Here, as in so many other ways, the fur-traders learned from the natives, whose life they so largely shared and whose attitude to women was so eloquently expressed to Samuel Hearne in 1770 by his Chippewyan guide, Matonabee, who himself had eight wives:

'Women,' added he, 'were made for labour; one of them can carry, or haul, as much as two men can do. They also pitch our tents, make and mend our clothing, keep us warm at night; and, in fact, there is no such thing as travelling any considerable distance, or for any length of time, in this country, without their assistance. 'Women,' said he again, 'though they do everything, are maintained at trifling expense; for as they always stand cook, the very licking of their fingers in scarce times, is sufficient for their subsistence.'

The image of the native woman as slave-like drudge did not apply to all the Indian communities of Canada; among the agrarian Iroquois, for example, women were more independent and had at least some say in the government of tribal affairs. But it was with the northern Indians, like the Chippewyans and the Woods Cree, that the fur-traders had the closest contact. Although in the early days the Hudson's Bay Company had rather moralistically tried to limit the relations between their employees and native women, by the period of which we are writing they had followed the example of the North West Company, which had continued the practice of the *coureurs de bois*: taking as common-law wives, *à la façon du pays*, either native women or, later, the women of the Métis, the mixed-blood community that by the late eighteenth century was growing in numbers and importance.

Native and Métis women came to be accepted as necessary for the proper carrying out of the fur trade. In 1802 the traders at York Factory stressed their importance in the operations of the trading posts:

> . . . they clean and put into a state of preservation all Beaver, and Otter skins brought in by the Indians undried and in bad condition. They prepare Line for Snow shoes and knit them also without which your Honors servants could not give efficient opposition to the Canadian traders, they make Leather shoes for the men who are obliged to travel about in search of Indians and furs and are useful in a variety of other instances.

By 1821, however, when the two rival companies had been united, and Governor Simpson was beginning his task of rationalizing their operations and cutting down on staff and dependents, the numbers of women were beginning to alarm the members of the Committee in London, who wrote to Simpson:

> We understand that there are an immense number of Women and Children supported at the different Trading Posts, some belonging to men still in the service and others who have been left by the Fathers unprotected and a burden on the Trade.

John West, who arrived as Anglican chaplain at Red River in 1820, was deeply shocked at the attitude of some of the fur traders to the women they had taken according to the fashion of the country.

> They do not admit them as their companions, nor do they allow them to eat at their tables but degrade them *merely* as slaves to their arbitrary inclination.

And Nicholas Garry—a travelling member of the Company's London Committee after whom Fort Garry was named—added his own comment on the men involved in these irregular unions.

> Perhaps nothing shows Debasement of Mind so much as their having lived themselves in an unmarried state, giving up their Daughters to live the same life as their Mothers, and this Feeling, or rather its Justification, had been general all over the Country.

One of the worst offenders in this respect was Governor Simpson himself, discarding more than one mixed-blood companion with her children before he finally married a Scottish girl in 1827, and referring to these women with whom he had lived—with a repellent combination of male chauvinism and colour prejudice—as 'the commodity', the 'bit of Brown' and, collectively, 'the Browns'.

Not every Hudson's Bay man proved quite such a consummate cad as Simpson in his behaviour towards native women. In fact Garry was able to record with satisfaction that the Reverend West had persuaded no less than 65 former Company officers settled on Red River to legitimize their marriages; and quite a number of gentlemen and even *engagés* were so happy in their relationships that they often expressed the wish to take their mixed-blood families back to Scotland or England with them. In 1822 Simpson reported that in a couple of cases 'I was induced to comply being aware that they had the means of providing for them so as to prevent their becoming a burden on the Company, and some labourers are in like manner permitted to take their children home.'

In a passage that has since become famous, James Douglas wrote to one of his friends in 1842:

> There is indeed no living with comfort in this country unless a person has forgot the great world . . . . To any other being . . . the vapid monotony of an inland trading post, would be perfectly insufferable, while habit makes it familiar to us, softened as it is by the many tender ties, which find a way to the heart.

The tender ties were those that bound Douglas to his wife Amelia, the daughter of Chief Conolly and his Cree common-law-wife Susanne. Douglas and his Amelia stayed together until his death, and to all appearances happily; eventually she ascended with him into the honorary aristocracy of the time, when he became Sir James and she became Lady Douglas. Another marriage marked by exemplary devotion was that of Daniel Harmon, who married a Métis girl in 1805, and became so devoted to her that he ignored the advice of his fellow fur-traders when he left New Caledonia in 1819 and took her back to his native Vermont, where they lived happily for the last 26 years of his long life. His mixed-blood children were so well accepted and educated that eventually one of his daughters was able to run a fashionable school for girls in Ottawa.

Douglas and Harmon may have been able to maintain their relationships at least in part because they lived out their fur-trading lives away from the centres of civilization. By the 1830s the little society of Red River was changing through the arrival of European women with social pretensions. There had been white women there since Lord Selkirk's settlers arrived in 1812, but they belonged to the Scottish farming community, which maintained a fairly close cohesion and kept to itself. It was when men like Simpson and Chief Factor John George McTavish went home to Scotland and returned with Scottish brides in 1829 that imported social pretensions began to invade the colony, just as they invaded India when the memsahibs began to arrive and destroyed the old easy relationship between the racial groups. New standards of behaviour were introduced. The veteran fur-trader Colin Robertson was openly snubbed when he attempted to introduce his Métis wife to Mrs Simpson. 'I told him distinctly'—said Simpson—'that the thing was impossible which mortified him exceedingly.' As James McMillan remarked wryly, 'Mrs Simpson's presence here makes a change in us.'

Ironically, one of those who bowed to the wind of change was Douglas's father-in-law William Conolly who, after many protestations of devotion, in 1832 got rid of Susanne, the mother of his six children, and went off to Montreal, where he married his rich cousin Julia Woolrich, who had the broad-minded decency to support Susanne after Conolly's death.

The effects of this changing social order were felt not only by the native women but also by the white women who supplanted them, for many could endure neither the rigours of western life nor the isolation their false social position imposed on them. Simpson protected his wife Frances from all contact with the local women, and then complained: 'She has no Society, no Friend, No Relative here but myself . . . .' She left Red River in 1833 and never returned.

With settlement the family took the place of the irregular and often ill-matched unions of the fur trade. There was little distinction of race between men and women, since immigrant groups tended to be endogamous and at least in the first years of settlement hard times and hard work forced on both man and woman a certain rough-and-ready equality. The exigencies of early pioneering forced the settler's wife into the same role of active producer as an Indian woman's, and often on a level hardly less primitive. But necessity made the woman who survived this hard life resourceful, and resourcefulness often made her shrewd and independent of mind. Writing in 1861 of the farms in Upper Canada, James Croil remarked:

> Whatever qualifications the farmer should have, mental or physical, all are agreed upon this point, that *a good wife* is indispensable. What is the aim of the husband to accumulate, it becomes the province of the wife to manage, and wherever we hear of a managing wife, we are sure to find a money-making farmer.

Beginning with the *habitants* of Quebec, continuing with the settlers who after 1814 began to transform the dense backwoods of Upper Canada into rich farmlands, and ending with the people of many races who broke the great grasslands of the Prairies from the 1880s onwards, pioneer life was a struggle first for subsistence, which was gained only by the cultivation of a kind of self-sufficiency that townspeople in Europe and even in North America had long forgotten.

John Howison, who visited Upper Canada shortly after the end of the War of 1812, described the kind of habitation in which the pioneer wife might expect to live and work and bear and rear her children.

The usual dimensions of a house are eighteen feet by sixteen. The roof is covered with bark or shingles, and the floor with rough hewn planks, the interstices between the logs that compose the wall being filled up with pieces of wood or clay. Stones are used for the back of the fire place and a hollow cone of coarse basket work does the office of a chimney.

And Catharine Parr Traill, in *The Canadian Settler's Guide*, tells us with what resourceful simplicity that house might be furnished:

The shanty, or small log-house of the poorer emigrant, is often entirely furnished by his own hands. A rude bedstead, formed of cedar poles, a coarse linen bag filled with hay or dried moss, and bolster of the same is the bed he lies on; his seats are benches, nailed together; a table of deal boards, a few stools, a few shelves for the crockery and tinware; these are often all that the poor emigrant can call his own in the way of furniture. Little enough and rude enough. Yet let not the heart of the wife despond. It is only the first trial; better things are in store for her.

How the women coped in such circumstances is suggested by a passage in the diary of Anne Langton, written during 1838 at Sturgeon Lake in Upper Canada where she had gone to keep house on her brother's farm.

We certainly have been a rather bustling family this summer, and when I look back I sometimes wonder how we managed for those months when we had no fire in the house, and every culinary operation, from baking bread to heating water, was performed on a dilapidated cooking stove, while eight or nine meals were regularly served each day and ten or twelve mouths fed with bread. This stove stands about ten yards from the back door, under a little shed. It measures 2 feet 7 inches each way. The chimney pipe rises at the top, an oval kettle fits into one side, a deep pan, with a steamer above it the other side, and a large boiler on a bake-pan at the bottom, each hole having an iron lid, when the vessels are not in, in which you may then place smaller saucepans, or heat irons, etc. The front of the stove, has an upper and lower door and a little hearth—formerly there was something of an oven within, but it was out of repair before I was acquainted with it, now there is only an iron plate, which enables you to have your fire on the upper or lower story. Here was many a nice dinner cooked with all proper varieties for a party of five or six (sometimes more) besides the eternal almost daily bread-baking, and everlasting frying for breakfasts and suppers.

The diaries of pioneer women often record an abundance of food to produce such meals. For example, on 27 November 1828 Mary O' Brien (as she later became) notes of her brother's wife Mary Gapper that she is

having a hundredweight of sausages made to furnish our winter breakfast, and Bill and Anthony are building a smoke house for drying the bacon and hams on three pigs for the coming year. The wall for the ice house is finished.

And a little later, towards the end of the same winter, she remarks:

> . . . we are still eating fresh beef from the ox which was killed at Christmas and we shall probably have it for a month or two longer. It is kept in the ice house and brought indoors to be thawed before we want it.

But the Langton and Gapper and O'Brien men were gentleman settlers who had come with enough means to establish good farms and tide themselves over hard times. When poor crops and hard times did come in the 1830s even people of their class complained about prices—like Ann Macauley, writing in 1837 to her son John, who at this time was surveyor-general of Upper Canada:

> I am afraid provisions will be dear this winter. Within 2 weeks flour has risen from 5 to 9 and ten dollars. I bought 2 Barrels to day for 19 dollars and it is expected to rise still more.

In the summer of the same year the diary of an English emigrant farming family, the Woods, noted in two consecutive days the way the tight economic situation of the year of rebellion affected settlers who were not among the poorest class.

> *Wednesday August 16*
> Mr Pugsley went up to Dover to procure us some flour if possible which he returned with this evening   17 lbs very dear at the rate of £12 4s per barrel   hard hard times however we are glad of it at any rate   having tasted little besides potatoes a long time . . . .

> *Thursday August 17*
> . . . Thank God we have bread once more and good it is to a hungry soul filled with nothing more for the last ten days but potatoes and cucumbers with a little milk as a treat.

A pioneer woman in Lower Canada, and later in Upper Canada and finally on the Prairies, had to return to something very like the versatile self-sufficiency of a peasant housewife in medieval Europe. She bore children and nursed and often educated them. She cooked and kept house. She looked after the chickens and often the kitchen garden as well; she preserved food in a number of ways and concocted simple home remedies; she helped with the harvest and fed the neighbours when they gathered in barn-raising bees. But she also operated as a primitive manufacturer, making from substances grown on her own farm or gathered in her neighbourhood all kinds of products that her urban sisters bought from shops. She made candles from tallow into which strings were dipped, and she made soap by an elaborate process that seems almost alchemical in the description Nellie McClung gave of it in her autobiography, *Clearing in the West.*

The leach was a small barrel of ashes, set up on a trestle, high enough to cover a black iron pot. The barrel had small augur holes bored in the bottom, and the innumerable pails of water poured on the ashes would at last run through in reluctant black drops, and then the leach was said to be running.

The lye thus extracted was used for making soap, and the day the soap was made was a day of high adventure. The operation took place outside in a big black kettle that was never used for anything else. No ordinary day would do; it had to be a clear bright day with no wind, and the moon had to be on the increase or the soap might not set. Over a blazing fire, made in a hole lined with stones, the grease and lye were fused in the old black pot and stirred all the time, from left to right, with a hickory stick . . . .

. . . My mother, in a sprigged blue print dress, tucked tightly between her knees and her head rolled in a red handkerchief stood on the windward side, stirring with a quick motion. Wooden boxes stood ready to receive the soap when it was done. No one must speak to her or interrupt in any way when the boiling was going on, for there was a moment when the pot must be removed, and if that moment were correctly guessed the soap would harden.

Clothes, and the cloth to make them, were also produced on the pioneer farm. Nellie McClung recorded how unhappy she was as a child to be sent to a prairie school in homespun rather than store-bought clothes.

Catharine Parr Traill talked of the 'great spinning-wheels' used in the Canadas, at which the spinster 'walks to and fro, guiding the yarn with one hand while with the other she turns the wheel,' and Joseph Howe described a 'Carding Machine' that some entrepreneur had set up in Nova Scotia 'to which you may see all the old and young women of the neighbourhood going backwards and forwards, with their waggons loaded to overflowing with immense sacks of wool, and their lovely persons mounted on the topmost pinnacle of the fleecy pyramids.'

Howe was given to the hyperbole that comes naturally to politicians, but Andrew Macphail, in his lucid gem of a book on the early life of Scottish settlers on Prince Edward Island, *The Master's Wife*, described in sober detail how the women on farms produced their textiles from the wool of the farm and the dyes of the woodlands. The whole passage is a tribute to his mother's resourcefulness and to her knowledge of the traditional methods of a pre-mechanical society.

Before the sheep was shorn the lamb must be reared. The wool was to be washed at the stream in water warmed in an iron pot over an open fire; dried in the sun, picked free of chaff, burrs and seeds; carded, spun and woven into cloth light enough for a woman's dress, heavy enough for blankets or great-coat for a man. The cloth itself after it left the loom must be scoured, thickened, combed, and dressed under hot irons.

Nor was this all. The white wool and the black wool made white or black cloth; white warp and black woof made various patterns; blended white and black became grey. Warp died in indigo could be bought, but all other colours were made in the house. The dyes were found in the woods—oak and hemlock-bark for browns, various species of lichens known as *crotals* or *crottles* for other shades. Combined with copperas these materials produced colours from green to inky black.

In addition to hard work that demanded a great deal of stamina and ingenuity, the pioneer women and their families were subjected to sicknesses that they often had to endure and cure without medical assistance. Notable among them was 'ague', a malarial fever whose appearance was attributed to such causes as the effluvia from rotting vegetables in ill-kept cellars; nobody thought to blame the mosquitoes from whose bites in summertime everyone complained. Catharine Parr Traill declares:

Few persons escape the second year without being afflicted with this weakening complaint; the mode of treatment is repeated doses of calomel, with castor-oil or salts, and is followed up by quinine. Those persons who do not choose to employ medical advice on the subject, dose themselves with ginger-tea, strong infusion of hyson, or any other powerful green tea, pepper, and whiskey, with many other remedies that have the sanction of custom or quackery.

Anna Jameson, observing mainly women of her own class who were trying to keep up English appearances in the Canadian backwoods, wrote:

I have not often in my life met with contented and cheerful-minded women, but I have never met with so many repining and discontented ones as in Canada. I never met with *one* woman recently settled here who considered herself happy in her new home and country; I *heard* of one, and doubtless there are others, but they are exceptions to the general rule.

But most writers on immigrant experiences said that on the whole working people found pioneer life an improvement on what they had left in Britain, especially after the first very hard years of land-clearing and house-buildings. Even Catharine Parr Traill, who made her own special terms with the Canadian environment through her interest in its fauna and flora, could remark after a quarter of a century in Canada, in *The Female Emigrant's Guide, and Hints on Canadian Housekeeping* (1854), that 'the hardships and difficulties of the settler's life . . . are felt peculiarly by the female part of the family.' Yet the enduring of these difficulties was not always a matter for complete regret. Hard work had its compensations. The material ones are stated and the immaterial ones implied in a passage in *Roughing It in the Bush* in which Susanna Moodie tells of sugaring off:

I was heartily sick of the sugar-making long before the season was over; however, we were well paid for our trouble. Besides one hundred and twelve pounds of fine soft sugar, as good as Muscovado, we had six gallons of molasses, and a keg containing six gallons of excellent vinegar. There was no lack, this year, of nice preserves and pickled cucumbers, dainties found in every native Canadian establishment.

Even when the pioneer age had ended on the Prairies, and farms were no longer self-contained subsistence economies, the life of the farmer's wife continued to be a hard and strenuous one. In 1910 Mrs George (Marion Dudley) Cran wrote, in *A Woman in Canada*, her own recollections of the farm wife's day at the end of our period.

In seeding time she will be up at 4 a.m. to get the men their breakfast. Then she will have to milk, and separate the cream afterwards, if they have a separator. If there are several cows it is quite a back-breaking task. Then there will be the house to clean, the breakfast things to wash up, the beds to make, and she must not waste time over that part of the day for there is dinner to cook for hungry men by 11.30. After washing up again the afternoon will mean breadmaking, or clothes washing and ironing, or jam-making, or butter-churning—one of the endless things like that anyway, and at 7.30 or 6.30 (according to the season of the year) she must have 'tea' ready. Tea is nearly as big as dinner and the last meal of the day. After that she must wash up, then milk two cows and separate her milk before she can think of going to bed. Probably there will be some darning or mending to do even then. That is a straightforward day, but it is greatly complicated when the children begin to come.

Getting help in their multiple tasks was one of the constant problems of farming women. From the officers' wives of Upper Canada in the 1830s down to prairie women in the 1890s the complaint of the scarcity echoes through letters and journals and recollections. Servants were difficult; they were undisciplined; they went off to get married or they were just unobtainable. Nellie McClung recalled:

It was hard to get help in the house for the farmer's daughters all had plenty of work at home and there were no unemployment Bureaus for women in the cities and very few women had come from the Old Country. There were the Crofters from Scotland who lived in a settlement in the Tiger Hills, but they had their own small farms and seemed to have work enough for all their women to do. I remember one woman who lived in Wawanesa at this time lament the fact that everyone in the country was so well off that no one needed to work for anyone else.

By custom farm women gained a little financial independence because eggs and cream and garden products were often their 'perquisites', which they could sell and keep the proceeds for their own use. Often the lack of help prevented them from earning as much as they would like, and even what they had produced they often found difficult to market profitably. As Elizabeth Mitchell observed in her book, *In Western Canada Before the War* (1915),

> The farmer's wife might drive in ten miles or more, in time she could ill afford, and go to the first store to offer her goods, butter, eggs, cream, vegetables, all very perishable in hot weather. A low price would be offered, which she would refuse, but before the second store was reached the second store-keeper would be warned by the first, by telephone, not to go above his price.

Yet rural life in Canada during the Victorian age was not without its relaxations. Many kept Sunday as a day of rest, and once the isolation of early pioneer farming had ended and small communities had begun to coalesce, church and Sunday School became gathering places, of which we shall have more to say in another context. Nor were secular amusements lacking. As Nellie McClung remarked, remembering her young womanhood in a small prairie community of the 1880s, '. . . we had no telephones, picture-shows, radios, phonographs, daily papers or lending libraries. We made our own fun—and we had plenty—the sort of fun you can remember for forty years and find it still warms your heart.' There were socials and amateur theatricals and musical evenings where each person showed his or her particular way of entertaining friends and neighbours. And in summer there were picnics, sometimes vast political affairs at which statesmen would orate and bands would play under resplendent banners, and sometimes gatherings of neighbours in which the local women would compete in making good food from limited materials.

> Down by the river the tables were set, and benches from the boarding-house brought down for seats. There were raisin-buns and cinnamon buns, curled like snail shells, doughnuts, cookies (ginger and molasses), and railroad cake; lettuce cut up in sour cream, mustard and sugar, cold sliced ham, home cured, and mother had made half a dozen vinegar pies, using her own recipe. The filling of a pie is rather a delicate matter if you have no fresh fruit, or eggs, but she made her filling of molasses and butter, thickened with bread crumbs, and sharpened and flavored with vinegar and cinnamon.

And though many households were ruled with a puritan strictness, particularly among the Methodists and Baptists, life was not always so staid as the repute of the Victorian age might lead one to suppose. It was not only the upper class who danced the night through at those 'nasty Quebec balls', at one of which Frances Monck recorded, 'the runaway wife of Mr. Herbert of the Guards danced the fast dances with a rose in her mouth, and then leaped a kind of *hurdle race* over the seats, with an officer.' Country dances could also welcome the dawn, like the one described by Lucy Maud Montgomery that took place after an out-door wedding at Cavendish on Prince Edward Island in 1900.

> After supper the minister considerately went home and the rest of us betook ourselves to dancing. They had a splendid big dancing pavilion built in the garden and roofed over with maple boughs. It made an ideal ballroom, for the night was dewless and the air kept so cool and pure all the time. We had three fiddlers; there were lots of boys from town who were dandy dancers, so we had a pretty good time. We danced the night out and the sun was just rising when we finished the last lancers.
>
> Then we had breakfast and a rather fagged-looking lot we were in the merciless daylight. But afterwards I took a picture of all the survivors and then I drove the bridal pair to the station.

Out of discontent, which sometimes amounted to despair, the women of the period often developed an amazing self-reliance. It has been pointed out that in Susanna Moodie's writings—her personal letters as well as her books—the men are always either weak or wicked, to be sustained or to be avoided. Susanna actually records an old peasant woman who said to Dunbar Moodie: 'I have seen a good deal in my time; but I never saw a gentleman from the old country make a good Canadian farmer. The work is rough and hard, and they get out of humour with it, and leave it to their hired helps, and then all goes wrong. They are cheated on all sides, and in despair take to the whisky bottle, and that fixes them . . . . I tell you what it is, mister—I give you just three years to spend your money and ruin yourself; and then you will become a confirmed drunkard, like the rest.' Susanna wryly comments: 'The first part of the prophecy came true. Thank God! the last has never been fulfilled, and never can be.' Her husband may have been inept, but he did not succumb to cheap Canadian whisky!

This was part of Susanna Moodie's experience, and being forced to take control of difficult situations not only doubtless strengthened her as a person, but also turned her from a writer of inferior sentimental fiction into the creator of a successful kind of reportage in which observation and experience were ordered by a shaping imagination. In other words, though she had quite strong political convictions and may have wielded some political influence behind the scenes, it was largely by changing her pattern of work that she began, like many other Canadian women, to emerge from the traditionally subordinate role of the female half of the population. She did so by her writing, other women by creating farms and a social life in the wilderness.

For unmarried women—both immigrants and those who grew up on the farm—working for wages provided liberation, or at least independence of a sort. Most of the jobs open to them, however, were menial, and all of them were poorly paid. Heading the list of unskilled job opportunities was domestic service (up to $7 a month), apprenticeships in dressmaking and millinery (unpaid for the first six months, when up to $2 a week might be given), factory work (a wide range of salaries, depending on the factory, below $10 a week); waitresses earned $2 and $3 a week plus meals (except on Sunday) and saleswomen about $5 a week. Domestic service, with its long hours and confinement in the employer's home, was rightly regarded as too restrictive, and towards the end of the century young women increasingly shunned it when they left home to find work. An editorial in *The Farmer's Advocate* (1900) explained the problem:

> From one side comes the cry of the worried and harassed housekeeper: 'Where, and oh! where are our household helpers gone?' And from the other side comes the reply: 'To the factories and to the stores, where, if our positions are not always of certain tenure, and our salaries leave something to be desired by way of margin, after our board bills are paid, yet, oh! glorious privilege, we are, after business hours, our own mistresses, and we can go to the theatres and band concerts, to big balls and little 'hops', with Jack to-day and Tom to-morrow, and who shall say us 'nay'?'

In Montreal and Toronto the employment of women was already widespread at the end of our period, but in general the number of wage-earning women was not great. It amounted to less than 14 per cent of the labour force in 1901, as against about 30 per cent in Britain at the same time and 41 per cent in Canada in 1981. This was partly because employers were reluctant to employ unmarried women as temporary labour outside certain restricted occupations, like the clothing industry and retail trade. Moralists feared they might be lured away from their roles as wives and mothers; workmen feared that, like the Chinese, they would be used as cheap labour and depress the general wage level.

It was not an entirely unjustified fear. Women's earnings as late as 1911 were 52.8 per cent of the men's; the Ontario Board of Industries produced figures in 1889 showing that women over eighteen, working an average of 259 days a year, earned an average of $216 annually, or $18 a month, for a 54-hour week, which meant just over 10 cents an hour. Many earned such sums by hard piece work, like that described by Minnie Phelps in an article on 'Women as Wage-Earners', published in 1889.

> Let me give a few instances of the wages paid to women in the great industry of underwear for women. We hear now-a-days of the cheapness of these garments. 'So much cheaper,' you say, 'than you could make them yourselves.' You wonder at it. Here are the reasons, and the only reasons. For the underclothing that some of you are wearing at this very hour, some poor, needy sister has been paid the sum of 48 cents per dozen, or 4 cents a piece, for the manufacture of the same. She has been paid 40 cents a dozen for coarse drawers; night-dresses, tucked and trimmed,

$1.30 a dozen, while for the white skirts, tucked ruffles, she gets $1.00 per dozen. This is not all. These women work nine and one-half hours per day, if late five minutes are fined five cents. These facts are from the City of Toronto,—'the city of churches', and while you are reading these things, the rush of the shuttle and the hurrying needle is being plied while some of us wear these garments which mean life and virtue to some poor girl.

In the same year the anonymous author of a publication called *Montreal by Gaslight* recorded this impression of one of the local cigar factories, which were even worse than the garment sweatshops.

Here in stifling air foul with odors of tobacco, machine oil, perspiration, and a thousand other evil-smelling substances, are seated the slaves of the leaf. Young and old, women and men, boys and girls, from seven o'clock in the morning until six o'clock at night, with one short hour for dinner, they toil for three dollars a week and sometimes two. There are no toilet appliances, no fire escapes, no facilities for ventilation: there is nothing but work and a brutal foreman to enforce it.

For women employed in such industries work offered no liberation. It presented merely another way of wearing themselves out without the satisfaction of working for the good of their families, and without the standing in the household and the community that the pioneer wife often achieved. Less menial positions as stenographers, bookkeepers, cashiers, library assistants, and non-professional nurses were also available to women, but they paid little more than unskilled jobs. The situation of women who fought their way into the professions was somewhat different, largely because most of them began with social and economic advantages: they started off in the middle class.

The first professions that Canadian women entered with notable success were writing and teaching. We have already encountered some of the women writers who made names for themselves during the period, and we shall meet many more—as novelists, as poets, as social commentators. Writing was perhaps the easiest of all the professions to enter. It had no professional guilds, no qualifying examinations, no structures that men might capture and defend; it was not even unladylike to write. Journalism was another matter, and though a number of women did break into this male enclave very successfully, some idea of their difficulties is offered by the fact that Sara Jeannette Duncan had to assume a male guise under the nom-de-plume of 'Garth Grafton' when she began to write in the 1880s for the Toronto *Globe* and the *Washington Post* and to act for the Montreal *Star* as the first women parliamentary correspondent in Ottawa.

Duncan, like many other Canadian women writers, such as Lucy Maud Montgomery and Nellie McClung, started her journey towards independence by way of the Normal School and teaching. Until the

1840s such public education as existed in Canada had been carried out mainly by men, and women were relegated to teaching small children in 'dame-schools' and young ladies in academies devoted to the graces of living. The universalization of education, beginning with Egerton Ryerson's reforms in Canada West from 1843 onwards, entirely changed the pattern. Ryerson found a great deficiency of potential male teachers, so he established a Normal School and opened it to women. Soon elementary education was almost entirely in the hands of women teachers, and educational administrators were declaring, as the British Columbia School Superintendent did in 1872, that women 'possessed greater aptitude for communicating knowledge' and that they had proved themselves 'usually better disciplinarians, especially among younger children, than males.'

This did not mean that women gained equality in their professions. They were employed in great numbers largely because school boards in the country found they could pay them less than men. They usually worked, except in one-room schools, under male principals; a woman rarely ascended to a supervisory position. And when they married, even if they did not leave of their own accord, they were usually dismissed to make way for single women, younger and less well paid. Almost everywhere in Canada women teachers were paid less than men in comparable posts, and Minnie Phelps, who wrote of the plight of women in the garment trade, also revealed that in Ontario in 1890 the average salary for male teachers in the city was $776 and in the country $427, while that for women was $358 in the city and $287 in the country. Three years later another writer, Miss E. Binmore, told of the plight of the even worse-paid teachers in Montreal.

> The women teachers of this city presented a petition that the scale of their salaries be increased, and especially that $245 ($250 less superannuation) is too little for anyone to live upon for twelve months. Let me prove this statement. Board in this city is $3.50 to $4.50 per week, *i.e.* $182 to $234 per annum, according to the locality of the school. For, when a teacher cannot afford to drive, she must live near the school. That is, the unfortunate teacher has $11 to $63 from which to pay annually for clothing, doctor's bills, books, church contributions, and finally, though by no means least, take advantage of the educational advantages the city holds out to her so temptingly. Perhaps you believe I exaggerate or make an error in mathematical calculation, because so many do come forward to receive this exceedingly small sum. On enquiry, you will find these live with their parents and are exempted from board, or pay a more nominal account, or else kind friends [are] compassionate with them and receive them into their homes during the summer months.

Yet for all these discriminations, teaching was a profession that gave women a role in society outside the home, and their entry into it was a stage on the long climb towards equality. So was the recognition, in Ryerson's programs of universality and similar programs in other provinces, that education itself was a right of both sexes, and also the breakdown of sexual distinctions implied by the early acceptance of co-education. But there was still far to go, for discrimination among staff and student alike continued in the school far into the twentieth century. And this was one of the reasons why the teaching profession became a breeding ground for suffragettes, and why one can so often trace a clear course from the Normal School and the classroom into the professions and into the task of awakening the female political consciousness.

An example is that of Emily Howard Stowe, the first Canadian woman to qualify as a doctor. Stowe started as a teacher, attending Ryerson's Normal School in the early 1850s. While working as a teacher she became convinced that it was demeaning for a women to have no alternative but to consult a man in sickness and in childbirth, and that the male monopoly of the medical profession was unjust and impractical. Since no medical training for women existed in Canada at this time, Stowe went to the United States and in 1867 graduated from the New York College of Medicine. Operating on the margin of the law because she was not given a licence until 1880, she started to practise immediately upon receiving her degree. To obtain her licence she, with two other women who aspired to the profession, had to attend a session in 1879 at the School of Medicine in Toronto. More than thirty years later, in a lecture at the Osler Club of Queen's University, at a time when women doctors were becoming accepted, Elizabeth Short recollected her conversations with Dr Stowe and other women involved in that exercise:

> From the lips of one of these ladies I heard the most staggering accounts of their experiences. Little incidents, such as having to observe their seats from a convenient loophole before entering the classroom, lest, as occurred on more than one occasion, they had to be cleared and cleaned before being occupied. Other playful activities of some members of the school were in the way of obnoxious sketches on the wall. There were so many artists or at least sketches, that the walls of a classroom had to be whitewashed four times during that session. But more trying and more frequent were the needless objectionable stories told by 'enemy' lecturers to the class to instigate its worst element to make noisy and vulgar demonstrations. It was so unbearable on one occasion that one of the ladies went to the lecturer afterwards and asked him to desist from that sort of persecution or she would go to his wife and tell exactly what he said. His lectures were more bearable after that.

Some of the confusion that existed in the male mind over the entry of women into the medical profession was shown in the well-meaning remarks of Principal Grant when in the same year of 1879 he announced classes for women in the Medical Faculty at Queen's. The professors had agreed to this, he declared, even though it meant double work for them, 'for it is generally recognized that co-education is out of the question in medical and surgical studies.' It was this view that made the foundation of Women's Medical Colleges at both Toronto and Kingston in 1883 an incomplete victory for women. They were allowed into the medical profession, but segregated within it.

Until the 1890s the acceptance of women in the legal profession was similarly resisted, as four stanzas from 'The Law and the Lady' (*Grip*, September 1892; probably written by a woman, 'Ananias Limberjaw, QC') makes clear:

> I think all lawyers must agree
> On keeping our profession free
> From females whose admission would
> Result in anything but good
>
> . . .
>
> Soon the invading female ranks
> Will fill the warehouses and banks;
> The pulpit next, no doubt will fall
> And men be driven to the wall.
>
> Oh, say, my brethren! shall not then
> One refuge be reserved for men,
> One male monopoly where we
> Can claim our old supremacy,
>
> One relic of that good old day
> When man held undisputed sway,
> And women knew no more than crave
> To be some husband's toy or slave?

Many of the women involved in the professional struggles of the time were also engaged in the wider struggle for female emancipation and especially for women's suffrage. Here again Emily Stowe was an example, for in 1876, in the midst of striving for recognition as a doctor, she founded the Toronto Women's Literary Club, which was the first organization in Canada to devote itself to the cause of votes for women, and in 1889 she was the real activator of the Dominion Women's Enfranchisement Association, of which she became the first president.

The last decades of the nineteenth century were a period when women's organizations proliferated, but this is not the place to convey their rather complex history. Each, in its own way, showed the growing determination of women to take greater control of their own lives, but by no means all of them were politically radical. The Women's Institute movement long retained the conservative slant imparted by Adelaide Hoodless, who founded the first Institute at Stoney Creek, Ontario, in

1897, directed the movement towards a concern for the education of women and their training for domestic life, and, believing that the place for women was in the home, never supported the suffragist cause. The National Council of Women, presided over in the beginning by Lady Isabel Aberdeen, wife of the Governor General, also avoided taking a political position, and in the Preamble to its first Constitution in 1893 declared the preservation of family and state its major objectives:

> We, Women of Canada, sincerely believing that the best good of our homes and nation will be advanced by our own greater unity of thought, sympathy and purpose, and that an organized movement of women will best conserve the greatest good of the Family and the State, do hereby band ourselves together to further the application of the Golden Rule to society, custom and law.

It was, curiously, from a revived puritanism evoked by the temperance movement that the most radical support for women's suffrage emerged. The movement started in the Prohibition Woman's League of Owen Sound, Ontario, in 1874, metamorphosed into the Women's Christian Temperance Union, and by 1880 had spread over the country. Its support came from younger women and also from older women in the Protestant churches who were haunted by memories of the bad old days (good old days for drinkers), when whisky was twenty-five cents a gallon, made in the local distilleries that sprang up in every small town, and brought by the bucket-load to community occasions like barn-raisings and other bees. Women and children, it was argued, were as much the victims of alcoholism as the drinkers themselves, through the unemployment, sickness, and consequent poverty that followed from it. The temperance militants believed that the difficulty in introducing effective legislation against drinking was due to male domination of the political process. For this reason the temperance movement began to agitate for women's suffrage from the 1890s onwards, and many of the most ardent advocates of the enfranchisement of women were former temperance militants, of whom Nellie McClung was perhaps the best known and the most effective.

Canadians were too divided and too sensible for prohibition to have any widespread and lasting success, even though an attempt would be made to impose it temporarily during the First World War. Until that time temperance advocates had to be content with local successes in two of the most puritanical provinces, Nova Scotia and Prince Edward Island. The movement for women's rights, on the other hand, showed a cumulative success. In 1882 the right of married women to own their own property was granted, before it was gained by women in Great Britain. Women who owned property had been able to vote in Lower and Upper Canada until the Act of Union in 1840, and this right was returned for municipal elections in Ontario in 1872 and during the 1880s in most other provinces. Women also became eligible to vote for school trustees, and from the early 1890s motions in favour of women's suffrage began to appear on the order papers of provincial legislatures. Perhaps the major turning-point came in 1910 when the National Council of Women finally came out in favour of votes for women. The adhesion of this numerous and powerful organization enabled a massive and cumulative campaign to be launched that continued into the early years of the Great War. And something of the spirit in which it was sustained is shown by the peroration to a speech that Sonia Leathes made to the National Council in Montreal in 1913:

> . . . women today say to the governments of all the world: You have usurped what used to be our authority, what used to be our responsibility. It is you who determine today the nature of the air which we breathe, of the food which we eat, of the clothing which we wear. It is you who determine when, and how long, and what our children are to be taught and what their prospects as future wage-earners are to be. It is you who can condone or stamp out the white slave traffic and the starvation wage. It is you who by granting or refusing pensions to the mothers of young children can preserve or destroy the fatherless home. It is you who decide what action shall be considered a crime and how the offender, man, woman or child, shall be dealt with. It is you who decide whether cannons and torpedoes are to blow to pieces the bodies of the sons we bear. And since all these matters strike at the very heartstrings of the mothers of all nations, we shall not rest until we have secured the power vested in the ballot; to give or to withold our consent, to encourage or to forbid any policy or course of action which concerns the people—our children every one.

It was militant talk, and it gave expression to a militant movement that, during and immediately after the war, would gain its objectives when the vote would first be given in provincial elections (beginning with the three Prairie Provinces in 1916), and eventually, by 1918, in federal elections.

The right for women's suffrage would not be the end of the battle for equality between the genders, but the very winning of it showed there had been profound changes in the attitudes of both sexes and in the relations between them. A growing vanguard among women had ceased to be content with the influence that by strength of personality or hard work in farm and home they could wield in family and community. They sought more overt recognition of their equality with men; a share in the control of the world outside their families; a right to compete with men in professions and trades; a right to equivalent education. They wished to have their say in shaping the moral order of the society in which they and their children belonged. They marched, they orated, they lobbied, they petitioned, they publicized, and, without using the sensational direct action favoured by many of the English suffragettes, they advanced notably towards achieving their goals in the century between 1814 and 1914. Nellie McClung was not entirely unjustified when she declared exultantly to the Political Equality League of Manitoba, also in 1913:

> But the dawn is breaking and the darkness flees away. Women who long have sat in their boudoirs like the Lady of Shalott, looking at life in a mirror, are now throwing the glass aside and coming down into the conflict. The awakened womanhood, the aroused motherhood is the New Citizenship.

In a new way, the matriarchal power was reasserting itself. If men were not willing to change their world, women were eager to do it for them.

7

The Noble Chieftain:
Myth and Reality

It was amidst the blaze of a united salvo from the demi lune crowning the bank, and from the shipping, that the noble chieftain, accompanied by the leaders of those wild tribes, leaped lightly, yet proudly to the beach; and having ascended the steep bank by a fight of rude steps cut out of the earth, finally stood amid the party of officers waiting to receive them . . . .

Had none of those officers ever previously beheld him, the fame of his heroic deeds had gone sufficiently before the warrior to have insured him their warmest greeting and approbation, and none could mistake a form that, even among those who were a password for native dignity, stood alone in its bearing; but Tecumseh was a stranger to few.

This is how, in 1840, John Richardson, who a few years before in *Wacousta* had wrung his readers' imaginations in horror with his description of Pontiac's great massacre of the whites at Michilimackinac, introduced in *The Canadian Brothers* the heroic figure of Tecumseh, the noble savage, arriving at Amherstburg in a fleet of fifty canoes.* These contrasting presentations offer the double viewpoint that Canadians in the early nineteenth century harboured towards the native peoples: one unrealistically benign, the other unnecessarily malign.

The concept of the noble savage had been current in Europe at least since the seventeenth century, when accounts of the pre-Columbian American civilizations circulated widely in Europe, and it had already entered literature in works like Aphra Behn's *Oroonoko* (*c*.1688) and in John Dryden's *The Conquest of Granada* (1670):

> I am as free as nature first made man
> Ere the base laws of servitude began,
> When wild in wood the noble savage ran.

Dryden's lines almost summarize the way the concept of the noble savage would be used by the thinkers of the Enlightenment, whose aim was to show that man had a natural tendency towards goodness that was perverted by the creation of organized religions and authoritarian political structures. 'Government, like dress, is the badge of our lost innocence,' said Tom Paine; 'the palaces of kings are built on the ruins of the bowers of paradise.' It was believed that in an early stage of their development human societies led a freer and more natural existence than still obtained among primitive people. 'The savages of northern America have governed themselves in this way to our day, and they are very well governed,' said Jean Jacques Rousseau in *The Social Contract*. The more skeptical Voltaire, in *L'Ingénu*, used the idea of the noble savage with a double satiric intent: to make gentle fun of Rousseau's rather naïve vision of man in the natural state, but also to use an innocent natural man—a Huron—as a foil for his depiction of the corruption and injustice of what we call civilization. A century later Friedrich Engels would tie a Rousseauesque vision into the Marxist vision: somewhat anachronistically, writing in 1884 *The Origin of the Family*, he praised the kinship system he saw at the base of the confederacy 'under which the Iroquois lived for four hundred years and are still living today.'

> And a wonderful constitution it is, this gentile [i.e. kinship] constitution, in all its childlike simplicity! No soldiers, no gendarmes or police, no nobles, kings, prefects or judges, no prisons, or lawsuits—and everything takes its orderly course.

---

*I leave Wacousta out of the present equation, since I believe this grotesque character in no way reflects Canadian attitudes towards Indians. In creating him Richardson was not really concerned with the white man's relations with Indians, but rather with his relationship with the wilderness.

In Canada those likely to be affected by the myth of the noble savage were not so much social ideologues as men who, in a frontier society, would actually come into contact with Tecumseh and other 'noble' Indians; British officers who read Thomas Gray and sketched for pleasure, and early immigrants with some literary pretensions, like Walter Scott's brother Thomas, who settled in the Brantford area in 1815, and wrote with admiring enthusiasm to the novelist about his encounters with Chief Joseph Brant—whose striking presence, rendered often by Regency portraitists, combined with the memory of Tecumseh to create a local Canadian image of the noble savage, existing in real life and not merely in Enlightenment theory.

> I prefer the manners of the native Indians to the insipid conversation of our own officers. The Chief of the Five Nations speaks twelve languages, besides English, French, German and Spanish. He translated your 'Lady of the Lake' as well as the Scriptures into Mohawk, and yet with the most polished manner of civilized life, he would not disdain to partake of the blood of his enemy at the banquet of sacrifice; yet I admire and love this man.*

But these were exceptional Indians. Brant was much Anglicized through his long association with Sir William Johnson during the War of the Spanish Succession, and with Johnson's son Sir John during the American War of Independence, and Tecumseh was remarkable among Indians for his repugnance towards the torture-killing of prisoners. Brant flattered the English by imitating them; Tecumseh reassured them by seeming to prove that their vision of the noble savage was accurate.

The malign image of the native as savage, variants of which were doubtless held by a majority of Loyalists and French Canadians, was bred of an experience of Indian ways gleaned from living among them and particularly from the bitter guerilla warfare waged along the frontiers of settlement by Iroquois who played an important part in the fur-trade rivalry between English and French. In the middle of the seventeenth century the Jesuit missionary Jérôme Lalemant spoke of the incalculable menace of their raids.

> They come like foxes through the woods. They attack like lions. They take flight like birds, disappearing before they have really appeared.

Lalemant's own death by torture was only one of the many cruel incidents that led simple and frightened people to see the Indians as fiends in human form. Moreover, the bitterness of Indian warfare was often increased by the fact that the contending groups of white intruders, French and English, used the natives as auxiliaries in their own wars

---

*Joseph Brant had actually died in 1807, eight years before Scott wrote this letter, yet these are Brant's accomplishments, which he was obviously attributing to a successor.

and encouraged them in cruelty as a means of instilling fear into their opponents, even at times imitating them; there were occasions when French *habitant* militia would torture captured Iroquois to death.

Yet by the time of the settlement of Upper Canada these fears had largely died down. Indians—even the dreaded Iroquois—had been allies in two wars against the Americans and those members of less warlike tribes encountered by immigrant settlers seemed harmless people who passed almost like wraiths through the new world that was taking shape as their familiar forest hunting-grounds were felled and replaced by fields. Catharine Parr Traill recollected, when she was writing *The Canadian Settler's Guide* in the 1850s, that

> In the early state of the settlement in Douro, now twenty years ago, it was no uncommon occurrence for a party of Indians to enter the house (they never knock on any man's door), leave their hunting weapons outside, spread their blankets on the floor, and pass the night with or without leave, arise by the first dawn of day, gather their garments about them, resume their weapons, and silently and noiselessly depart. Sometimes a leash of wild ducks hung to the door-latch, or a haunch of venison left in the kitchen, would be found as a token of gratitude for the warmth afforded them.

Often, in peripheral ways, the Indians became incorporated into the new community. On New Year's Day 1836 Mary O'Brien wrote of the Indian postman at Shanty Bay who 'calls regularly at very irregular hours'.

> He comes in at the front door and from thence to the parlour so noiselessly that I generally think that some accident had unclosed the door till I see his dark figure hesitating in the opening. On being perceived, he comes up to the fire, takes off his bag which he deposits on the table, lays aside his walking stick, and answers as well as he can our queries. Perhaps he lights his pipe or dries his mocassins till I conduct him to the kitchen to get his meal. As soon as this is concluded, he returns, relights his pipe, resumes his bag, gets a warming by the fire which he seems to prefer to the stove, and glides out again.

The insubstantiality that the Indian assumes in both these accounts is not without significance. Dispossessed, increasingly outnumbered, the natives were no longer a threat, yet they were still present—inconvenient but benevolently tolerated survivors. Nobody at that time foresaw how obstinately they would continue to survive.

In other parts of Canada the image of the Indian as a violent and amoral being continued long after Indians had been submerged in the settled areas. Until the 1870s war parties still roamed the prairie and travellers reaching the Pacific Coast were often deeply shocked by what they considered the barbaric acts they saw perpetrated by the local tribes, who nevertheless had elaborate social hierarchies and extraordinary artistic traditions. On his way across Canada in 1845 Paul Kane had already been perturbed by the lodges of the Chippewa:

> The filth, stench and vermin make them almost intolerable to a white man; but Indians are invariably dirty, and it must be something very terrible indeed that will induce them to take half an hour's trouble in moving their lodge. As to removing the filth, that is never done.

Such generalizations as 'Indians are invariably dirty' may give a clue to the imperfections we shall later observe in Kane's artistic presentation of the peoples he encountered on his way across the West, but there was clearly something much more than a stereotyped response in his shocked reaction to an incident that happened shortly after his arrival at Fort Victoria in 1847.

> One morning while I was sketching, I saw upon the rocks the dead body of a young woman, thrown out to the vultures and crows, whom I had seen a few days previously walking about in good health. Mr Finlayson, the gentleman in charge of Fort Victoria, accompanied me to the lodge she belonged to, where we found an Indian woman, her mistress, who made light of her death, and was doubtless the cause of it. She told us that a slave had no right to burial, and became perfectly furious when Mr Finlayson told her that the slave was far better than herself. 'I' she exclaimed, 'the daughter of a chief, no better than a dead slave!' and bridling up all the dignity she could assume, she stalked out, and next morning she had up her lodge and was gone. I was also told by an eye-witness, of a chief, who, having erected a colossal idol of wood, sacrificed five slaves to it, barbarously murdering them at its base, and asking in a boasting manner who amongst them could afford to kill so many slaves.

A system of conspicuous consumption that, in the case of the potlatch, went so far in competitiveness as to be prodigal with property and human lives was hard for any puritanically tinged Victorian to understand, and even more incomprehensible were the bizarre ceremonials of the secret societies among the West Coast Indians who, during their winter rituals, indulged in some very realistic presentations of ritual cannibalism. Arriving at the remote coastal trading post of Fort Simpson in 1857, almost exactly a decade after Kane had reached Victoria, William Duncan, a young Yorkshireman freshly out from the Church Missionary Society's college at Highbury, was faced with another case of slave slaughter. A chief's daughter had suffered an injury and he had ordered a woman slave to be killed on the beach, probably to wipe out the disgrace of the original injury. What happened was described by Duncan in terms whose vividness was probably at least partly directed to potential supporters of the missionary cause.

> Presently two bands of furious wretches appeared, each headed by a man in a state of nudity. They gave vent to the most unearthly sounds, and

the two naked men made themselves look as unearthly as possible, proceeding in a creeping kind of stoop, and stepping like two proud horses, at the same time shooting forward each arm alternately, which they held out at full length for a little time in the most defiant manner . . . . For some time they pretended to be seeking the body, and the instant they came where it lay there commenced screaming and rushing round it like so many hungry wolves. Finally they seized it, dragged it out of the water, and laid it on the beach, where I was told the naked men would commence tearing it to pieces with their teeth. The two bands of men immediately surrounded them, and so hid their horrid work. In a few minutes the crowd broke again into two, when each of the naked cannibals appeared with half the body in his hands. Separating a few yards, they commenced, amid horrid yells, their still more horrid feast. The sight was too horrible to behold. I left the gallery with a depressed heart. What a dreadful place is this!

What Duncan did not realize—at least at the time, when he precipitately departed—was that this was largely an elaborately mimed ritual; members of the Cannibal Society—the Hamatsa, the leading quasi-religious fraternity on the Pacific Coast—did not actually eat the corpses used in their ceremonials. A later understanding of that fact would lead Duncan eventually to oppose the administering of Holy Communion to the coastal peoples, lest they confuse the symbolic eating of the body of Christ with their own ritual cannibalism. However, a more significant outburst of Duncan's at this time was an agonized notation in his journal.

How the land is defiled with blood. Blood, blood from end to end. And here there are none to come to the rescue—plenty who deplore the state of things—plenty who pour furious language upon the murderer—but none to rescue—none to guide the wretched creature to paths of peace and love.

Appalled though he might be by what he had seen, Duncan would not assume that the native was irremediably bad; he could, with help and understanding, be transformed into a different kind of being. In fact the two groups of people who in the earlier period of white penetration were most closely involved with native peoples assumed neither of the extreme views; they saw the Indian neither as noble savage nor as monster. The missionaries thought him redeemable. And the fur-traders were willing to accept him as he was, with a minimum of moral criticism.

By 1814 the relationships between Indians and traders had developed into one of mutual dependence. Once they had found muskets superior to bows and arrows, steel hatchets more dependable than stone ones, iron pots more durable than primitive clay vessels, and both tobacco and rum enjoyable, the Indians slipped into a pattern in which their daily lives were devoted to securing furs to purchase trade goods, and their movements were oriented towards the trading forts. The fur-traders consciously promoted this dependence, but at the same time they too were dependent on the Indians. They penetrated the wilderness only by adopting ways of travel, by birchbark canoe, dog sleigh, and snowshoe, that native peoples had already developed. Pioneers—like Henry Kelsey, Anthony Henday, and Samuel Hearne, who went without white companions into the Barren Lands and the great plains—were dependent entirely on the Indians with whom they travelled and on the survival techniques they learnt from them.

Samuel Hearne, journeying in the 1770s, produced the earliest first-hand account of the Indian way of life by one who shared it. And it was fur-traders who for many years offered the best accounts of Indian life, notably David Thompson and Daniel Harmon, who wrote during our period. Harmon's description of the Carrier in his *Journal of Voyages and Travels in the Interior of North America* (1820) has an objective clarity that recalls the scientist-travellers of later Victorian decades. Even when he is describing their gambling habits and sexual customs he shows an exemplary tolerance, though he seems to have been a devout Christian and somewhat puritanical, for it had distressed him to take a wife *à la façon du pays* in a country where there was no means of solemnizing a marriage, and he regularized his situation as quickly as he could. He tells us that:

> Both sexes, of almost every age, are much addicted to play, or rather gambling. They pass the greater part of their time, especially in the winter season, and both days and nights, in some kind of game; and the men will often lose the last rag of clothes, which they have about them. But so far from being dejected by such ill-fortune, they often appear to be proud of having lost their all; and will even boastfully say, that they are as naked as a dog, having not a rag with which to cover themselves. Should they, in such circumstances, meet with a friend, who should lend them something to wrap around their bodies, it is highly probable, that they would immediately go and play away the borrowed garment. Or, if the borrower belonged to another village, he would be likely to run off with it, and the owner would never hear of him afterward; for I never knew a Carrier to be grateful for a favour bestowed on him . . . .
>
> The Carriers are remarkably fond of their wives, and a few of them have three or four; but polygamy is not general among them. The men do most of the drudgery about the house, such as cutting and drawing fire wood, and bringing water.
>
> As the Carriers are fond of their wives, they are, as naturally might be supposed, very jealous of them; but to their daughters, they allow every liberty, for the purpose, as they say, of keeping the young men from intercourse with the married women. As the young women may thus bestow their favours on whom, and as often as they please, without the least censure from their parents, or reproach to their character, it might naturally be expected they would be, as I am informed they actually are, very free with their persons.

Harmon's detachment mirrors the aloofness that characterized the attitude of the fur-traders to the Indians. Except for those like Hearne, and Dr John Rae in later years, who travelled with natives on extensive explorations, living off the land as they went, few of the traders dwelt in proximity to them. Their contact was usually mediated by the French-Canadian and later the Métis *voyageurs* who acted as interpreters, for often the Gentlemen did not understand the local languages, and even traded outside the forts. It is true that some of the Gentlemen married the daughters of native chiefs. But these were alliances entered into as cold-bloodedly on both sides as the dynastic marriages of European monarchies. To the chiefs they offered prestige and access to firearms for use in their sporadic wars with other groups. To the Hudson's Bay Company, which at times encouraged such marriages even if it did not command them, they offered assured markets and allies in case of need—and occasionally immediate windfalls. In 1823 Chief Trader Archibald McDonald married the daughter of the powerful Chief Concomly of the Chinook tribe on the Columbia River, and it is recorded that when McDonald went to the chief's great clan house to receive his bride, the path from the river bank to the palace of cedar planks was carpeted with beaver pelts and the skins of sea and land otters, which were presented to the bridegroom who, according to the rules of the trade, handed them over to the Company.

In effect, the fur-traders stood in relation to the natives as suzerains rather than as sovereigns. They claimed no right to interfere in the way the Indians conducted their lives, individually or socially. On the other hand, in their own interests they would at times feed starving Indians and support old hunters, and doubtless on these occasions calculation was diluted by natural benevolence. But the relationship was never one that could lead to any true *rapprochement*, since in real terms a class system had emerged, a situation of primitive capitalism similar to that in which, before the rise of the factory system, entrepreneurs employed handweavers to work in their homes and bring the product of their toil to a central depot: the Indians who brought their pelts to the trading forts for the eventual use of the furrier or the felt-maker became the equivalent of a European proletariat. Decimation by white men's diseases, demoralization by alcohol, and eventually hunger resulting from the destruction of game animals by white men's weapons led the natives to accept this situation with growing docility.

In consequence, a variety of attitudes emerged on the part of the fur-traders. Harmon's sympathetic detachment was counterbalanced by the cavalier indifference of R.M. Ballantyne, the famous Victorian writer of boys' novels who started out—a boy himself—as an apprentice clerk in the fur trade, and whose first book was an account of his experiences in Rupert's Land and in the remoter parts of Quebec as a young Gentle-

man in the service of the Company. *Hudson's Bay* (1848) is mainly concerned with the way fur-traders lived and with the experience of travelling
a country of climatic extremes and dramatic settings, all of which Ballantyne describes with great verve and colour. But essentially it is the
life of young Scots and Englishmen liberated from schoolhouse toils to
roam the great world that Ballantyne represents, and he tells of the
natives only in so far as their lives contribute to the profits of the fur
trade. There is a vivid passage about a night in the life of an Indian
trapper that gives promise of a good popular adventure-story writer,
but it is evident that Ballantyne took little trouble to understand the
society to which the trapper he described belonged, and his summary
of native religious beliefs is as contemptible as it is contemptuous.

> The Supreme Being among the Indians is called Manitow; but he can
> scarcely be said to be worshipped by them, and the few ideas they have
> of his attributes are imperfect and erroneous. Indeed, no religious rites
> exist among them, unless the unmeaning mummery of the medicine tent
> can be looked on as such.

Though few fur-traders had Ballantyne's gift of words, most of them
probably shared his limitations of perception. Even such an ornament
of the trade as Governor Simpson himself could indulge in facetious
contempt, as witness his description of his meeting with the Chippewyan chiefs on Rainy Lake in 1841:

> They had all dressed or rather decorated themselves for the occasion—
> their costumes being various enough to show that fashion, as it is called,
> had not yet got so far to the westward. Their glossy locks were plaited all
> round the head into tails, varying in number according to the thickness
> of the bush or the taste of the owner; at the ends of the different ties were
> suspended such valuable ornaments as thimbles, coins, buttons, and clip-
> pings of tin; . . . and their necks were encircled with rows of beads at
> discretion and large collars of brass rod.
>
> As to clothing properly so called, everyone had leggings and a rag round
> the loins, while some of the chiefs, with the addition of scarlet coats and
> plenty of gold lace had very much the cut of parish beagles.

Such pragmatic aloofness was not possible for the missionaries, at
least if they were worthy of their mission. They had to create some
channel of understanding with the people they set out to convert. James
Evans, the Wesleyen missionary of the 1840s, spoke for all serious-
minded proselytizers when he asked: 'How can a man reach these people
if he doesn't speak their language? To work through an interpreter is
like hacking one's way through a forest with a feather.' Evans went
beyond learning the language of the Cree whom he taught at Norway
House in what is now the far north of Manitoba. He invented a system
of syllabic characters for the Cree language that is still in use, and then

he faced the more physical problems of communicating through that language. On 28 November 1840 he noted in his diary:

> For a fortnight I have been endeavouring to cast type to print the Cree language, but every attempt hitherto has failed. I have no proper materials, neither type materials nor any other thing requisite. I hope, however, to conquer the difficulties and begin printing in a few weeks or a few months at the furthest.

In fact he succeeded within a fortnight, casting the type for his new characters in lead obtained from bullets and the linings of tea chests, and printing a sixteen-page booklet of hymns and scriptural texts, in an edition of one hundred copies, with an ink of soot and fish-oil on birch-bark; the booklets were bound in deerskin.

To the problem of communication was added the problem of understanding, for it would be impossible to enter the minds of one's converts without gaining some idea of their thought patterns. While most of the fur-traders almost deliberately avoided this kind of enquiry, the best of the missionaries found it necessary. Perhaps the superb ethnographical and linguistic studies carried out by the Oblate Father, A.G. Morice, among the Dené peoples of northern British Columbia during the 1890s were exceptional, and went beyond missionary functions as ordinarily conceived; but there were other men whose attempts to understand the beliefs of others while holding to their own were impressive.

The work of the Methodist missionary John McDougall provides a good example. He came of a missionary family; his father George Millward McDougall had gone to the Prairies in 1860 and died in a blizzard near Calgary in 1874 while working for his faith. John McDougall carried on his father's work in the Northwest for another thirty years, and he wrote about this in a series of books published during the 1890s: *Forest, Lake and Prairie*, *Saddle, Sled and Snowshoe*, and *Pathfinding on Path and Prairie*. Written in a racy and exuberant prose that seems strangely immature, considering that McDougall was over 50 when he wrote the first of them, they project work in the mission field as an adventure comparable in its thrills and dangers with exploration or fur-trading. In this they reflect the curiously adolescent quality of the Muscular Christianity of the period. No journey comes to an end without a narrow escape, a brush with death.

At the same time McDougall conveys an interest in native ways of life and thinking that, though necessary to him as a missionary, amounts to a show of respect. One of the most vivid passages of *Pathfinding on Path and Prairie* is a quite elaborate—and remarkably objective—account of the Thirst Dance of the prairie natives. McDougall talks of it as a 'religious festival', without any offensive talk of 'mummery', and writes:

> This religious gathering has been for ages an annual occurrence. It is an occasion for the fulfilment of vows, and an opportunity for the more religious of this pagan people to make sacrifices and to endure self-inflicted tortures and hardship in meeting the requirements of the traditional faith of their fathers.

He describes how the people are called together from various parts of the Prairies, how the preliminary sacrifices are performed, how the 'big lodge' for the festival is erected, and how the 'idol tree' that will stand in its centre is selected, cut down, and brought to the site.

> When the idol tree is raised in place the conjurors make a special effort with medicine-rattles and religious singing. Some make the 'nest' in the idol tree, or, as it might be called, the sacrificial table, and fasten in and on this the sacrifices which had been purchased long before at the trading-posts for this purpose. All the timbers in place, the whole is covered with the lodges of the principal men of the camp, it being thought an honor to have these used in this way. And now the high priest approaches. He has a big buffalo head mask, both himself and the head well covered with earth. Stepping slowly, and wailing as he walks, he enters the temple. Immediately on his entrance is made the inner circle of those who have vows and will dance through the long hours. Then a spot in the temple is selected for the drummers and singers, and these come in turns, so that the choir is continuous day and night during the festival. Fire is placed in four places, and on these fires are put sweet smelling herbs, which as they burn create incense . . . . In the inner circle, and immediately around the 'idol tree', the real dancers who are to undergo torture arrange themselves.
>
> Some of these attach long lines to the 'idol tree', and then passing the end through the muscles of their arms they dance and swing around the circle. Others hang guns to the tendons of their back, and dance with these swinging and jerking about them. Others go from out the camp, and finding a bull's skull with horns attached, pass a line through the eyelets, and then hitch themselves to the other end of the line through the tendons of the back, and drag the head to the temple, entering amongst the dancers for the rest of the festival.
>
> The self-tortured and the dancers do not eat or drink until the afternoon of the third day. At that time the warriors in costume come in a body to the temple, the bravest ten in the lead, all singing as they march, either on foot or on horseback, and forming a circle just outside the 'thirst lodge'. Then come those who make gifts, and horses, guns, blankets, etc., are placed in the ring as a general offering, being afterwards distributed to the needy and the infirm.

It will be observed that McDougall never denies the 'religious' character of this ceremony, or the sincerity of the 'pagans' who carry it out. Implicitly he praises the fortitude of the self-tortured and points out the care for the 'needy and the infirm' that pagan, like Christian, beliefs enjoin. Yet he is never in doubt of the urgency of converting the natives to his own religion, and he sees the process as a cultural as well as a religious conversion, for, like many other missionaries, he set out to make his mission at Pigeon Lake a centre where natives could learn the skills that would fit them for entry into the white man's world.

> Our duties to and amongst these people were manifold. We had to supply the object lesson in all new industries. In fishing, net making and mending, chopping and sawing, planting and weeding, and even in economical hunting, we found that we must not only take a part but lead. I was doctor, lawyer, judge, and arbitrator, peace commissioner, pastor, teacher and brother man.

The essential paternalism implied in such an attitude had been present in missionary-founded communities ever since the first days of New France. Then the conversion of the heathen had been regarded as one of the main reasons for the colony's existence, but conversion in terms of faith was regarded as dependent on cultural absorption; both the clergy and the royal officials looked forward to the day when the natives would gradually lose their identity in an increasingly homogenous French-speaking population. This aim lay behind the effort and the tragedy of the inevitably unsuccessful Jesuit project of turning Huronia into a model Christian community.

The tradition of the Jesuit fathers did not entirely die out, and in the nineteenth century members of other orders, notably the Oblates, encouraged mission settlements, mainly among the Métis. The prime intent was religious; a settled agrarian community with a chapel in its midst was more likely to keep Catholics—which the Métis nominally were—in the paths of faith than in a nomadic way of life with all its temptations to return to paganism and loose living. Certainly in the case of many of the Fathers there was the more mundane altruistic thought that if the hunters could be induced to start farming, they would be less vulnerable to the consequences of the extinction of the buffalo, which by the early 1870s many far-sighted people envisaged. The settlements began as groups of houses where the hunters could winter around the missions and cultivate plots of land when they were not out on the hunt. Some have survived as viable communities, like the village around the mission Father Thibault founded at Lake St Anne in Alberta in the late 1840s. Among the less permanent settlements the most interesting was the one Father André established at St Laurent with Gabriel Dumont's help in 1873. Ruled by a council elected according to the old customs of the buffalo hunt, it set up a court for trying disputes and established codes relating to hunting, land use, and timber use. There was a clear political aim, as well as a disguised religious one—to establish order and organization where none yet existed, as the Métis stressed in their statement on establishing the commune:

. . . they see themselves as loyal and faithful subjects of Canada and are prepared to give up their own organization and submit to the laws of the Dominion as soon as Canada brings into their midst official magistrates with sufficient power to uphold the law of the land. (*Translation.*)

(Such dedication to order is particularly striking in view of the fact that the founders of the commune of St Laurent would be among the leaders of the rebellion into which the Métis were at least partly goaded by governmental procrastination in 1885.)

These Métis settlements consisted of people who, as well as being already Catholic, were also at least partly French in language and culture. Some of the Protestant missionaries attempted the greater task of transforming pagan natives into Victorian Christian working-men by establishing communities aimed not only at isolating them from their traditional existence but also at equipping them to live an adequate and prosperous life in a world dominated by white men's practices and values.

Probably the most striking example of these missionaries—who anticipated the Social Gospel movement later in the century by regarding it as their duty to save the whole person, not only the soul, of everyone to whom they ministered—was William Duncan, whose first perturbed encounter with the native society of coastal British Columbia was cited earlier.

Duncan, a lay preacher who never agreed to be ordained, was a product of the early-nineteenth-century Evangelical movement. This Low Church trend, which had been closely associated with William Wilberforce's campaign against slavery, emphasized a Christianity stripped of ritual and liturgical extravagances and open to men of all colours and conditions. It was a movement of class as much as of doctrine. Into an Anglican ministry that traditionally had been the province of gentlemen, there came a host of young clerks and shop assistants (Duncan had worked in a leather business) who—when they were kept out of English rectories and vicarages—turned their attention to what was known then as 'the mission field'.

Duncan quickly came to the conclusion, in opposition to accepted Victorian wisdom, that the natives' troubles were due not merely to their heathenism, but also to the destructive influence of the whites who preyed on them in various ways. His solution was to remove his followers physically from the temptations of Fort Simpson, and in 1862 he led a party of converts to some ancient village sites at Metlakatla near Prince Rupert, where he set about creating a model village.

It was a kind of exorcism of the Devil by Beelzebub (though Duncan would not have seen it in that way), for he proposed to rescue the natives from the wiles of the white man by turning them into imitation white men. He did it so successfully that Bishop Bompas, the great missionary of the desolate North, visiting from his diocese in the Yukon territory, would ruefully contrast Duncan's success in teaching Victorian manners with his own failure.

> An Indian congregation, worshipping in the Mission Church on the coast of British Columbia, would not be distinguished from an English congregation in their outward dress and demeanour, and the natives there are very careful of their clothes, preserving their Sunday Suits so successfully in cedar-wood boxes, that they seem to be always new. To the east of the Rockies, the Indians of the forests are very careless of their clothes, and a native may purchase a suit of fine black cloth, and in a few weeks tear it to rags in travelling through the woods.

Duncan's 1,100 Indians worshipped in a church built with their own hands that was larger than any cathedral north of San Francisco. They lived in uniformly designed houses for single families, set in neat garden plots with picket fences, instead of in old communal longhouses. To their traditional basic occupation of fishing, they added various new industries, such as weaving, sawmilling, brickmaking, rope-making, and furniture-making. They had their own councillors, their constables, their celebrated brass band, their trading schooner, their store, and they seemed to be moving rapidly towards self-government through co-operation.

Philanthropic Victorians made their way to Metlakatla, and among them were Lord and Lady Dufferin in 1876. The Indians sang 'dirges' for them from canoes. Lady Dufferin sketched the village, and in her diary wrote enthusiastically of the church and the school, where 'the pupils all learn to read English, which they prefer for reading to their native tongue—their own words are so very long. They translate what they read into Tschimshyau.' Lady Dufferin was also intrigued by the prison, which to Rousseau and Engels would have seemed the mark of lost Paradise:

> . . . it is a funny little tower, painted black below and white above. It is divided into two rooms, the 'black' prison being more disgraceful than the 'white'. On the top of this building there is a stand for the band!

The members of the vice-regal party were so impressed that they deposited on top of the alms box a pile of $20 gold coins too large to go through the narrow slit that represented Duncan's low expectations of outside help.

Duncan was an autocrat. When the Indian Commissioner I.W. Powell visited Metlakatla in 1879, he declared it to be 'one of the most orderly, respectable and industrious communities to be found in any Christian country', but he also remarked that Duncan's 'individuality seemed to me to pervade everything connected with the town.' Yet Duncan inspired great devotion, and in 1887, when he finally split with the High Church bishops who had come to British Columbia and decided to shift the village to Annette Island in Alaska, 90 per cent of the Metlakatlans followed him.

Such loyalty was undoubtedly in part because Duncan had always shown himself resolutely on the side of the natives. He was not one of those who imagined that their race was doomed to extinction, which George Monro Grant thought 'not unlikely' and Goldwin Smith thought certain:

> Musical Indian names of places and rivers, Indian relics in museums, Indian phrases, such as 'going on the warpath' and 'burying the hatchet'— these and nothing more apparently will remain of the aboriginal man in British Columbia. His blood is not on the head of the British Government, which has always treated him with humanity and justice.

Duncan not only believed that if the Indian had appropriate help he could survive and take his part as an equal in the modern world. He also believed the native peoples had rights that, officially and unofficially, the white men were violating. As early as 1861 he denounced the rapacity with which the Indians' land was being seized. 'It is his country, given him by the Maker and Governor of the universe, that we occupy.' This attitude was not popular among his fellow whites in British Columbia, where there were not even treaties with most of the natives guaranteeing them reserves. But it found an echo among the northern tribes, who were encouraged by Duncan and other missionaries in their region to demand recognition of their aboriginal title. Their discontent was expressed by one of the chiefs addressing a Commission—the first of many—that was sent to the Nass River in 1887 to enquire into grievances.

> What we don't like about the Government is their saying this: 'We will give you this much land.' How can they give it when it is our own? We cannot understand it. They have never bought it from us or our forefathers. They have never fought and conquered our people and taken our land that way, and yet they say now that they will give us so much land—our own land.

This is not the place to consider in detail the famous series of eleven treaties concluded by the Dominion government between 1871 and 1921, under which the natives in Canada east of the Rockies were induced to barter away their birthright of land in exchange for meagre reserves, medals and uniforms, a little money, and some scanty aid in converting themselves from hunters into farmers. The contrast between the pageantry and fine speeches of these occasions and their actual benefits to the natives never did become apparent to Canadians who saw the opening of the western lands for settlement as an urgent matter, and who realized that the land could not be occupied while the natives roamed freely across it. Most Canadians in the Victorian era would probably have subscribed to Goldwin's Smith's view—expressed in 1891 *after* the North West Rebellion had exposed the inadequacy of the treaties—that the Indian in Canada had always been treated 'with humanity and justice'. And most would probably have given the same answer to Principal Grant's rhetorical question that he himself gave:

> What is the secret of our wonderful success in dealing with the Indian? It can be told in very few words. We acknowledge their title and right to the land; and a treaty once made with them, we keep it.

The fact that the treaties had dissolved the 'title and right' for trivial considerations obviously did not occur to Grant and his readers.

Grant, of course, was one of the advocates of western expansion; he would not otherwise have undertaken the journey from the east to the west of the country described in *Ocean to Ocean* (1872). And during the later part of the nineteenth century Canadians were as much indebted for their knowledge of the native peoples of the West to such travelling observers as they were to the traders and missionaries who spent large parts of their lives among them.

Often the travellers were British gentlemen—and occasionally gentlewomen—who had more leisure and means than their Canadian contemporaries, and perhaps even more willingness to penetrate what still seemed to the Canadians a threatening wilderness. And they tended to look upon natives with more sympathy and understanding than their Canadian contemporaries did. Anna Jameson, who could describe her fellow whites with great acerbity, showed a genuine empathy towards the natives she met. She confessed to disappointment at first encountering them on an occasion when they had come together to accept gifts from the government.

> On the whole, the impression they left, though amusing and exciting from its mere novelty, was melancholy. The sort of desperate resignation in their swarthy countenances, their squalid, dingy habiliments, and their forlorn story, filled me with pity and, I may add, disappointment; and all my previous impressions of the independent children of the forest were disturbed.

The noble savage had not become ignoble—which might have been endurable—but pathetic.

Yet Jameson persisted and, for an English woman of her time, she put a great deal of time and effort into visiting and studying the natives. In this she was helped by Henry Schoolcraft, the American ethnologist whom she met at Sault Ste Marie when he was Superintendent of Indian Affairs in Michigan, and she wrote of native beliefs with an understanding rarely shown by her male fellows in the travelling fraternity.

> It is a mistake to suppose that these Indians are idolators; heathens and pagans you may call them if you will; but the belief in one Great Spirit,

who created all things and is paramount to all things, and the belief in the distinction between body and soul, and the immortality of the latter—these two sublime principles pervade their wildest superstitions; but though none doubt of a future state, they have no distinct or universal tenets with regard to the condition of the subject, and some doubtless never think about it at all. In general, however, their idea of a paradise (the land of spirits) is some far off country towards the south-west, abounding in sunshine, and placid lakes, and rivers full of fish, and forests full of game, whither they are transported by the Great Spirit, and where those who are separated on earth meet again in happiness, and part no more.

Not only man, but everything animate, is spirit, and destined to immortality. According to the Indians, (and Sir Humphry Davy), nothing dies, nothing is destroyed; what we look on as death and destruction is only transition and change.

The independent travellers who wandered over the West in these early days tended often to find among the native peoples qualities that they themselves valued, such as endurance and independence. A relatively early wanderer in 1860, the Earl of Southesk, was particularly taken with the Métis, who in his view—he was judging mainly by the people settled on the Red River—combined respectability and independence.

I doubt if a half-breed, dressed and educated like an Englishman, would seem at all remarkable in London society. They build and farm like other people, they go to church and to courts of law, they recognize no chiefs (except when they elect a leader for their hunting expeditions), and in all respects they are like civilized men, no more uneducated, immoral, or disorderly, than many communities in the Old World.

Viscount Milton and Dr Cheadle depended on native guides and servants for their very survival in the quixotic journey they made across Canada to the Cariboo gold fields in 1862, and praised the Métis, without disparaging the Indians, for the qualities necessary for good wilderness travellers.

Of more powerful build, as a rule, than the pure Indians, they combine his endurance and readiness of resource with the greater muscular strength and perseverance of the white man.

Captain William Francis Butler, the volatile Anglo-Irish soldier-adventurer who made two long journeys into the Northwest in 1870 and 1872 (and wrote two flamboyant and verbose books about them—*The Great Lone Land* and *The Wild North Land*) had reservations about the Métis. He gave a vivid description of a hunter's camp on the South Saskatchewan in 1872 that was almost certainly the one presided over by Gabriel Dumont before the foundation of the commune of St Laurent:

Huts promiscuously crowded together; horses, dogs, women, children, all intermixed in a confusion worthy of Donnybrook Fair; half-breed hunters, ribboned, tasselled, and capôted, lazy, idle, and, if there is any spirit in the camp, sure to be intoxicated; remnants and wrecks of buffalo lying everywhere around; robes stretched and drying; meat piled on stages; wolf-skins spread over framework; women drawing water and carrying wood; and at dusk from the little hut the glow of firelight through parchment windows, the sound of fiddle scraped with rough hunter hand, and the quick thud of hunter heel as Louison, or Bâtiste, or Gabriel foot it ceaselessly upon the half-hewn floors.

Unquestionably these French half-breeds are wild birds—hunters, drinkers, rovers, rascals if you will—yet generous and hospitable withal; destined to disappear before the white man's footprint, and ere that time has come owing many of their vices to the pioneer American, whose worst qualities the wild man, or semi-wild man, has been ever sure to imitate.

Worst of all, to Butler, a typical British animal-lover, was the way the 'half-breeds' treated their sleigh dogs.

The cruelty so systematically practiced upon dogs by their half-breed drivers is utterly unwarrantable. In winter the poor brutes become more than ever the benefactors of man, uniting in themselves all the services of horse and dog—by day they work, by night they watch, and the man must be a very cur in nature who would inflict, at such a time, needless cruelty upon the animal that rendered him so much assistance.

For the natives, on the other hand, Butler held an almost unrestricted admiration, particularly when comparing them with the 'civilizers'— 'these brutal pioneers of Anglo-American freedom, with their many stages between unblackened boots and diamond breast pins' for whom 'I have felt nothing but loathing and disgust'—who were pouring into the Prairies. For Butler the 'freedom' proclaimed by the white invaders of the Prairies was clearly a false one; but the freedom of the native was a true one that he, as a fellow free spirit, hailed.

This wild man who first welcomed the new-comer is the only perfect socialist or communist in the world. He holds all things in common with his tribe—the land, the bison, the river, and the moose. He is starving, and the rest of the tribe want food. Well, he kills a moose, and to the last bit the coveted food is shared by all. That war-party has taken one hundred horses in the last raid into Blackfoot or Peagin territory; well, the whole tribe are free to help themselves to the best and fleetest steeds before the captors will touch one out of the band . . . . Poor, poor fellow! his virtues are all his own; crimes he may have, and plenty, but his noble traits spring from no book-learning, from no schoolcraft, from the preaching of no pulpit; they come from the instinct of good which the Good Spirit has taught him; they are the whisperings from that lost world whose glorious shores beyond the Mountains of the Setting Sun are the long dream of his life. The most curious anomaly among the race of man, the red man of America, is passing away beneath our eyes into the infinite solitude.

The possession of the same noble qualities which we affect to reverence among our nations makes us kill him. If he would be the African or the Asiatic it would be all right for him; if he would be our slave he might live, but as he won't be that, won't toil and delve and hew for us, and will persist in hunting, fishing, and roaming over the beautiful prairie land which the Great Spirit gave him; in a word, since he will be free—we kill him.

This was a celebration of the 'noble savage' at its most extreme, and it is not surprising that Butler felt somewhat disappointed when he saw these free lords of the Prairies making fools of themselves by imitating white men's fashions.

The universal passion for dress is strangely illustrated in the Western Indian. His ideal of perfection is the English costume of some forty years ago. The tall chimney-pot hat with round narrow brim, the coat with high collar going up over the neck, sleeves tight-fitting, waist narrow. All this is perfection, and the chief who can array himself in this ancient garb struts out of the fort the envy and admiration of all beholders. Sometimes the tall felt chimney-pot is graced by a large feather which has done duty in the turban of a dowager thirty years ago in England. The addition of a little gold tinsel to the coat collar is of considerable consequence, but the presence of a nether garment is not at all requisite to the completeness of the general get-up. For this most ridiculous-looking costume a Blackfeet chief will readily exchange his beautifully-dressed deerskin Indian shirt— embroidered with porcupine quills and ornamented with the raven locks of his enemies—his head-dress of ermine skins, his flowing buffalo robe: a dress in which he looked every inch a savage king for one in which he looks every inch a foolish savage.

Butler equated settlers with exterminators, even though his own travels helped to open the way for them. But at the same time other men were travelling the Prairies, some with scientific inclinations, whose aim was to assess the West in terms of development and settlement. George Monro Grant, whom we have already seen journeying with the railway engineer Sandford Fleming, was one of them; and so was Captain John Palliser, who headed a British government expedition in 1857 to assess the agricultural possibilities of the Prairies. Palliser's observations never got beyond a government report. But those of the geologist Henry Youle Hind, who led two expeditions on behalf of the Canadian government into territory it did not yet own, appeared in a lengthy and in many ways an enlightening book, *Narrative of the Canadian Red River Exploring Expedition of 1857 and of the Assiniboine and Saskatchewan Exploring Expedition of 1858* (1860). Hind's enthusiastic account of the possibilities of the land undoubtedly strengthened the intention of Canadian politicians to acquire the West, and it is significant that his view of the natives was on the whole negative. He harboured no myth of the noble savage, and while like Butler he seems when he started on his journey to have seen the natives as members of a vanishing race, for him it was clearly a matter of pathos rather than of tragedy. This one infers from his account of a meeting with Ojibway at the head of Lake Superior:

> Just before starting a large body of heathen Indians, from the camp on the opposite side of the river, came over in a number of small canoes and commenced a dance outside of the pickets of the fort. They were painted and feathered in various ways, and furnished an admirable subject for our artists. Having danced on the outside of the fort for some minutes, they entered and arranged themselves in a semicircle in the quadrangle. The medicine-man and his assistant, gaudily painted and decked with eagles' feathers, sat on the ground beating a drum, and near to them squatted some half dozen squaws, with a few children. About sixty men and boys, headed by the chief, painted and feathered similar to the medicine man, danced or jumped round the ring. Our party being collected in front of the chief, he made a short speech, which was interpreted by a half-breed attached to the expedition to the following effect:- 'They were happy to see us on their soil, they were hungry and required food, and trusted to our generosity and the plenty by which we were surrounded.' The pipe of peace was then lit, and handed in turns for each to take a whiff. The picture of a hand across the mouth and cheek was admirably drawn in black on the faces of the chief and medicine-man. The Ka-Ki-whe-on, or insignia, consisted of eagle's feathers stuck in a strip of red cloth about four feet long, and attached to a cedar pole. The whole scene was highly ridiculous, and many of the performers were wretched looking creatures, being dreadfully affected with scrofula. Some of the men, however, possessed splendid looking figures, but the progress of civilization will soon close the history of these wretched Indians of the Kamistiquia.

But an encounter with a band of Cree who were engaged with macabre vigour in slaying bison in a pound seems to have modified Hind's views of the ease with which the 'progress of civilization' might penetrate the West. They seemed a very different people from the pathetic mendicants on Lake Superior. Mist-tick-oos was their chief.

> Mist-tick-oos, or 'Shortstick', is about fifty years old, of low stature, but very powerfully built. His arms and breast were deeply marked with scars and gashes, records of grief and mourning for departed friends. His son's body was painted with blue bars across the chest and arms. The only clothing they wore consisted of a robe of dressed elk or buffalo hide, and the breech cloth; the robe was often cast off the shoulders and drawn over the knees when in a sitting posture; they wore no covering on the head, their long hair was plaited or tied in knots, or hung loose over their shoulders and back. The forms of some of the young men were faultless, of the middle-aged men bony and wiry, and of the aged men, in one instance at least, a living skeleton.

One of the old men was believed by the local Métis to be 100 years old.

Encounters such as this led Hind to stress the need for proper negotiations to deal with native claims to the land:

> In Rupert's Land, where disaffected Indians can influence the savage prairie tribes and arouse them to hostility, the subject is one of great magnitude; open war with Sioux, Assiniboines, Plain Crees or Blackfeet, might render the prairie country unapproachable for many years, and expose the settlers to constant alarms and depredations.

His final conclusion was not far from that of the missionaries, for he saw their future as

> dependent upon the steps which may be taken by the future government of the country, to provide for their instruction in the Christian religion; their assumption of a settled mode of life, and their consequent advancement in civilization.

The natives, in other words, could survive only by ceasing to be the free and noble 'wild man' of Captain Butler's imagination.

The Victorian era was the age of the picturesque as well as of the moralist, and inevitably there were some who saw the Indian not as noble or 'wild' or potentially Christianized into an imitation white man, but as a colourful exotic who could adorn a traveller's tale. Here is a description of Indian torchlight fishermen by Captain R.G.A. Levinge, who was stationed with the 43rd Regiment in New Brunswick in the 1840s and wrote his recollections in *Echoes from the Backwoods* (1846):

> When the salmon make their appearance on the Nashwak, fleets of canoes, each containing a couple of Indians, leave Fredericton to spear them by torchlight. The fish, checked by the falls, are collected in great numbers in the pools below. Nothing can be more exciting than this scene, the canoes hurled about in all directions by the foaming tide, the skill displayed by the Indians in forcing them up the rapids, and fending them off the rocks, or allowing them to plunge head-foremost down stream, when they suddenly bring them to, and transfix their fish. The eagerness of the chase, the contrast of the flaming torches with the black masses of the woods, and the fine attitudes of the men, dashing at the salmon with their spears, form a wild and most animating picture.

In the nineteenth century the picture and the picturesque were often not far apart, and Indians play a usually minor but still significant role in the art and writing of the period. Many of the artists were less concerned to encounter the native peoples as they actually were than to seek in their way of life the virtues that had been leached out of their own. Affected by the romantic preoccupations of the era, these artists were often willing to falsify what they found in order to do justice to what they sought.

Paul Kane showed this inclination. He was not the first artist to paint Indians in Canada. They often appear as incidental figures in the paintings of topographers like Thomas Davies, and there are anonymous early nineteenth-century sketches of Micmac that show a close interest in native customs. But Kane was the first Canadian painter to set out deliberately to make a visual record, in frank imitation of what George Catlin had done in the United States. He saw himself as destined to preserve in paint an obsolescent way of life, which he sought in the fastnesses of the West:

> . . . those who would see the aborigenes of this country in their original state, or seek to study their native manners and customs, must travel far through the pathless forest to find them.

The great journey that Kane embarked on, with the assistance of Governor Simpson, took him from Toronto through the western plains and over the mountains to the Pacific coast, and lasted from 1845 to 1848. He was often disillusioned with the natives—not only with the filth of the Chippewa and the cruel treatment of slaves on the Pacific coast, but also with the indiscriminate and wasteful slaughter of bison in the buffalo pounds.

> The Indians in this manner destroy innumerable buffaloes, apparently for the mere pleasure of the thing. I have myself seen a pound so filled up with their dead carcases that I could scarcely imagine how the enclosure could have contained them while living. It is not unusual to drive in so many that their aggregate bulk forces down the barriers. There are thousands of them annually killed in this manner; but not one in twenty is used in any way by the Indians, so that thousands are left to rot where they fall. I heard of a pound, too far off my direct road to visit, formed entirely of the bones of dead buffaloes that had been killed in a former pound on the same spot, piled up in a circle similarly to the logs above described.

But Kane persisted, sketching often unwilling natives, warts and all. He came back with 240 of these rapid notations in oil and watercolour, as well as a journal from which he wrote one of the best early books on the West, *Wanderings of an Artist Among the Indians of North America* (1859). His sketches were so immediate and vivid that a century and a half later they still retain their freshness of impact and constitute Kane's title to be considered a historic Canadian painter. Yet back home in Toronto, referring to these sketches, he painted what he had sought rather than what he found in a series of grandiose canvases that seem to combine the myth of the noble savage with the nineteenth-century romantic notion of the world of medieval chivalry. Grandly posed Indian warriors ride spirited steeds that seem of Arabian breed, and fight with a melodramatic ferocity that recalls the romantic violence of the French painter Géricault.

In literature John Richardson projected a similar ambivalence to Kane's. Having experienced the War of 1812, he cannot have been unaware of the flesh-and-blood Indian, as distinct from the myth that quickly de-

veloped around Tecumseh and that was sealed by his death in battle
and the gothically mysterious disappearance of his body. Yet Richardson's poem *Tecumseh* is a romantic presentation of the noble savage so
conventional in intent that he chose Byron's all-too-familiar *ottava rima*
as the form in which to present it.

Charles Mair had more on his mind than reliving the old battles of
1812 when, a generation after Richardson, he too made the Indian leader
the protagonist of a great disorganized closet drama, also called *Tecumseh*. The romanticized image of the noble savage is still present—
rather surprisingly in one who, in 1869, had been so anxious to promote
the Canadian acquisition of the West. So is the doctrine of aboriginal
rights, which is embodied in a soliloquy on Tecumseh's recollections of
the time when the Indians lived their own lives without interference or
intruders:

> Once all this mighty continent was ours,
> And the great spirit made it for our use.
> He knew no boundaries, so had we peace,
> In the vast shelter of his handiwork,
> And, happy here, we cared not whence we came.
> We brought no evils thence—no treasured hate,
> No greed of gold, no quarrels over God;
> And so our broils, to narrow issues joined,
> Were soon composed, and touched the ground of peace.

This is noble savagery at its purest; the idyllic vision of primitive
society that in the same period haunted Mair's contemporaries, such as
Kropotkin and Engels and even Karl Marx. It fitted the utopian thinking
of the time even though it bore little relation to actual Indian existence.
But Mair was not concerned merely with the noble savage and romantic
utopianism. He also had a nationalist cause at heart, and Tecumseh's
role as one of the great opponents of the American invasion was not
forgotten, nor were the implications for Canadians. Tecumseh's soliloquy ends thus:

> But we shall yield no more! Those plains are ours!
> Those forests are our birth-right and our home!
> Let not the Long-Knife build one cabin there—
> Or fire from it will spread from every roof,
> To compass you, and light your souls to death!

When he published his play in 1886, Mair saw the Indian cause as lost,
but he was still concerned with the preservation of Canada as a nation
from American (Long-Knife) assault, and he found in Tecumseh a suit-
able symbolic figure to support the notion of ongoing resistance.

Other poems of the period also adapted the Indian heritage to their
own uses. Isabella Valancy Crawford used imagery derived from it to

splendid effect in poems like 'The Camp of Souls' and 'Said the Canoe', but put it to the service of an imagination that sublimated her own frustrated fantasies. What we have in the end, as in the final stanzas of 'Said the Canoe', is an autonomous and highly coloured vision that pays glancing acknowledgment to the darker authenticity of Indian life.

> They hung the slaughtered fish like swords
>   On saplings slender; like scimitars,
>   Bright, and ruddied from new-dead wars,
> Blazed in the light the scaly hordes.
>
> They piled up boughs beneath the trees,
>   Close round the camp, and at its curtain
>   Pressed shapes, thin, woven and uncertain
> As white locks of tall waterfalls.

Only towards the end of the nineteenth century did a Canadian poet attempt to perceive the condition of Indian life as it was and to make poetry out of it. Duncan Campbell Scott strikingly displayed the ambivalence of Canadian attitudes and even actions. He was a federal civil servant who had entered the Department of Indian Affairs as a boy of seventeen and stayed there all his working life, until he retired in 1932 as deputy superintendent general. As a civil servant he did not act in a particularly enlightened way. Without much overt questioning he implemented the often harsh and usually insensitive policies of his superiors; yet he was not insensitive to the hardness and pathos of Indian life as he observed it and heard about it during his journeys into the northern forest lands. Out of his empathetic understanding emerged a series of poems—like 'On the Way to the Mission', 'The Forsaken', and 'At Gull Lake: August, 1810'—that have a special authenticity because they not only embody compassionate perceptions of native life but also belong in feeling and in form to Scott's own evolving literary culture. 'The Forsaken' is a familiar enough poem, with its wholly plausible presentation of an Indian life: that of a young woman who gives her own flesh as bait to catch fish and feed her child in the frozen wilderness, yet who in old age is abandoned by the same child because she will be a useless burden on the clan. There is no moral criticism:

> But in the frost of the dawn,
> Up from the life below,
> Rose a column of breath
> Through a tiny cleft in the snow,
> Fragile, delicately drawn,
> Wavering with its own weakness,
> In the wilderness a sign of the spirit,
> Persisting still in the sight of the sun
> Till day was done.
> Then all light was gathered up by the hand of God and hid in his breast,

Then there was born a silence deeper than silence,
Then she had rest.

For this rather successful reconciliation of Indian actuality and white reaction, the Keatsian and Tennysonian verse forms that had suited Scott's contemporaries and associates, such as Lampman and Carman and Roberts, were no longer adequate. Scott began to evolve a freer form, and in his Indian poems—and some later almost imagistic pieces, like 'En Route'—we can see the beginning of a transition between the Canadian Victorian romantics and the Canadian modernists of the 1920s and 1930s, whose careers actually overlapped Scott's.

While the white men were reacting in their various ways to their encounter with aboriginal inhabitants of Canada, some natives were moving from an oral to a literary age. But the treaty gatherings, beginning in 1871, still furnished them with occasions to display the oratorical eloquence they had shown in their own conciliar gatherings in the past. The sentiments expressed were always broad and generous, and the imagery, like that of Homer and the great oral bards of the Old World, tended to run in rather conventionalized channels, as one can see by reading the speeches of the treaty-signing chiefs that Alexander Morris, then Lieutenant-Governor of the Northwest Territories, recorded in *The Treaties of Canada with the Indians of the North-west* (1880).

Here is Mawedopenais of the Ojibway declaring in 1873:

> . . . what has been done here today has been done before the Great Spirit and before the nation; and now in closing this council I take off my glove, and in giving you my hand I deliver over my birthright and lands; and in taking your hand I hold fast all the promises you have made, and I hope they will last as long as the sun rises and the river flows, as you have said.

Here is the Cree, Chief Sweet Grass, speaking at Fort Carlton in 1876:

> When I hold your hand I feel as if the Great Father were looking on us both as brothers. I am thankful. May this earth here never see the white man's blood spilt on it. I thank God that we stand together, that you all see us: I am thankful that I can raise up my head, and the white man and red man can stand together as long as the sun shines.

And here is old Crowfoot signing on behalf of his people at Blackfoot Crossing in 1877 and alone giving a hint of the dark necessities that were forcing the Indians to come to the best terms they could get with the white men.

> The advice given me and my people has proved to be very good. If the police had not come to this country, where would we all be now? Bad men and whiskey were killing us so fast that very few of us would have

been alive today. The Mounted Police have protected us as the fathers of a bird protect it from the frosts of winter. I wish them all good, and I trust that all our hearts will increase in goodness from this time forward. I will sign the treaty.

Reading such statements, one is struck by the pathos they assume in historical retrospect, in their naïve assumptions that these were indeed treaties between equal powers, and in their lack of attention to the greater disaster that was about to overcome all the native societies of the West through the collapse of their ancient economy when the buffalo came no more. There was even more passion, and also more poetry, in the outcries of the malcontents who realized that the old way of life was doomed and who refused to 'go gentle into that good night'.

The Ojibway chief Pequis had welcomed the Selkirk settlers in 1812 and had refused to join in the efforts of the North West Company and the Métis to destroy the Red River Settlement. He had even been converted and had taken the name of William King as befitting his rank. But before his death in 1864 he spoke out bitterly on the destruction of his people's environment by the coming of the whites.

> Before you whites came to trouble the ground, our rivers were full of fish and woods of deer. Our creeks abounded with beavers and our plains were covered with buffalo. But now we are brought to poverty. Our beavers are gone for ever; our buffalo are fled to the land of our enemies. The number of our fish is diminishing . . . . The geese are afraid to pass over the smoke of our chimneys and we are left to starve while you whites are growing rich on the very dust of our fathers, troubling the plains with the plough, covering them with cows in the summer and in the winter feeding them with hay from the very swamps whence our beavers have been driven.

The Cree chief Piapot refused to be converted, and considered native beliefs better than those the missionaries offered. In the 1880s he defied the government by practising the illegal rain dances, and when the authorities removed him from his office of chief, the tribe still treated him as their leader.

> You can kill me and scalp me but you cannot scare me [Piapot declared]. Nobody will find the Great Spirit through fear. That is not his plan. His voice can be heard by Indians as well as whites, but Indians are the best listeners. I have more faith in what I have heard from the Great Spirit than in what I have heard from you.

Such men were defending with dignity a culture that was being threatened more than they knew and could not survive long into the nineteenth century. By surviving and increasing as a people, the Indians might refute those who prophesied their extinction, but their ways of life and their artistic traditions could not possibly continue in the pristine forms in which white men first encountered them. Yet some astonishing outbursts of creativity attended the demise of the aboriginal patterns of living. There is one anecdote, at once pathetic and inspiring, that seems to set a light in the darkness of that passage in Canadian history. It concerns Nancy Shanadithit, the last survivor of the Beothuk Indians of Newfoundland, who were almost literally hunted to their death in the first quarter of the nineteenth century. Nancy was captured in 1823 and looked after by missionaries until her death six years later. In *Newfoundland and Its Missionaries* (1866) the Rev. William Wilson told about her behaviour shortly after her capture.

> A gentleman put a looking-glass before her and her grimaces were most extraordinary, but when a black pencil was put into her hand and a piece of white paper laid upon the table, she was in raptures. She made a few marks on the paper apparently to try the pencil; then in one flourish she drew a deer perfectly, and what is most surprising, she began at the tip of the tail.

So, in such spontaneous ecstasy, the paleolithic artists of Lascaux and Altamira must have drawn their marvellously fluent bulls and bison, reflecting that strange empathy between the hunter and the hunted that helped to shape primitive man's view of his world and its inhabitants, that complex of creatures whom the Buddhist would later embrace with the phrase 'all living beings'.

A striking aspect of the story of Nancy Shanadithit is her quickness to use materials she has never seen before. Presumably—since the Beothuks painted themselves with red ochre (which led the inhabitants of the Americas to become known as Red Indians)—they made drawings with this tincture, using sticks as brushes. Nancy adopted with ease the transfer from drawing on rock with a stick and ochre to drawing with a pencil on paper. In the same way the wood-carvers of the Pacific coast—who had already created masterpieces of sculpture in wood, using jade adzes and chisels made from beaver teeth for their finer work—seized immediately on the metal tools brought to their coast by Captain Cook and the Spanish explorers and the sea traders whom they variously called King George's Men (British) and Boston Men (American). Having obtained steel knives and chisels, the Haida, Tsimshian, and Kwakiutl artists for a generation—roughly from 1870 to 1900—worked at the height of their powers and, with acquired tools and traditional concepts, created what, with a modicum of exaggeration, Claude Lévi-Strauss has described as 'an art on a par with that of Greece or Egypt'.

Canadian Indians during this period of transition produced nothing in literature comparable to the achievements of Pacific Coast Indians in the plastic arts. Nevertheless, while ethnologists, with Henry Schoolcraft in the lead, began to collect the traditional tales and legends of the native peoples of what later became Canada, the missionaries were having an influence on literature analogous to that of the chisel-selling trader on West Coast sculpture. As the natives of Ontario—the Chippewa and the Ojibway—became converted during the first half of the nineteenth century, some of their most intelligent young men, who had connections with chiefs, were educated in English, and eventually produced the first works written by Canadian Indians in that language.

The most important of them, George Copway and Peter Jones, became Methodist ministers (though Copway was later converted to Roman Catholicism), and their works showed a striking similarity of pattern. Each produced an autobiography: respectively these were *The Life, History and Travels of Kah-ge-ga-gah-bowh (George Copway), a Young Indian Chief of the Ojibway Nation, a Convert to the Christian Faith, and a Missionary to His People for Twelve Years* (1847), and *Life and Journals of Kah-Ke-Wa-Quo-Na-By (Rev. Peter Jones) Wesleyan Minister* (1860). Each also wrote a history of the Ojibway people. Their intentions were frankly didactic rather than literary; Copway in fact proclaimed that he wrote to 'awaken in the American heart a deeper feeling for the race of red men, and induce the pale-face to use greater effort to effect an improvement in their social and political relations.'

Part of the strategy of both Copway and Jones was to diminish the distance between Indians and white men by portraying traditional Indian life in an appealing way, and suggesting that peoples like the Ojibway already had moral and religious attitudes that predisposed them towards Christianity and thus made them worthy of the help of Christians in adapting themselves to the new world that was growing up around them; in fact, Copway added 'an appeal' in these terms to his autobiography. They made their writing personal and anecdotal, and wrote of the old Indian life in a way that would attract the sympathy of white readers by stressing the community of need and feeling between the two peoples. Here is a typical story from Copway's autobiography:

> To obtain furs of different kinds for the traders, we had to travel far into the woods, and remain there the whole winter. Once we left Rice Lake in the fall, and ascended the river in canoes as far as Belmont Lake. There were five families about to hunt with my father on his ground. The winter began to set in, and the river having frozen over, we left the canoes, the dried venison, the beaver, and some flour and pork, and when we had gone farther north, say about sixty miles from the white settlements, for the purpose of hunting, the snow fell for five days in succession, to such a depth, that it was impossible to shoot or trap anything. Here we were, the snow about five feet deep, our wigwam buried, the branches of the trees falling all about us, and cracking with the weight of the snow.
>
> Our mother boiled birch-bark for my sister and myself, that we might not starve. On the seventh day some of us were so weak they could not guard themselves, and others could not stand alone. They could only

crawl in and out of the wigwam. We parched beaver skins and old mocassins for food. On the ninth day none of the men could go abroad except
my father and uncle. On the tenth day, still being without food, the only
ones able to walk about the wigwam were my father, my grandmother,
my sister and myself . . . .

On the eleventh day, just before daylight, my father fell into a sleep;
he soon awoke, and said to me: 'My son, the good Spirit is about to bless
us this night; in my dream I saw a person coming from the east walking
on the tops of the trees; he told me we should obtain two beavers about
nine o'clock. Put on your mocassins, and go along with me to the river,
and we will hunt beaver, perhaps, for the last time.' I saw his countenance
beamed with delight and hope; he was full of confidence. I put on my
mocassins and carried my snow-shoes, staggering along behind him about
half a mile. Having made a fire near the river, where there was an air-
hole through which the beaver had come up during the night, my father
tied a gun to the stump with the muzzle towards the air-hole; he also tied
a string to the trigger, and said, 'Should you see the beaver rise, pull the
string and you will kill it.' I stood by the fire, with the string in my hand;
I soon heard the noise occasioned by the blow of his tomahawk; he had
killed a beaver and brought it to me. As he laid it down, he said, 'Then
the great Spirit will not let us die here;' adding, as before, 'if you see the
beaver rise, pull the string;' and he left me. I soon saw the nose of one,
but I did not shoot. Presently, another came up; I pulled the trigger, and
off the gun went. I could not see for some moments for the smoke. My
father ran towards me with the two beavers, and laid them side by side;
then, pointing to the sun, 'Do you see the sun?' he said; 'the great Spirit
informed me that we should kill these two about this time in the morning.
We will yet see our relatives at Rice Lake. Now let us go home and see if
our people are yet alive.' We arrived just in time to save them from death.

This story shows narrative skills very similar to the traditional Indian
tales that ethnologists were beginning to collect in this period. But it is
also clearly written with the intention of stressing the intervention of
Providence in human affairs, a conclusion that was congenial to the
Victorian mind.

Something of the dilemma in which converted Indians found themselves can be seen by reading the writings of the half-Indian Peter Jones.
In his *History of the Ojebway Indians* (1861) he indicates how ill the white
men repaid the Indians who wished to be friendly towards them:

Our fathers held out to them the hand of friendship. The strangers then
asked for a small piece of land on which they might pitch their tents; the
request was cheerfully granted. By and by they begged for more, and more
was given them. In this way they had continued to ask, or have obtained
by force or fraud, the fairest portions of our territory.

Yet in a sermon preached in 1830, Jones was clearly willing to accept a
heavenly rather than an earthly resolution, through conversion rather
than through restitution:

My white friends, there was a time when all this country belonged to our Indian fathers. Our fathers used to fish in these rivers and hunt through these woods; and where your houses now stand, there stood their wigwams. But the white men came across the great waters,—and the Indians drank the fire waters and they died. And now we are almost all gone, there are a few in the west, and a handful of us in the north. And what do the Indians ask of you? do we want our land back again? NO: we do not want our land back again! Do we want your fine houses, or your fine farms? No: we do not! All we say is, Send us the gospel—send us missionaries, and we are satisfied.

The first Indian to write with a literary intent, and the first to produce a body of poetry in English that would attract wide public attention, was Pauline Johnson (1861-1913). The daughter of a Mohawk chief and an English mother—and Sara Jeannette Duncan's contemporary in the schools of Brantford, Ontario—she was one of the earliest Canadian poets to develop a public-reading circuit, appearing both in conventional evening-dress and in an Indian costume of buckskin. This dual guise reflected the ambivalence of her poetry, for though she presented herself as an Indian, and featured her own 'Indian' poems, her work was moulded by the same Victorian romantic influences that shaped the writing of her non-Indian contemporaries in Canada. A good example is 'Ojistoh', a rather sensational 'noble savage' narrative poem that tells of a young woman, in love with a Mohawk brave, who is forced to marry a Huron she despises; she murders her would-be husband as he is taking her to his home, and flees to rejoin her lover. The last verse, which is not without spirit, could have been written by a disciple of Sir Walter Scott:

> Ha! how I rode, rode as a sea wind-chased,
> Mad with sudden freedom, mad with haste,
> Back to my Mohawk and my home. I lashed
> That horse to foam, as on and on I dashed.
> Plunging thro' creek and river, bush and trail,
> On, on I galloped like a northern gale.
> And then my distant Mohawk's fires aflame
> I saw, as nearer, nearer still I came,
> My hands all wet, stained with a life's red dye,
> But pure my soul, pure as those stars on high—
> 'My Mohawk's pure white star, Ojistoh, still am I.'

With her deep feelings, her histrionic power, and shallow literary pretensions, Pauline Johnson almost personified a dilemma of the times: the educated Indian, suspended between the collapse of the old cultures and the rise of a new sense of identity, who was left to wander, like Matthew Arnold's traveller, 'between two worlds, one dead,/ The other powerless to be born'.

8

Neighbours and Strangers

For the poet-politician Thomas D'Arcy McGee, that most sympathetic of Canadian founding fathers, ours seemed a land where liberties and minorities might flourish. That was one of his reasons for leaving the United States. In 1865, eight years after he had shaken from his footsoles the dust of the Land of the Free, he eulogized the flexibility of Canadian society, as distinguished from the rigidity in the United States:

> To the American citizen who boasts of greater liberty in the States, I say that a man can state his private, social, political and religious opinions with more freedom here than in New York or New England. There is, besides, far more liberty and toleration enjoyed by minorities in Canada than in the United States. I would rather be the serf of a Russian boyar than of that many-sided monster, public opinion, that will not permit me to have my own private opinions on subjects social, religious, national and political.

McGee was an open-minded Irishman seeking refuge from the narrow fanaticism of the Fenians, which led him to leave New York for Montreal: for this the Fenians regarded him as a traitor to the cause of Ireland, and eventually they would kill him on his Ottawa doorstep in 1868. He needed to see Canada as an open haven, as hundreds of thousands of people have done since, fleeing from unendurable persecution or, more often, from unendurable poverty.

But the reality has never been quite so benign as it seemed to McGee in his euphoric moments. During our period the relations, first of all between the French and the English, and then between those 'founding peoples' and the other peoples who arrived in the great migrations of the nineteenth and early twentieth century, were often more tortuous, more ridden with hostilities and heartbreaks than those who have tried to see Canada as a working pluralist society might admit.

The tensions between communities that emerged in this period have a great deal to do with the immense demographic changes of the century. In 1814 the French-speaking and English-speaking inhabitants of the Canadas were numerically roughly equal. And it is likely, though we have no clear date, that the number of native peoples in the whole of British North America—before the great epidemics of smallpox, measles, and influenza—was more or less equal to that of white people. By 1901 the proportions had shifted so much that the 100,000 or so surviving natives represented about 2 per cent of a population of about five and a half million, and despite a phenomenal birth-rate and an enormous increase in numbers, French-speakers had fallen to about 30 per cent of the population. At the same time the settlement of the Prairies brought in hundreds of thousands of people who were neither French nor British in origin or language. In 1901 they formed 12 per cent of the population and by the Great War they had reached 15 per cent.

I cite these demographic figures merely to indicate the great proportional changes in the population of Canada that took place during the century between the War of 1812 and the Great War. The chief concern of this chapter is the way the people of the time saw and were affected by these changing relationships, and how they accepted them.

Even a few years after the end of the War of 1812 visitors noticed the way the population of the Canadas was being differentiated. In 1820, in a pamphlet entitled 'A Few Plain Directions . . .', 'an English Farmer' still talked of an Upper Canada where the American Loyalist element remained dominant.

> The inhabitants of Upper Canada consist of British and Americans, with several families of German, and some of French extraction. From this mixture arises a great diversity of manner and customs in the province. But as the emigrants from the United States form by far the greater moiety of the people, the rest are, in some measure, compelled to conform to their habits and usages.

By 1830 the situation had already changed markedly. The first great waves of immigrants, as yet almost entirely from the British Isles, were arriving in Quebec and Montreal and mostly spilling over into the unoccupied backwoods of Upper Canada. William Lyon Mackenzie, writing in 1830, welcomed the influx of working people from Scotland, doubtless because he saw it as counterbalancing the great influx at the same time of members of the English gentry and middle class.

> I perceive that shiploads of industrious and active mechanics are arriving with their families from Scotland—and truly I am right glad of their immigration—North America will hold them all, and the curse of poverty, oppressive taxation, and corn bills they will feel no more. I have found much reason to rejoice and be glad of the day when I left my native town for this country, now ten years back—and when I read of the hunger and hardships which an industrious and hard-working people are enduring at the hands of that landed gentry and borough-mongers of Scotland, I regret that the means of emigration, both from highlands and lowlands are not more easy and extensive—many are too poor to come here.

In those days the level of tolerance for strange customs, and what seemed to the majority eccentric beliefs, seems to have been relatively high. William Dunlop (though he seems to have confused Quakers and Mennonites because they both held pacifist beliefs) spoke well, if somewhat condescendingly, of the German and Dutch sectarians who had come to Upper Canada with the Loyalists and for a long time remained the principal community in the Canadas that stood outside the pattern of Franco-English relations:

> There are a good many Quakers and Low Dutch among the inhabitants of this region; and these, though generally ignorant, and prejudiced in favour of the wisdom of their ancestors, to such an extent that many of them commence sowing, reaping and other agricultural operations on the day of the month that tradition has sanctified as the proper day for such labours, without paying the slightest attention to existing circumstances, are almost uniformly men of sober, steady, and industrious habits, and such, in all countries, will render success in business probable, but in this case certain.

It was when the emigrations began to swell in numbers in the 1830s—consisting often of poverty-stricken Irish or of English paupers who carried with them year after year into Canadian cities the plague of cholera—that attitudes towards the newcomers became more apprehensive. In September 1832 John Strachan wrote to an unnamed correspondent:

> We are just beginning to breathe from the cholera. Next to Quebec and Montreal, this place [York] suffered most; some indeed say that it has been more fatal here, than in any other place on the continent. The stream of emigration has been very great this season; upwards of 50,000 have already landed at Quebec and four-fifths of this number direct their course to Upper Canada—the majority of them reaching this place. The journey from Quebec (600 miles) is so long and tedious, that it exhausts the little pittance they had on landing; so that a great portion of them arrive here penniless. The terrible disease attacked them as they journeyed hither; many died on the way; others were landed in various stages after they

came among us. In short, York became one general hospital . . . . It is computed that one in four of the adults of this town were attacked, and that one-twelfth of the whole population died. Our duty, as you will understand, throws us, clergymen, into the very midst of such calamities; at no time, more than during such contagious sicknesses, do people require the consolations of religion.

Strachan did not spare himself. In epidemic after epidemic we see him on duty visiting the cholera hospitals, seeking out sufferers in private houses, and burying the dead eight and nine at a time, with no apparent thought that his safety might be more important than what he regarded as his Christian obligations. At such times he showed his most admirable qualities. But his patience began to wear thin. Writing in 1847, at the end of the year of great migration when the Irish had fled their country in tens of thousands as a result of the potato famine, he spoke sadly this time of the death of 'many of our inhabitants when charity induced them to minister to the necessities of these unhappy strangers.' And he ended in a tone that seemed to dismiss the Irish as immigrants who might contribute effectively to the life of their new country.

What adds greatly to the calamity, the poor emigrants who survive are seldom able or disposed to be industrious. Many are old and feeble and totally incapable of work; many are children not yet old enough to be useful; and a large proportion of them who are able to do something are so awkward and ignorant of the methods of the country.

These sickness-ridden migrations aroused fear and resentment among Canadians, but the resentment was more often against the British authorities who had allowed them to come and the absentee landowners who had been glad to rid their Irish estates of thousands of starving peasants. Shipowners who had not provided adequately for their passengers were also criticized, and Patrick Shirreff in *A Tour Through North America* (1835) was one of many who condemned the entrepreneurs who transported poor immigrants from Montreal to Upper Canada in *bateaux* towed behind passenger steamers:

. . . in one . . . I counted 110 immigrants of all ages, who were doomed to pass the night on board. Men, women and children were huddled together as closed as captives in a slave-trader exposed to the sun's rays by day and river-damp by night, without protection.

Indignant compassion often overcame prejudice in references to the immigrants, as in this protest from the *Quebec Mercury* of 3 August 1854:

We regret to learn that owing to want of attention on the part of the Board of Health, the emigrants as they are landed are allowed to stay whole days and even nights on the wharves of the Lower Town, awaiting the steamers in which they are packed like cattle for the upper country. A shipload of these creatures remained on the Napoleon wharf all day Tuesday, and when the heavy thunder showers of the night fell, they were still unprotected from either the rain or cold or night air. There were a great number of females and children among them, and for want of proper provisions or a place to cook them, they were to be seen feeding upon raw pork and unripe apples and cherries.

Despite his concern, the writer could not resist showing his superiority by alluding to the immigrants as if they were abused animals—'creatures' rather than human beings, 'females' rather than women. But the experience of the shared life of the backwoods could be a remarkable solvent of deeply held prejudices. Susanna Moodie wrote an unconsciously revealing letter on Boxing Day 1868 to an old English friend, Allen Ransome:

So here we are—living in a little cottage with just room enough to hold us, but beautifully situated on the edge of our lovely bay, with a fine common in front covered with noble trees through which we see the spires of Belleville about a mile distant, and for which we pay a rent of 12 pounds and the rate 10 dollars.

A further twelve pounds went on the wages of her servant Margaret—

for I am too old, now 65, for hard work and am able to earn the money that pays her wages. She is a good and faithful woman though *Irish* and a *Catholic*, and lived with us in our prosperity and will not leave us in age and poverty, and whom I regard as a tried and valued friend.

Clearly a double process was at work here. Shared experience brought together people whose backgrounds might have made them strangers in their native settings. Yet the very geography of the unsettled land often made contact intermittent, and therefore not oppressive.

It is true that these British immigrants brought with them the racial, religious, and political battles they had been fighting for centuries in their homeland. The Catholic Irish carried as part of their scanty baggage an inherited hatred of English oppression; yet, unlike their compatriots in the United States, they did not organize themselves into Fenian commandos dedicated to attacking British institutions. Perhaps this was because they quickly emerged from a minority situation once they reached Canada; in 1871, among the English-speaking inhabitants of the new Dominion, they numbered nearly 850,000, as against 700,000 English and half a million Scots; the Welsh were a scanty fourth. The home-grown enemy accompanying the Catholic Irish from Ireland were the Protestants. Some of the latter in nineteenth-century Canada—like the Baldwins and the Blakes—were among the least-tainted politicians; but others imported from Britain the officially discountenanced traditions and rituals of the anti-Catholic Orange Order. William Lyon Mackenzie included the Order among the many objects of his denunciation:

Orange Lodges in this Colony are a dangerous nuisance, of the most strictly exclusive kind, from which Catholics are always kept, and their main objects is to oppose and oppress the Catholics.

He went on to ask: 'How, then, comes it that the heads of government here, trifling with the powers entrusted to them, are cherishing this public pest?'

His apprehensions were not without foundation, for the Orangemen converted many of the descendants of the Loyalists to their conservative cause, and the processions marching on the 12th of July to the beat of drums, with King Billy's surrogate riding on his white horse at the head, became a part of Ontario folk culture that persisted well into the present century. Politically, too, as Mackenzie had feared, the Orange Order became powerful within the Conservative Party, and for decades virtually controlled municipal affairs in Toronto.

Even local feuds were transported intact from the old country. One of them, in 1880, resulted in a famous Canadian murder, when five members of the Donnelly family were slaughtered by otherwise respectable neighbours in pursuance of a vendetta that had found its way, via the emigrant ships, from Tipperary to Biddulph County, Ontario. The murderers were well known, and their guilt was proved in court by eyewitnesses; but no local jury dared convict. These were only the most sensational deaths. Provocative Orange marches and Catholic parades often resulted in assaults and deaths. But during these violent decades the Irish fought mainly with each other. They eventually merged into the general mass of Anglo-Celtic Canadians that sustained no deep intergroup conflicts based on race or faith.

Common language proved to be a great counter-force against the differences that spilled over from the British homeland. There was also the fact that no racial group settled compactly in a single area. The Scots were settled from Cape Breton in the East to the Red River in the West, the Irish were strong in Newfoundland and Upper Canada, and the English were to be found everywhere from St John's to Victoria—as, in much smaller numbers, were the Welsh.

This was in sharp contrast to the French Canadians, who never moved out in large numbers to the major areas of settlement in the West, and remained concentrated in a compact area consisting of Quebec, the Acadian regions of New Brunswick, and the areas of northern Ontario where French-Canadian farmers had pushed over the border from Quebec. To this close geographical unity was joined a complex cultural unity in which a shared language and a shared religion were combined with a shared sense of being a conquered people determined to survive.

But though the French population lived mainly in a closely defined region—one province and adjacent parts of two others—that area was not homogeneously French. In 1851 no less than 25 per cent of the population of Canada East was English-speaking, concentrated mostly in the two main cities of Montreal and Quebec and in the Eastern Townships, which had been settled by the Loyalists in the 1780s. In the earlier part of the century visitors were impressed by the varied peoples to be encountered in the streets of Montreal. Writing in 1841, Sir Richard Bonnycastle, an officer in the Royal Engineers, remarked:

> In this city, one is amused by seeing the never-changing lineaments, the long queue, the bonnet-rouge, and the incessant garrulity, of Jean Baptiste, mingling with the sober demeanour, the equally unchanging features, and the national plaid, of the Highlander; whilst the untutored sons of labour, from the green isle of the ocean, are here as thoughtless, as ragged, and as numerous, as at Quebec. Amongst all these, the shrewd and calculating citizen from the neighbouring republic drives his hard bargains with all his unwonted zeal and industry, amid the fumes of Jamaica and gin-sling.

Not all the English lived in the cities or the Eastern Townships. Some of the merchants had acquired seigneuries in rural Quebec, where they were liable to become targets of particular resentment on the part of insurrectionary *habitants* during the Rebellion of 1837-8. One renowned English beauty caught in such a precarious situation was Katherine Jane Balfour, who in 1834 had married Edward Ellice, son of the famous 'Bear' Ellice who negotiated the union of the North West Company and the Hudson's Bay Company. Edward Ellice accompanied Lord Durham to Canada as his secretary, and when the second Lower Canadian rebellion broke out in November 1838, he and Jane were staying at the family's seigneury at Beauharnois. On the evening of 4 November, she wrote an excited note in her diary (now in the National Archives of Canada):

> It's an odd thing that last night when we went to bed both Tina & I said we thought something was going to happen—Twice I awoke Edward, because we heard the dogs barking & *Turkeys* making a noise—About 1 o'clock a messenger came saying there was a disturbance at Chateauguai & several British farmers had fled from the Canadian rebels—E.E. had hardly come to bed again when we thought we heard a *hallo*—he opened the window & listened but all was still, & just as he was getting into bed a yell like *the Indian war cry*, burst close to the house & guns fired at the same moment—struck the house on all sides, breaking the windows &c. Edward jumped into his clothes, & drag'd Tiny & I along, *en chemise*, without shoes or stockings downstairs & put us thro' a trapdoor into the cellar—The house was surrounded on all sides, Edward & Mr. Brown taken prisoners, and were carried off we knew not where, leaving Tina & I alone, *en chemise* in the middle of a group of the most 'Robespierre' looking ruffians, all armed with guns, long knives and pikes, without a single creature to advise us, every respectable person in the village having been taken prisoner—What a day we passed sitting hand in hand, in the

midst of a heap confusion, comforting each other, & praying for protection to Him who orders all things well. But it was severe trial—The ruffian looking men coming in every now & then quite drunk—In the evening the priest came to see us, & we got leave to come to his house.—What a wretched day & yet how much worse it might have been.

Eventually the Ellices were rescued, though Jane spent several anxious days under a kind of house arrest; she did not lose her spirit, and one day painted a water-colour, vibrant with haste, of pike-bearing *habitant patriotes*. They looked remarkably like the Victorian image of Parisian *sans culottes*, and this was undoubtedly how upper-class Britons in Lower Canada, scared by the second insurrection, saw the rebels and perhaps even the majority of the Québécois at the time. Clearly this was what Lord Durham had in mind when he talked of the 'deadly animosity' he saw separating 'the inhabitants of Lower Canada into the hostile divisions of French and English'.

Yet all cannot have been animosity; otherwise there would not have been the assimilations that so surprised André Siegfried around the turn of the century, when he realized that

in the province of Quebec one finds families of Englishmen, Irishmen, and especially Scotsmen, becoming French Canadians within two generations. They call themselves Fraser, Barrie, Macleod, but they speak our [French] language with an unmistakable Norman accent, without any trace in it of British pronunciation.

There is no doubt that, by assimilation, by heavy breeding, by infiltrating the cities and the Eastern Townships, the French eroded the British presence in their province; by 1901 it had fallen to 18 per cent. Yet there remained hard, uncompromising nuclei of the British presence, enclaves whose inhabitants seemed to have assumed much the same attitude towards the 'natives' as was held by the sahibs and memsahibs inhabiting their cantonments on the peripheries of Indian cities. André Siegfried, an untypical Frenchmen who was often sharply critical of the French Canadians, was strongly aware of this situation in both Quebec and Montreal:

Quebec . . . does not give the immediate impression of a city of ours; many sensitive observant visitors have felt that. In this city of 69,000, of whom not more than 10,000 are English, there are more parts where French is not understood; perhaps it is more accurate to say where people *will* not understand it. On the railways it is tolerated at best. At the Chateau Frontenac, that marvel of comfort and elegance created by the Canadian Pacific, the principal employees do perhaps understand it, but they refuse to speak it . . . . The French Canadians have come to put up with this kind of not very pleasant obstinacy. They learn English, and in that they are wise enough; but they have never been able to get their rivals to learn French. And therein we cannot but recognize a really significant defeat.

It is the same in Montreal. Visitors may pass whole weeks there, frequenting hotels, banks, shops, railway stations, without ever imagining for a moment that the town is French by a great majority of its inhabitants. English society affects unconsciousness of this fact, and bears itself exactly as though it had no French neighbours. They seem to regard Montreal as their property.

Things were in fact not much different in the Westmount district of Montreal—an English enclave—than they were in Simla, and in both cases it was because the British of a certain class and kind felt entitled to hold on to the fruits of conquest. These Anglophones had their spokesman in Goldwin Smith who, in one of his more obnoxious moments, declared: 'Either the conquest of Quebec was utterly fatuous or it is to be desired that the American Continent should belong to the English tongue and the Anglo-Saxon civilization.'

Goldwin Smith made his statement as late as 1891. More than fifty years before, an even more distinguished student of North American history had issued his warning against such an attitude. He was the French politician Alexis de Tocqueville, author of *Democracy in America* (4 vols, 1835-40), writing a personal letter of advice in January 1838 (that time of Canadian crisis) to his friend Henry Reeve, the clerk to the British Privy Council:

French Canadians are a separate people in America, a people of a distinct and vivacious national character, a new and healthy people whose origins are entirely warlike, with its language, its religion, its laws, its customs, a nation more densely populated than any other in the new world; which could be conquered but not dissolved by force to be absorbed into the milieu of the Anglo-Saxon race.

Not long afterwards, Lord Elgin—who in his term as Governor-General had more time to observe the two principal peoples of the Canadas than his father-in-law, Lord Durham—had similar things to say:

You may perhaps *Americanize*, but, depend upon it, you will never *Anglicize* the French inhabitants of the province. Let them feel on the other hand that their religion, their habits, their prepossessions and prejudices if you will, are more considered and respected here than in other portions of this vast continent which is being overrun by the most reckless, self-sufficient and dictatorial section of the Anglo Saxon race, and who will venture to say that the last hand which waves the British flag on American ground may not be that of a French Canadian?

Long before Hugh MacLennan wrote *Two Solitudes* (1945), people on both sides of the Canadian cultural frontier were aware of the failing communication between Canadians speaking two different languages. Goldwin Smith declared: 'To make a nation there must be a common life, common sentiments, common aims and common hopes. Of these, in the case of Quebec and Ontario, there is none.' A French Canadian who was far from being committed, like Smith, to the submergence of Canada in a continental structure, voiced similar sentiments about the relations between anglophone and francophone Canadians. He was Pierre Chauveau, who had dedicated a great deal to the cause of a unified Canada. He had been Quebec's first premier after Confederation, became Speaker of the Dominion Senate in 1873, and for more than twenty years edited the bilingual *Journal of Public Instruction*. Yet in 1876, after many years of trying to bring the two groups together, he was moved to remark:

> English and French, we climb by a double flight of stairs toward the destinies reserved for us on this continent, without knowing each other, without meeting each other, and without seeing each other, except on the landing of politics. In social and literary terms, we are far more foreign to each other than the English and French of Europe.

We have already glimpsed what happened in terms of *rapprochment* between English and French Canadians 'on the landing of politics'. In social and literary terms there was, so far as the French Canadians were concerned, a double pattern of withdrawal and assertion.

Late twentieth-century French-Canadian nationalists have claimed control over every aspect of collective life within their linguistic territory. Their counterparts in the later nineteenth century seemed willing not only to accept the control that English-speaking entrepreneurs had established over their commerce, industry, and financial institutions, but to see their society as a land-oriented one, based on the *habitants* who were still the most numerous class in Quebec; young men with education entered the priesthood, or became lawyers and notaries, doctors, and surveyors—roles that were all-important in a land-oriented society. A mystique of the land began to take shape in the minds of conservative French-Canadian nationalists that they associated with a willing surrender of the evils of industry and finance to the Anglo-Celtic heretics.

The most ardent prophets of an agrarian revolution were not stay-at-homes who knew nothing beyond the life lived on the long strip farms beside the St Lawrence. One of the most eloquent, Edmond de Nevers, had travelled widely in Europe, studied in Berlin under the historian Theodor Mommsen, and worked for the Havas Agency in Paris. Returning to Quebec, he became a zealous supporter of a back-to-the-land movement that aimed at colonizing the still-undeveloped northern parts of the province. In his influential book, *L'Avenir du peuple canadien-français* (1896), he declared:

> Certainly it cannot be too often repeated, that the most solid basis for a nation is the possession of the land; that the question of 'repatriation', that is of the return of the agricultural districts of the province of Quebec,

remains the order of the day. Lay hold of the land, as far as circumstances will permit.

Jules-Paul Tardivel, even more active in the same cause, was born in Kentucky; his mother was an American of British descent. But when he came to Canada as a youth, starting a journalistic career shortly afterwards, he became an ardent ultramontanist, writing a biography of Pope Pius IX and a strident nationalist polemic, *L'Anglicisme voilà l'ennemi* (1880). He sought the proper goal for French Canadians by looking fervently backward to pre-Conquest days in the spirit of *reculer pour mieux sauter*.

> God planted in the heart of every French-Canadian patriot a flower of hope. It is the aspiration to establish, on the banks of the St. Lawrence, a New France whose mission will be to continue in this American land the work of Christian civilization that old France carried out with such glory during the long centuries.

He too preached the gospel of an agrarian order, which he argued was the only means the people of Quebec had of preventing themselves from becoming Americans like any others.

> It is no longer that we possess industry and money. We would no longer be French Canadians but Americans almost like the others. Our mission is to possess the earth and spread ideas. To cling to the soil, to raise large families, to maintain the hearths of intellectual and spiritual life, that must be our role in America.

It was perhaps out of the concentration of resources implied in this withdrawal to the land and the home that the affirmation so evident in literary terms at this period in Quebec is at least partly attributable. This affirmation, it has often been said, began as a reaction to what the Lower Canadians regarded as one of the most offensive passages of Lord Durham's Report, a passage that seemed to proclaim their cultural poverty:

> There can hardly be conceived a nationality more destitute of all that can invigorate and elevate a people, than that which is exhibited by the descendants of the French in Lower Canada, owing to their retaining their peculiar language and manners. They are a people with no history and no literature.

Durham was only partly wrong. Lower Canada had a far richer history than the English-speaking provinces of North America, but its characteristic literature was as slow to develop as that of English Canada. The real beginnings of that literature lie in the efforts of a small cluster of brilliant men in the mid-nineteenth century to challenge Durham and create among their fellow Québécois a pride in their past.

The first, and perhaps most influential, of these writers (who in no sense formed a group or set out to create a movement) was François-

Xavier Garneau. His three-volume *Histoire du Canada depuis sa découverte jusqu'à nos jours*, which appeared between 1846 and 1848, actually brought the story of Canada only as far as 1791. As he told Hippolyte Lafontaine, his aim was 'to impress upon this nationality a character that would make it respected in the future'. Greatly influenced by the freedom of thought he had encountered in France during the July monarchy, and also by his discussions with Louis-Joseph Papineau during the period of the book's gestation, Garneau set out to write a liberal-minded book aimed at giving a historical foundation to the concept of a nation, French in culture and language, situated on the North American continent. And, far from retreating into a glorious past, he sought to relate the achievements of that past to his people's present struggles to maintain their identity.

> When we contemplate the history of Canada as a whole, from the time of Champlain till our own day, we first remark its two great divisions,—the period of French supremacy, and that of British domination. The annals of the former are replete with the incidents of wars against the savages and the people of the coterminous British colonies, since become the United States; the other portion is signalized by parliamentary antagonism of the colonists to all infractions of their nationality and designs against their religion.

For Garneau the two stages were inter-fluent, and there is no doubt that he was the first writer to give French Canadians a real sense of their history as a continuing whole. His secularism at first offended the clergy, and led Garneau to make substantial revisions in the 1850s; but the book quickly became the standard work on the past of Quebec and remained so until the middle of the present century, inspiring poets and novelists as well as historians with a heroic account of the survival and the vitality of a small nation living under perpetual challenge.

The first significant French-Canadian novels began to appear in the 1840s. Pierre Chauveau, whom we have already encountered as a politician in his later years, published (anonymously) in 1846 a novel—*Charles Guérin*—in which he projected the classic frustration experienced by the Québécois intellectual until the 1960s:

> In French Canada one must be doctor, priest, notary or lawyer. Outside of these four professions it seems that there is no salvation for the young educated Canadian. If by chance one of us had an invincible distaste for all four; if it was too painful for him to save souls, mutilate bodies, or lose fortunes, there remained only one course for him to take if he were rich, and two if he were poor; to do nothing at all in the first case, to exile himself or starve to death in the second.

Not long afterwards, in the first novel of a brilliant young journalist, Antoine Gérin-Lajoie, the currents of withdrawal and affirmation seemed to come together. *Jean Rivard, le défricheur* (1874) is the story of a young man who finds himself by abandoning professional ambition and returning to the land, establishing a pioneer village in the Eastern Townships that young men join instead of taking the road to the milltowns of New England. This novel, which combines realism and didacticism, can be read with interest even today as a record of a movement aiming at social renewal. It influenced literature by helping to turn young French-Canadian writers away from the double temptation of a negative self-pity—to which Chauveau's *Charles Guérin* is somewhat prone—and an over-romantic immersion in the past.

Evoking the past—in a way that was not wholly romantic, but that struck chords of emulation in readers' minds—was the chosen task of two other important prose writers of this crucial transitional time, the confusing de Gaspés: Philippe Aubert de Gaspé the elder and his son of the same name. Confusion was compounded because Philippe the younger was the first to appear on the literary scene. His rather fragile work, *L'Influence d'un livre*—actually the first French-Canadian novel, published in 1837—was a late-Gothic tale of black magic beside the St Lawrence. Its main interest nowadays lies in its accessories—the legends of the *canadiens*, with which it is studded—rather than in its meagre and derivative plot. More than a quarter of a century later Philippe the elder made his remarkable entry into the literary scene at the age of 76 with a historical romance, *Les Anciens Canadiens*. Immediately on its publication in 1863 it became a classic in Quebec that endures to this day, largely because it evokes so well, in its description of seigneurial life in Canada at the time of the Conquest, the lasting mixed emotions felt by French and English Canadians towards each other. (It became well known in English as *The Canadians of Old*, 1890, translated by Charles G.D. Roberts.) As well as being a novel in the ordinary sense, it is also a great fictional chronicle, crammed with folk-tales and descriptions of old Québécois customs—and as such it was read by generations of Québécois, seeking to call up the romance of a lost past.

Les Anciens Canadiens has an elegiac tone that was largely echoed in the work of the two leading poets of this formative period in French-Canadian literature, Octave Crémazie and Louis Fréchette—though they also expressed an almost aggressive pride. Crémazie was Aubert de Gaspé's contemporary. A bookseller with radical inclinations, he established a high reputation as a poet in the 1850s, but left for France in 1862, pursued by rumours of questionable financial deals. In Paris he tried in vain to make a new literary career for himself under the name of 'Jules Fontaine', and died in near-poverty in 1879. He was remembered in Canada for the poems that celebrated, as ambitiously as Garneau's prose narrative, the great past of New France, such as his poem of 1858, 'Le drapeau de Carillon', which tells of Montcalm's victory at Ticonderoga.

Louis Fréchette, the only other Québécois poet of importance before the appearance of Émile Nelligan and his associates of the École Littéraire de Montreal in the 1890s, contributed to the mid-century literary movement the one Canadian historical poem written in French that rivals those of E.J. Pratt in English. *La légende d'un peuple* (1887) celebrates the heroes and heroic deeds of the French-Canadian past in a series of forty-seven tableaux set in eloquently evoked landscapes. The historical details are not always accurate, but one never doubts the sincerity of the patriotic passion that makes this loose and massive work a Québécois classic, even though at times the expression may seem overwrought.

There is a kind of incipient hysteria in such poems that doubtless arose from the lack of a compelling symbolic issue at the time—one that could give definition to the dialectic of French-English relations. The rebellions were over, and their leaders in many cases had moved into the national mainstream of politics. Following Confederation, which it was hoped would solve the problems created by the Act of Union in 1840, the centralism of Sir John A. Macdonald in the 1880s was forcing Canadians of all groups to reconsider what they meant by federalism, and provincial-rights movements were becoming strong. In Quebec the old fears of English domination were emerging and centring on the Parti National, founded in 1871 and now falling increasingly under the leadership of the maverick Liberal demagogue, Honoré Mercier.

The times demanded an issue, and it emerged in 1885 when the Métis leader Louis Riel was condemned to death in Regina. This led to a veritable explosion of emotion in Quebec that took on social and cultural as well as political overtones, and changed not only the shape of Canadian politics but also the way French Canadians saw their position within a confederated Canada.

There are some curious aspects in this outburst. Quebec's interest in western Canada had diminished rapidly when Montreal ceased to be the depot for the fur trade after the union of the two great companies in 1821. During the Red River Rebellion of 1869-70 Louis Riel's provisional government aroused little interest and got scanty support in Quebec. After the creation of Manitoba in 1870, only a few small French-speaking groups responded to the call to emigrate westwards. In 1885 more than 500 French-Canadian volunteers joined the force led by General Middleton against Gabriel Dumont's tiny army at Batoche, and few protested their departure. It is true indeed that even before the troops set out for Batoche, some French-language papers called for commissioners of enquiry to be sent instead of soldiers, and raised the matter of race by suggesting that the Métis were being persecuted for their

French origins and Catholic religion; *L'Étendard* appealed for support for the rebels in the name of 'the voice of blood'. But the leaders of the Catholic Church, who had given both moral and material support to the uprising in 1870, denounced the Northwest Rebellion, and described Riel, for his anti-clerical pronouncements, as a heretic and an enemy of the Church.

Even while the fighting was going on in May 1885, and while Riel was being tried in July, the atmosphere remained muted. It was when he was condemned to death, and the debate over his reprieve began, that racial passions—which it was hoped had been lulled into somnolescence by the political compromises of Confederation—were brought to the surface. Riel might be a member of the Métis nation that the people of Quebec had so long neglected and perhaps secretly despised; he might be a heretic condemned by the clergy; he might represent the problems of western Canada, which had been ignored east of the Ottawa River. Yet the image of a French-speaking rebel at the mercy of his English-speaking enemies touched a chord of sympathy among French Canadians—just as the thought that he might go unpunished stirred the anger of Orangemen in Ontario. The French press attacked the *Orangeiste* policies of the government and raised Riel to the status of a Gallic hero. *L'Électeur* declared:

> History will consecrate a glorious page to you, and your name will be engraved in the hearts of all true French Canadians . . .. Your personal faults will be effaced by the sanctity of the noble cause whose champion you have made yourself. Joan of Arc! Napoleon! Chenier! Riel! it is with the deepest respect that we pronounce your sacred names. Chenier has his monument, and you, Riel, will have yours.

On 22 November, the Sunday following Riel's execution, one of the most important gatherings in nineteenth-century Canada took place—though it has not always been recognized as such. In the greatest public meeting yet held in the province of Quebec, fifty thousand Montrealers poured into the Champ de Mars to surround the three platforms on which thirty-seven orators spoke in turn, with *tricolor* and *fleur-de-lys* banners floating above them. There were veteran ultramontane *castors* like Senator François-Xavier Trudel, who compared Riel with Christ; and less exalted *bleus*, like Israel Tarte and Alphonse Desjardins, former supporters of Cartier and Macdonald. There was Wilfrid Laurier, leader of the Quebec *rouges* and soon to become leader of the dominion-wide Liberal Party, whipping the crowds to enthusiasm when he declared, far away from the battlefield:

> Had I been born on the banks of the Saskatchewan, I would myself have shouldered a musket to fight against the neglect of governments and the shameless greed of the speculators.

And there was Honoré Mercier, who virtually propelled himself into the premiership of Quebec two years later with the bitter speech he made in the Champ de Mars, pitting hatred against hatred, and denouncing not only Sir John A. but also the Québécois ministers who had stood by him over the question of Riel's execution.

> Riel, our brother, is dead, victim of his devotion to the cause of the Métis of whom he was the leader, victim of fanaticism and treason—of the fanaticism of Sir John and some of his friends, of the treason of three of our brothers who sold their brother to keep their portfolios.
> In killing Riel, Sir John has not only struck a blow at the heart of our race, but above all he struck the cause of justice and humanity which, represented in all languages and sanctified by all religious beliefs, begged mercy for the prisoner of Regina, our poor brother of the North-West.

One of the results was an outburst of Ontarian anger. Papers like the Toronto *Mail* talked of dismantling Confederation, of fighting the War of the Conquest over again. 'Lower Canada may depend upon it, there will be no new treaty of 1763. The victors will not capitulate next time.' The *Orange Sentinel* talked of 'an appeal to arms' that would be heard 'in all parts of Canada'.

The rest of the story belongs to political history. The meeting on the Champ de Mars was the first wave of a storm that would change the whole political landscape, destroying the old Conservative alliance of Ontario Orangemen and Quebec *castors*, sweeping the Tories out of power first in Quebec and then in the Dominion, and ushering in a long era in which the Liberals would be the party most often in control. But, in spite of Mercier and the Orangemen, Confederation did not break apart, and at the end of our era, on the eve of the Great War, the two 'founding peoples' became linked uneasily as they had been at the beginning. Laurier went on to become the leader of a great national party in which the Ontario Grits were allied with the Quebec *rouges*. Something of the ambivalences of his position, and of the position of a Canada with dual traditions, can be seen in a statement Laurier made in the House of Commons in 1910.

> I do not pretend to be an imperialist. Neither do I pretend to be an anti-imperialist. I am a Canadian first, last and all the time. I am a British subject by birth, by tradition, by conviction—by the conviction that under British institutions my native land has found a measure of security and freedom it could not have found under any other régime. I want to speak from that double standpoint, for our policy is an expression of that double opinion.

The stress on duality, though expressed in a different way, ran through the thoughts of Laurier's Nationalist counterpart and rival, Henri Bourassa, the grandson of Louis-Joseph Papineau, who had assumed the leadership of those dedicated to the preservation of Quebec's traditions after Honoré Mercier had been discredited and fallen from power in 1891. Bourassa founded the Ligue Nationaliste in 1903 and established Quebec's greatest newspaper, *Le Devoir*, in 1910, but he was far from being a separatist. Indeed, he was one of the forerunners of a true Canadian nationalism, for what he sought was an acceptable arrangement between English and French in Canada that would preserve both cultures alike from the demands of British imperialism and from absorption by the United States. In 1907 he lamented that 'there is no Canadian patriotism, and we can have no Canadian nation when we have no Canadian patriotism.' The vision he gave of Canada in 1912 was one of a nation united rather than divided by its divergent cultures, a nation that should gain rather than lose from its differences:

> A free Anglo-French Confederacy, in the northern part of America, united by bonds of amity and kinship with Great Britain and France, the two great nations from which it has derived its races, its civilization and its thoughts, and offering to the trade and the intellectuality of the world a friendly rival and counterpoise to the expanding civilization of the United States, would become one of the greatest contributions to humanity.

Human societies develop as much through conflict as through sympathy, and there is a good deal of truth in the simple statement of Amor de Cosmos that 'political hatreds attest the vitality of the state.' Certainly in the relations between French and English in Canada the times of conflict have done as much to bring about mutual understanding as the quiet decades in which the two cultures went their own ways, ignorant and ignoring. It may indeed be that, as F.R. Scott once said: 'There are two miracles of Canadian history. The first is the survival of French Canada, and the second is the survival of Canada.' The experience of the century that is our period displayed the tenacity of the irrational bonds that both held the two peoples together and pulled them apart in a strange alternating pattern.

In contrast to the tolerance and humanity of the statement by Bourassa quoted above is the undisguised prejudice that characterized his statement on the subject of immigration in 1904, when he rose in the House of Commons to declare:

> It was never in the minds of the founders of the nation, it was never in the minds of the fathers of confederation, the men these so-called Liberals are so fond of evoking, that in order to be broad—or even in order to make land speculators rich—we ought to change a providential condition of our partly French and partly English country to make it a land of refuge for the scum of all nations.

The background to these remarks was the great turn-of-the-century flood of immigrants who were neither French nor English in language or in culture. The year 1885, which had changed Anglo-French relations through the execution of Riel, also saw the completion of the Canadian Pacific Railway. The settling of the Prairies then became not only possible but also necessary in order to justify the railway's continued existence. Even before the railway was finished, a trickle of immigrants had arrived in Manitoba and begun to percolate westward into the Saskatchewan territory. These included the first appreciable groups originating in countries outside the British Isles since the Hanoverians went to Nova Scotia and settled in Lunenberg during the eighteenth century and the Pennsylvania Dutch and Germans arrived in Upper Canada with the Loyalists. In 1872 a few Danes arrived in New Brunswick and set up a cheese-making settlement called New Denmark, from which some of them later gravitated to western Canada. 1873 saw the arrival of two fairly large groups—of Icelanders pulling up roots because an eruption of Mount Hecla had destroyed many of their farms, and of German-speaking Mennonites fleeing from persecution in Tsarist Russia.

The Icelanders settled first in Muskoka, Ontario, but went on to Manitoba, where they settled an area on the shores of Lake Winnipeg that they called New Iceland. They named their little town Gimli, which in Norse mythology means 'the great hall of heaven'. They were used to transplanting their traditions and established one of Canada's most durable minor cultures; there are still Icelandic newspapers and Canadian poets of repute writing in the Icelandic language.

The German-speaking Mennonites who had fled persecution in Tsarist Russia were another people tenacious of traditions, though theirs tended to be religious and moral rather than cultural in the narrower sense. Their habit of living in closely knit communities guided by elders gave them a social stability that helped enable them to cope with the harsh conditions of a new land, and their having lived for generations on the Russian steppes made them familiar with the techniques of dry farming needed for success on the open prairie. But it was their sobriety and industriousness that appealed to those who encountered them and that lodged in the official mind the thought that European peasants might be good settlers. A large Mennonite settlement established itself on Rat River in Manitoba in 1875 and it soon had 7,000 inhabitants. Typical of the positive reactions to them was a report made to a House of Commons Committee in 1878 by John Lowe, an official in the Department of Agriculture:

These people were put down on the naked prairie in the middle of the summer, barely three years ago, about 14 miles distant from any wood, and at a still greater distance and out of sight of any human habitation. They had to dig wells for water for their daily use on their arrival, and sleep, with their women and children, under the shelter of their wagons. They broke a little sod for the beginning of a crop the first year, and built temporary huts or houses . . . the first winter. They subsequently built the substantial houses and outbuildings of the villages we saw . . . besides carrying on the large farming operations . . . and besides furnishing the Winnipeg market with eggs, poultry and other farm produce . . . The secret of this result I found to be that every man, woman and child in the settlement is a producer. We saw women ploughing in the fields as we drove into the settlement. We next saw a woman thatching the roof of a building, a girl plastering the outside of a house . . . We saw very young children take out and bring in the cattle . . . We saw men, women and children going out into the fields to work before the morning was grey.

There was little sign that prejudice arose against these early immigrants of Germanic and Scandinavian origin. They kept to themselves; they were industrious; they were, if not British, at least North European, which was the next best thing; they were Protestant, even if somewhat eccentrically so in the case of the Mennonites; and the Canadian West was still so empty that they offered little real competition for land or for employment.

When Clifford Sifton became Minister of the Interior in 1896 he realized that vast areas of the West were still unsettled; he decided that if the Prairies were to be sufficiently populated to remove temptation from the land-hungry Americans, he must draw on sources of immigrants beyond the British Isles and Northern Europe. The obvious place to search was among the land-starved and politically repressed peasants of central and eastern Europe. But as soon as he decided to change immigration policy and turn to the Slavic peoples, apprehension and hostility began to spread among the existing population.

Between 1897 and the Great War no less than 200,000 Poles and Ukrainians, who were then called Galicians, as well as small groups from other parts of eastern Europe, settled in the West, and their arrival so affected the population that today those of British descent are a minority, and those of French descent are a tiny minority throughout the Prairie Provinces. The critics of Sifton were many, and it was in reply to them that he made his famous defence of the newcomers:

When I speak of quality I have in mind, I think, something that is quite different from what is in the mind of the average writer or speaker upon the question of Immigration. I think a stalwart peasant in a sheep-skin coat, born on the soil, whose forefathers have been farmers for ten generations, with a stout wife and half-dozen children, is good quality.

But many Canadians—some of them intelligent and on other issues broad-minded people—were troubled by the situation Sifton seemed to be creating, one in which Canada might become a country of unassimilable minorities.

We have already seen the extreme reaction of a normally sane and compassionate man like Bourassa on seeing the possibility that the precarious balance of French and English in Canada might be disturbed. But even the men of God were troubled. The Anglican church protested as a body against Sifton's policies, and the famous Social Gospeller J.S. Woodsworth, then a Methodist minister actively giving material and moral aid to immigrants in the All People's Mission in Winnipeg, had great misgivings about the perils to the cultural and linguistic unity of English-speaking Canada. In 1905 he told a gathering of his co-religionists:

> If Canada is to become in any real sense a nation, if our people are to become one, we must have one language. Hence the necessity of national schools where the teaching of English—our national language—is compulsory. The public school is the most important factor in transforming the foreigners into Canadians.

There was no talk then of multiculturalism. Even the liberal-minded mainly agreed with Woodsworth in regarding with horror the prospect of Canada's becoming what we now accept as an accommodation of different peoples and cultures. They felt the differences should be eliminated as quickly as possible, that assimilation should be rapid, and that a breed of homogeneous, unhyphenated Canadians should be quickly created. The idea of the melting pot was then fashionable; the concept of the mosaic did not begin to emerge until the 1920s.

Much of the opposition to the new wave of immigrants was considerably more bigoted. The Orange leader and Tory MP J.C.Sproule declared in 1903: 'Canada is today the dumping ground for the refuse of every country in the world.' Somewhat more mildly, the Toronto *Mail and Empire* remarked that the Canadian West was becoming 'a sort of anthropological garden', whose inmates were 'the waifs and strays of Europe, the lost tribes of mankind and freaks of creation'. Even trade-union leaders and the small body of organized labour reacted with alarm to the prospect of competitive cheap labour, and a wandering English observer, W.L. Griffith, noted somewhat disapprovingly in his book *The Dominion of Canada* (1911) that 'the labouring class, like all other classes in Canada, are a heterogeneous body, and they're not only divided but strongly antagonistic towards each other on questions of race and religion.'

The inclination of the majority of the immigrants—as it usually is with people seeking to create a new life in a strange country—was to accept whatever was required of them so long as they were allowed to establish themselves in peace. And though in later years a strong urge would emerge among second-generation immigrants, particularly among the Ukrainians, to revive their traditional culture in the land they had adopted, most of the first generation were eager to fit in, to learn new ways, and among them (unlike French Canadians) there was little thought that their identity was bound up with their language. They accepted education in English for their children and did their best to learn it themselves. And they entered freely into the developing pattern of local institutions. Prairie settlers were never, in fact, so concerned about immigration policies as people in the cities. When they began to discover that they had common enemies—such as the CPR, the grain merchants, and the eastern manufacturers who enjoyed protective tariffs under the National Policy that militated against western consumers—they came together regardless of origins. Members of all the ethnic groups collaborated in forming the first prairie farmers' organizations in the early years of the twentieth century and began to take on various co-operative functions; while through school boards, and later in other ways, immigrants of Slavic origins became involved quite early in the municipal politics of the West. In 1913, in Alberta, the first Ukrainian was elected to a provincial legislature, and this degree of acceptance meant that by the time the Great War, tensions between the various peoples in the Prairies had largely died down and, in the Canadian manner, an accommodation had been achieved without very much being said about it.

The situations of continuing prejudice and strife were those in which minorities stubbornly held to their differences and refused to accommodate to the majority pattern. The most striking case both intrinsically, and because of the way it reflects on the nature of Canadian democracy at the time, was that of the Doukhobors. They were pacifists with strong communitarian traditions who had been harshly persecuted in Tsarist Russia and finally—through the intervention of Leo Tolstoy and Peter Kropotkin, aided by the Canadian political economist James Mavor— were allowed to immigrate to Canada in 1899. About 7,400 arrived that year. The *Lake Huron*, bearing the first 2,300, docked at Halifax early in June, and there Canadians had a first inkling of the strangeness of this 'peculiar people' (as Aylmer Maude once called them without exaggeration) they had admitted into their midst. With the Doukhobors came Tolstoy's son, Sergei, and a young disciple of the novelist named Leopold Sulerzhitsky, who later became a close associate of Stanislavsky in the Moscow Arts theatre, and wrote an account in Russian of his journey to Canada, misleadingly titled, in translation, *To America with the Doukhobors* (1905). At Halifax the Doukhobors, respected as veterans of persecution and stubborn resistance, were welcomed by solemn Philadelphia Quakers and by Canadian trade-union representatives. And then, as Sulerzhitsky remarked, 'something unexpected happened that utterly amazed all the English':

The whole crowd of Doukhobors sighed and suddenly went down on their knees and bowed right down to the ground. People lay prostrate and the majority of the English looked at this picture of people bowing before them with great perplexity. Many apparently were greatly startled, as they stood with open mouths. Even the captain, who continually chewed a wad of tobacco, and who had been listening with partly closed eyes, stopped his occupation for a minute and looked at the Doukhobors in amazement. The old Quaker looked over his glasses, stretching out his neck and raising his eyebrows high with a face expressing deep perplexity. The workers' representative stood with his hands in his pockets. On his face could be seen a resigned acceptance tinged with disgust. Poor Doctor Mercer was confused and embarrassed to tears as he had just been telling the correspondents about the dignity of the Doukhobors . . . .

Finally, the Doukhobors moved, arose in a deep silence, and it seemed, had more dignity than before. Solemnly stepping forward and bending politely to [Prince] Hilkoff and pointing to the English, Vasya Popoff said: 'Dmitri Alexandrovich, tell them please that we did not really bow to them even though they may think so. We bowed to the spirit of God which has appeared among them and to the God who lives in all hearts which have been moved to accept us as brothers in their home.'

The Doukhobors travelled to the Prairies, running into trouble with the labour movement in Brandon because, living in the immigration hall with few expenses, they innocently accepted employment for small remuneration. The English-speaking labourers of the locality demonstrated at a meeting where the placards read 'Down with the Doukhobors', and an orator shouted, 'Protect yourselves against the new Chinese', introducing an issue to be touched on later. The Doukhobors took notice, refused to be exploited at the expense of others, and by the time they had moved to the land allotted to them on the Prairies, the incident was forgotten.

Altogether the Doukhobors established 59 villages in what later became Saskatchewan, and the early stages of their settlements reverted to the primitive communism that was traditional to their sect. James Mavor visited and described one of their early villages:

These villages were composed of a few large houses in each of which several families were accommodated. The houses were built of logs luted with clay. In the centre of the floor a large plain stove supplied heat. On two sides of a single room of which each house consisted there were two tiers of bunks, each bunk being about seven feet long and five feet wide. A bunk was provided for each family. There were in it fourteen bunks.

In these houses meals were prepared and eaten in common.

The Doukhobors' communal customs and their pacifism both aroused uneasy criticism, though they had their defenders, including Clifford Sifton, who stood up in the House, recalled the persecutions they had endured, and remarked:

> I doubt if there are five men in this House who would show the moral courage, who would show the tenacity, who would show the fortitude which these people have shown in preserving the faith which they believe to be the true faith.

Fortitude in preserving their faith would be the undoing of the Doukhobors on the Prairies. Under the Dominion Land Act all settlers were supposed to take up individually their quarter-sections, and to make an oath of allegiance to the Queen. This was repugnant to the beliefs of the Doukhobors. Just before Sulerzhitsky left Canada to return to Russia, he was involved in these discussions, and found the Doukhobors asking that the appropriate amount of land be assigned to them without any farm's becoming the property of an individual Doukhobor.

> 'Why do you wish this?' I asked them.
> 'Because, as we understand it, the land is God's. It belongs to God and no person can buy it and become its master,' answered the Doukhobors.
> 'The same as air, or say, water,' others explained. 'No one can sell them. God has released them for the use of all creatures equally. Not only for man but for all insects. So it is with land. Work as much as you can handle, feed yourself and other good people—that is the law. But to have a piece of land as your own or my own—that would be sinful. That's where sin comes from.'

This was an extreme minority viewpoint that in the Canada of the turn of the century could not be accepted. After several years of indecision, the government decided the law must be kept to the letter, and in June 1907 a quarter-of-a-million acres were taken from the Doukhobors and opened to the public, resulting in the biggest land-rush in prairie history. Most of the Doukhobors left for British Columbia, where they established the great Christian Community of Universal Brotherhood, which has already been described. The strife with government in which the Doukhobors then became involved reached its height after our period. But once again it was a matter of a democratic society attuned to the ideas of the majority, and therefore having no room for eccentric social or economic minority viewpoints—particularly if they led beyond theory into action and resulted in social enclaves that followed different ways of life from the accepted ones.

When they reached British Columbia, the Doukhobors in fact entered a region with its own special ethnic make-up and a history of racial conflict that would develop the most extreme degrees of racial discrimination and prejudice to be encountered anywhere in Canada. Until the Fraser Valley Gold Rush of 1858, the area that in that year became British Columbia had been inhabited by a few hundred British traders and Métis *voyageurs* among a fairly large Indian population. The discovery of gold changed that situation very quickly. People of all ethnic origins, including a considerable number of Chinese and blacks, found their way into the area, first of all from the goldfields of California, but later from many other regions. When George Monro Grant reached the little city of Victoria in 1872, he was astonished at the variety of its peoples.

A walk through the streets of Victoria showed the little capital to be a small polyglot copy of the world. Its population is less than 5,000; but almost every nationality is represented. Greek fishermen, Kanaka sailors, Jewish and Scottish merchants, Chinese washermen, French, German and Yankee officeholders and butchers, negro waiters and sweeps, Australian farmers and other varieties of the race, rub against each other, apparently in the most friendly way. The sign boards tell their own tale. 'Own Shing, washing and ironing;' Sam Hang, ditto; 'Kwong Tai & Co., cigar store'; 'Magazin Français;' 'Teutonic Hall, lager beer;' 'Scotch House;' 'Adelphic' and 'San Francisco' saloons; 'Oriental' and 'New England' restaurants; 'What Cheer Market' and 'Play me off at ten-pins,' are found within gunshot, interspread with more common-place signs.

The Chinese, who were among the first participants in the Gold Rush, were perhaps the most stable of all groups, since while other people might depart when prosperity declined, they remained. Frugal in their habits, they were able to extract enough to live on and to save some money from working deposits white miners thought too meagre, or even from repanning the piles of tailings left behind by other miners. When the gold gave out they remained, working for low pay as farm labourers, as navies on public works, and as domestic servants, meeting a labour shortage at the time. Others came in the 1870s, imported directly from the rural villages of Kwantung, and by 1881 there were 4,350 of them, almost a fifth of the non-Indian population of British Columbia. (Their numbers elsewhere at this time in Canada were negligible.) There was a dramatic increase in 1882 when Andrew Onderdonk, the contractor for the western section of the Canadian Pacific Railway, faced with an acute shortage of unskilled labour, imported another six thousand Chinese from Hong Kong. Sir John A. Macdonald defended his action, saying in the House of Commons, 'Either you have this labour, or you can't have a railway.'

At the same time Macdonald admitted that he did not believe the Chinese could 'assimilate with our Arian population'. In saying this he gave expression to a widespread apprehension that the Chinese were a people so alien in culture, and in the set of their minds, that it was hard to imagine their fitting into a society that, even if it was developing in the New World, derived all its values and most of its perceptions from the Christian civilization of Europe west of the Vistula. A similar attitude was adopted towards the Japanese and the Sikhs, who by the turn of the century were beginning to enter British Columbia. In 1914 Richard McBride, then Premier of British Columbia, remarked: 'We realize that Western and Oriental civilizations are so different that there could never be an amalgamation of the two.' And a Royal Commission on Chinese and Japanese Immigration expressed a similar view even more harshly when it said that Asians were 'unfit for full citizenship' because they were 'obnoxious to a free community and dangerous to the state'.

The idea that the Chinese were an unassimilable element was somewhat confirmed by their own attitudes, for in the main they saw themselves as sojourners rather than immigrants. They were men who came alone, with the intention of earning money to send back to their families, and where they lived they created small replicas of China with their joss-houses (as their Buddhist shrines were commonly called), gambling haunts, and crowded dwellings. Though they often entered Canadian houses as servants, they showed little interest, in that early period, in taking any more active part in local society than that of ill-paid menials and small-scale entrepreneurs. Canada was the land where they could earn the money they needed to fulfil their modest ambitions to provide for their families in China.

Canadian attitudes towards the Chinese at this time tended to differ according to class: the rich were more tolerant than the poor. The reasons were obvious. The presence of the Chinese enabled the well-to-do to live surrounded by servants as they might have done in Shanghai or India. Chinese provided employers with cheap and reliable labour, particularly useful when strike-breakers were needed. They even provided in Vancouver and Victoria exotic sites for tourists to visit in their joss-houses.

It was from among the establishment that the defenders of the Chinese came. Appearing in 1887 before one of the many Royal Commissions investigating Asian immigration, Matthew Baillie Begbie, the Chief Justice of British Columbia, defended them firmly against charges of excessive immorality or criminality; on the latter point he obviously spoke from his experience as a judge. He went on:

> Their religion, notions of honour and rank, mode of thought, dress, amusements, sense of beauty, are not to our taste. Their language appears to us ridiculous. Yet they as evidently despise all our attainments and ways and they come here and beat us on our own ground in supplying our own wants. They are inferior in weight and size of muscle and yet they work more steadily and with better success on the average than white men.

And the Rev. Matthew MacFie, a Congregationalist minister who wrote an early account of the Pacific Coast colonies (*Vancouver Island and British Columbia*, 1865), earnestly urged on his readers the virtues of tolerance.

> Let the colonists show the fruits of a superior civilization and religion, not in ridiculing and despising these Pagan strangers, but in treating them with the gentle forbearance due to a less favoured portion of the family

or mankind, and they will continue to be useful and inoffensive members

of society. The prejudice which characterises race or colour as a disqual-
ification for the exercise of civil rights reflects dishonour upon the civilized
community that indulges it.

Neither Begbie nor Macfie wrote from a position of assumed equality.
Their sense of superiority to the Chinese is evident, but their sense of
security, of being unchallenged and unthreatened, is equally clear. Their
forbearance was mixed with aloofness from these self-effacing sojourners
from another land.

The people who did resent and fear the Chinese, and who saw doom
in their increase, were of two kinds. There were those who irrationally
feared people whose looks and manners were different from their own.
They were swayed by dire warnings about the 'Yellow Peril' that
originated among racist writers in Europe during the 1890s and quickly
spread to North America, where the Pacific coast seemed more immediately threatened by the fast-breeding hordes from Asia who, according
to certain fanatic prophets, would one day replace the whites as the
master-race of the world. But there were also those who felt threatened
in their very livelihood, and they were vociferous and successful in
influencing official policy.

In the 1860s, as Dr John Sebastian Helmcken of Victoria remembered,
'the Chinese were believed by all to be an advantage and an improvement', since these 'heathen' soon 'monopolized the market garden and
the washing trade . . . Previous to their advent the supply of vegetables
had been scant, for Indians never took to this business, excepting in so
far as they grew potatoes in small quantities.' The attitude towards the
Chinese began to change when they became numerous enough to compete in the general labour market. White workers began to fear for their
jobs after the completion of the CPR in 1885 caused a scarcity of work.
Even in the 1870s the leading labour organization of the time, the Knights
of Labour, had abandoned their claim to work for the benefit of all
workers without regard to skill, sex, or race, and denounced the use of
Chinese labour, claiming that the Knights' aim was 'to elevate the working man, to keep his broad heritage for our sons and not for a race of
aliens'. In response to this agitation, the British Columbia government
in 1878 banned the employment of Chinese in public works. In 1879 the
British Columbia politician Amor do Cosmos, whose adopted name proclaimed him a lover of the universe, presented to the Dominion parliament a petition from 1,500 British Columbian working-men calling for
an end to Chinese immigration, and in 1880 he came with another. While
efforts by the provincial government to exclude Chinese were disallowed
by Ottawa, the Dominion government itself, in 1885, imposed a head-

tax on Chinese entering the country and specifically excluded 'a person of Mongolian or Chinese race' from the franchise under an Electoral Franchise Act.

Such measures did not prevent the first anti-Chinese riots in 1887. The continued arrival of Chinese, and after them of Japanese and Sikhs, fed the rage of the Canadian workers. 'Western civilization is and will be threatened,' declared one of the union leaders as an Asiatic Exclusions League was formed, and in September 1907 a demonstration of the League in Chinatown and the adjoining Japanese quarter of Vancouver turned into a destructive riot that was halted only when the Japanese turned on their attackers. In a message to Lord Grey, the Governor General, Sir Wilfrid Laurier reported in a manner that said a great deal about his own racial attitudes:

> . . . the Japs showed fight, turned upon their assailants, and routed them. This is at once a cause for rejoicing and for anxiety; rejoicing because the rowdies got a well-deserved licking; anxiety because it may make the Japs more saucy, and renders the adjustment of the trouble very difficult.

I have concentrated on the relations between the Chinese and the host community because they were the first group to become involved in this situation of rejection and prejudice, and the most numerous group of that kind. The experience of the Japanese and the Sikhs before the Great War was generally similar—though different, of course, in detail. In 1908 there were some 2,000 Sikhs in British Columbia. A famous attempt to promote further immigration took place in May-July 1914 in Vancouver with the arrival of the freighter *Komagata Maru*, filled with Sikhs, who were detained on board for two months until the ship was forced to leave. Largely unresolved by the time of the war, the situation was eventually arbitrarily controlled in the immediate post-war years by Draconian exclusionist laws, so that few Asians entered Canada until the early 1960s, when the racially discriminatory provisions of Canadian immigration policy were eliminated.

With this background later Canadians inherited—and took many decades to eliminate—a situation of racial conflict that arose partly from the economic fears of workers, aggravated by the tendency of employers to engage Asians more cheaply; partly from a fear of the unknown, and the misunderstood, that during the nineteenth century was largely due to limitations of education; and partly from attitudes of racial superiority. In the twentieth century the two great countries of North America have been the first places of refuge and hope chosen by disadvantaged people from around the world. In Canada the conflict that developed between whites and Asians was the greatest of all the failures of the majority to accept people from outside the original cultures of the French and

English. This is a passage of our history that in the late twentieth century we tend to look back on with astonishment and a degree of shame. Yet it is part of the century that made us. Its scars are sadly evident today wherever prejudice against—or a hardly less maiming indifference to—those whose cultures are alien to us persists.

9

Entering the Land

In the preceding essays I have attempted to delineate the broad areas of attitudes and ideas—the tension between authority and rebellion, the dialectics of class, gender, and race—that help us to define the Canadian character and, in the widest sense, our culture. I now wish to narrow in on an influence that produced the first vital expression in the arts: the land itself.

For people to know the land they had to travel over it. Improvements in transport that made travel speedier and more comfortable inevitably brought increased knowledge of Canada to a growing number of Canadians and changed their attitudes to the land. Instead of a remote wilderness, a menace lurking in the mind, it became a penetrable and perceptible reality. When the War of 1812 ended, Canada stood at a pivotal point in transportation between the use of human and animal strength (still reflected in the curious survival of the term 'horse-power') and mechanical power created by various non-animate sources—water and wind, steam, and eventually electricity. Apart from the first rudimentary steamships, everything was still non-mechanical; but the rapidity of change—even by the 1850s, a mere four decades later—was shown by Henry Youle Hind's remarks in the opening pages of his *Narrative of the Red River Exploring Expedition of 1857 . . . :*

In those days of canoe transportation, merchandise was conveyed up the Ottawa, across the height of land to Lake Huron, thence by the north shore of Lake Superior to Fort William, the starting point of the long journey into the great interior valleys of Red River, the Saskatchewan, and the Mackenzie. In these days ships can sail from European or Atlantic ports, and without breaking bulk, land their cargoes at Fort William for less than one-fiftieth part of the cost involved during the period when the North-West Company became a powerful, wealthy and influential body.

The completion of the Sault Ste. Marie Canal, in May, 1855, established an uninterrupted water communication for sea-going vessels between Lake Superior and the Ocean.

To strangers just arrived in Canada the canoe could be an object of admiration and wonder when it was propelled by an efficient crew with perfect co-ordination. That is how Lieutenant-Colonel Charles Grey, the brother-in-law of Lord Durham, saw it when he visited the Ellices at Beauharnois in 1838.

> Mr. Ellice comes out to meet us in a bark canoe, belonging to the Hudson's Bay Company, manned by Indians who come paddling up at a great rate singing the whole time. It has been the most extraordinary effect possible to see a canoe of this sort coming up to you. The short red blades flashing in and out of the water incessantly in time to the music. It is like an animal with so many legs on each side.

The canoe brigades that travelled in the days of the North West Company from Montreal into the Athabaska country and over the mountains into New Caledonia (British Columbia) took a whole season, between late spring and early autumn, to get from Montreal to the farthest points of the Northwest. When the governor of the Hudson's Bay Company, George Simpson, pressing on with selected crews of Iroquois paddlers, travelled a hundred miles on a favourable day, that was considered exceptional, and to judge from Simpson's own account, it demanded an almost intolerable discipline:

> Weather permitting, our slumbers would be broken about one in the morning by the cry of 'Lève, lève, lève!' In five minutes, woe to the inmates that were slow in dressing; the tents were tumbling about our ears; and within half an hour, the camp would be raised, the canoes laden, and the paddles keeping time to some merry old song. About eight o'clock, a convenient place would be selected for breakfast, about three quarters of an hour being allotted for the multifarious operations of unpacking the equipage, laying and removing the cloth, boiling and frying, eating and drinking; and, while the preliminaries were arranging, the hardier among us would wash and shave, each person carrying soap and towel in his pocket, and finding a mirror in the same sandy or rocky basin that held the water. About two in the afternoon we usually put ashore for dinner;

and, as this meal needed no fire, or at least got none, it was not allowed to occupy more than twenty minutes or half an hour.

Such was the routine of the journey, the day, generally speaking, being divided into six hours of rest and eighteen of labour.

Although Simpson made some extraordinary journeys by canoe, including an especially perilous trip through the Fraser River canyon in British Columbia, he was mainly responsible for the supersession of canoes by wooden York boats and bateaux, which were more commodious, less liable to be damaged, and required smaller crews. By the late 1820s boats on the larger rivers, and schooners on the lakes, carried most of the freight and passengers into the Northwest, though canoes were still used in the smaller, more tortuous waterways.

Travelling by boat was less romantic than by canoe, since the vessels were heavier though safer, and lacked the almost perfect functional beauty of the birchbark canoe. Anna Jameson travelled on a bateau on Lake Superior, rowed by five *voyageurs*, in 1837:

> The boat might have carried fifteen persons, hardly more, and was rather clumsy in form. The two ends were appropriated to the rowers, baggage and provisions; in the centre there was a clear space, with a locker on each side, on which we sat or reclined, having stowed away in them our smaller and more valuable packages.

Even if it was more durable and dependable than the canoe, the boat still required a great deal of skill, as the pioneer Mountie Sam Steele remembered in his memoirs of the last days of the Old West:

> On approaching a rapid which has to be run, the bowman always stands up in his place and steers, long paddle in hand, braced against the stem, his keen and practiced eye on the rushing water. The voyageur in the stern, who has shipped a long oar in the stern rowlock, keeps the boat from swinging in the current. Down the torrent the craft rushes, propelled by the desperate efforts of the six oarsmen. They row as for their lives so that there may be steerage way for the bowman who, by skilful use of his paddle brings the vessel safely through the rocks and whirlpools of the passage.

While the watermen of the West were carrying out a minor revolution by changing from light canoes to sturdy boats and from paddles to oars, their counterparts in the East were involved in a major revolution, the first application of mechanical power to transport. This began some years before the period of this book when John Molson's little steamboat, the *Accommodation*, which was equipped with a six-horse-power engine and two open-side paddle wheels, in 1809 took thirty-six hours of actual sailing time to go from Montreal to Quebec. Three years later his second ship, the *Swiftsure*, was launched from Logan's Shipyard, Quebec, before a crowd of three thousand people, including the Governor-in-Chief Sir George Prevost and his lady.

> At that instant a detachment of Capt. Dunlop's company, commanded by Mr. Andrews, fired a salute of 19 guns with a correctness not to be surpassed by any regular artillery on a similar occasion.

From this point the development of steam navigation on the St Lawrence continued to the point where, according to the *Quebec Gazette* (25 July 1816), 'The Steam boats have already ruined the prospects of the Old River Craft, many of which long ago ought to have been condemned as unfit to receive the property of the merchant.' By 1819 there were seven steamships plying the St Lawrence.

Very soon after Molson's ventures on the St Lawrence, steam navigation spread to the Great Lakes, where the *Frontenac* began to operate in 1817. For several years this was the only steamer, making, as William Lyon Mackenzie remembered, 'sometimes two, oftener three and rarely four trips in the month between Kingston and Fort George.' In 1830 he remarked, 'there are some eight or ten tight steamers, plying in every direction in quest of freight and passengers at moderate rates, and a considerable steamboat proprietor is so much encouraged by the present state of affairs that he has now on the stocks a steamship on a new and elegant model, the estimated cost of which is £15,000.'

The continuing importance of water transport in the earlier part of our period was shown by the spread of the canal system, built for commercial as well as strategic purposes, during this period. The Lachine Canal, built to replace the portage around the rapids there; the Rideau Canal between Ottawa and Kingston; and the first Welland Canal between Lake Ontario and Lake Erie, bypassing the Niagara River and the Falls—were all built between 1819 and 1834. In the latter year a start was made on the even more important Trent Canal system, which traced its way across western Ontario to Georgian Bay on Lake Huron, linking up natural waterways and small lakes and stimulating the settlement of this area away from the shores of the Great Lakes. Sir J.E. Alexander, a staff officer with the British forces during the 1840s, described the rigours of a steamboat voyage on the Rideau Canal in his *L'Acadie; or Seven Years' Exploration in British America* (1849).

> In the beginning of June, we embarked on the small steamer, 'Otter', towing barges containing the men of the detachment of the 14th Regiment, and began the navigation of the Rideau Canal . . . .
> We found the Rideau a hot ditch at this season, and beginning to be infested with musquetoes; there was no casing to the hot funnel of the steamer, which also added to our discomfort. It was painful to witness the hundreds of acres, which had unavoidably been drowned by reason of the dams, and to see the dead trees of the forest standing, with their

grey trunks and leafless boughs, like ghosts in the water. Sometimes we navigated the lakes, and in the evening had an opportunity of fishing for bass, or paddling in a canoe . . . .

By the 1850s the steamboats were beginning to alter the patterns of transport and communication on the prairie. The canoe routes had already been transformed into York-boat routes, but for the carriage of bulk freight, these had been supplemented on land by brigades of Red River carts, usually driven by Métis. George Monro Grant described the Red River cart as 'a clumsy looking but really light box cart with wheels six or seven feet in diameter, and not a bit of iron about the whole concern', since it was virtually tied together with shaganappi, or buffalo raw-hide thonging.

> These small-bodied high-wheeled carts cross the miry creeks, borne up by the grass roots, and on the ordinary trail the horses jog along with them at a steady pace of four or five miles an hour. Ordinary carts would stick hopelessly in the mud at the crossings of the creeks and marshes and travel slowly on a good trail. A cart without an ounce of iron was a curiosity to us at first, but we soon found that it was the right thing in the right place.

The Red River carts had provided the transport in the last days of the buffalo hunts, going out several hundred at a time on those seasonal expeditions. The Métis hunter Louis Goulet recollected in his memoirs, which he dictated to Guillaume Charette before his death (as *Vanishing Spaces* they were eventually published in 1980):

> We would travel at the speed of an ox towards the setting sun through the vast fragrant air of the endless plain, stopping only for meals and to camp at night in tents or under the stars if the weather looked promising for the next day.

As traffic into the Northwest increased towards the middle of the nineteenth century, trains of Red River carts supplemented the canoe and boat brigades, following the Carlton trail across open prairie. They took forty days to cover 480 miles from Fort Garry to Carlton House on the Saskatchewan River, and another forty days to reach Fort Edmonton. Even larger trains took a month to travel the 350 miles from Fort Garry to St Paul, Minnesota. In 1855 the trader Norman Kittson organized a train of 500 carts to take the products of the buffalo hunt and of fur trading from the Red River district to the American market.

Both the Red River cart and the York boat were doomed to obsolescence when the paddlewheeler *Anson Northup* sailed down the Red River from Minnesota to Fort Garry in 1859. The steamboats did more than carry greater bulk; they carried it at a much greater speed. They also made travel in the West more comfortable than it had ever been. Steaming down from the American cities—with their ornate staterooms, their musicians, their elaborate meals—they brought a first whiff of culture into the wilderness.

In the next decade, at the height of the Cariboo Gold Rush, steamboats reached the rivers of the Far West, and Viscount Milton and Dr Cheadle were among the first to use them on the upper Fraser. On 15 October 1863 they reached Soda Creek on the Fraser, having crossed the mass of Canada by land, and boarded the *Enterprise* going northward to Quesnel. Cheadle vividly portrayed in his diary the character of travel in that frontier region:

> FRIDAY, OCT. 16th. Steamer came in at 2 o'clock bringing a host of miners 2 of whom were very drunk and continued to imbibe every 5 minutes . . . . After we had been on board a short time the Captain, finding out who we were, gave us the use of his cabin, a comfortable little room & supplied us with cigars & a decanter of cocktail, also books & papers. We were fetched out every few minutes to have a drink with some one, the Captain taking the lead by standing champagne all round. We had some dozen to do before supper; no one the least affected, Milton & I shirking in quantity. The 'Cap' told us the boat was built on the river, all the timber sawn by hand, the shaft in 5 pieces packed on mules, cylinders in two, boiler plates brought in same manner. Boat cost $75,000!
>
> SUNDAY, OCT. 18th. Arrived about 9, at Quesnel mouth, a little collection of about 20 houses on the wooded banks of the Fraser. Quesnel at the north side of the Fort. Large new stores & carts all lying about the street . . . . Captain Done met us in street half seas over & insisted to treat us to champagne, etc., at every bar in the place.

Wherever the steamboats went they took communication with them, knitting the out-of-the-way places with the greater world in a way earlier forms of transport had failed to do; they carried a greater quantity and variety of goods from outside and they made contact quicker and easier. This change emerges in the diaries of the time. Mary O'Brien writes in May 1836 on the importance of the first call of the steamboat at Shanty Bay on Lake Simcoe after the long winter.

> The long awaited steamboat has at length arrived and been received with a degree of excitement which is almost ludicrous, but towards the end of winter everything in the way of carriage and travelling becomes dependent on the arrival of the steamboat, so that in reality all your comfort, if not your existence, comes to be connected with it. I, for instance, depending on the butcher shop she carried within her, had not exerted myself to obtain a fresh supply of meat.

And Feo Monck, travelling on a small Ottawa River steamer in 1864 that stopped 'at about fifty small places', remarks that 'when there were any inhabitants they all flocked down as if no boat had ever been there before, and there was shouting and screaming.'

With steamships the idea of speed as a necessary attribute of a civilized life that was growing in commercial and political complexity became increasingly important to the Canadians. In order to achieve it before the advent of the railways, an improvement of the old portage system was developed by which steamships connected, often in quite complicated ways, with stage coaches that spanned the intervening stretches of land. Here the much-travelled Colonel Henry Grey gives a vivid account in his diary (1838) of the complexity of a journey he made from Montreal to Ottawa, or Bytown as it was then called. He started off in a friend's jaunting car for Lachine, and there, above the rapids, he took a steamboat, the *Chieftain*, upriver to Cascades.

> A number of passengers on board. Three officers of the Royal Regiment en route for Niagara, Captain E of the King's Dragoon Guards ditto, Mister C., wife, wife's sister, and three children on their way to some place in the Upper Province where the gentleman is to leave his encumbrances. It is an odd story. I fancy he is to be separated from his wife in consequence of having taken illegitimate means, with the assistance of his wife's maid, to increase his family. He is son of the Bishop of St.—and is a Lieutenant in the 66th Regiment.
>
> . . . At Cascades, which we reach a few minutes under two hours, we are all transferred to stages, five in number, each having nine inside. Captain Whipple fortunately takes us under his special protection and arranges one coach for myself and Caroline, the three Royals, the Dragoon and the marrying Medico of the Coldstream, seven in all, and we get over the 16 miles to Coteau du Lac tolerably comfortably, tho' the road is execrable from the late heavy rain. Embark in the *Neptune*, 44 Cabin Passengers in all—and lots of steerage ones. Leave Coteau at three. Dine on board at four and arrive at Cornwall at half past eight. Here we are again transferred to stages to go 12 miles to Dickinson's Landing. But there being only four coaches they are all crammed full, inside and out, and one coach contains ourselves, the C— family and maid, two Royals and the Dragoon, in all nine grown up People and three children. A dreadful road and being dark do not reach the Landing till half past eleven, when we turn in tolerably comfortably on board the Brockville.

That evening, after stopping on the way at Prescott, Brockville, and Gananonoque, at all of which he went ashore, Grey reached Kingston. He had to stay a whole day there, and embarked at six the next morning on the *Cataraqui*, which took him through the Rideau Canal to Bytown, arriving at two o'clock on the afternoon of the second day. Such progress, which seems to us extremely slow, was far quicker than journeys had been in the days of canoe transport.

The ability to penetrate the wilderness that water transport already provided finds its expression not only in the journals of travellers, but also in imaginative literature. In this respect Charles Sangster's long poem, *The St. Lawrence and the Saguenay* (1856)—despite its extraordinary conservatism of diction and form—showed a significant shift in sensibility. Sangster was not merely using romantic forms and images in a way that an English Regency poet like Samuel Rogers might have done. He applied romantic feeling directly to the Canadian landscape, beginning somewhat dimly to see it for itself, rather than as merely real-estate to be exploited, as he described his journey by sailboat from Kingston down the St Lawrence and then up the Saguenay into what was then wilderness country. By this time such a trip was more likely to be taken by steamboat, but the means by which Sangster travelled is less important than the shift in perception he displays. He is no longer the immigrant facing Lower Canada with open hostility, like Standish O'Grady in the early 1840s:

> Thou barren waste; unprofitable strand,
> Where hemlocks brood on unproductive land,
> Whose frozen air on one bleak winter's night
> Can metamorphose *dark brown hares to white*.
> (*The Emigrant*,1842)

Instead, as David Latham said in *The Oxford Companion to Canadian Literature*, Sangster in his poem was taking 'a journey away from civilization towards nature and the divine creator', and to judge from the praise his poem received, many Canadian readers were prepared to accompany him mentally when he sailed past Cape Eternity on the Saguenay into Trinity Bay:

> A deep and overpowering solitude
> Reigns undisturbed along the varied scene.
> A wilderness of Beauty, stern and rude,
> In undulating swells of wavy green;
> Soft, airy slopes, bold, massive and serene;
> Rich in wild beauty and sublimity,
> From the far summits on their piney sheen,
> Down to the shadows thrown by rock and tree
> Along the dark, deep wave, that slumbers placidly . . . .
>
> Is there a soul so dead to Nature's charms
> That thrills not here in this divine retreat . . . ?

Here is no talk of 'barren waste' or earth to be conquered, but an early acceptance of the wilderness—as the native peoples had recognized it—as a place where one communes through nature with the divine.

Even at its speediest, water transport ceased to satisfy Canadians as the railway age dawned. Canadian actually entered that age quite early. In 1836, only eleven years after the historic opening of the Stockton to Darlington Railway in Great Britain, the Champlain and St Lawrence Railway was built to replace a portage between the St Lawrence and Richelieu Rivers. Three hundred people sailed on a special steamer from

Montreal to witness the opening in mid-July. Two of the small cars were attached to the locomotive and the rest were drawn by horses over the iron-stripped wooden rails, presumably to exhibit the superior powers of steam. And, as the *Montreal Gazette* reported:

> The locomotive, with its complement, shot far ahead of the other cars, which passed along the road just as fast as the nags (which were none of the fleetest) could drag them. The motion was easy and elicited from many comparisons far from favourable to the usual comforts of travelling by stage road.

The train took 59 minutes to cover the 14$^1/_2$ miles from La Prairie to St John's on the Richelieu, where the passengers were entertained at a champagne dinner. A similar line was built around the Lachine Rapids in 1841. But these tiny railways were mere adjuncts to the water-transport system, and even in that role they did not for a long time replace stage coaches. By 1850 there were still only 66 miles of railroad in the whole of British North America.

When advocates of railroads observed the much more rapid progress of the system in the United States, and took into account that the steamship-and-stagecoach network virtually ceased to operate during the long months of winter, they grew suitably eloquent. One of them was a young civil engineer of Loyalist descent, Thomas Coltrin Keefer, who in 1850 published a pamphlet rather pretentiously called *Philosophy of Railroads*. He complained that while Americans built railways, Canadians only talked about them. And he raised the spectre of winter immobility:

> Old Winter is once more upon us, and our inland seas are 'dreary and inhospitable wastes' to the merchant and to the traveller;—our rivers are sealed fountains—and an embargo which no human power can remove is laid on all our ports. Around our deserted wharves and warehouses are huddled the naked spars,—the blasted forest of trade,—from which the sails have fallen like the leaves of autumn. The splashing wheels are silenced,—the roar of steam is hushed,—the gay saloon, so lately thronged with busy life, is now but an abandoned hall,—and the cold snow revels in solitary possession of the untrodden deck. The animation of business is suspended, the life blood of commerce is curdled and stagnant in the St. Lawrence, the great aorta of the North. On land, the heavy stage labours through mingled mud and frost in the West,—or struggles through drifted snow and slides with uncertain track over the icy hills of Eastern Canada. Far away to the South is heard the daily scream of the steam whistle,—but from Canada there is no escape: blockaded and imprisoned by ice and Apathy, we have at least ample time for reflection—and if there be comfort in philosophy may we not profitably consider the PHILOSOPHY OF RAILROADS?

When the railway boom really began to gather momentum in Canada, it was less a matter of philosophy than of profits and politics. Sir Allan

MacNab, who was prime minister of the Province of Canada in 1854, made the famous declaration, 'Railroads are my politics', and it was another celebrated politician of the times, Joseph Howe, who foresaw, in a speech he made in Halifax as early as 1851, the eventual role of the railways in the continent-wide Canada that as yet was no more than a vision.

> I am neither a prophet, nor a son of a prophet, yet I will venture to predict that in five years we shall make the journey hence to Quebec and Montreal, and home through Portland and St. John, by rail; and I believe that many in this room will live to hear the whistle of the steam engine in the passes of the Rocky Mountains, and to make the journey from Halifax to the Pacific in five or six days.

Not until 1871 did the government of the recently created Dominion, in accordance with its promise to the newest province, British Columbia, even begin to plan the great enterprise that Howe had foreseen twenty years before. But in the Province of Canada, created in 1841, the relatively small local railways had spread rapidly, and by 1871 they extended over 2,645 miles, arousing in those who travelled in them the most exalted ideas. In 1857, for example, Susanna Moodie wrote enthusiastically to her English publisher, Robert Bentley:

> We went down to Kingston by the rail road. It was the first time I had ever been in the cars, and I felt very much inclined to shout with joy at their wondrous speed. It seemed to realise dreams I have had about flying. The sight of these great machines affects me greatly. I cannot divest myself of the idea, that they possess a certain degree of intelligence. That the spirit of man is working in them the same as the spirit of God works in us. The perfect time they keep, the harmony of their motion is beautiful. The poetry of mechanism.

Railways had a romantic attraction, and their openings could be great occasions, particularly when the presence of leading public figures gave them social cachet, as at the turning of the first sods for the Toronto, Grey and Bruce Railway, performed at Weston, Ontario, on 6 October 1869 by Queen Victoria's son, Prince Arthur, later the Duke of Connaught. As the *Globe* remarked, 'no other railway in the Dominion can boast of having had its first sod turned by a Royal Prince.'

> A few hundred yards west of the village a platform was built close to the track. This led through a beautiful arch decked with evergreens, and surmounted by ensigns and crowns and bannerets, bearing appropriate mottoes innumerable, into a quadrangle surrounded on all sides with sloping galleries crowded with schoolchildren and people of the neighbourhood all of whom were evidently in the highest state of expectancy to catch a glimpse of his Royal Highness.

The ladies of Toronto were, according to the reporter, particularly pushing.

It may be mentioned in closing that when the Prince had tumbled his two sods out of the barrow, a most indiscriminate scramble took place as to who should obtain possession of the precious earth. Ladies and gentlemen joined in the melee, and the two sods were soon torn all to pieces, and several parties in the cars homeward were seen to draw from their pockets a good sized turf and show it to their less fortunate fellow travellers with as much gusto as if they had some relics from the ruins of Pompeii or the ancient palace of Thebes.

Once the decision had been made to build the Canadian Pacific Railway, the construction of the great 'iron belt' to the Pacific continued intermittently but inexorably until it was completed in 1885. The whole operation seemed to take on a life of its own, as P. Turner Bone, who worked on it, recalled in his memoirs, *When the Steel Went Through* (1947):

> End of track was something more than just the point to which track had been laid. It was a real life community, a hive of industry, in which teamsters, tracklayers, blacksmiths, carpenters, executive officers, and other trades and professions all had a part. They had their quarters on a train composed of cars loaded with rails and other track material, followed by large boarding-cars for the workmen, and by sundry smaller cars for the executives. This train was pushed ahead as track-laying proceeded; and at the end of a day's work, it might be three or four miles from where it was in the morning.

The length of Canadian railways increased until in 1901 there were 18,140 miles. Even that was not enough; not one but two railways were projected to open up the northern parklands not served by the CPR. These were the Canadian Northern and the Grand Trunk Pacific, and they became matters of low as well as high politics. André Siegfried described a 1904 election meeting in Winnipeg in aid of the Liberal candidate Mr Bole, in which the walls of Selkirk Hall were emblazoned with the stirring message:

> THE WEST WANTS COMPETITION ON RAILWAYS!
> LAURIER, BOLE, AND PROSPERITY!
> THE GRAND TRUNK MEANS 125 MILLIONS FOR WINNIPEG!
> PROSPERITY—DO YOU FEEL IT IN YOUR POCKETS?
> VOTE FOR THREE YEARS MORE OF PROSPERITY
> VOTE FOR BOLE AND YOUR OWN WELFARE!
> VOTE FOR THE GRAND TRUNK AND HIGH WAGES!

By 1914 the total length of Canadian railways had reached 30,795 miles, while the population of the country was still less than $7\frac{1}{2}$ millions, which meant that there was one mile of track to every 250 people, a ratio higher than in any other country. The virtual bankruptcy of two of the three competing transcontinental railways—and their absorption into the state-run Canadian National—was the result.

All this may be represented as vast economic folly, to say nothing of political corruption, but socially and culturally the railways transformed the country. Moving forward into the West, protected by the recently created North West Mounted Police, and challenged continually by the Indians who recognized all too clearly the meaning of its advent, was the spearhead of a ruthless new civilization—'its hour come round at last', as W.B. Yeats might have said.

Hard on the heels of the construction of the CPR came the first of the thousands of settlers who began to swarm in to the prairie in the 1880s, travelling in Spartan style, as J.C. Stead describes in an early prairie realist novel *The Homesteaders* (1916):

> So John Harris and his bride took the passenger train from her city home, while their goods and chattels, save for their personal baggage, rumbled on in a box-car or crowded stolidly into side-tracks as the exigencies of traffic required.
>
> At a junction point they were transferred from the regular passenger service to an immigrant train. Immigrant trains, in the spring of 'eighty-two, were somewhat more and less than they now are. The tourist sleeper, with its comfortable berths, its clean linen, its kitchen range, and its dusky attendant, restrained to an attitude of agreeable deference by his antici-pation of a gratuity, was a grey atom of potentiality in the brain of an unknown genius. Even the colonist car, which has done noble service in later days in the peopling of the Prairie West, was only in the early stages of its evolution. The purpose of immigrant trains was to move people. To supply comforts as well as locomotion was an extravagence undreamed of in transportation.
>
> The train was full. Every seat was taken; aisles were crowded with standing passengers who stumbled over burdens and valises with every pitch of the uncertain railroads.

When they reached their stations on the bare prairie, homesteaders like the Harrises still had to travel to the remote spots where their land was located. One such pioneer family in real life was that of Nellie Mooney who later became Nellie McClung. They took up land on the Souris River in 1880, and long afterwards Nellie described their journey there in her autobiography *Clearing in the West* (1936):

> Fortunately there were many travellers on the road and the mud-holes were the drag nets which brought them all together. Sometimes it took three yokes of oxen to draw a wagon out of a bad spot and even then the long grass beside the road had to be cut and thrown into the slippery, gummy mud to give the oxen a foot-hold.
>
> The men wore long boots of leather and overalls of brown or blue duck, but I do not remember seeing any rubber boots . . . . It was like a night-mare to see the oxen go down, deep into the mud. But they did not get excited as horses would have and they did their best, without urging. In the worst part of the road we were fortunate to have Lord Elphinstone

and his traders, and they gave assistance to all the wagons on the road. The traders who had been travelling the trail for years, were always serene and cheerful and said the road was not as bad as it used to be, and that no wagon had actually been lost for quite awhile.

When the railway was completed in 1885, the more fortunate travellers rode in the comfort promised in a promotional booklet describing the CPR's cross-country sleeping-cars:

> These cars are of unusual length and size, with berths, smoking and toilet accommodation correspondingly roomy. The transcontinental sleeping cars are provided with BATHROOMS . . .
>   The seats are richly upholstered, with high-backs and arms, and the central sections are made into luxurious sofas during the day. The upper berths are provided with windows and ventilators, and have curtains separate from those of the berths beneath. The exteriors are of white mahogany and satinwood, elaborately carved.

The railways opened the Canadian West both to exploitation and to an appreciation of the beauties of the wilderness. The economic possibilities of the land had been canvassed by Ontario newspapers during the 1860s, and in the 1870s travel narratives like Captain Francis Butler's *The Great Lone Land* had made some of the reading public aware of the vastness and splendour of the prairie and of the western mountains. But it was the Northwest Rebellion of 1885, and the transport of thousands of Canadian militiamen through the Shield country and into the Prairies over the still uncompleted Canadian Pacific Railway, that stirred the imagination of the general public, since the reporters who travelled with General Middleton's expedition would sometimes, on days when there was nothing of military interest to write about, devote their despatches to describing the land. Later Sir William Van Horne and his associates of the CPR virtually created a tourist industry in the Rockies, and people began to travel merely to see the land.

At the end of their journey the travellers arrived at the fast-growing new city of Vancouver, with its splendid harbour and its magnificent mountain and ocean setting. Some of them were depressed by its dedication to trade and exchange and its relative lack of the obvious civilized graces.

> It is a purely business town, a thing of stores and banks and meagre wooden houses, with no public buildings of account . . . . The stranger is amazed at the profusion of solid banking houses; it would almost seem as if the inhabitants must be a race of financiers, concerned merely with money and stocks and shares . . . . And, in point of fact, this is a land of speculation, in mining properties, lumber lands, fruit lands, and, above all, in city lots, the pick of which has doubled in value in the last two years.

Those were the views of the English writer and economist J.A. Hobson when he visited Vancouver at the turn of the century. Yet things may not have been quite what they seemed to him, for the merchants and speculators of the city, who appeared to him so materialistic in their outlook, had shown enough appreciation of the beauty of their environment for the city's first council to petition the federal government to give them at a nominal rent in perpetuity the great area of wild land known as Coal Peninsula, which was being held as a military reserve. This act of environmental foresight, extraordinary for its time, led to the opening of Stanley Park in 1888—dedicated explicitly to use by people of all races—which Jan Morris has described as 'the most beautiful of all' the great parks of the Empire.

Certainly the recollections of Ethel Wilson, who reached Vancouver in 1898 when the city was a mere twelve years old and wrote a largely autobiographical novel—*The Innocent Traveller* (1949)—about those early days, suggest that Vancouver people paid attention to things other than trade and profit and that they responded to the dual beauties of mountain and sea.

> The West End was wooded . . . . The houses all had wooden trimmings and verandahs, and on the verandah steps when day was done the families came out and sat and walked and counted the box pleats on the backs of the fashionable girls' skirts as they went by; and visitors came and sat and walked, and idly watched the people too, and watched the mountains grow dark, and the stars come out above the mountains. And then they all went in and made a cup of coffee . . . .
>
> . . . It was not long before the contours of the mountains became part of their lives. There was the Sleeping Beauty, lying nobly to the sky. There were the Lions rising, sculptured, remote, indifferent. Smoke of fires trailed delicately through the trees. Along the topmost generous curve of the westward hills, pine trees cut sharply against the coloured evening skies and there were always the sounds of the sirens of the ships and the cries of the sea-gulls—sounds of ocean.

In the last pages of *Ocean to Ocean* George Monro Grant writes an eloquent passage on the way travel, aided by transportation, makes it possible to conceive the magnificence of Canada and its extraordinary diversity within unity.

> Looking back over the vast breadth of the Dominion when our journeyings were ended, it rolled out before us like a panorama, varied and magnificent enough to stir the dullest spirit into patriotic emotion. For nearly 1,000 miles by railway between different points east of Lake Huron; 2,185 miles by horses, including coaches, waggons, pack and saddle-horses; 1,687 miles in steamers in the basin of the St. Lawrence and on Pacific waters, and 485 miles in canoes or row-boats; we had travelled in all 5,300 miles between Halifax and Victoria, over a country with features and resources more varied than even our modes of locomotion.

From the sea-pastures and coal-fields of Nova Scotia and the forests of New Brunswick, almost from historic Louisburg up the St. Lawrence to historic Quebec; through the great Province of Ontario, and on lakes that are seas; by copper and silver mines so rich as to recall stories of the Arabian Nights, though only the rim of the land has been explored; on the chain of lakes, where the Ojibbeway is at home in his canoe, to the plains, where the Cree is equally at home on his horse; through the prairie Province of Manitoba, and rolling meadows and park-like country, out of which a dozen Manitobas shall be carved in the next quarter of a century; along the banks of

> A full-fed river winding slow
> By herds upon an endless plain,

full-fed by the exhaustless glaciers of the Rocky Mountains, and watering 'the great lone land'; over illimitable coal measures and deep woods; on to the mountains, which open their gates, more widely than to our wealthier neighbours, to lead us to the Pacific; down deep gorges filled with mighty timber, beside rivers whose ancient deposits are gold beds, sands like those of Pactolus and channels filled with fish; on to the many harbours of mainland and island, that look right across to the old Eastern Thule 'with its rosy pearls and golden-roofed palaces,' and open their arms to welcome the swarming millions of Cathay; over all this we had travelled, and it was all our own.

> 'Where's the coward that would not dare
> To fight for such a land?'

And in fact, parallel with the opening of the land by transportation systems, with the telescoping of its distance by a series of inventions like the electric telegraph and that innovation associated with Canada, the telephone, there had come about a changing attitude to the environment and the beginning of a process by which fear of the land, a desire to subdue and conquer, was replaced by a mystique of the land, a desire to cherish and to understand what had once seemed entirely impenetrable. Here I am talking of something quite different from the nineteenth-century French-Canadian preoccupation with the land, which I noted in the last chapter. That concept of *la terre de nos aieux* (land of our forefathers) emerged in an established, religiously oriented society and was expressed by writers who saw almost mystical links between the soil, the people, and the faith; it was culturally intensive, based on the intimacy of a long-established agrarian society. The English-Canadian mystique of the land was extensive, and in a paradoxical way it combined the desire to conquer and exploit the vast unoccupied spaces with a parallel desire to cherish and understand the wilderness that had once seemed entirely hostile and impenetrable.

It is true that even at the end of our period, despite the incursions of settlement, nine-tenths of the land was still wilderness—forest and semi-desert, lake and tundra—with only the verges of it eaten into by loggers and criss-crossed by the trails of trappers and prospectors. The great unexplored North, the Meta Incognita of Elizabeth I, pressed down upon the fragile South, imprisoning it in walls of weather and remoteness. Even city-dwelling Canadians still lived in a series of clearings, though these were much larger than the stumpfields within the looming primeval forest the Moodies and their kind had confronted. The bush was still a presence, menacingly alive, and, as anyone who has travelled in Canada's areas of abandoned land will know, it was only waiting to return and take over—nature triumphing where man retreated.

Yet as the nineteenth century progressed, men and women began to look with different eyes on their slowly changing environment. In various ways historians and critics have shown how defensive—and almost uniformly so—was the attitude of early pioneers and visitors to the country they travelled through or settled in. Northrop Frye's metaphor—transferred from the military history of early Canada and from novels of the time like *The History of Emily Montague* and *Wacousta*—of colonial Canada as a garrison enclosed upon itself, can be supplemented by the image of the shack in the tiny clearing from which the settler fought his way against the forest, every tree an enemy, to unite his portion of the open sky with that of his neighbours. The native peoples saw themselves as part of the scheme of nature, in spiritual relationships with the land and even with the animals they killed in order to survive; there might be evil forces within their world, but the land itself was beneficent, the source of life. The early settler, and the early traveller, saw the land as hostile, an entity to be conquered before it could be lived in. Early accounts show travellers appalled by the landscape's vast monotonies, by the great barriers of forest to be hacked through, by the expanses of prairies to be traversed day after day. Adjectives like 'forlorn' and 'dreary' and 'gloomy' are endlessly repeated in the narratives of men like George Vancouver and Simon Fraser and even of relatively sensitive diarists like David Thompson, and it was only grudgingly that Susanna Moodie in the end admitted that 'the wilderness was not without its rose, the hard face of poverty without its smile.'

When the men and women of that early era first began to come to terms with the land, it was less by recognizing it for what it was than by seeking and finding in it the characteristics of a more civilized and familiar setting. William Cobbett, who spent some years as a private soldier in New Brunswick, saw it in his later recollections as the ideal setting for the kind of settled rural life that was already fading away in the counties of England. Highly responsive to the relatively gentle beau-

ties of the Maritime landscape, he discussed it with an eye to its use for
bucolic pleasure and profit. In his *Advice to Young Men* (1829) he described
the woodlands of New Brunswick as if they were the perfect setting for
the kind of Regency park that Humphrey Repton might have landscaped.

> Here were about two hundred acres of natural meadow, interspersed with
> patches of maple trees in various forms and of various extent; the creek
> (there about thirty miles from its point of joining the St. John) ran down
> the middle of the spot, which formed a sort of dish, the high and rocky
> hills rising all round it, except at the outlet of the creek, and these hills
> crowned with lofty pines; in the hills were the sources of the creek, the
> waters of which came down in cascades, for any one of which many a
> nobleman in England would, if he could transfer it, give a good slice of
> his fertile estate.

Cobbett of course was a transient and never returned to Canada. But
writers who were Canadian-born and had known the land from child-
hood still described it in terms of Augustan pastoral, as Oliver Goldsmith
the younger did in the decade when Cobbett wrote the above passage.
There is a strong element of making a virtue of necessity in *The Rising
Village*, whose intent seems to have been to refute the original Oliver
Goldsmith's vision in *The Deserted Village* of the New World as a 'horrid
shore' beset by 'various terrors':

> Those matted woods, where birds forget to sing,
> But silent bats in drowsy clusters cling;
> Those pois'nous fields with rank luxuriance crown'd,
> Where the dark scorpion gathers death around; . . .
> Where crouching tigers wait their hapless prey,
> And savage men more murd'rous still than they . . . .

Many travellers and pioneers, and especially those who abandoned
the Americas with disgust, would have agreed with this passage from
The Deserted Village. The older Oliver had wanted to contrast the idyllic
village of the days before the enclosures with the wilderness to which
its people were forced to immigrate. But young Oliver had to present a
reassuring picture of the settled rural areas of New Brunswick for the
very simple reason that he and his fellow Loyalists had nowhere else
to go. They had to come to some kind of terms with the land, but the
spirit of *The Rising Village* is not that of acceptance, since the poet uses,
with less felicity, exactly the same kind of diction and imagery that his
great-uncle had used to describe a British village half a century before;
he can only make the Canadian landscape comprehensible by translating
it into English pastoral conventions:

> There smiling orchards interrupt the scene
> Of gardens bounded by some fence of green;
> The farmer's cottage, bosomed 'mong the trees,

Whose spreading branches shelter from the breeze;
The winding spring that turns the busy mill,
Whose clanking echoes o'er the distant hill;
The neat white church beside whose wall are spread
The grass-clad hillocks of the sacred dead . . . .

This failure to describe—perhaps even to see—one's surroundings with fresh and original insight was accompanied by a surprising lack of interest among poets and fiction writers, as well as newspaper journalists and the public who read them, in the western and northern hinterlands whose exploration continued apace during the nineteenth century and which Confederation would bring into the same great country as the original provinces. The sense of a country so vast and so varied and so grand—almost grandiose—in the dimensions of its natural features had not yet penetrated the creative imagination revealed in Canadian writings of the time. Canadians were much less passionately involved in the tragedy of Franklin's expedition on the frozen coasts to the north of their country than the English were. The records of the explorers who almost yearly to the end of the nineteenth century were adding to the accumulated knowledge of the territory that became Canada inspired no imaginative writing on our country. In fact few of the explorers, by sea or by land, were Canadian born. It was not until the journeys of the Tyrrell brothers through the Barren Lands in the late 1880s and the early 1890s that a tardy tradition of native-born explorers emerged. It was left for an English poet, Samuel Taylor Coleridge, to make poetry in *The Rime of the Ancient Mariner* out of the great Arctic voyages.

Undoubtedly this indifference was partly due to the pioneer life in which the perception of the environment was conditioned by the experience of hardship. Anne Langton, an Englishwoman trapped like Susanna Moodie in the backwoods of Upper Canada, wrote home in 1839:

The old world is the world of romance and poetry. I dare say our lakes, waterfalls, rapids, canoes, forests, Indian encampments, sound very well to you dwellers in the suburbs of a manufacturing town; nevertheless I assure you there cannot well be a more unpoetical and antiromantic existence than ours.

In her generation and circumstances complaints like this were much more often expressed than lyrical appreciation of the beauty of the land.

But travellers from England, already imbibing romantic ideas of the sublimity of nature and accustomed to the care taken by Regency landscapists to give an illusion of the natural to the great parks of England, were shocked by the savage thoroughness with which the pioneers destroyed the magnificent forest covering of Upper Canada. In 1837 Anne Jameson lamented:

A Canadian settler *hates* a tree, regards it as his natural enemy, as something to be destroyed, eradicated, annihilated by all and any means. The idea of useful or ornamental is seldom associated here even with the most magnificent timber trees, such as among the Druids had been consecrated, and among the Greeks would have sheltered oracles and votive temples. The beautiful faith which assigned to every tree of the forest its guardian nymph, to every leafy grove its tutelary deity, would find no votaries here. Alas! for the Dryads and Hamadryads of Canada!

And forty years later the Earl of Southesk looked on pioneer industriousness with the alarm of a man coming from a country where the woods were treasured because the forests had vanished long ago:

It grieves the heart of a lover of trees to travel through America. For hundreds and thousands of miles his eyes behold nothing but wholesale destruction of these noblest ornaments of the earth. Fire everywhere, the axe everywhere, the barking-knife and the bill-hook—joint ravagers with the storm, the lightning and the flood—all busy pulling down nature's handiwork—and who builds up anything in its stead?

For those who felled them, the trees of course seemed menacingly abundant, and even those who felt the appeal of the great forests could sense the thrill of domination that came from their destruction—as Isabella Valancy Crawford did when, in her narrative poem about the pioneers, *Malcolm's Katie* (1884), she combined a lyrical evocation of the beauties of the wilderness—

> Said the high hill, in the morning, 'Look on me—
> Behold, sweet earth, sweet sister sky, behold
> The red flames on my peaks, and how my pines
> Are cressets of pure gold; my quarried scars
> Of black crevasse and shadow fill'd canyon
> Are traced in silver mist; how on my breast
> Hang the soft purple fringes of the night . . . .

—with a glorification of its subjugation.

> The mighty morn strode laughing up the land,
> And Max, the labourer and lover, stood
> Within the forest's edge, beside a tree;
> The mossy king of all the woody tribes,
> Whose clatt'ring branches rattl'd, shuddering.
> As the bright axe cleaved moon-like thro' the air,
> Waking strange thunders, rousing echoes link'd
> From the full, lion-throated roar, to sighs
> Stealing on dove-wings thro' the distant aisles.
> Swift fell the axe, swift follow'd roar on roar
> Till the bare woodland bellow'd in its rage,
> As the first-slain slow toppl'd to his fall.
> 'O King of Desolation, art thou dead?'

Thought Max, and laughing, heart and lips, leap'd on
The vast, prone trunk. 'And have I slain a King?
'Above his ashes will I build my house—
'No slave beneath its pillars, but—a King!'

Yet, as the poem ends, the wilderness is represented, not as a hostile place, but as a refuge:

. . . these wild and rocking woods
Dotted with little homes of unbark'd trees,
Where dwell the fleers from the waves of want, . . .

A degree of detachment seemed necessary to separate the hardships of pioneer life from the beauty of the setting, and this, as an urban poet, Crawford had. Those who had the leisure and the opportunity to experience the land without toiling on it could see it with new eyes, just as Europe's mountains had ceased to be dreary and forbidding during the romantic era and had become inviting and beautiful.

It was not merely a matter of aesthetics. Already in Canada there had been occasional artists like Thomas Davies in the late eighteenth century who had presented the landscape in loving detail, and there had been beauty spots like Montmorency Falls and—somewhat later—Niagara Falls and Lake Memphramagog that became the centres of pilgrimage for those with leisure, sensibility and the means of transport, from Frances Brooke to Feo Monck, who described her visit to the lake with her usual wit and perceptiveness:

Towards nightfall we neared Georgeville at the side of Lake Memphramagog. The drive was too beautiful—the burial places at the side of their houses—every family its own burial place. We saw such quantities of 'snake fences', angry wind clouds over the deep deep blue mountains, the dark green 'forests primeval', and the blue lake—it was all like what one might dream of in an inspired moment, but rarely see in real life. The lake is quite surrounded with mountains covered with forests, and at the foot of one of the highest of them, stands the Mountain House, or inn, the only house for miles round. It is wooden and built with galleries all round it, and it is very picturesque-looking . . . . After more than an hour's steaming in *The Maid of the Mist*, we got to the Mountain House. A crowd from the hotel was assembled in the dark night to see us land. We had great fun at dinner; the knives would not cut, and such hacking you never saw. It was a rough, clean inn, and we had a floor to ourselves.

Here we are reminded of the cult of the picturesque that had made pilgrimage places of spots—such as Llangollen or Land's End, the Lake District or Snowdonia—whose lingering traces of wildness offered a contrast to the rest of an England that was already far advanced in urbanization and industrialization. The new element that entered into the Canadian mystique of the land was the idea of scale, a concept that goes beyond the merely aesthetic because it embraces vastnesses that cannot be encompassed by sight but can only be apprehended by the intelligence. Yet it is at the same time an idea as deeply rooted in the physical as any delight in the beauty or grandeur of an immediate landscape, for it can only be aroused when means are taken to unite and make accessible the remotenesses that the imagination must apprehend in a continuum of space and time. The extent of Canada, which covers five of the world's twenty-four time zones, can never be divorced from the concept of time. It was no accident that the originator of the very idea of time zones should be an engineer, Sandford Fleming, working on the opening out of the great Canadian spaces through the construction of railways.

It was with this broader penetration of the territories beyond the Canadian Shield, which the fur companies had long protected from outside intrusion, that a mystique of the land began to emerge. The first writer in whose work it appears strongly is Henry Youle Hind, whose expedition was really intended as a challenge to the fur-traders' suzerainity over the plains. Henry Youle was the brother of William G.R. Hind, Canada's one authentic Pre-Raphaelite painter, and he seems to have shared William's visual sensibility, for his *Narrative* is full of splendid descriptive pieces that show a painterly eye for evocative detail as well as a due sense of the sublimity of phenomena—which travelling fur traders seem to have regarded as merely annoying or dangerous. Here is one of his descriptions of a prairie that had been burnt over.

> In the afternoon we arrived at a part of the prairie where the fire had run; as far as the eye could see westward, the country looked brown, or black, and desolate. The strong north-westerly wind which had been blowing during the day drove the smoke from the burning prairies beyond Red River, in the form of a massive wall towards us; a sight more marvellously grand, and at the same time gloomy and imposing, could scarcely be conceived than that approaching wall of smoke over the burnt expanse of prairie stretching far away to the west. The upper edge was fringed with rose-colour by the rays of the sun it had just obscured; and as it swept slowly on, the rich rose-tints faded into a burnt-sienna hue, which gradually died away as the obscuration became more complete, until, though early in the afternoon, with a bright cloudless sky towards the east, a twilight gloom began to settle around and the rolling fold of smoke over the prairie rapidly enveloped all things in a thin but impenetrable haze. When the sun was still some degrees above the horizon the light was that of dim twilight; the prairie hens flew wildly across the trail, and without, as is usual with them, any determined or usual direction; our horses appeared to be uneasy or alarmed, and the whole scene began to wear an aspect of singular solemnity and gloom.

What especially characterized Hind's attitude, and distinguished it from that of earlier travellers, was his willingness to see nature as a unity, in which aspects that might be hostile to the interests of men might nevertheless have their own sublime beauty, and it was in this further manifestation of the grandeur of the wilderness that he observed the great plagues of grasshoppers that swept destructively over the vast plains.

> Lying on my back and looking upwards as near the sun as the light would permit, I saw the sky continually changing colour from blue to silver to white, ash grey and lead colours, according to the numbers in the passing cloud of insects . . . . The aspect of the heavens during the greatest flight was singularly striking. It produced a feeling of uneasiness, amazement and awe in our minds, as if some terrible, unforeseen calamity were about to happen.

Not only was the sublimity of the new land seen by the mid-Victorians in its grander and more terrible aspects: they also, Blake-like, dwelt on its smallest details. One morning in July 1872 George Monro Grant noted in his diary an awakening to the first view of the prairie:

> Awakened at 8 a.m. by hearing a voice exclaiming, 'thirty-two new species already; it's a perfect floral paradise.' Of course, it was our botanist, with his arms full of the treasures of the prairie. We looked out and beheld a sea of green sprinkled with yellow, red, lilac, and white, extending all round to the horizon. None of us had ever seen a prairie before, and, behold, the half had not been told us! As you cannot imagine what the ocean is without seeing it, neither can you in imagination picture the prairie. The vast fertile beautiful expanse suggests inexhaustible national wealth. Our uppermost thought might be expressed in the words, 'Thank God, the great North-west is a reality.'

'Our botanist' was James Melville Macoun, a fine field naturalist who wrote his own book on the prairies, *Manitoba and the Great North West* (1882). But if he had something of Blake's ability to see 'heaven in a wild flower', and if Grant could conjure the prospect of wealth out of a view of endless grassland, it was William Francis Butler, that great champion of the untamed Indian, who saw the sublime in almost every feature of the West, and expressed it with true Victorian magniloquence:

> An immense plain stretched from my feet to the mountain—a plain so vast that every object of hill and wood and lake lay dwarfed into one continuous level, and at the back of this level, beyond the pines and the lakes and the river-courses, rose the giant range, solid, impassable, silent— a mighty barrier rising midst an immense land, standing sentinel over the plains and prairies of America, over the measureless solitudes of the Great Lone Land. Here, at last, lay the Rocky Mountains.

Another example of the change in attitudes that appeared among Canadians as transport and communications knit the country together can be seen in the work of Charles Mair, who never took enough time out from his various activities to become a really accomplished poet, yet whose work had greater authenticity than that of his predecessors because from the beginning he tried to express actual perceptions of the environment rather than represent it by outworn conventions. His early poetry, in *Dreamland*, which he published in 1868 before his foray into the Red River colony, is jerky and unpolished, often harsh in tone, and sometimes archaic in phrasing. Yet in his poem 'August' it is evident that Mair observed carefully the effects of summer drought, and tried to record them directly, rather than relying on the Augustan clichés that Goldsmith and Sangster inherited and handed on. August for him is the 'dull' month of 'sultry days',

> When every field grows yellow, and a plague
> Of thirst dries up her herbage to the root,
> So that the cattle grow quite ribby-lean
> On woody stalks whose juices are all spent;
> When every fronded fern in mid-wood hid
> Grows sick and yellow with the jaundice heat,
> Whilst those on hill-sides glare with patchy red;
> When streamlets die upon the lichened rocks,
> And leave the bleaching pebbles shining bare,
> And every mussel shell agape and parched
> And small snail-craft quite emptied of their crews . . . .

Mair's lines are not entirely innocent of awkward poeticisms ('mid-wood', 'agape, etc.), and the final image of snail-shells as 'craft quite emptied of their crews' is naïvely absurd. Nevertheless one senses that he had carefully observed the particularities of his surroundings and tried to record them faithfully. More than any other early poet—with the exception of Isabella Valancy Crawford—he anticipated the task Charles G.D. Roberts and his associates later on set themselves, that of seeing the Canadian world anew and trying to evolve a fresh way of giving expression to their perceptions.

But Mair is more than a meticulous note-taker putting into verse what he saw on his nature walks. The later Mair generalizes where earlier he had particularized, and in *Tecumseh* he achieves an equation of myths that illuminates an important aspect of nineteenth-century Canadian attitudes: the equation of the Noble Savage with the Benign Wilderness, in what often reads like Canada's first conservationist manifesto but is really a threnody for a spoilt world:

> There was a time on this fair continent
> When all things throve in spacious peacefulness . . . .
> The prairie realm—vast ocean's paraphrase—
> Rich in wild grasses numberless, and flowers
> Unnamed save in mute Nature's Inventory,
> No civilized barbarian trenched for gain.

The rivers and their tributary streams,
Undammed, wound on forever, and gave up
Their lonely torrents to weird gulfs of sea,
And ocean wastes unshadowed by a sail.
And all the wild life of this western world
Knew not the fear of man, yet in those woods,
And by those plenteous streams and mighty lakes,
And on stupendous steppes of peerless plain,
And in the rocky gloom of canyons deep,
Screened by the stony ribs of mountains hoar
Which steeped their snowy peaks in purging cloud,
And down the continent where tropic suns
Warmed to her very heart the mother earth,
And in the congeal'd north where silence self
Ached with intensity of stubborn frost,
There lived a soul more wild than barbarous;
A tameless soul, the sunburnt savage free—
Free, and untainted by the greed of gain:
Great Nature's man content with Nature's food.

Yet *Tecumseh* is not entirely elegiac either in intent or effect. In this massive closet drama, which took decades to write and was published in 1886, the year after the North West Rebellion and the completion of the CPR, Mair was not merely celebrating a hero and his long-dead way of life; he was also speaking of a wilderness that still survived over vast areas of the land, even though the buffalo and the proud warriors of the plains had been pushed away into the past. And he was describing it for Canadians, just as he had done—in different language—when, as a Canada Firster, he had agitated for the annexation of the great plains to the newly established dominion.

Tecumseh has its place—a small one—in the Canadian literary tradition. But it was never widely read and must be regarded as a sign of the times rather than as an influence on general perceptions. Its appearance, however, coincided with the beginning of a major change in the Canadian attitude towards the wilderness and in the image of the land Canadians carried in their minds. In its most conscious forms, that change became manifest in the painting and literature of the late nineteenth and early twentieth centuries.

W.G.R. Hind, *The Leather Pass, Rocky Mountains*, 1862. McCord Museum of Canadian History.

10

The Visual Imagination and
the Mystique of the Land

In the westward expansion of Canada, material motives and aesthetic experience were linked in an almost casual manner. Economic aims had taken the original fur-trading explorers across the country. And while some of the later nineteenth-century travellers—who went west like Southesk, and Milton and Cheadle—did so in a spirit of globe-trotting adventure, and Paul Kane uniquely travelled in search of subjects he could paint, those to whom we owe some of our most vivid impressions of the Old West, before settlement changed it, headed there originally for a combination of political and economic reasons linked with the termination of the Hudson's Bay Company's suzerainty over Rupert's Land. Henry Youle Hind went on a geographical expedition whose real aim was to assess the economic potentialities of the Prairies. William Butler set out on his travels in 1870 as part of the Red River Expedition investigating the results of the Red River Rebellion. And in 1872 and 1883 George Monro Grant accompanied Sandford Fleming on western trips in connection with surveys for the transcontinental railway. All three were astonished and captivated by the scenery which—as good late-Victorians—they appreciated for its sublimity as much as they were impressed by considerations of the region's untapped resources.

The most striking contemporary aesthetic response to this newly opened land, however, was that of the landscape painters and photographers who journeyed there—in the case of the photographers in the 1870s and of the painters in the 1880s. They too, like Kane in the 1840s, went under the auspices of the dominant economic interest (the fur-trade in Kane's case, and the railways in that of his successors). Their response to the landscape there combined romantic admiration of the grandeur of nature, national pride, and a genuine aesthetic feeling that was typical of the era—with its Ruskinian tendency to confuse the representational and the formal aspects of the visual arts, and to blend artistic practices with socio-political intents. They came, they saw, and—unlike Caesar—they were conquered.

In a young country the visual arts have many functions. Before photography, drawings and paintings—and the engravings that printers used to disseminate them to a wider public through books and periodicals—were the only means of transmitting a visual sense of peoples, places, and events. When we look at a painting by an early nineteenth-century artist, our first impulse is to read its informative or anecdotal content; only later do we sort out the works whose lasting significance is merely documentary from those that survive for their formal qualities.

Early landscape painting in Canada was executed by British officers who had attended the Royal Military Academy, Woolwich, and learned topography and water-colour painting along with their military training. One of the treatises they were introduced to was John Hassell's *The Speculum; or The Art of Drawing in Water Colours; and Instructions for Sketching from Nature*, which combined rather mechanical remarks on composition and perspective with an interpretation of the natural as being very near the picturesque. Hassell warned his readers that nature rarely presents 'a finished picture', so that 'the component parts of your view are not an absolute portrait of the place'; and he exhorted them to strive for 'simplicity'. What the majority of the officer-artists produced in Canada—those whose aim was not solely to present an informative sketch of a particular place that was the object of military attention—was a rather tamely picturesque and localized view of the terrain and the people. Several of them, however, were true artists who were skilled in the medium of watercolour and had an individual eye, a personal way of looking at nature and life: they created many treasured depictions of early Canada. Thomas Davies, George Heriot, and James Pattison Cockburn all trained at the Academy—Heriot and Cockburn under Paul Sandby. Davies and Heriot were active before our period begins. Cockburn produced a large body of paintings—mainly of Quebec City and its environs—which, for accuracy of detail, charm of composition, and their

James Pattison Cockburn, *The Lower City of Quebec from the Parapet . . .*, 1833. Colour aquatint. Metropolitan Toronto Library.

sometimes anecdotal inclusion of people, offer a record of a time, the 1830s, and a place that is both historically valuable and artistically pleasing.

During the decades between the end of the War of 1812 and the lull after the Rebellions of 1837, the country that became Canada was shaking itself into political shape, and British North Americans were coming to recognize that they were neither British nor American in the narrow sense of either term. They would soon need a mental picture of a land that was their own, and the artists were naturally the first to help them fill this gap in their imaginary panorama of the world.

Artists were among the first people, other than fur traders, to make their way into the West. Peter Rindisbacher was one of the earliest. A young Swiss of precocious ability, he came to Red River with his family in 1821, when he was fifteen, and on the way from York Factory to the settlement he made the first sketches ever done of the Hudson's Bay Company's posts and their surrounding terrain. But Rindisbacher was an anecdotal rather than a landscape artist; we remember him principally for his marvellously detailed and expressive watercolours of western natives, the first paintings of their kind. (See page 138.)

Almost a quarter-of-a-century later two artists who were concerned with landscape travelled through the Canadian West and made their visual records of it. One was the professional painter Paul Kane, who set off in 1845 across Rupert's Land, bound for the Pacific coast, to record the natives' ways of living before they were submerged by the inexorable advance of an alien civilization, with its materialist ethos and its dominant myth of progress. The other was Henry Warre, a lieutenant in the British Army and one of the last in the tradition of officer painters. In 1845 Warre was sent on a secret mission by the British government to investigate the American encroachment into the Oregon territory. Warre's report did not prevent the British government from pusillanimously giving away to the Americans, under the Oregon Boundary Treaty, the land that should have extended Canada southward to the Columbia River. But he did bring home enough drawings to make up a volume of monochrome studies (*Sketches of North America and the Oregon Territory*, 1848) that—perhaps because Warre was not an academic professional, and because he came late in the officer-topographer tradition—show a true perception of the landscape and have a romantic feeling that elevates them above the merely topographical.

The very extent of Warre's experience of the land took him beyond the merely local perceptions of so many early genteel water-colourists in Canada. In his *Diaries* one finds the beginning of the sense of a wilderness sought, and finally accepted, that characterized the notable landscapists of the later nineteenth century.

> Not a vestige of human life to be seen, nay! so far as we knew existed for miles around . . . . The scenery through which we passed onward was grand beyond description—but oh how desolate! Mountains upon mountains reared their bleak heads high above the mists, which rolled upwards from the valley below: pine & fir trees broken by storms & wonderfully picturesque in shape grew together in the ravines or stood like sentinels scattered amidst the rugged rocks. The trackless vallies were smooth with unbroken snow. No living thing dared to brave the awful loneliness.

No living thing but the artist! Here is foreshadowed the spirit of excitement and adventure that from the mid-century onward increasingly prompted Canadian artists to journey into the remotenesses of their great land.

Much of that excitement is projected in the text of Paul Kane's *Wanderings of an Artist Among the Indians of North America* (1859), as it is in the landscape sketches he prepared, which have the same kind of direct and spontaneous vision as his sketches of natives. But Kane did not carry that kind of perception forward into his finished landscapes any more than he did into his finished paintings of Indians. The various studies he made of Boat Encampment on the Columbia River exemplify

Paul Kane, *Boat Encampment*. Watercolour. Courtesy Stark Museum of Art, Orange, Texas.

this difference. He went there twice. On the first occasion he was somewhat hastily passing through on his way to the Pacific coast, and on 15 November 1845 he noted:

> On leaving Boat Encampment, I did not take any sketches, although the scenery was exceedingly grand; the rapidity with which we now travelled, and the necessity for doing so owing to the lateness of the season, prevented me, and as I was determined to return by the same route, I knew that I should then have time and opportunity.

In the following autumn Kane returned and stayed there for almost three weeks, waiting to accompany the fur brigade back across the mountains. In his diaries he gives very little detail about his painting activities; the only direct reference states:

> We had almost constant rain, accompanied by immense snow-flakes, which obscured our view of the mountains nearly the whole time of our remaining here. I, however, managed to pick out some few bright hours for sketching.

When they were about to leave Boat Encampment he noted that he and his companions 'were all heartily tired of our gloomy situation.'

Nevertheless Kane made several good landscape sketches, which in their faithfulness to the terrain compare rather well with later photographs. He also did a sketch of the camp at Boat Encampment and later a finished oil painting actually entitled *Boat Encampment*, probably painted the year after his return to Toronto. In the oil a fairly authentic-looking camp in the foreground is surrounded by towering grandiose mountains and darkly romantic forests. In the watercolour sketch of the same scene the mountains do not overpower the landscape but belong to it so intimately that their white slopes echo the white slopes of the foreground tent, and the whole view—sombre in the oil—is bathed in the clear sunlight of high altitudes. It gives a sense of Kane's fresh and vivid perceptions of the original scene, and suggests his capacity for understanding and for rendering a landscape's intrinsic patterns, which he put aside when making paintings for the market. What Kane produced in the region most associated with his work was far better than what he produced on his return to Toronto. There, in completing his canvases, he allowed a true regional insight to be overwhelmed by a deadening academic cosmopolitanism.

No painter of any great significance followed Kane into the West until William G.R. Hind reached the Prairies in 1862. In the days before the camera was sufficiently developed to be useful to travellers, artists were taken along on exploratory expeditions to make visual records and illustrate reports. The brother of the geologist and explorer Henry Youle Hind, William Hind—very likely stimulated by his brother's account of his two expeditions to the Northwest in the late 1850s—accompanied the geological-survey expedition his brother led to Labrador in 1861. The pencil drawings and watercolours of local Indians William produced—several of which were reproduced as woodcuts and chromo-lithographs in the published report—transcend their documentary function and are works of art. Henry Youle Hind was also deeply interested in the arts and sometimes wrote about them when he was editing the *Canadian Journal* in the 1850s. There is a pictorial quality in his descriptive set pieces that one can imagine appealing to the landscape painters of the time. An example is this evocation of the prairie's changing aspects:

It must be seen at sunrise, when the boundless plain suddenly flashes with rose-coloured light, as the first rays of the sun sparkle in the dew on the long grass, gently stirred by the unfailing morning breeze. It must be seen at noon-day, when refraction swells into the forms of distant hill ranges the ancient beaches and ridges of Lake Winnipeg, which mark its former extension; when each willow bush is magnified into a grove, each distant clump of aspens, not seen before, into wide forests, and the outlines of wooded river banks, far beyond unassisted vision, rise into view. It must be seen at sunset, when, just as the huge ball of fire is dipping below the horizon, he throws a flood of red light, indescribably magnificent, into the illimitable waving green, the colours blending and separating with the gentle roll of the long grass in the evening breeze, and seemingly magnified towards the horizon into the distant heaving swell of a parti-coloured sea. It must be seen, too, by moonlight, when the summits of the low green grass leaves are tipped with silver, and the stars in the west disappear suddenly as they touch the earth. Finally, it must be seen at night, when the distant prairies are in a blaze, thirty, fifty, or seventy miles away; when the fire reaches clumps of aspen, and the forked tips of the flames, magnified by refraction, flash and quiver on the horizon, and the reflected lights from rolling clouds above tell of the havoc that is blazing below.

There cannot be much doubt of a close connection between perceptions of this kind and William Hind's subsequent decision to join the Overlanders in their trek across the Prairies and through the Rockies to the Cariboo in 1862. He responded in a most idiosyncratic way; greatly influenced by William Morris, he turned Cariboo miners into Morrisite Vikings in moments of relaxation. His landscapes—like those of such Pre-Raphaelite painters as J.E. Millais and Holman Hunt—are characterized by meticulous foreground detail, but they tend to become grandiose and formalized in their distances. (See the headpiece to this chapter.)

Pre-Raphaelitism was one of a number of external factors, some of them stylistic and others mechanical, that affected Canadian landscape painting during the nineteenth century and helped give it a shape of its own. Thanks largely to foreign travel by Canadian painters, by the beginning of the Great War almost all the leading movements abroad—including not only Pre-Raphaelitism, but also Impressionism, Fauvism, early twentieth-century Scandinavian landscape painting, Art Nouveau, and the romantic luminism of such contemporary American painters as Albert Bierstadt—had made their mark on Canadian painting. The rise of photography also had its effects in changing modes of perception and attitudes towards composition. Equally important for its extension of the chromatic and tonal possibilities of landscape painting was the invention of new vivid paints based on aniline and other coal-tar derivatives. These paints, which the Pre-Raphaelites began to use early on to create their sharp and lucent colouring, were of particular value in the Canadian setting, where the clear air and vivid tints of rocks and vegetation lent themselves to these new strong pigments. In the 1870s the Canadian painter Allan Edson used the new brilliant paint to build up light effects that rivalled those of the Impressionists, and—especially in spectacular works like *Giant Falls* (Montreal Museum of Fine Arts), completed in 1872—contributed notably to the upsurge of Canadian landscape painting even before the great trek to the West that followed Confederation.

From the 1870s onward landscape painting in Canada flourished largely through its ambiguous links with the relatively new art of photography. In the 1860s pioneer photographers like William Notman offered to the public prints derived from detailed realistic landscape drawings by artists like John A. Fraser; and famous landscape painters of the same period, like Otto Jacobi, would sometimes reverse the process, painting—without any apparent sense of plagiarism—landscapes that were virtually identical with the photographic views on Notman's stereographic cards.

For a long time painting and photography seemed to take parallel courses in discovering the new land. It can be argued that the best of the early images of the West were produced by photographers, and especially by two men who worked with Sandford Fleming in the early days when he was planning the first surveys for the Canadian Pacific Railway. Benjamin Baltzly, an associate of William Notman, accompanied a survey party in British Columbia in 1871. In 1872 Charles Horetsky went along with Fleming on the expedition described by George Monro Grant in *Ocean to Ocean*. The nature of their assignments implied that their photographs—like the drawings of the British officers half a century before—would be primarily topographical in intent, yet both men had strong aesthetic judgement and an appropriate sense of awe in relation to the mountain country through which they separately passed.

Baltzly's expedition made its way up the North Thompson River and tried to break through the dense forest in the direction of the Yellowhead Pass. A typical entry in Baltzly's journal refers to his attempts to photograph the Garnet River cascade near Mount Cheadle.

> Thinking the land opposite our camp was the mainland, I got LaRue to take me across in the canoe. Then I started through the willow, alder, and tall cranberry trees and ferns, wet with the last night's rain, to go to the cascade to see whether there was any prospect of getting views near the falls. After plodding on about three-fourths of a mile through the above bushes, across bear tracks (one evidently very large judging from the marks of his claws), shooting a grouse, and passing an old deserted Indian hunter's camp and cabin, I found, by coming to a slue or arm of the river, that I was only on a large island. So I returned, deeply chagrined, and when I got opposite the camp, Hammond and La Rue came over with the canoe. I told them my mistake, and also that I was determined to go to the falls, this time with the canoe; so away we went downstream. The river flows very rapidly, thus without much paddling it took us only twenty-five minutes to reach the cascade. The cascade, as seen from the foot of the falls, is grand beyond conception. It is by far the boldest scenery of the kind I ever witnessed. It made my heart throb with wonder and amazement as I stood for a few moments and looked upon this beautiful sheet of water as it dashes and tumbles down over the rocks with a deep thundering and roaring noise. The height of the fall is altogether about 400 feet. Far above, it runs down a narrow canyon in angry foaming sheets, and then makes a bold leap over a perpendicular rock for many feet down, and dashes its course a little to the right, again it makes another fearful leap, but is again arrested by another rock which has a front of about 900 feet. Here the water separates, the most part running over a rocky precipice on the right, and on the left the water flows down over the brow in thin sheets to a distance of 150 feet, and before it reaches the rocks beneath it breaks into a shower of spray, and looks much like a white veil against the dark rocks over which it flows.

B.F. Baltzly, *Making Portage of Canoes over the bluff at the Upper Gate of Murchison's Rapids, in the North Thompson River, B.C.*, 1871. National Archives of Canada.

Such intricate description accords with the close detail of Baltzly's photography, confined in the narrow valleys and hemmed in by forest. One print of the party dragging a dugout canoe across the stones of a portage on the North Thompson remains among the most striking images in Canadian photography.

Charles Horetsky, leaving the main Fleming party at the end of 1872, went far to the north, with the unwilling botanist John Macoun in tow; they went through the Peace River country, across the mountains and over to the Nass river. Horetsky was almost as laconic about his photography as Kane had been about his painting. A typical entry is this one for the beginning of January 1873 on the Nass River:

> Before the canoe left, we boiled our kettle and lunched on tea and dried salmon. Pending the preparations, I got out my photographic apparatus and succeeded in getting a negative of the bay, which must be lovely in

the summer season, but at this time was cold and gloomy, snow lying on the ground to a depth of three feet.

He was working in far more open country than Baltzly was trapped in, and his images were at once more austere and more panoramic,which fitted in with Horetsky's arrogant and intractable nature.

There is no doubt that such photographs helped to stir Canadian interest in the landscape of the Cordilleras and of the West in general, making it seem a promised land at the end of a promised railway. In May 1879, when that indefatigable lover of art, the Marquis of Lorne, opened the gallery of the Art Association of Montreal, he lectured his audience of powerful and wealthy anglophones:

> And in the scenery of your own country, the magnificent wealth of water in its great streams, in the foaming rush of their cascades, overhung by the mighty pines or branching maples, and skirted with the scented cedar copses; in the fertility of your farms, not only here, but throughout Ontario also; or in the sterile and savage rock scenery of the Saguenay—in such subjects there is ample material, and I doubt not that our artists will in due time benefit this country by making her natural resources and the beauty of her landscapes as well known as are the picturesque districts of Europe, and that we shall have a school here worthy of our beloved Dominion.

The association of the Canadian Pacific Railway—and especially of William Van Horne—with the great age of landscape painting in the Canadian West cannot be ignored. Van Horne, as an administrator, was alert to the uses of publicity. In the final stages of building the CPR, through the Rockies and the even more difficult Selkirks, he encouraged the newspapermen who came to celebrate the engineering feats and the scenery in the purple prose favoured by the press in that age. He also devised his own methods of publicity, which he keyed in with the advertising campaigns of the immigration officials who, under the guidance of Clifford Sifton, were promoting in Europe and the United States 'The Last Best West'. The settlers who were attracted during the late 1890s and the early 1900s scattered all across the Prairies and provided the CPR with ample returns in traffic and in land sales. Meanwhile Vancouver justified itself largely through imports from the Orient.

But the almost uninhabited territory between Calgary and Kamloops, where the railway passed through three major mountain ranges—the Rockies, the Selkirks, and the Monashee—provided little traffic. To increase it, Van Horne set about transforming the 'sea of mountains', so derided by Edward Blake in his Aurora speech, into a destination for tourists: 'Since we cannot export the scenery, we must import the tourists,' he declared. Chance helped him in 1883 when workers on the line

James Wilson Morrice. *Winter Street with Horses and Sleighs*, c. 1905.
Oil on panel. Art Gallery of Ontario.

through the mountains discovered sulphur hot springs at the place that
became Banff. Spas were still fashionable, and to forestall speculators
the government of Sir John A. Macdonald acted with unusual foresight
in deciding to reserve the springs and twelve square miles around them
for the public; thus was the concept of the national park, which originated south of the border with the creation of Yellowstone Park in 1872,
naturalized in Canada.

But as well as being a great entrepreneur, Van Horne had a genuine
interest in the arts and considerable taste. An enthusiastic and competent
Sunday painter, he would often sketch *en plein air* with his artist friends
among the mountains he opened up to them. He was a discriminating
collector of the avant-garde art of his time—Impressionist and later Post-
Impressionist—and he had a remarkable eye for talent. More than anyone else he was responsible for setting James Wilson Morrice on his
course as Canada's first painter of international repute. Van Horne was

the first to purchase a painting by the young Morrice; and he talked the artist's father into sending him to study in Paris where his real career began and where, in those heady artistic years of the 1890s, Morrice won recognition from Europeans before he gained it from Canadians. Matisse spoke of Morrice as 'the artist with the delicate vision, taking delight with a touching tenderness in the rendering of landscapes . . .', and in Somerset Maugham's *The Magician* there is a clear reference to Morrice as

> one of the most delightful interpreters of Paris I know and when you have seen his sketches—he's done hundreds of unimaginable grace and beauty and feeling and distinction—you can never see Paris in the same way again.

Yet despite his wanderings, which made Matisse think of him as being 'like a migrating bird', Morrice never forgot his Canadian setting, or the 'healthy, lusty colour which you see in Canada' that he celebrated in his great Quebec sketches, and that so many of his contemporaries would discover, often with much help from William Van Horne.

Van Horne commissioned photographs to record the building of the railway and to illustrate promotional material designed to attract tourists. John A. Fraser, the painter who had once been a partner of William Notman, painted some landscapes from photographs on a commission from Van Horne. But in general Van Horne had no need to commission artists to paint the mountains and the varied British Columbian land- and seascapes beyond. The mystique of the land was dawning on them; eager to enter this new realm of possibilities, they seem to have been content with the free passes Van Horne offered them. Some of them became regular visitors to the Cordilleras and to the Pacific coast, where Van Horne would sometimes join them with his easel and paints. Often their reputations became attached to what they did in these regions.

At the outset many of the painters were confused and benumbed by what they saw as, in the words of John A. Fraser, the train went

> up, up, ever up, past peak after peak, glaciers innumerable, over madly roaring boiling torrents, toying with and playfully flinging here and there on their snowy crest, trees.

Fraser confessed that at first he found it difficult to render the mountains in paint, and he talked of a fellow artist who wandered in bewilderment for days; his hands 'hung helplessly in the presence of those peaks over which the clouds, with their ever-changing lights and shades, travelled carelessly.' But what they saw awakened in some of the artists an almost messianic sense of purpose, and Thomas Mower Martin, a dogged crafts-man painter with occasional flashes of visionary illumination, declared his sense of a mission to 'interpret the beauties of nature into a language that all can understand.'

Yet, once the artists had adjusted their sights to the splendour of the western mountains, these years became the peak of the best era of Victorian landscape painting, in which several of the finest artists of the period did some of their best work: the evocative mountain distances of Lucius O'Brien and the bolder and more direct scapes of John Fraser, as well as Mower Martin's extraordinary *jeu d'esprit*, a masterpiece of luminous and intricate colour, the *Interior of the Great Illecilleweet Glacier*.

Some of the excitement evoked by this new country can be gleaned from the enthusiastic letters many of the artists sent home. One of the most eloquent letter-writers was Lucius O'Brien. His mother Mary had noted in her diary on 12 February 1834 the first stirrings of the urge that brought him eventually to the Rockies.

> I don't say that my boy is a born artist, but he sometimes torments me very inconveniently to supply him with the implements to 'Dera, dera.' Sometimes by the same passion I get him off my hands for an hour together. The productions of his pencil as far as I can judge are very much like and quite equal to those of any other young gentleman of a year and a half old.

Half a century later her son was not only one of the leading Canadian painters but had developed a facility with words sufficient to make us understand a great deal of what the painters were seeking and finding in the far Canadian West. He first reached the mountains in the summer of 1886, and was even more impressed by the Selkirk range than by the Rockies, writing a series of letters that were published in the Toronto *Mail*.

> We have been unable to tear ourselves away from these lovely mountains of the Selkirk range . . . . The interest of this scenery is inexhaustible, not only from the varied aspects it presents from so many different points of view, but from the wonderful atmospheric affects. At one moment the mountains seem quite close, masses of rich, strong colour; then they will appear far away, of the faintest pearly grey. At one time every line and fork is sharp and distinct; at another the mountains melt and mix themselves up in the clouds so that earth and sky are almost undistinguishable. Now the mountain sides are of the softest velvet, and presently they look like cast metal. The foregrounds, too, away from the desolation made by the railway cuttings and banks, are rich and luxuriant; large-leafed plants and flowers clothe the slopes. The trees, where the timbermen have not culled out the finest, are most picturesque.

The word 'picturesque' in this context is ambiguous. Clearly O'Brien was thinking first of all about what might make a picture, and in this sense 'picturesque' can be taken to mean 'paintable'. But undoubtedly he also had in mind the more popular Victorian connotation of the word,

Lucius O'Brien, *Wagon Road on the Fraser*, 1887. Watercolour. National Gallery of Canada.

which might be defined as 'romantically pleasing'. The adjective recalls a lavish work of Victorian-Canadian iconography, *Picturesque Canada* (2 vols, c. 1882), of which O'Brien was art director and George Monro Grant was editor. It contains some 540 illustrations, most of them wood-engravings based on paintings (seventy-nine by O'Brien), with, for the West, photo-engravings based on photographs—all of them serene, beautifully composed vistas that are nothing if not picturesque. The complementary text by numerous authors—celebrating the present and the imagined glorious future of the people, cities, towns, and regions of Canada—is suffused with pride and complacency.

Because O'Brien looked at landscapes with the eye of a painter as distinct from that of a poet, what he saw—and fairly precisely de-scribed—was not Wordworthian sublimity so much as atmospheric ef-fects on the forms and colours of the landscape he intended to paint. But he could also realize that there were other ways of coming to terms with the mountains and of being taken into the mystique of the land. One was the sense of adventure, and of the challenge presented by the land, which he projects when he talks of travelling by train down the Kicking Horse Pass.

> The railway has to follow its descent as best it can, clinging to the slopes in a serpentine path which often overhangs the stream, flashing white through the treetops hundreds of feet below. The sides of the pass are dominated by the highest mountains on the line, Mount Stephen and Cathedral Mountain being seven thousand feet above the track. The grade of the railway is extraordinarily steep, making the bare possibility of a runaway train or carriage frightful to contemplate. But every possible precaution was taken and one feels that the risks are controlled and the line is practically safe; still enough is left for pleasing excitement and a stirring of the nerves . . . .
>
> If, by special favour, one is permitted to go on the front of the forward engine, the grandeur of the pass and the forces of nature overcome and controlled by the hand of man are fully realised. There can be but few things in the way of locomotion to compete with the sensation of a spin down the Kicking Horse on the front of the engine.

And he could also understand the appeal that the mountains were beginning to have for ordinary, unartistic people seeking physical health or visual stimulation. Of Banff, where in 1887 a great railway hotel was rising beside the hot spring whose virtues Van Horne's publicity men were assiduously extolling, O'Brien remarked:

> This place seems designed by nature for the purpose for which the country, with one consent, has appropriated it. The aspect and sentiment of the scenery is as different from the stern majesty of the Selkirks as it is possible to conceive. The mountains are as high, but the valley is wider, and they stand off to be admired instead of towering over one's head. There is no want of grandeur, but one is filled with a sense of beauty rather than of awe. Among the Selkirks and in the desolate wilderness at the summit of the Rockies, the tourist is an intruder and an offence. Here the pleasure seekers and the invalids who come to the healing waters for relief for their maladies, are welcome guests, and add the kindly human interest which is appropriate to the place.

Despite O'Brien's irritable reference to the presence of tourists in the desolate places, it is clear that, at this time when landscape painting found itself in the mountains, painters were reflecting a widespread turning towards the land that was also echoed in the works of writers who were trying to come to terms with the environment in their poems and in the animal stories they began to write at this period. It is not accidental that two of the leading younger poets of the time, Archibald Lampman and Duncan Campbell Scott, should have made fairly frequent and often insightful references to contemporary painting in the column 'At the Mermaid Inn', which during the early 1890s they shared with

Wilfred Campbell in the Toronto *Globe*. They wrote on exhibitions; they wrote on such locales of artists as the national parks; and in February 1893 Lampman published an interesting column about landscape painting that showed his own strong visual perceptiveness, and also expressed an attitude parallel to that which began to guide Canadian *plein air* painters during the same decade.

> It seems to me that Canadian painters have a great and comparatively unbroken field before them, if they will only take advantage of it, in the colour effects of our midwinter landscape. On some of these splendid February mornings it cannot but occur to one that there is some wonderful painting to be done, which had perhaps not yet been even attempted. In the winter dawn, with every gradation of red and gold and blue; even in the early forenoon, when the towers of our northern capital stand westward, pale luminous, touched with rose, against a pale, greenish-blue sky, when every roof fronting the sun is a sheet of dazzling cream, and every roof not sunlit and every shadow a patch of the clearest crystalline violet; in the coming of the winter night, with its gorgeous changes of colour, subtle and indescribable, what an infinite variety of choice there is for the hand of the painter, and how simple in many cases, yet always how perfect, the beauty with which he would have to deal.

Lampman's preoccupation with true light and colour in this passage had already found a limited expression in the work of a few Canadian painters—notably Allan Edson—concerned with presenting the clarity of Canadian light and the effects of atmosphere upon it, and by the time this was written it had been greatly developed by the European Impressionists and by other painters, the American James McNeill Whistler, for example. Several young Canadian painters—John Hammond, Maurice Cullen, and James Wilson Morrice—were in contact with Whistler and were aware of his methods of manipulating tones to enhance the shapes in a painting and thereby produce an aesthetic pleasure quite distinct from the conceptual pleasure derived from recognizing an image. These three painters all went to Paris and imbibed the ambiance of the French artistic world at its most vital period. Because of his prolonged absence abroad, Morrice's main influence on Canadian painting was delayed until after his death. But Cullen came home to do the very things with Canadian winter landscapes that Lampman had advocated, filling them with searching light and showing the true relationships of natural Canadian colours. He saw Nature as a book 'with most of its pages uncut', and in showing the world as he perceived it he aroused much derision but also made it possible for young Canadian artists to become experimental without going abroad.

Canada travelled far in artistic terms from the soldier topographers of the end of the Napoleonic wars to the dedicated professionals who, on the eve of the Great War, were beginning to create a tradition of painting (though not of sculpture, which did not flourish in our period, apart from church sculpture in Quebec) that would not only project a national spirit but, by the strength of its practitioners' skills and insight, would stand in a valid relation to world movements. This development was due largely to the peripatetic rhythm that began to dominate the practice of Canadian painting in the later decades of the nineteenth century. The image of the travelling artist is always present in our view of that period. The most originative Canadian painters of the time were those who shook free of their frail bonds to locality and to academic standards, and either went west to broaden their awareness of the land that better transportation had now opened to their perceptions, or went east to learn beyond the Atlantic in the old centres of artistic creation. By going west a painter vastly increased his store of potentially valuable subject matter. By going east he improved his techniques and entered a realm where, increasingly, art was valued for its intrinsic qualities, whether by the aesthetes like Whistler, or by the late Impressionists like the older Monet and their Fauve successors like Matisse, beside whom in the end Morrice worked in the equality of genius.

Such developments were bound up with the emergence during the nineteenth century of landscape as the most important category of Canadian painting, and the partial eclipse of such important early forms as portraiture and genre painting. Landscape enjoyed a long period of vigour and variegation during the mid-nineteenth century and down to the eve of the Great War, and because of its connection with a growing pride in the land, it was often seen as a manifestation of incipient nationalism; the members of the Group of Seven, who emerged on the eve of the Great War, were in fact self-consciously nationalist in their declarations.

The variegation of Canadian landscape was intimately linked with the growing tendency of painters to travel and to become visual explorers of the land in all its extensiveness. But its vigour came largely from an acceptance of the environment, a loosening of pioneer fears of the land, that was not necessarily linked with travel. Indeed, some of the best landscape painters of the time—even if not the most spectacular—were men who did not stir far once they had found a landscape they could respond to. Horatio Walker learnt much from French painters of the pastoral tradition, like Millet and Troyon and also Corot, but he found the inspiration for the great works he began to paint in the 1880s in the small terrain of the Ile d'Orléans. He explained, in an undated note that lies in the files of the National Gallery, what this favoured environment had contributed to his work:

The pastoral life of the people of our countryside, the noble work of the Habitant, the magnificent panoramas which surround him, the different aspects of our seasons, the calm of our mornings and the serenity of our evenings, the movement of ebb and flow of our tides which I have observed off my island, which truly is the sacred temple of the muses and a gift of the gods to men, such are the preferred subjects of my paintings. I have passed the greatest part of my life in trying to paint the poetry, the easy joys, the hard daily work of rural life, the sylvan beauty in which is spent the peaceable life of the habitant, the gestures of the wood cutter and the ploughman, the bright colours of sunrise and sunset, the song of the cock, the daily tasks of the farmyard, all the activity which goes on from morning to evening, in the neighbourhood of the barn.

Another important Canadian landscape painter of the static inclination, who never strayed far from the Ontario woodlands around his beloved Doon, was Walker's contemporary and friend, Homer Watson. Watson—who lived long enough to object to the general condemnation of the Group of Seven in the 1920s—was praised by Oscar Wilde when the celebrated aesthete visited Canada in 1882. 'Mr Watson,' said Wilde, 'is the Canadian Constable and Barbizon without ever having seen Barbizon.' Like so many of the Irish writer's statements, this remark conveyed more than was immediately evident. For the great contrast in early nineteenth-century British landscape painting was that between Constable, the pastoral painter who did not have to go far to find his subjects, and Turner, who wandered restlessly in search of the striking aspects of nature from which he could extract pictorial drama. In this sense, Walker and Watson both resembled Constable, while Turner would have found his affinities in their contemporaries who were now beginning to travel far over the Dominion. But Watson made a statement that conveyed a new sense of the land as a pictorially conceived entity that was present as much in his work as it was in that of his contemporaries like Lucius O'Brien or F.M. Bell-Smith or John A. Fraser, who wandered so often and so restlessly across the country:

There is at the bottom of each artistic conscience a love for the land of their birth. It is said that art knows no country but belongs to the world. This may be true of pictures, but great artists are no more cosmopolitan than great writers, and no immortal work has been done which has not as one of the promptings for its creation a feeling its creator had of having roots in his native land and being a product of the soil.

Watson was making a sensible distinction between the 'pictures' that at the point of completion discard the umbilicus linking them to antecedent circumstances and achieve the autonomy and universality of the masterpiece, and the 'promptings' that led to their creation. We can accept the distinction all the more easily because so few Canadian works

Homer Watson, *Log-cutting in the Woods*, 1894. Oil on canvas. The Montreal Museum of Fine Arts.

in landscape or any other pictorial genre have reached the level of universal masterpiece; both the ultimate relevance and the circumstances of creation of most Canadian art remain local. Thus the development of a true Canadian landscape tradition, culminating in the work of the Group of Seven, is not important solely for its intimate links with the development of a general awareness of the Canadian land as described in the foregoing chapter. Its principal achievement in a collective sense was to elevate that awareness, through the imaginative use of pictorial skills, into a visually conceived myth.

Even in Canada the last years before the Great War were a time of changing artistic perspectives. French styles spread to the New World. In early 1912 Emily Carr exhibited in Vancouver paintings she had recently completed in France, startling viewers with their broad Fauve brushwork and intense colours. That summer she visited the Indian villages of the Queen Charlotte Islands, employing her newly acquired technique in depicting totem poles and their lush blue-green background. Another Canadian Fauve painter named David Milne was represented at the famous Armory show of the Post-Impressionists held in New York in 1913. Art Nouveau had penetrated, mostly through commercial art, and had found a stronghold in the Toronto studios of Grip Limited, an art firm that at various times employed most of the painters who later formed the Group of Seven. The Japanese influences that had affected Whistler and the French Impressionists began to show themselves, particularly on the Pacific coast. There Charles John Collings combined Japanese and English watercolour styles to produce minute and luminous mountain scenes, which his fellow western artist, Walter J. Phillips, described as revealing 'much behind and beyond the ordinary vision, not expressed by abstractions, but by color and form related to nature.'

Thus by the time the Group of Seven began to form between 1911 and 1914 the response of Canadian artists to the land was changing in many ways; to refer to them as 'young revolutionaries', as J. Russell Harper does in his *Painting in Canada*, is to accord them too much credit. Even their linking of landscape with nationalism, and much of their technique in the early 1900s, had been anticipated by C.W. Jefferys, who experimented boldly with colour and light in his paintings of the West and remarked that 'It is inevitable that a country with such marked characteristics as Canada should impress itself forcefully on our artists.' And Jefferys in fact was among the first to recognize the national character of the work of painters who later formed the Group when in 1911 he wrote, after seeing some sketches by J.E.H. MacDonald:

> Mr. MacDonald's art is native—native as the rocks, snow or pine trees that are so largely his theme. In these sketches there is a refreshing absence of Europe, or anything else, save Canada.

By the end of our period there was enough going on in painting to presage the revival of landscape as a major Canadian genre, now linked to the country's emergent nationalism, which the Group of Seven would eventually and emphatically represent. Jefferys and others associated with him were already giving landscape a new credibility, after the fading out of the railway-inspired school of the 1880s, by the time the members of the Group began to come together, with the offices of Grip— that haven of transported Art Nouveau—as their focus. A.Y. Jackson had been to Europe of 1910 and again in 1912 and had returned imbued with the spirit of Impressionism. He was especially impressed by Gauguin, whose early paintings of Brittany had a considerable influence on several members of the Group. There were other equally important foreign influences on this school, which is so often regarded as distinctively Canadian. In 1913 J.E.H. MacDonald and Lawren Harris went to Buffalo to see an exhibition of Scandinavian painting that showed them how a landscape as bleak and elemental as that of the Precambrian Shield might be interpreted in aesthetic terms and—for Harris at least—in mystical terms. The paintings of Harald Sohlbert and Gustav Fjaested impressed them most. As Harris remembered a generation later:

> This visit turned out to be one of the most stimulating and rewarding experiences that either of us had had. Here was a large number of paintings that gave body to our rather nebulous ideas. Here were paintings of northern lands created in the spirit of the lands. Here was a landscape seen through the eyes, felt in the hearts, and understood by the minds of people who knew and loved it. Here was an art, bold, vigorous, and uncompromising, embodying direct experience of the great earth.

But such influences would probably have had little effect had the painters involved not undergone a revelatory experience of the land that was as stimulating to them as the first sight of the Rockies had been to their predecessors a quarter of a century before.

In 1911 one of the Grip artists, William Broadhead, took Tom Thomson up to the northern-lakes country in Algonquin Park on the edge of the Shield. Thomson was immediately inspired and activated by the rock forms, the splendid autumn colours, the atmospheric effects, and began to paint oil sketches in great number *en plein air*, returning to Toronto in the winter to do his studio work. In 1913 he wrote from the North: 'When I take these sketches down to Toronto, the experts will all scoff at them, but those were the colors that I saw.' The 'experts' might scoff, but the young painters Thomson was getting to know did not, and very soon Jackson was accompanying him to the lakes and writing back in 1914:

> Tom seems quite enthusiastic and I expect is quite an inspiring chap to work with. You need a man with you who tries to do the impossible. To do what you know is easily within your powers has never given rise to a great school of art or anything else.

And in another letter he reported: 'Tom is doing some exciting stuff . . . . He plasters on the paint and gets fine quality.'

By 1914 other artists—Fred Varley, Arthur Lismer, and Frank Carmichael—had joined Jackson, MacDonald, and Harris in the yet informal group, and all of them were accompanying Thomson on his painting trips. In winter Harris, Jackson, Thomson, and MacDonald lived in the newly opened Studio Building in the Rosedale Valley of Toronto, which was built by Harris for the use of artists. At this stage, and until his death by drowning in 1917, Thomson was undoubtedly the leader in more ways than one, a guide to the painting country, and a pioneer perceptive eye. When he died, A.Y. Jackson wrote:

Tom Thomson, *Parry Sound Harbour*, 1914. Oil on board. National Gallery of Canada.

> . . . without Tom, the north country seems a desolation of bush and rock.
> He was the guide, the interpreter, and we the guests partaking of his
> hospitality so generously given . . . . [M]y debt to him is almost that of a
> new world, the north country, and a truer artist's vision, because as an
> artist he was rarely gifted.

Undoubtedly had Thomson lived he would have been the most important painter in Canada during the years immediately after the First
World War, not least because he saw the land as a visual rather than a
political entity and was less touched by nationalist ideologies than some
of his associates. Even without him, the movement that would change
Canadian painting and eventually create its own orthodoxy had acquired
an impetus that in hindsight seems to have been inevitable. The group
was informally assembled; the stylistic influences were coming together;
the philosophy was forming. The stage was set for landscape to re-
emerge as the dominant genre in Canadian painting, and travel, opening
new aspects of the country, had once again played its part.

11

The Liberation
of the Literary Imagination

At the beginning of his classic study *On Canadian Poetry*, E.K. Brown recollected Matthew Arnold's complaint in the 1880s about the assumption that there might be an American literature in some way separate from English literature. The language, Arnold believed, united all the literatures that used it into a single tradition. 'Imagine the face of Philip or Alexander at hearing of a Primer of Macedonian Literature! Are we to have a Primer of Canadian Literature, too, and a Primer of Australian?' Writing in 1943, Brown answered in the affirmative. Indeed, we must have a Primer of Canadian Literature, he believed, because in his view there was 'a Canadian Literature, often rising to effects of great beauty'—though he admitted that even in the mid-twentieth century it had 'stirred little interest outside Canada'.

At the time of Arnold's remark, there was much less confidence among Canadians about their literary achievements. Edward Hartley Dewart, the patriotic enthusiast who published *Selections from Canadian Poets* in 1864, admitted: 'Our colonial position, whatever may be its political advantages, is not favourable to the growth of an indigenous literature.'

About the same time Arnold's friend in Canada, Goldwin Smith, declared that 'cooped up as it is and severed from the great literary and publishing centres', Canada was 'not a field in which literary distinction is to be earned.' And even Archibald Lampman, for all his conviction that the achievements of Charles G.D. Roberts called on Canadian writers 'to be up and doing', did not believe, in 1880, that a Canadian literature yet existed. Its emergence, in his view, was dependent on wider cultural developments.

> If our country becomes an independent, compacted, self-supporting nation, which is, or ought to be, the dream of all of us, its social and climatic conditions will in the course of time evolve a race of people having a peculiar national temperament and bent of mind, and when that is done, we shall have a *Canadian* literature.

His argument tended to be a circular one, for in what way, one might ask, could a 'national temperament and bent of mind' evolve without a language and a literature through which it might define itself? What actually happened in the long run was that the development of a national consciousness and the development of a national literature supported each other and ran parallel with the development of political independence. But in the late nineteenth century the possibility of such an eventuality could only be envisaged by someone with the kind of uncritical romantic enthusiasm that W.D. Lighthall displayed in his introduction to the ultra-patriotic *Songs of the Great Dominion* (1889):

> The poets whose songs fill this book are voices cheerful with the consciousness of young might, public wealth and heroism. Through them, taken all together, you may catch something of great Niagara falling, of brown rivers rushing with foam, of the crack of the rifle in the haunts of the moose and caribou, the lament of vanished races singing their death-song as they are swept on to the cataract of oblivion, the rural sounds of Arcadias just rescued from surrounding wildernesses by the axe, shrill war whoops of Iroquois battle, proud traditions of contest with the French and the Americans, stern and sorrowful cries of valour rising to curb rebellion. The tone of them is courage.

Clearly Lighthall was in the business of myth-creating, of abstracting a heroic pattern from deeds that were not necessarily thought heroic in their own context. Canadian culture certainly differs from older cultures in the ways its myths and its literature have come into being. The contemporary critic Victor Hopwood, writing in the *Literary History of Canada* (1965), developed an insight that applies in all areas of early Canadian writing:

> Unlike European consciousness, which goes back directly to ritual and myth, Canadian consciousness, especially that of English-speaking Canada, was born literate into history.

It received the 'rituals, myths, legends' of European culture only in dilution and in written form.

The fact is that Canadian literature was not only born literate: it was born literate in a bad time, for the models the early Canadian writers followed were the late products of declining styles. The Loyalists of the eighteenth and early nineteenth centuries started off with degenerate late-Augustanism, and the British immigrants of the 1830s and 1840s brought with them the sentimental mannerisms that emerged like pale maggots from the decay of romanticism. Henrietta Prescott, publishing her *Poems, Written in Newfoundland* in 1839, was not the worst, but perhaps one of the best of them.

> And let us look upon the snow, as white and pure it lies,
> When the vales are gently sloping, or the hill's tall summits rise;
> Let us mark each branch and twig in the frequent 'Silver-frost,'
> And confess that, e'en now, the trace of Beauty is not lost.

The worst were the earnest moralists, like the temperance-minded Phoebe Mills, whose *Vesper Chimes* appeared in 1872:

> Alas for all her glowing dreams,
> Her new-found joys where are they now?
> Upon her cheek shame's hectic gleams,
> A hot flush mantles o'er her brow.
>
> What is it rends her feelings so?
> What is it wounds her woman's pride?
> Ah, she has learned the truth to know,
> She is a moderate drinker's bride.

Doubtless such styles—at their best in poets like Goldsmith and Sangster and Heavysege—were suited to the production of escapist forms of writing that would lull their readers into enduring a hostile or unsympathetic environment. But they were entirely unsuited to the real task of literature, which is to mediate positively between the reader and his world, and it was probably a half-conscious realization of this inadequacy that through so much of the nineteenth century made Canadians disregard literature as a valid interpretation of their ways of life. This attitude, shared by many people and combined with the functional illiteracy of large sections of the farming population up to the mid-nineteenth century, bred an indifference to literature that many cultured people complained of sadly. Anna Jameson noted that in Niagara she asked for a bookseller and found 'there is not one in town, but plenty of taverns', though in Buffalo she found 'several good booksellers' shops'. E.H. Dewart, writing about a quarter of a century later, in 1864, expressed this view:

There is probably no country in the world, making equal pretension to intelligence and progress, where the claims of native literature are so little felt, and where every effort in poetry has met with so much coldness and indifference, as in Canada.

And Archibald Lampman wrote in very much the same vein as late as 1892.

Hitherto English literature in Canada has been cultivated by so scanty a population, scattered at great distances over so vast a country, that it has not been a matter of great public interest whether our native writers produced good works or bad. Consequently anything like an efficient critical press has been out of the question.

It was not merely that the indifference to writing brought no effective criticism of writers' works. It brought only a scanty living for the writers themselves, as Duncan Campbell Scott remarked, writing, like Lampman, in the 'Mermaid Inn' column they shared in the Toronto *Globe*:

I think it would be impossible to find a more loyal group of men in Canada than her writers. Although from no fault which can at present be remedied our country furnishes for the literary man absolutely no chance of living by his art, desertions from her ranks of the men of letters have been small indeed, and, where they have occurred, probably the severance was not of the spirit at all. If a man is forced to live by his pen in Canada, or wilfully determines to do so, there is only one refuge for him—journalism—and if what all my journalistic friends tell me is true, even that field is not covered very thickly with clover. So that it happens that all our country can bestow on her writers is in some cases only a very modest (or, perhaps, a prudish would be the better word) income, in others, no income at all.

It is true that there were Canadian writers—like James De Mille and May Agnes Fleming—who, by working deliberately for an American market, could make a living by their writing by the 1860s. And there were even, as early as the 1890s, Canadian bestsellers like Gilbert Parker and especially Ralph Connor whose works sold worldwide in the millions; the total sales of Connor's first three novels, *Blackrock* (1898), *The Sky Pilot* (1899), and *The Man from Glengarry* (1901) reached five million copies by the time of his death. But in the nineteenth century, as in the twentieth, it was only a tiny minority of writers who became bestsellers, and usually they were writers whose work is no longer read because its appeal was based on a popularizing facility that produced neither literary art nor a true reflection of the society from which it emerged.

More typical of the lot of Canadian writers in the nineteenth century was that of Susanna Moodie, whose letters are filled with accounts of the difficulties of making ends meet and of writing while being obliged to carry on the occupations of a pioneer housewife. In *Roughing It in the*

Bush (1852) she tells how she 'actually shed tears of joy over the first twenty dollar bill I received from Montreal' and how, after the 'labours of the day', she 'sat up and wrote by the light of a strange sort of candle that Jenny called "sluts", and which the old women manufactured out of pieces of old rags twisted together and dipped in pork lard and stuck in a bottle.'

Her letters to her publisher are full of indications of precarious finances. In the summer of 1853, discussing *Life in the Clearings* with Richard Bentley, she said:

> Should you like the work, I would most *thankfully* accept your kind offer of advance upon it. For though we contrive with rigid economy to make both ends meet, it is hard pinching. The money earned by the two works you have published has paid off a mortgage on our little estate of 18 acres, and that alone saves the interest money of 15£ per annum on a small mortgage of 150 pounds. Usurers thrive here. This is 10 per cent, but I have known 20 given upon loans.

And a few months afterwards she described to Bentley, with a wry, half-amused irony, 'the poor Blue-stocking's various daily employments':

> First, I rise at six, read a chapter to the children, with short appropriate prayers. Get breakfast ready with the assistance of one servant, all I can afford to keep. After that important business is discussed. I make my own bed and put my chamber neatly in order. Make bread, or pies as required. Give orders for dinner and sit down to write. By the time I have put down a few sentences on paper, the Irish help pops her head into the room, 'Please Mistress, you are w..nted,' and this interruption is more or less continued until after dinner, when I get a little rest, take a walk, or sew *pro bono publico*. In the evening I generally write until I go to bed as my eyes are not strong enough to sew by candle light. I have little time for reading, though I do continue to enjoy this luxury sometimes.

Susanna Moodie, and her sister Catharine Parr Traill, were at least fortunate in having publishers and a readership in Britain, for Canada itself had nothing that could reasonably be called a publishing industry until late in the nineteenth century when a few Canadian publishers, notably William Briggs at the Methodist Book and Publishing House in Toronto, began resolutely publishing Canadian authors. The Canadian market was flooded with American pirated editions of English books, which in spite of a 30-per-cent tariff were cheaper than imported English editions; such Canadian publishing houses as existed were little more than jobbing distributors. As early as 1857 D'Arcy McGee described the functioning of the system in a way that held good for almost a century afterwards; he argued how vital it was to change it if a genuine Canadian culture were to emerge:

. . . The Montreal and Toronto houses are mere agents for New York publishers, having no literary wares to exchange with Harper, or Putnam, or the Sadliers, or Appleton. Economically, this is an evil; intellectually, it is treason to ourselves. If the design is to Massachusettize the Canadian mind, this is the very way to effect that end; if, on the other hand, we desire to see a Canadian nationalism freely developed, borrowing energy from the American, grace from the Frenchman, and power from the Briton, we cannot too soon begin to establish a Grand Trunk of thought, which will be as a backbone to the system we desire to inaugurate.

More than a quarter of a century later, in 1884, the Canadian publisher George McLean Rose was putting the same point in a rather different way:

After many years experience in the publishing business I have come to the conclusion that it is almost useless to attempt building up a large and profitable publishing trade in our country, unless our government take the matter of copyright in hand . . . . As the British copyright is at present understood and worked it is all one sided, that is it gives the United States author entire possession of our markets.

The scantiness of Canadian publishing meant that there was no direct link between Canadian writers and Canadian readers, and only if published in the United States could a writer find even a local readership of any importance, as writers like Ralph Connor of course did.

Yet another reason that writers of the time, as well as some later observers, adduced for the scanty support given to Canadian writing during the greater part of the nineteenth century was the overwhelming materialism that developed as Macdonald's National Policy began to bear fruit. The novelist Robert Barr, who eventually departed for the greener literary fields of England, complained bitterly in 1889 that Canadians would sooner spend their money on whisky than on books, and that 'it is not lack of money that makes Canada about the poorest book market in the world outside of Senegambia.' A later novelist, Arthur Stringer, who went to New York to establish himself as a writer, saw the situation even more pessimistically when he argued that perhaps, in comparison with the energetic entrepreneurs of the time, writers had become irrelevant. He gave his gloomy message in the New Year's edition of the Toronto *Globe* in 1910:

The sad truth is that our whole busy bunch of novelists and storytellers and verse writers today constitute nothing more than an attenuated choir of street sparrows chirping disconsolately from the rafters of a locomotive round house. Canada's great artists today are Shaughnessy and Mann and Mackenzie and Charlie Jays [railway builders and officials] and those epic-minded workers who are writing a new kind of blank verse in town sites and railway iron and grain routes.

Stringer was not alone among Canadian writers in the late Victorian and Edwardian eras in responding to the spirit of economic and political imperialism that was sweeping the land. The novelist Robert J.C. Stead was also a rather facile verse writer who published in 1908 a volume of poems entitled *The Empire Builders*, and declared with naïve enthusiasm:

> Sweet is the breath of the prairie, where peace and prosperity reign,
> And joyous and sound of the city, where all is expansion and gain.

It is true that Canadian writers in the nineteenth century had to start off without the support of a pre-literate body of myth and tradition; that an intelligent and substantial readership was slow to develop; that Canadians who wished to make a living from their writing had to seek it abroad; that the infant Canadian publishing industry was almost strangled in the cradle by the mass importation of books, particularly from the United States; that writers were often hypnotized by the very cult of material progress, which made it difficult to create a genuine national culture. But the principal reason for the slow development of what anyone was willing to regard as a Canadian literature lay within the literature itself. The fact of being 'born literate into history' prevented the free development of a literature, responsive to its time and setting, that occurred in cultures that had moved simultaneously out of both prehistory and preliteracy. The first writers in the New World—whether Canadian or American, whether speaking French or English—started out with second-hand tools that were appropriate to Old World literatures.

The situation was complicated, as we have seen, by the defensive conservatism of pioneer societies, which to begin with seek in a self-protective way to rebuild the old culture in the new world and therefore do their best to avoid cultural change. One consequence of that evasion is a reluctance to see the new environment for what it is, which inhibits the evolution of new forms of expression appropriate to it. It is difficult to think of any pioneer writer in the nineteenth century who would have had the insight shown by the English Imagist T.E. Hulme—an outsider, drifting through the West during the Edwardian decade—who confessed in one of his historic lectures on modern poetry:

> Speaking of personal matters, the first time I ever felt the necessity or inevitableness of verse was in the desire to reproduce the peculiar quality of feeling which is induced by the flat spaces and wide horizons of the virgin prairie of western Canada.

More typical of the pioneer was the mentally paralysing reaction recorded by the poetical clergyman Joshua Marsden in his *Narrative of a Mission, to Nova Scotia* . . . (1816):

There is . . . a solitary loneliness to the woods of America to which no language can do adequate justice. It seems a shutting out of the whole moral creation.

What we see among Canadian writers, at least until the last years of the nineteenth century, is less an effort to develop new forms or to seek a changed language appropriate to the new environment than an attempt to find a traditional form that can best be used in the new circumstances. Some of these traditional forms—especially the more complex ones like the novel, the drama, and the more sophisticated kinds of verse—are usually the products of well-established societies and mature cultures. This is undoubtedly why the first genuinely original poets came, as we shall see, so late in the period; why the interesting plays that were written remained unactable closet dramas like Charles Heavysege's *Saul*; and why, as John Bourinot wrote in 1893, in a book appropriately entitled *Our Intellectual Strength and Weakness:* 'there is one respect in which Canadians have never won any marked success, and that is in the novel or romance.' This was true enough of fiction in its larger forms up to the time he wrote, and even afterwards; despite the popular success of writers like Ralph Connor and the artistic success of writers like Sara Jeannette Duncan in *The Simple Adventures of a Memsahib* (1893) and *The Imperialist* (1904), no more than a handful of significant Canadian novels had been published by the time of the Great War.

The early writers who were most successful, and who are still read today, sought and adapted less-ambitious genres. The most felicitous and also the most characteristic prose writing by British North Americans until the end of the nineteenth century fell into three categories: the autobiographical memoir consisting of a series of episodes and reflections, like Susanna Moodie's *Roughing It in the Bush*; the satirical sketch; and the animal tale. None required the elaborate constructive skills needed for the novel or for drama. All could be related directly to experiences in Canada, yet all also derived from European models.

The satirical sketch appeared first in Nova Scotia, which for a brief period in the early nineteenth century was undoubtedly the most culturally sophisticated of the English-speaking North American colonies. It was probably a more uniformly literate society than that of Upper Canada, since the English-speaking farmers in Nova Scotia had for the most part come originally from New England, where the standards of education were relatively high. Both the first newspaper in what later became Canada (the *Halifax Gazette*, 1752) and the first literary journal (the *Nova Scotia Magazine*, 1789) appeared there. The intellectual life was represented by the group of Anglican patricians, mostly Loyalists, who centred on King's College at Windsor, by the Scottish Presbyterians who were linked with the Pictou Academy, and by the more plebeian Halifax intelligentsia whose leader Joseph Howe became.

The most representative figures in the first two groups were also the most noteworthy early Nova Scotian writers and pioneers in the tradition of Canadian satirists. Thomas McCulloch (1776-1843) was the founder of the Pictou Academy, and Thomas Chandler Haliburton (1796-1865), born in Windsor and educated at King's College, served as a judge and was therefore an ornament of the establishment for more than a quarter of a century. The two men respected each other, and although he was an Anglican Tory, Haliburton, in disagreement with some of his fellow conservatives, supported in the colonial assembly the making of a grant to McCulloch's Pictou Academy, which stood firmly outside the Anglican establishment. The two men shared a critical view of their fellow Bluenoses and of the state of Nova Scotia at the time, and they sought to remedy it by showing the Nova Scotians to themselves. Sam Slick, the Yankee clockmaker, spoke for them both when he said, in one of Haliburton's later books (*The Attaché; or, Sam Slick in England*, 1843):

> To my mind there is no vally in a sketch if it ain't true to nature. We needn't go searching about for strange people or strange things; life is full of them. There is queerer things happening every day than an author can imagine for the life of him. It takes a great many odd people to make a world, that's a fact. Now, if I describe a house that has an old hat in one window, and a pair of trousers in another, I don't stop to turn glazier, take 'em out, and put whole glass in, nor make a garden where there is none, and put a large tree in the foreground for effect; but I take it as I find it, and I take people in the dress I find em in, and if I set em a talkin I take their very words down. Nothing gives you a right idea of a country and its people like that.

Both writers set out to offer a mirror to society. But, as we know from experience, a mirror not only displaces right to left and vice versa; it also flatters or depreciates by exaggerating features according to the way the light falls on them. Thus satire, which works in the same way, by selecting and highlighting certain features that exist, is a work of exaggeration rather than falsification.

Rash as it may be to place too much importance on social conditions in seeking the origins of literary trends, one is led to speculate on the reason why two such important satirical writers should have emerged in early nineteenth-century Nova Scotia. Even assuming that Haliburton imitated McCulloch, the fact that he found the satirical sketch and the ironic manner so appealing suggests that he and McCulloch were reacting to a situation they shared and saw in the same way; it was the situation of an intellectually fairly advanced society afflicted by the economic uncertainty and drifting political values that followed the end of the Napoleonic wars. Like most satirists, they sought to bring people back to the ideas of a moral and rationally functioning order. Here we must remember that while Haliburton was a Tory, McCulloch was a Dissenting Whig of strong Presbyterian convictions in spite of his reformist sympathies.

McCulloch was the pioneer, and Northrop Frye has justly credited him with being 'the founder of genuine Canadian humour: that is of humour that is based on a vision of society and is not merely a series of wisecracks on a single theme.' McCulloch's *Letters of Mephibosheth Stepsure* (1862) first appeared in the *Acadian Recorder* between 1821 and 1823, and Haliburton did not begin to publish until 1835 in the *Nova Scotian* the sketches on which *The Clockmaker; or, The Sayings and Doings of Sam Slick of Slickville* (1836) was based, so it is clear in which direction the strain of influence operated.

There was a practical reason for the choice by both writers of a discontinuous fiction form for their homiletic tales. The periodical essay or episodic sketch was the kind of writing that could easily find a place in the semi-literary journals that had been appearing in Nova Scotia since the 1790s, and it was also the kind of writing in which a critical view of society could be built up cumulatively, each individual piece making its point with equal emphasis and the continuity being one of theme rather than of structure.

McCulloch and Haliburton were undoubtedly influenced by Augustan English essayists like Addison and Steele, but the particular kind of mocking social sketch they developed went farther back, at least as far as the Restoration, to writers less smooth and respectable than the creators of *The Spectator*—Tom Brown and Ned Ward, for example. McCulloch particularly recalls at times, in the roughness of his treatment, these earlier and more plebeian writers.

He is inclined towards broader caricature than Haliburton, and the letters he attributes to Stepsure tend to be populated by types rather than characters, as their names, like Sham and Clippet, suggest. Sometimes the names—Soakum the tavern-keeper or Tubal Thump the blacksmith—reflect with broad humour the occupations of the characters. The most complex of all is Stepsure, because of McCulloch's ambiguous use of him. Stepsure presents himself as a virtuous and hard-working young man who stands for 'industry, domestic comfort, and religion', all the positive attributes that McCulloch seeks to prescribe for his feckless fellow Nova Scotians. Yet at the same time, with his calculating piety and his joy at the deserved misfortunes of others, Stepsure is a somewhat repellent character; his cold virtues are exaggerated to provide a contrast with the dissipated and improvident life of unregenerate Bluenoses who sleep through the sermons of Dr Drone and ignore his exhortations. The *Letters* is impressive even now for the sharp realism—and a humour at times surprisingly scatological (as when McCulloch evokes the 'huge accumulation of odoriferous sweets' in a barnyard)—of the portrait they present of a society crude in its piety as well as its profanity. McCulloch's sustained irony leaves the impression that he is content with neither his Bluenose targets nor with Stepsure, which is not surprising in a man whose broad education, scholarly bent, and reformist sympathies show him to have been a more sensitive and generous man than his protagonist.

Haliburton abandoned McCulloch's letter form, which was a hangover from earlier days of English fiction, but he followed him in making each chapter of *The Clockmaker* a kind of self-contained sketch, consisting largely of dialogue so skilful in its use of variant speech patterns and dialect forms that it constitutes a first real attempt to find a North American language to deal with North American situations. Sam Slick's rich colloquial vocabulary is built up in catalogue-like harangues:

> Them old geese and vet'ran fowls, that are so poor the foxes won't steal 'em for fear o' hurtin' their teeth: that little yaller, lantern-jaw'd long-legg'd, rabbit-eared runt of a pig, that's so weak it can't curl its tail up; that old frame of a cow, a standin' there with her eyes shot to, a-contemplatin' of her latter end; and that varmint-lookin' horse, with his hocks swelled bigger than his belly, that looks as if he had come to her funeral . . .

And in sketches like the episode of Sam Slick and Deacon Flint, word-play is mingled with the anal humour to which Haliburton and McCulloch were both partial, and Sam shows his knowledge of human nature—the basic psychology by which he makes use of people's capacity to deceive themselves. He begins by using 'soft sawder' and a bit of coarse byplay on the Deacon:

> We had hardly entered the house, before the Clockmaker pointed to the view from the window, and addressing himself to me, said, 'If I was to tell them in Connecticut there was such a farm as this down east here in Nova Scotia, they wouldn't believe me. Why there ain't such a location in all New England. The Deacon has a hundred acres of dyke—'
>
> 'Seventy,' said the Deacon, 'only seventy.'
>
> 'Well, seventy; but then there is your fine deep bottom, why I could run a ramrod into it—'
>
> 'Intervale, we call it,' said the Deacon, who though evidently pleased at this eulogium, seemed to wish the experiment of the ramrod to be tried in the right place.
>
> 'Well, intervale if you please—though Professor Eleazer Cumstick, in his work on Ohio, calls them bottoms—is just as good as dyke. Then there is that water privilege, worth three or four thousand dollars, twice as good as what Governor Cass paid fifteen thousand dollars for. I wonder, Deacon, you don't put up a carding mill on it: the same works would carry a turning lathe, a shingle machine, a circular saw, grind bark, and—'
>
> 'Too old,' said the Deacon, 'too old for all those speculations . . .'

'Old,' repeated the Clockmaker, 'not you; why you are worth half a dozen of the young men we see nowadays. You are young enough to have—' Here he said something in a lower tone of voice, which I did not distinctly hear; but whatever it was, the Deacon was pleased. He smiled and said he did not think of such things now.

Having softened up the Deacon, Sam brings in a 'gawdy, highly varnished, trumpery-looking' clock, and remarks that it is already bespoken, and that the neighbour of the Flints has shown an interest in it, but he would like them to keep it until his return to save him the trouble of taking it home. So the clock is installed on the chimney-piece.

'That,' said the Clockmaker, as soon as we were mounted, that I call "*human natur*"! Now that clock is sold for forty dollars; it cost me just six dollars and fifty cents. Mrs Flint will never let Mrs Steel have the refusal, nor will the Deacon learn until I call for the clock that having once indulged in the use of a superfluity, how difficult it is to give it up. We can do without any article of luxury we have never had, but when once obtained, it is not "*in human natur*" to surrender it voluntarily. Of fifteen thousand sold by myself and partners in this Province, twelve thousand were left in this manner, and only ten clocks were ever returned; when we called for them they invariably bought them. We trust to "*soft sawder*" to get them into the house, and to "*human natur*" that they never come out of it.'

Haliburton was as aware as McCulloch of the moral backslidings of Nova Scotian society—the thriftlessness and the dissipation that were widespread in town and country alike—but he was, after all, a latitudinarian Anglican who himself loved the good things of life, and the economic and political ills of his country weighed more heavily on his mind than the moral ones. He saw the land badly used, the corruption of officialdom, and the lack of a true sense of responsibility among local politicians. And choosing Sam Slick—the brash and slangy Yankee, whose democratic pretensions Haliburton scorned—to act as his principal spokeman in exposing the faults of his own society was a brilliant literary inspiration.

Even the episodic forms of McCulloch's and Haliburton's books suited the parochial nature of British North American society in the early nineteenth century. Just as there was no overriding unity of national vision in the North American colonies until well after the mid-nineteenth century, so there was no overriding unity in either *The Clockmaker* or *The Stepsure Letters* (as they have become in modern editions). The structure is loose, each letter or chapter being capable of standing easily on its own as an essay or a short story. Yet a different, less structured unity was derived from the continuity of character and the consistency of tone provided by both writers.

Haliburton's writings were a great deal more admired abroad than in his own province, where they cut too near the bone to be read with comfort, and his more discerning readers, even at the time, recognized how much the success of his fiction depended on its innovative use of language. The English wit and poet, Walter Savage Landor, emphasized this aspect of the Nova Scotian's work in the doggerel tribute he offered him in 1858:

> Once I would bid the man go hang
> From whom there came a word of slang;
> Now pray I, tho' the slang rains thick
> Across the Atlantic from *Sam Slick*,
> Never may fall the slightest hurt on
> The witty head of Haliburton,
> Wherein methinks more wisdom lies
> Than in the wisest of the wise.

The next Canadian humorist to gain an international reputation similar to Haliburton's was also his true successor, Stephen Leacock (1869-1944). That Leacock's following in Britain and the United States should have been so considerable is not inappropriate, for like Haliburton, Leacock owed his success largely to his ability, when he was writing at his best, to stand outside his world and to present it with comic objectivity. His English origins, his unhappy early years in Canada, and the influence of the great Scandinavian-American political economist Thorstein Veblen, who developed the idea of conspicuous consumption that Leacock so often used in his satires on the rich, all contributed to his ironic sense of detachment—without disinvolvement—from Canadian life. Leacock's ability to observe Mariposa (Orillia, Ontario), and its real-life equivalents, with such Olympian amiability was due to his lack (in comparison with contemporaries like Charles G.D. Roberts and Archibald Lampman) of a strong localized attachment to his country, which, like Goldwin Smith, he tended to view in continental terms.

> I am a Canadian, but for the lack of any other word to indicate collectively those who live between the Rio Grande and the North Pole, I have to use 'American'. If the Canadians and the Eskimos and the Flathead Indians are not American, then what are they?

Influenced by Mark Twain as much as by Dickens, and always reluctant to admit the excellences of Haliburton, his Canadian forerunner, Leacock was much aware of being part of an American tradition, even though he was clearly less inclined than Sam Slick's creator to experiment with North American speech patterns. He was highly conscious of the importance of his American readers in providing his steady income, and it may well have been to please them that *Arcadian Adventures of the Idle Rich* (1914) is set nominally in a large American city, though the book is obviously about the Wasp financiers he observed in Montreal.

Leacock's traditions, however, run much farther back than the American humorists, for he has Swift's satiric trick of drawing our attention to human follies by shifting proportion, and part of the effect of *Sunshine Sketches of a Little Town* (1912) lies in the way we are shown the large in the small and the way the narrator constantly moves his focus so that the proportions change.

> Of course, if you come to the place fresh from New York, you are deceived. Your standards of vision is all astray. You do think the place is quiet. You do imagine that Mr Smith is asleep merely because he closes his eyes as he stands. But live in Mariposa for six months or a year and then you will begin to understand it better; the buildings get higher and higher; the Mariposa House becomes more and more luxurious; McCarthy's Block towers to the sky; the 'buses roar and hum to the station; the trains shriek; the traffic multiplies; the people move faster and faster; a dense crowd surges to and fro in the post-office and the five and ten cent store . . . .
>
> . . . it's a thriving town and there is no doubt of it. Even the transcontinental trains, as any townsman will tell you, run through Mariposa. It is true that the trains mostly go through at night and don't stop. But in the wakeful silence of the summer night you hear the long whistle of the through train for the west as it tears through Mariposa, rattling over the switches and past the semaphores and ending in a long, sullen roar as it takes the trestle bridge over the Ossawippi. Or, better still, on a winter evening about eight o'clock you will see the long row of the Pullmans and diners of the night express going north to the mining country, the windows flashing with brilliant light, and within them a vista of cut glass and snow-white table linen, smiling negroes and millionaires with napkins at their chins whirling past in the driving snowstorm.

Mariposa is, in fact, Leacock's Lilliput, just as the mining country and the city are his Brobdingnag, where everything is monstrous. But the two are intimately linked, as is shown in the story of the Mariposa election: Josh Smith wins by waiting until an hour before the polls close and wiring to the city the news of his victory, which is wired back for the edification of the Mariposans, who then swarm into the polling booths to be on the right side.

Leacock's best books were his earliest—those written before the First World War: *Literary Lapses* (1910), *Nonsense Novels* (1911), *Sunshine Sketches* and *Arcadian Adventures*. In these books his wit is fresh, his social vision is clear, and his awareness of literary pretences is acute. And this, I suggest, is because they belong in feeling, as Leacock himself belonged in experience, somewhere between the worlds that—so to speak—were changing guard during his first years of writing. During the years immediately preceding the Great War, Canada was going through the crucial change from a predominantly rural to a predominantly urban society. Leacock's youth had been lived in a small-town ambience on the shores of Lake Simcoe; he spent his mature years in Montreal, teaching at McGill, but he never gave up his links with the country and maintained a summer home at Orillia until his death. It was the interplay between the narrator's present as a city man and his past as a native of Mariposa that gave *Sunshine Sketches of a Little Town* its special quality of ironic indulgence. The people of Mariposa are no less self-seeking or self-deceiving than the magnates of Plutoria in *Arcadian Adventures of the Idle Rich*, but their vices are on a small and harmless scale and so can be regarded with benevolent amusement, while the same vices magnified in the *Arcadian Adventures* merit the sharper and more judgemental satire the later book projects. Mariposa in its own way is a microcosm, containing everything that Plutoria contains, but the very smallness of the scale reduces the enormities of social injustice: the simple and the humble can survive in the small town but they become instant victims in the city. The complexity and inhumanity of urban society is one of Leacock's constant themes, presented with Chaplinesque poignancy in the little man bewildered by the great world of finance in 'My Financial Career' (*Literary Lapses*). In such sketches Leacock's more serious persona, the student of Veblen, is not far in the background; but he almost takes centre stage in *Arcadian Adventures*, which at times reads like a homily on the evils of conspicuous consumption.

Leacock really closed the cycle that began with McCulloch, and it is hardly accidental that both authors' works feature a Dr Drone who personifies the futility of trying to make men good merely by exhortation. Leacock's stories evince little sense of human perfectability; we are led to believe that the flaws and weaknesses will persist, and will be kept harmless only if we limit the scale on which they can operate.

Along with Haliburton, McCulloch and Leacock represent, in terms of intention, an attempt to create a genuine *polis*, an order based on moral values and on the recognition of social responsibility—the goal of most satirists. In this context they were Aristotelians, seeing the ideal community as one small enough for men and women to know each other by name or local repute, if not directly, and to interact urbanely with each other. In feeling, these three satirists belong to pre-industrial and pre-metropolitan orders. Their ideal is a society in which people behave well not because they are told to or even because they are virtuous, but because their ambitions and opportunities are limited and because the good opinion of their neighbours is still a potent inducement to decency. The ironic mood projected by these writers links them with an important tradition in Canadian writing, and perhaps with a general Canadian cast of mind that intensified as the nineteenth century continued and Canadians began to see themselves as a people who—in spite of their geographical pretensions—were doomed by their relatively small numbers to a spectator role in the great world. Certainly the ironic detachment of the marginal personality is expressed constantly in mature Canadian fiction, from Sara Jeannette Duncan down to Robertson Davies and Mavis Gallant, and in modern Canadian poetry as well, where F.R. Scott and Earle Birney provide typical examples.

One might say that McCulloch, Haliburton, and Leacock represented one side of the Victorian and Edwardian shift of consciousness that enabled men and women to adjust to the wild land of Canada. Like Mrs Traill and Mrs Moodie, though in different ways, they too were seeking to turn a pioneer proto-society into a kind of civilization, adapted to the circumstances of the New World. The satirists, however, were all men of the clearings and campuses, comfortable at a distance from the frontier. One gets little sense in them of an empathy with the natural world, and even less of an attraction towards the wilderness. It is the world of human society they attempted to come to terms with and they gave us the first authentic fictional reflections of it in Canada.

The originators of the animal story in Canada take their place at the other pole. If the humorists were seeking to evoke the civic virtues in a society preoccupied with its task of taming and cultivating the wilderness, Charles G.D. Roberts and Ernest Thompson Seton were intent on breaking down the barriers between civilized men and the wilderness that the pioneer experience had created. They were intent on showing that the world of wild nature was not hostile and negative, as the elder Goldsmith and even Joshua Marsden later on had pictured it. To be reconciled with the wilderness and its creatures, to understand and cherish them, would enrich us morally and in many other ways, as Roberts argues in the introductory essay to his volume of stories, *The Kindred of the Wild* (1902).

> The animal story, as we now have it, is a potent emancipator. It frees us for a little from the world of shop-worn utilities, and from the mean tenement of self of which we do well to grow weary. It helps us return to nature, without requiring that we at the same time return to barbarism. It leads us back to the old kinship of earth, without asking us to relinquish by way of toll any part of the wisdom of the ages, any fine essential of the 'large result of time.' The clear and candid life to which it re-initiates us, far behind though it lies in the long upward march of being, holds for us this quality. It has ever the more significance, it has ever the richer gift of refreshment and renewal, the more humane the heart and spiritual the understanding which we bring to the intimacy of it.

A great deal of argument has built up over the matter of priorities. Did Roberts or Seton invent the characteristic Canadian type of animal story, which departs strikingly from both the European fable and from the anthropomorphic type of English animal story like *The Wind in the Willows* in which—as it has often been said—the animals are human beings in fur coats? Seton published what was really a kind of fictionalized animal biography—'The Life of a Prairie Chicken' in the *Canadian Journal*—as early as 1883. Roberts published 'Do Seek Their Meat from God' in *Harper's* in 1892; in its episodic structure it is a truer short story than Seton's piece. But more relevant than any question of precedence is the appearance of these stories at a time when people were ready to accept, and indeed to turn into bestsellers, tales that projected a view of wild animals and their habitats that differed from the attitude held by fur traders, farmers, lumbermen—the primary exploiters of animals. Margaret Atwood, in *Survival*, explained the presence and the popularity of animal stories in Canada by trying to fit them into her victor-victim theory of the motivations of Canadian writers: Canadians see wild animals as victims, and, being a colonially victimized people, they identify themselves with them.

What strikes one on actually reading the stories is that neither Roberts nor Seton consistently presents his animals as victims. Rather they are presented so as to arouse our admiration as much as our compassion. We admire their resourcefulness, their power of leadership, their skill at circumventing the wiles of their principal enemy, man. The overt Darwinian message is clear: the fittest survive. But none escape eventual death, though the animal will often die with what the writers suggest is true dignity, as much hero as victim. Indeed, both Roberts and Seton go to considerable lengths to emphasize the nobility of their animal heroes. They are shown as reasoning beings within the limitations of their special intelligences, and the writers stress the need to accept them as fellow participants in the scheme of nature.

Seton was the more didactic of the two, perhaps the more accurate field naturalist, but given to moralizing in ways that made him a distant pioneer of the animal-rights movements. He was also a less skilful writer of fiction than Roberts. An example of his manner and his limitations is the ending of the story 'Redruff', about the last of a local race of birds, dying in a trap.

> Have the wild things no moral or legal rights? What right has man to inflict such long and fearful agony on a fellow-creature, simply because that creature does not speak his language? All that day, with growing, racking pains, poor Redruff hung and beat his great, strong wings in helpless struggles to be free. All day, all night, with growing torture, until he only longed for death. But no one came. The morning broke, the day wore on, and still he hung there, slowly dying; his very strength a curse. The second night crawled slowly down, and when, in the dawdling hours of darkness, a great Horned Owl, drawn by the feeble flutter of a dying wing, cut short the pain, the deed was wholly kind.
>
> The wind blew down the valley from the north. The snow-horses went racing over the wrinkled ice, over the Don Flats, and over the marsh towards the lake, white, for they were driven snow, but on them, scattered dark, were riding plumy fragments of partridge ruffs—the famous rainbow

ruffs. And they rode on the winter wind that night, away and away to the south, over the dark and boisterous lake, as they rode in the gloom of his Mad Moon flight, riding and riding on till they were engulfed, the last trace of the Don Valley race.

It is obvious that Seton is less concerned with the aesthetics of the short story than with the ethics of man's relationship with wild creatures. He is presenting an argument, and drawing out of his broad field-naturalist's experience an instance to exemplify it. The anthropomorphic assumptions are obvious: '. . . he only longed for death'; '. . . the deed was wholly kind.' Seton was a polemical essayist, using fictional elements to strengthen his points, whose significance in the general picture of a Canadian literature coming to terms with the land is at best peripheral.

Roberts, on the other hand, stands at the centre, and not merely because of his importance in poetry. His animal stories indicate that while he may have been a less precise field naturalist than Seton, as a recorder of the habits of animals he was more of a natural philosopher, and more of what we would now call an ecologist; above all he was more of a perceptive artist seeking an authentic way of describing the environment and its non-human inhabitants. A good example is 'The Watchers in the Swamp', since this story is about fairly humble creatures and does not have the grand melodrama that sometimes mars his stories of the larger mammals. To illustrate what seem the more important aspects of his animal stories in relation to the literature of their time, here is a passage where action is stilled but description is active.

It was high morning in the heart of the swamp. From a sky of purest cobalt flecked sparsely with silver-white wisps of cloud, the sun glowed down with tempered, fruitful warmth upon the tender green of the half-grown rushes and already rank water grasses—the young leafage of the alder and willow thickets—the wide pools and narrow, linking lanes of unruffled water already mantling in spots with lily pad and arrow weed. A few big red-and-black butterflies wavered aimlessly above the reed tops. Here and there, with a faint, elfin clashing of transparent wings, a dragon fly, a gleam of emerald and amethyst fire flashed low over the water. From every thicket came a soft chatter of the nesting red-shouldered blackbirds.

And just inside the watery fringe of the reeds, as brown and motionless as a mooring stake, stood the bittern.

Not far short of three feet in length, from the tip of his long and powerful, dagger-pointed bill to the end of his short, rounded tail, with his fierce, unblinking eyes, round, bright and hard, with his snaky head and long, muscular neck, he looked, as he was, the formidable master of the swamp. In coloring he was a streaked and freckled mixture of slaty grays and browns and ochres above, with a freckled whitish throat and dull buff breast and belly—a mixture which would have made him conspicuous amid the cool, light green of the sedges but that it harmonized so perfectly with the earth and the roots. Indeed, moveless as he stood, to the indiscriminating eye he might have passed for a decaying stump by the waterside. His long legs were a dull olive which blended with the shadowy tones of the water.

The story moves on into action, to the bittern's packed day of killing and avoiding being killed, with dramatic encounters with a weasel and a goshawk, both triumphant. But the really interesting aspects of the story, in terms of the general development of Canadian literature at the time are, first, its attempt to present the *actual* Canadian scene with objective clarity, and, secondly, its recognition of the poetic value of the clear image, the verbalization of the visualized, which takes Canadian writing in the late nineteenth century on a course parallel to that of Canadian landscape painting.

Reading 'The Watchers in the Swamp', I was reminded, through its patient accuracy of detail, of the contemporary English nature writers Richard Jefferies and W.H. Hudson, with the poets John Clare and Edward Thomas in the background, but also of the clear, sharp, bright detail of pre-Raphaelite painting and poetry. I also recalled Roberts' story of the influence upon him—and upon Bliss Carman—of George R. Parkin, whom we have already encountered as an apologist for Imperialism, but who was headmaster of the Fredericton Collegiate School where the two future poets were among his students:

> But it was outside school hours that Parkin did most for us two ardent boys . . . . He would take us favoured two for long hikes over the wooded hills behind Fredericton . . . . England just then was thrilling to the new music, the new colour, the new raptures of Swinburne and Rossetti; Parkin was steeped in them; and in his rich voice he would recite to us ecstatically, over and over until we too were intoxicated with them, the great choruses from 'Atalanta in Calydon', passages from 'The Triumph of Time,' and 'Rococo',—but above all, 'The Blessed Damozel,' which he loved so passionately that Bliss suspected him of sometimes saying it instead of his prayers.

It is hard to imagine, now that their paintings and poems have become such late-Victorian clichés, how new and pristine the vision of the pre-Raphaelites seemed in its time, as if they were seeing the world anew. In fact they were reviving and adapting Romantic conventions to suit their own purposes rather than inventing a wholly new approach like, say, the Impressionists in painting or the Imagists in verse, and the same applied to the Canadian poets of the 1880s and the 1890s. They endeavoured—and largely succeeded—to see the Canadian land as it was, but transmitted their perceptions by adapting Romantic and late Romantic form and diction. Yet because in general their perceptions were truer than those of contemporary novelists, it is in their works that we find the beginnings of what we might call a genuinely Canadian literature.

Again one can only speculate on the origins of a development that arose from the coalescence of thoughts in the minds of individuals who came together in the same period. It was left for Malcolm Ross in the late twentieth century to give the leading verse-writers of the time—Roberts and Lampman, Scott and Carman—the collective and not entirely appropriate title of the Confederation Poets. They never proclaimed themselves a movement or gave themselves a name as Charles Mair and his associates of Canada First had earlier done, but they were friends, mutually admiring and in fairly constant touch with each other, and they were highly aware of the potentialities of the new land that had emerged with Confederation. It is not accidental that they began to emerge, with Roberts's *Orion* in 1880, at a time when Macdonald's National Policy was in full swing and immigrants were moving west ahead of the railroad, or that their major publications appeared at the same time as the landscape painters were working in the Rockies. The writers too were touched by the mystique of the land. Yet the Keatsian remoteness their verse sometimes projects should not allow us to think they were all vague dreamers detached from events around them, though this to a degree may have been true of Carman. Two of them—Lampman and Scott—lived out their working careers in the recently created Canadian civil service. Roberts, associated with Goldwin Smith as short-time editor of *The Week*, was close to the centre of Canadian political thinking and often strident in his nationalism; Lampman went beyond nationalism to show his sympathy for Fabian socialism.

Considered as poets, these writers were no ordinary neo-Romantics. For example, compared with the English poets who were their models they seem infelicitous when they attempt love poetry. The pastoral, the elegiac, the patriotic—these were the modes they mainly followed. Their eroticism—and this applies even to a noted philanderer like Roberts—seems to have been subsumed in their concern for a reconciliation with the realm of nature—a concern that was apparently inimical to their mid-Victorian predecessors. Their poems were the first to suggest that they saw the world around them through their own eyes and translated it into poetry, without borrowing images from the English experience on which earlier Canadian poets had uncritically drawn. Like Roberts' animal stories at their best, these poems display an exactness of perception that irradiates a scene for what it is. This quality is perhaps most clear and candid in Lampman's marvellous poems of the Canadian seasons, poems like 'Late November':

> The hills and leafless forests slowly yield
> To the thick-driving snow. A little while
> And night shall darken down. In shouting file
> The woodmen's carts go by me homeward-wheeled,
> Past the thin fading stubbles, half-concealed,

> Now golden-gray, sowed softly through with snow,
> Where the last ploughman follows still his row,
> Turning black furrows through the whitening field.
>
> Far off the village lamps begin to gleam,
> Fast drives the snow, and no man comes this way;
> The hills grow wintery white, and bleak winds moan
> About the naked uplands. I alone
> Am neither sad, nor shelterless, nor gray,
> Wrapped round with thought, content to watch and dream.

It is the images of Canadian reality that are important in this poem, not the poet's thought. Lampman watches, records, translates what he sees into poetic form, and in the process the facts become the dream. Fine as his summer and autumn poems are—'Heat' and 'Sunset at Les Eboulements', for example—Lampman seemed at his best in winter scenes and moods, and one of his most beautiful poems, written just before his death in 1899, was 'Winter Uplands':

> The frost that clings like fire upon my cheek,
> The loneliness of this forsaken ground,
> The long white drift upon whose powdered peak
> I sit in the great silence as one bound;
> The rippled sheet of snow where the wind blew
> Across the open fields for miles ahead;
> The far-off city towered and roofed in blue
> A tender line upon the western red;
> The stars that singly, then in flocks appear,
> Like jets of silver from the violet dome,
> So wonderful, so many and so near,
> And then the golden moon to light me home—
> The crunching snowshoes and the stinging air
> And silence, frost and beauty everywhere.

The entranced poet and the entrancing land are rendered in words as crystalline as the air and snow; such poems convey an awareness of the environment and an urge to transmit that awareness in appropriate form. Since the time of Lampman and his associates this awareness has been the sign of what we think of as 'Canadianism' in our poetry.

Roberts was a far less even poet than Lampman, capable in his patriotic moods of some of the emptiest rhetoric ever written by a Canadian poet:

> O strong hearts of the North
> Let flame your loyalty forth
> And put the craven and the base to open shame . . . .

But at his best, as in 'The Tantramar Revisited', he can use remembered detail with striking nostalgic effect to recreate not only a past scene but also the emotion of recollecting it:

Miles on miles beyond the tawny bay is Minudie.
There are the low blue hills; villages gleam at their feet.
Nearer a white sail shines across the water, and nearer
Still are the slim, grey masts of fishing boats dry on the flats.
Ah, how well I remember those wide red flats, above tide-mark,
Pale with scurf of the salt, seamed and baked in the sun!
Well I remember the piles of blocks and ropes, and the net-reels
Wound with the bearded nets, dripping and dark from the sea!
Now at this season the nets are unwound; they hang from the rafters
Over the fresh-stowed hay in upland barns, and the wind
Blows all day through the chinks, with the streaks of sunlight, and sways them
Softly at will; or they lie heaped in the gloom of a loft.

In some of Roberts' fine sonnets, filled with sharp observation, brought together in 1893 in *Songs for the Common Day*, one can detect the beginning of a search for new and original ways of expression, sometimes mingling with tried and tired tropes. 'The Mowing' is an example:

This is the voice of high midsummer's heat.
The rasping vibrant clamour soars and shrills
O'er all the meadowy range of shadeless hills,
As if a host of giant cicadae beat
The cymbals of their wings with tireless feet,
Or brazen grasshoppers with triumphing note
From the long swath proclaimed the fate that smote
The clover and timothy-tops and meadowsweet.

The crying knives glide on; the green swath lies.
And all noon long the sun, with chemic ray,
Seals up each cordial essence in its cell,
That in the dusky stalls, some winter's day
The spirit of June, here prisoned by his spell,
May cheer the herds with pasture memories.

Some passages are archaically poetic: 'triumphing note', 'proclaimed the fate', 'cheer the herds with pasture memories'. And, though original, the insect metaphors for the noise of mowing machines—cicadas and grasshoppers—are overdone. But there is one perfect line that announces from the centre of the poem the emergence of a different kind of poetic sensibility: 'The crying knives glide on; the green swath lies.' In its stark directness and originality, the line is itself almost a cry, announcing a new mode of perception shared, in varying degrees and in their own ways, by all the four poets.

In the case of Carman, the least precise in rendering detail and image among the four poets, the new perception was diffused in a hypnotic mistiness of feeling that gave off a sense of ambient nature too poignant for words to express exactly, as in the justly famous last verse of 'Low Tide at Grand Pré':

> The night has fallen, and the tide . . .
> Now and again comes drifting home,
> Across those aching barrens wide,
> A sigh like driven wind or foam:
> In grief the flood is bursting home.

Of the four friends and fellow poets, Duncan Campbell Scott has been the least immediately penetrable. Only recently have critics recognized that he carried to the ultimate point that immersion in the natural world that characterizes so strikingly all the important Canadian poets of the time. The others set out to evoke with a fresh perception the aspects and moods of the settled areas and their adjacent countryside, and spoke of the emotional benefits human beings could gain from the acceptance of nature in its benign aspect. Scott, rather like Samuel Hearne a century and more before him, committed himself to the wilderness and accepted it in all its rigour. In this he was notably assisted by the special nature of his experience, for his whole career was spent as a civil servant in the Indian Branch (later the Department of Indian Affairs) in which he rose eventually to the position of Deputy Superintendent. His work led him to visit the Indians often, and in 1905 he made an extensive tour of the James Bay area that brought him close to the real circumstances of life for the native peoples of the North in that period of cultural disintegration. More than any of the other poets of his group, Scott peopled the land about which he wrote. Even though the perceiving eye in poems like 'The Forsaken' and 'The Onondaga Maiden' is that of an outsider, he presented genuine personal tragedies with great sensitivity. He sympathized with the predicament of the Indians with whom he worked and wanted to lessen the gap that had opened in his time between native peoples and latecomers.

In Scott's poetry, even more than in that of Lampman and Roberts, the mystique of the land is expressed in its full starkness. It appears not merely in his telling of the human tragedies inflicted by contact with the wilderness—which suggest that nature is supremely indifferent to our efforts to find fulfilment through identifying with her—but also in his evocation of a profound sense of the land as an enduring entity embracing and outlasting all human action:

> Gull Lake set in the rolling prairie—
> Still there are reeds on the shore,
> As of old the poplars shimmer
> As summer passes;
> Winter freezes the shallow lake to the core;
> Storm passes,
> Heat parches the sedges and grasses,
> Night comes with the moon-glimmer,
> Dawn with the morning-star;

> All proceeds in the flow of time
> As a hundred years ago. ('At Gull Lake: August, 1810')

Such a passage not only shows the philosophic attitude that underlay Scott's poetry. It also shows how his desire to express his impressions and feeling affected his verse in a formal way: it not only escapes into metrical irregularity, but also avoids archaic diction and almost avoids metaphor, speaking directly through observed facts—in other words, through images. Scott lived long enough—he died in 1947—for his career to overlap that of the radical young Canadian poets of the 1920s and 1930s. During this later phase, after the end of the period we are discussing, he wrote 'En Route', a poem that seems to carry to its farthest degree the desire of Scott and his companions to find authentic expression for their intense involvement in the natural setting. It represents the culmination of the nature poetry that emerged in Canada during the 1890s. This poem also offers a striking parallel to the Imagist perception from which modern poetry largely emerged. Its quiet concluding statement on the validity of the encounter between the concrete and the transitory is the essence of Imagist thinking:

> The train has stopped for no apparent reason
> In the wilds;
> A frozen lake is level and fretted over
> With rippled wind lines;
> The sun is burning in the South; the season
> Is winter trembling at a touch of spring.
> A little hill with birches and a ring
> Of cedars—all so still, so pure with snow—
> It seems a tiny landscape in the moon.
> Long wisps of shadow from the naked birches
> Lie on the white in lines of cobweb-grey;
> From the cedar roots the snow has shrunk away,
> One almost hears it tinkle as it thaws.
> Traces there are of wild things in the snow—
> Partridge at play, tracks of the foxes' paws
> That broke a path to sun them in the trees.
> They're going fast where all impressions go
> On a frail substance—images like these,
> Vagaries the unconscious mind receives
> From nowhere, and lets go to nothingness
> With the lost flush of last year's autumn leaves.

The Confederation poets, like the painters who shortly afterwards formed the Group of Seven, were a rare conjunction of talents in the Canada of their time. Most writers worked in isolation, and few shared with Lucy Maud Montgomery the fortune and the following that *Anne of Green Gables* so unexpectedly brought her in 1908, or the fame—fleeting through it was—that Ralph Connor reaped from his writing about the men of Glengarry. Their situation was well described by Archibald Lampman in a 'Mermaid Inn' column he published on 27 August 1892.

> Those who do accomplish anything in literature in this country have, at any rate, the grim satisfaction of knowing that if it is not what they would have done under more favourable circumstances, it is at least the product of sheer natural talent. The Canadian littérateur must depend solely upon himself and nature. He is almost without the exhilaration of lively and frequent literary intercourse—that force and vitality of stimulus which counts for so much in the fructification of ideas. The human mind is like a plant, it blossoms in order to be fertilized, and to bear seed must come into actual contact with the mental dispersion of others. Of this natural assistance, the Canadian writer gets the least possible, and, if out of the poverty of his opportunities he accomplishes something, let him not be blamed for being, perhaps, a little boastful and inclined to rate himself at a little more than his actual worth.

Whether suitably humble or understandably boastful, it was the satirists, poets, and above all the tellers of animal stories in the century that made us who gave birth to a genuine Canadian literature.

Epilogue

By the time the century that made us came to an end in the first of the great world wars, Canada existed not only as an imaginative concept in the minds of writers and artists, but also as a geographical and political entity. With the transfer of the Arctic archipelago to the Dominion by the British government in 1880, the great mass of Canada had become complete; only insular Newfoundland remained for another third of a century outside the continent-wide country. The great railways had carried settlers as well as artists from coast to coast, and Canadian society had grown more various, both ethnically and socially, as it expanded. Conservatism and rebellion, alternating and sometimes co-existing, had produced attitudes that were more élitist than the American, more democratic than the British.

Many trends that developed during the century that ended in 1914 reached fulfilment shortly afterwards. From 1916 onwards the suffrage became truly universal with the winning of the vote by women. The equality of Canada within the Empire, which the imperialists dreamed of, was achieved in the Statute of Westminster of 1931, though this led in the end to independence and not to a strengthening of the traditional ties. And the people began to see themselves no longer as colonials populating and defining the remoter edges of empire but as a new combination of peoples making their own way of life in a unique habitat and becoming Canadians.

A List of Sources

The bibliography that follows includes the sources cited in each chapter. Though many of these titles are available in new editions, only the year of first publication is given.

I have found guidance and information in so many other books and publications that a list of them would be unwieldy, even though it would act as a tribute to the vast expansion of historical writing in Canada during the past quarter-century. I must acknowledge, however, a notable debt to those notable synthesizing projects that nowadays ease the path of any writer of Canadian history: *The Dictionary of Canadian Biography*; the seventeen volumes already published of that history of Canada by many hands, *The Centenary Series*; *The Oxford Companion to Canadian Literature*; *The Canadian Encyclopedia*; and, for its numerous hints of directions in which to search, *Colombo's Canadian Quotations*, and other volumes associated with it. Without them my task, like that of any other contemporary historian, would have been immensely more difficult.

1. THE WAR OF 1812

BERTON, PIERRE. *Flames Across the Border.* Toronto, 1981. *The Invasion of Canada.* Toronto, 1980.

CHRISTIE, ROBERT. *The Military and Naval Operations in the Late War with the United States.* Quebec, 1818.

HITSMAN, J. MACKAY. *The Incredible War of 1812: A Military History.* Toronto, 1965.

MAIR, CHARLES. *Dreamland and Other Poems.* Montreal, 1868. *Tecumseh, A Drama.* Toronto. 1886

RICHARDSON, JOHN. *Tecumseh; or, The Warrior of the West.* London, 1828. *Wacousta; or The Prophecy.* Edinburgh, 1832. *The Canadian Brothers; or, The Prophecy Fulfilled. A Tale of the Late American War.* Montreal, 1840. *The War of 1812.* Brockville, 1842.

SANGSTER, CHARLES. *Hesperus, and Other Poems and Lyrics.* Montreal, 1860.

STANLEY, G.F.G. *The War of 1812.* Toronto, 1983.

2. CANADA IN 1814

DUNLOP, WILLIAM. *Statistical Sketches of Upper Canada for the Emigrants: by a Backwoodsman.* London, 1832.

HALL, FRANCIS. *Travels in Canada and the United States in 1816 and 1817.* London, 1818.

HOWISON, JOHN. *Sketches of Upper Canada . . .* London, 1821.

MacGREGOR, JOHN. *Historical and Descriptive Sketches of the Maritime Colonies of British America.* London, 1821.

HUGH, MACLENNAN. *Barometer Rising.* New York, 1941.

MOODIE, SUSANNA. *Roughing It in the Bush.* London, 1852.

MOORSOM, WILLIAM SCOTT. *Letters from Nova Scotia.* London, 1830.

O'BRIEN, MARY. *The Journals of Mary O'Brien, 1828-1838.* Ed. Audrey Saunders Miller. Toronto, 1968.

TALBOT, EDWARD ALLAN. *Five Years' Residence in the Canadas . . . .* London, 1824.

TRAILL, CATHARINE PARR. *The Backwoods of Canada.* London 1836.

3. GENTLEMEN AND OTHERS

AKRIGG, G.P.V.A., and HELEN B. AKRIGG. *British Columbia Chronicle, 1778-40.* Vancouver, 1975.

ALLISON, SUSAN. *A Pioneer Gentlewoman in British Columbia: The Recollections of Susan Allison.* Ed. Margaret A. Ormsby. Vancouver, 1876.

ANON. *A Few Plain Directions to Persons Intending to Proceed as Settlers to His Majesty's Dominions in Upper Canada, By a Settler.* London, 1820.

ATKIN, RONALD. *Maintain the Right.* Toronto, 1973.

At the Mermaid Inn: Wilfred Campbell, Archibald Lampman, Duncan Campbell

Scott in the Globe 1892-93. Toronto, 1979.

BERTON, PIERRE. *Klondike.* Toronto, 1958.

BICKERSTETH, JOHN BURGON. *The Land of Open Doors.* London, 1914.

COZZENS, FREDERICK S. *Acadia; or A Month with the Bluenoses.* New York, 1859.

DALHOUSIE, LORD. *The Dalhousie Journals.* Ed. Marjory Whitelaw. Ottawa, 1978.

DAVIS, ROBERT. *The Canadian Farmer's Travels . . .* Buffalo, 1837.

DUFFERIN, LADY. *My Canadian Journal, 1872-3.* London, 1891.

DURHAM, LORD. *Report on the Affairs of British North America.* London, 1839.

DUNCAN, SARA JEANNETTE. *The Imperialist.* Toronto, 1904.

FIRTH, EDITH. *The Town of York, 1815-1834.* Toronto, 1966.

GLAZEBROOK, G.P.DE T. *The Story of Toronto.* Toronto, 1971.

HEAD, SIR FRANCIS BOND. *A Narrative.* London, 1839.

HELMCKEN, JOHN SEBASTIAN. *The Reminiscences of John Sebastian Helmcken.* Ed. Dorothy Blakey Smith. Vancouver, 1975.

HOWE, JOSEPH. *Joseph Howe: Voice of Nova Scotia. A Selection.* Ed. J. Murray Beck. Toronto, 1964.

JAMESON, ANNA. *Winter Studies and Summer Rambles in Canada.* London, 1838.

KELLY, NORA and WILLIAM. *The Royal Canadian Mounted Police.* Toronto, 1973.

LAMPMAN, ARCHIBALD. *The Poems of Archibald Lampman (including At the Long Sault).* Toronto, 1874.

LEACOCK, STEPHEN. *Arcadian Adventures with the Idle Rich.* London, 1914.

LIZARS, ROBINA and KATHLEEN M. *In the Days of the Canada Company.* Toronto, 1897. *Humours of '37, Grave, Gay and Grim. Rebellion Times in the Canadas.* Toronto, 1897.

McCOURT, EDWARD. *Saskatchewan.* Toronto, 1968.

McDONALD, ARCHIBALD. *Peace River. A Canoe Voyage from Hudson's Bay to the Pacific by the Late Sir George Simpson in 1828. Journal of the Late Chief Factor Archibald McDonald . . . Who Accompanied Him.* Ottawa, 1872.

McGEE, THOMAS D'ARCY. Address to the Legislative Assembly, February 9, 1865. *Parliamentary Debates on the Subject of the Confederation of the British North American Provinces, 3rd Session, 8th Provincial Parliament of Canada.* Ottawa, 1865.

McLEAN, JOHN. *John McLean's Notes on a Twenty-five Years' Service in the Hudson's Bay Territory.* Ed. W.S. Wallace, Toronto, 1932.

MOODIE, SUSANNA. *Op. cit.*

MORTON, W.L. ed. *Monck Letters and Journals, 1863-68. Canada from Government House at Confederation.* Toronto, 1970.

ORMSBY, MARGARET. *British Columbia: A History.* Toronto, 1958.

PORTER, JOHN. *The Vertical Mosaic.* Toronto, 1965.

READ, COLIN and RONALD J. STAGG, eds. *The Rebellion of 1837 in Upper Canada.* Toronto, 1985.

SELLAR, ROBERT. *Gleaner Tales.* Huntingdon, Que., 1895. *True Makers of Canada: The Narrative of Gordon Sellar, who emigrated to Canada in 1825.* Huntingdon, Que., 1915.

SMITH, GOLDWIN. *Canada and the Canadian Question.* Toronto, 1891 *Reminiscences.* Ed. Arnold Haultain. New York, 1910.

STEELE, SAMUEL B. *Forty Years in Canada.* Toronto, 1915.

TOYE, WILLIAM. *The St Lawrence.* Toronto, 1959.

TRAILL, CATHARINE PARR. *Op. cit.*

WATTERS, R.E., ed. *British Columbia: A Centennial Anthology.* Toronto, 1958.

4. THE RADICAL THESIS

BROGE, PATRICK. *Sir John Beverley Robinson: Bone and Sinew of the Compact.* Toronto, 1984.

COOK, RAMSAY. *The Regenerators. Social Criticism in Late Victorian Canada.* Toronto, 1985.

DE MILLE, JAMES. *A Strange Manuscript Found in a Copper Cylinder.* New York, 1888.

DENT, JOHN CHARLES. *The Last Forty Years: The Union of 1841 to Confederation.* Toronto, 1881.

DUFFERIN, LADY. *Op. cit.*

DURHAM. LORD. *Op. cit.*

GIRAUD, MARCEL. *Le Métis canadien.* Paris, 1945.

HALIBURTON, THOMAS CHANDLER. *Sam Slick's Wise Saws and Modern Instances.* London, 1853.

HEAD, SIR FRANCIS BOND. *Op. cit.*

JAMESON, ANNA. *Op. cit.*

KEALEY, GREGORY S. and BRYAN D. PALMER. *Dreaming of What Might Be: The Knights of Labor in Ontario, 1865-1900.* Cambridge, 1982. *Essays in Canadian Working Class History.* Toronto, 1976.

KILBOURN, WILLIAM. *The Firebrand: William Lyon Mackenzie.* Toronto, 1956.

LeSUEUR, WILLIAM DAWSON. *William Lyon Mackenzie.* Toronto, 1979.

LINDSAY, CHARLES. *The Life and Times of William Lyon Mackenzie.* Toronto, 1862.

MACKENZIE, WILLIAM LYON. *The Selected Writings of William Lyon Mackenzie, 1824-1837.* Ed. Margaret Fairley. Toronto, 1960.

MOODIE, SUSANNA. 'Canada: A Contrast.' (Preface to first Canadian Edition of *Roughing It in the Bush.*) Toronto, 1871.

ORMSBY, MARGARET. *Op. cit.*

Queen v. Louis Riel. Intro. by Desmond Morton. Toronto, 1974.

RAE, J.E. 'William Lyon Mackenzie— Jacksonian?', *Mid-America* 50 (1968).

READ, COLIN and RONALD J. STAGG, eds. *The Rebellion in Upper Canada: A Collection of Documents.* Toronto, 1985.

Queen v. Louis Riel, with an introduction by Desmond Morton. Toronto, 1974.

ROBIN, MARTIN. *Radical Politics and Canadian Labour.* Kingston, 1968.

ROSS, ALEXANDER. *The Red River Settlement.* London, 1856.

SIEGFRIED, ANDRÉ. *The Race Question in Canada.* 1907; Ottawa, 1978.

SPRAGUE, D.N. 'The Manitoba Land Question'. *Journal of Canadian Studies.* XV, No 3 (Autumn), 1980.

THOMAS, CLARA. *Ryerson of Upper Canada.* Toronto, 1969.

THOMPSON, T. PHILLIPS. *The Politics of Labour.* Toronto, 1887.

WATT, F.W. 'Literature of Protest' in the *Literary History of Canada.* Toronto, 1965.

WOODCOCK, GEORGE. *Gabriel Dumont: The Métis Chief and His Lost World.* Edmonton, 1975. 'Henry Jones' in *Dictionary of Canadian Biography.* Vol. VIII, Toronto, 1985. 'Harmony Island: A Canadian Utopia' in *British Columbia: A Centennial Anthology.* Ed. R.E. Watters, Toronto, 1958.

5. THE TORY ANTITHESIS

BERGER, CARL. *The Sense of Power: Studies in the Ideas of Canadian Imperialism, 1867-1914.* Toronto, 1970. 'The True North Strong and Free' in *Nationalism in Canada.* Ed. Peter Russel. Toronto, 1966.

BROGE, PATRICK. *Op. cit.*

CREIGHTON, D.G. *John A. Macdonald.* 2 vols, Toronto, 1952-1955.

DUNCAN, SARA JEANNETTE. *Op. cit.*

DURHAM, LORD. *Op. cit.*

ENGELS, FRIEDRICH. *Letters to Americans 1848-1895, A Selection.* Ed. Alexander Trachtenberg. New York, 1953.

FLINT, DAVID. *John Strachan, Pastor and Politician.* Toronto, 1971.

FORBES, H.D. *Canadian Political Thought.* Toronto, 1985.

FOSTER, W.A. *Canada First: or, Our New Nationality.* Toronto, 1871.

HALIBURTON, THOMAS CHANDLER. *The Clockmaker; or The Sayings and Doings of Sam Slick of Slickville.* Halifax, 1836.

HEAD, SIR FRANCIS BOND. *Op. cit.*

MACKENZIE, WILLIAM LYON. *Op. cit. Sketches of Canada and the United States.* New York, 1833.

MARRYAT, FREDERICK. *Diary in America, with some Remarks on Institutions.* London, 1839.

MORTON, W.L. *Op. cit.*

PATTERSON, GRAEME. 'An Enduring Canadian Myth: Responsible Government and the Family Compact.' *Journal of Canadian Studies.* XII (1977).

POMEROY, E.M. *Sir Charles G.D. Roberts: A Biography.* Toronto, 1943.

READ, COLIN and RONALD J. STAGG, *Op. cit.*

ROBERTS, SIR CHARLES G.D. *Selected Poems.* Toronto, 1936.

SCHULL, JOSEPH. *Edward Blake.* 2 vols. Toronto, 1875, 1876.

SHRIVE, NORMAN. *Op. cit.*

SIEGFRIED, ANDRÉ. *Op. cit.*

SKELTON, OSCAR DOUGLAS. *Life and Letters of Sir Wilfrid Laurier.* Toronto, 1921.

STEWART, GORDON T. 'Political Patronage under Macdonald and Laurier, 1878-1911'. *American Review of Canadian Studies*, X (1980).

STRACHAN, JOHN. *Documents and Opinions.* Ed. J.L.M. Henderson. Toronto, 1969.

THOREAU, HENRY DAVID. *The Journals of Henry D. Thoreau.* Ed. Bradford Torrey and Francis H. Allen, New York, 1906.

TROLLOPE, ANTHONY. *North America.* London, 1862.

WALLACE, ELIZABETH. *Goldwin Smith: Victorian Liberal.* Toronto, 1957.

WISE, S.F. 'Sermon Literature and Canadian Intellectual History', *Bulletin of the Committee on Archives, the United Church of Canada.* Toronto, 1965.

WOODCOCK, GEORGE. *Amor de Cosmos.* Toronto, 1975,

6. PIONEERS! O, PIONEERS!

CAMPBELL, WILFRED. *Beyond the Hills of Dream.* Boston, 1899.

COOK, RAMSAY and WENDY MITCHISON, eds. *The Proper Sphere: Women's Place in Canadian Society.* Toronto, 1976.

CRAN, MRS. GEORGE. *A Woman in Canada.* London, 1910.

ELLIOTT, GORDON R. *Barkerville, Quesnel & The Cariboo Gold Rush.* Vancouver, 1958.

GALBRAITH, J.S. *The Little Emperor: Governor Simpson of the Hudson's Bay Company.* Toronto, 1976.

GLAZEBROOK, G.P.de T. *The Hargrave Correspondence, 1821-1843.* Toronto, 1938.

GRANT, GEORGE MONRO. *Ocean to Ocean: Sandford Fleming's Expedition Through Canada in 1872.* Toronto, 1973.

HEARNE, SAMUEL. *A Journey from Prince of Wales' Fort, in Hudson's Bay, to the Northern Ocean....* London, 1795.

HOWE, JOSEPH. *Western and Eastern Rambles: Travel Sketches of Nova Scotia.* Ed. M.G. Parkes. Toronto, 1973.

HOWISON, JOHN. *Op. cit.*

JAMESON, ANNA. *Op. cit.*

JOHNSON, ALICE M. ed. *Saskatchewan Journals and Correspondence, 1795-1802.* London, 1967.

LANGTON, ANNE. *A Gentlewoman of Upper Canada: The Journals of Anne Langton,* Ed. H.H. Langton. Toronto, 1950.

McCLUNG, NELLIE. *Clearing in the West: My Own Story.* Toronto, 1947.

MACPHAIL, SIR ANDREW. *The Master's Wife.* Toronto, 1939.

MITCHELL, ELIZABETH. *In Western Canada Before the War.* Saskatoon, 1915.

MONTGOMERY, LUCY MAUD. *The Selected Journals of L.M. Montgomery, Vol.1, 1889-1910.* Ed. Mary Rubio and Elizabeth Waterston, Toronto, 1985.

MOODIE, SUSANNA. *Op. cit.*

MORTON, ARTHUR S. *Sir George Simpson: Overseas Governor of the Hudson's Bay Company.* Toronto, 1944.

MORTON, W.L. *Op. cit.*

O'BRIEN, MARY. *Op. cit.*

ORMSBY, MARGARET. *Op.cit.*

PRENTISS, ALISON and SUSAN MANN TROFIMENKOFF eds. *The Neglected Majority: Essays in Canadian Women's History.* Vol. 1, Toronto, 1977. Vol.2, Toronto, 1985.

READ, COLIN and RONALD J. STAGG. *Op. cit.*

RICH, E.E., ed. *Minutes of Council of the Northern Department of Rupert's Land, 1821-31.* London, 1940.

TRAILL, CATHARINE PARR. *The Female Emigrant's Guide and Hints on Canadian Housekeeping.* Toronto, 1854. (Reprinted in a new edition as *The Canadian Settler's Guide*, Toronto, 1855.)

WEST, JOHN. *The Substance of a Journal During a Residence at the Red River Colony.* London, 1827.

7. THE NOBLE CHIEFTAIN

BALLANTYNE. *Hudson's Bay; or Every-day Life in the Wilds of North America.* London, 1848.

BUTLER, WILLIAM FRANCIS. *The Great Lone*

Land. London, 1872. *The Wild North Land*. London, 1873.

CHEADLE, JAMES and LORD MILTON. *The North West Passage by Land*. London, 1865.

COPWAY, GEORGE. *The Life, History and Travels of Kah-ge-gah-bowh* (George Copway) .... Philadelphia, 1847.

CRAWFORD, ISABELLA VALANCY. *The Collected Poems*. Ed. J.W. Garvin. Toronto, 1905.

GRANT, GEORGE MONRO. *Op. cit.*

HARMON, DANIEL WILLIAMS. *A Journal of Voyages and Travels in the Interior of North America* .... Andover, 1820.

HIND, HENRY YOULE. *Narrative of the Canadian Red River Exploring Expedition of 1857 and the Assiniboine and Saskatchewan Exploring Expedition of 1858*. 2 vols. Toronto, 1859.

JAMESON, ANNA. *Op. cit.*

JOHNSON, EMILY PAULINE. *Flint and Feather. Complete Poems*. Toronto, 1924.

JONES, PETER. *History of the Ojibway Indians*. London, 1861?. *Life and Journals of Kah-Ke-Wa-Quo-Na-By (Rev. Peter Jones) Wesleyan Missionary*. Toronto, 1860.

KANE, PAUL. *Wanderings of an Artist Among the Indians of North America*. London, 1859.

KENTON, EDNA, ed. *The Jesuit Relations and Allied Documents*. Toronto, 1954.

LEVIGNE, R.G.A. *Echoes from the Backwoods*. London, 1849.

McDOUGALL, JOHN. *Forest, Lake and Prairie*. Toronto, 1895. *Saddle, Sled and Snowshoe*. Toronto, 1896. *Pathfinding on Path and Prairie*. Toronto, 1898.

MAIR, CHARLES. *Tecumseh. A Drama*. Toronto, 1886.

MORICE, ADRIAN GABRIEL. *Fifty Years in Western Canada*. Toronto, 1930.

MORRIS, ALEXANDER. *The Treaties of Canada with the Indians of the Northwest*. Toronto, 1880.

MURRAY, PETER. *The Devil and Mr. Duncan*. Victoria, 1985.

O'BRIEN, MARY. *Op. cit.*

RICHARDSON, JOHN. *Tecumseh; or The Warrior of the West in Four Cantos with Notes*. London, 1828. *The Canadian Brothers; or The Prophecy Fulfilled*. Montreal, 1840.

SCOTT, DUNCAN CAMPBELL. *The Poems of Duncan Campbell Scott*. Toronto, 1926.

SHIPLEY, NAN. *The James Evans Story*. Toronto, 1966.

SIMPSON, SIR GEORGE. *Narrative of an Overland Journey around the World* .... London, 1847.

SMITH, DONALD B. *Sacred Feathers; The Reverend Peter Jones and the Mississauga Indians*. Toronto, 1987.

SOUTHESK, LORD. *Saskatchewan and the Rocky Mountains*. Edinburgh, 1875.

TRAILL, CATHARINE PARR. *The Canadian Settlers' Guide*. Toronto, 1855.

WILSON, WILLIAM. *Newfoundland and Its Missionaries*. Cambridge, Mass., 1866.

WOODCOCK, GEORGE. *Gabriel Dumont: The Métis Chief and His Lost World*. Edmonton, 1975.

YEIGH, FRANK. 'Scott, Carlyle, Dickens and Canada'. *Queen's Quarterly*, Spring 1930.

8. NEIGHBOURS AND STRANGERS

AN ENGLISH FARMER. *A Few Plain Directions for Persons Intending to Proceed to His Majesty's Province of Upper Canada*. London, 1820.

AUBERT DE GASPÉ, PHILIPPE. *Les Anciens Canadiens*. Quebec, 1863; tr. Charles G.D. Roberts as *The Canadians of Old*, 1890.

AUBERT DE GASPÉ, PHILIPPE, JR. *L'Influence d'un livre; roman historique*. Québec, 1837.

BONNYCASTLE, SIR R.H. *The Canadas in 1841*. 2 vols, London, 1841.

BOURASSA, HENRI. 'Imperialism and Nationalism', December 18, 1912. *Addressed Delivered Before the Canadian Club of Ottawa, 1911-12*. Ottawa, 1912.

CHAUVEAU, PIERRE-JOSEPH-OLIVIER. *Charles Guérin: roman de moeurs canadiennes* (published anonymously), Montreal, 1846. *L'Instruction publique au Canada*. Québec, 1876.

CRÉMAZIE, JOSEPH-OCTAVE. *Oeuvres complètes*. Montreal, 1883.

DUNLOP, WILLIAM. *Op. cit.*

DURHAM, LORD. *Op. cit.*

ELGIN, LORD. *The Elgin-Grey Papers, 1846-52*, Ed. A.G. Doughty. Toronto, 1937.

ELLICE, JANE. *Diary*. Manuscript in the National Archives of Canada.

FRÉCHETTE, LOUIS-JOSEPH. *La légende d'un people*. Paris, 1887.

GARNEAU, FRANÇOIS-XAVIER. *Histoire du Canada depuis sa découverte jusqu'à nos jours*. 3 vols. Québec, 1845-48.

GÉRIN-LAJOIE, ANTOINE. *Jean Rivard, le défricheur*. Montreal, 1874.

GRANT, GEORGE MONRO. *Op. cit.*

GRIFFITH, W.L. *The Dominion of Canada*. London, 1911.

HELMCKEN, JOHN SEBASTIAN. *Op.cit.*

MacFIE, MATTHEW. *Vancouver Island and British Columbia*. London, 1865.

McGEE, THOMAS D'ARCY. 'The New Nation and the Old Empire', *Montreal Gazette*, 9 Dec. 1865.

MACKENZIE, WILLIAM LYON. *Selected Writings*. Ed. Margaret Fairley. Toronto, 1960.

MILLER, ORLO. *The Donnellys Must Die*. Toronto, 1962.

MOODIE, SUSANNA. *Letters of a Lifetime*. Ed. Carl Ballstadt, Elizabeth Hopkins and Michael Peterman. Toronto, 1985.

NEVERS, EDMOND DE. *L'Avenir du peuple canadien-francais*. Paris, 1896.

ORMSBY, MARGARET. *Op. cit.*

RUMILLY, ROBERT. *Henri Bourassa: la vie publique d'un grand Canadien*. Montreal, 1953.

SHIRREFF, PATRICK. *A Tour through North America*. Edinburgh, 1835.

SIEGFRIED, ANDRÉ. *Op. cit.*

SMITH, GOLDWIN. *Canada and the Canadian Question*. London, 1891.

STRACHAN, JOHN. *Op. cit.*

SULERZHITSKY, L.A. *To America with the Doukhobors*, Tr. Michael Kalmakoff. Regina, 1982. (The original, *V Ameriku s dukhoborami*, was published in Moscow in 1905.)

TARDIVEL, JULES-PAUL. *L'Anglicisme voilà l'ennemi*. Québec, 1880.

TOCQUEVILLE, ALEXIS DE. 'A letter from Alexis de Tocqueville on the Canadian Rebellion of 1837'. Ed. Edgar McInnis. *Canadian Historical Review*, December 1938.

TOYE, WILLIAM. *Op. cit.*

WADE, MASON. *Canadian Dualism: Studies of English-French Relations*. Toronto, 1960.

WILLIAMS, DAVID R. 'The Man for a New Country': Sir Matthew Baillie Begbie. Sidney, B.C., 1977.

WOODCOCK, GEORGE. *Amor de Cosmos*. Toronto, 1975.

WOODCOCK, GEORGE and IVAN AVAKUMOVIC. *The Doukhobors*. Toronto, 1968.

WOODSWORTH, J.S. *Strangers Within Our Gates; or, Coming Canadians*. Toronto, 1909.

9. ENTERING THE LAND

ALEXANDER, SIR J.E. *L'Arcadie; or Seven Years' Exploration in British America*. London, 1849.

BONE, PETER TURNER. *When the Steel Went Through: Reminiscences of a Railroad Pioneer*. Toronto, 1947.

BUTLER, WILLIAM FRANCIS. *The Great Lone Land*. London, 1872.

CHARETTE, GUILLAUME. *Vanishing Spaces: Memoirs of Louis Goulet*. Tr. Ray Ellenwood. Winnipeg, 1980.

CHEADLE, JAMES and LORD MILTON. *Op. cit.*

COBBETT, WILLIAM. *Advice to Young Men*. London, 1829.

CRAWFORD, ISABELLA VALANCY. *Op. cit.*

GOLDSMITH, OLIVER (the elder). *The Deserted Village*. London, 1770.

GOLDSMITH, OLIVER (the younger). *The Rising Village*. London, 1825.

GRANT, GEORGE MONRO. *Op. cit.*

GREY, CHARLES. *Crisis in the Canadas, 1838-1839: The Grey Journals and Letters*. Ed. William Ormsby. Toronto, 1964.

HIND, HENRY YOULE. *Op. cit.*

HOBSON, J.A. *Canada Today*. London, 1906.

HOWE, JOSEPH. *Letters of the Hon. Joseph Howe*. Ed. William Annand. Halifax, 1858.

JAMESON, ANNA. *Op. cit.*

KEEFER, THOMAS COLTIN. *The Philosophy of Railroads.* Montreal, 1849.

LANGTON, ANNE. *Op. cit.*

McCLUNG, NELLIE. *Op. cit.*

MACKENZIE, WILLIAM LYON. *Selected Writings. Idem.*

MACOUN, JAMES MELVILLE. *Manitoba and the Great North West.* Guelph, 1882.

MAIR, CHARLES. *Dreamland and Other Poems. Tecumseh, a Drama. Idem.*

MOODIE, SUSANNA. *Letters of a Lifetime. Roughing it in the Bush. Idem.*

MORTON, W.L. *Op. cit.*

MORRIS, JAN. *Pax Britannica.* London, 1968.

O'BRIEN, MARY. *Op. cit.*

O'GRADY, STANDISH. *The Emigrant. A Poem in Four Cantos.* Montreal, 1841.

SANGSTER, CHARLES. *The St. Lawrence and the Saguenay, and other Poems.* Kingston, 1856.

SIEGFRIED, ANDRÉ. *Op. cit.*

SOUTHESK, LORD. *Op. cit.*

STEAD, ROBERT JAMES CAMPBELL. *The Homesteaders: A Novel of the Canadian West.* Toronto, 1916.

STEELE, SAMUEL B. *Op. cit.*

TOYE, WILLIAM, ed. *The Oxford Companion to Canadian Literature.* Toronto, 1983.

TOYE, WILLIAM. *The St Lawrence. Idem.*

10. THE VISUAL IMAGINATION
At The Mermaid Inn ... Idem.

BELL, MICHAEL. *Painters in a New Land: From Annapolis to the Klondike.* Toronto, 1973.

BUCHANAN, DONALD. *James Wilson Morrice.* Toronto, 1947.

DUVAL, PAUL. *Canadian Water Colours.* Toronto, 1954.

GRANT, GEORGE MONRO. *Op.cit.*

GREENHILL, RALPH. *Early Photography in Canada.* Toronto, 1965.

HARPER, J. RUSSELL. *Early Painters and Engravers in Canada.* Toronto, 1970. *Painting in Canada: A History.* Toronto, 1966. *William G.R. Hind.* Ottawa, 1976.

HARPER, J. RUSSELL and STANLEY G. TRIGGS. *Portrait of a Period: A Collection of Notman Photographs, 1856 to 1915.* Montreal, 1967.

HIND, HENRY YOULE. *Narrative of the Canadian Red River Exploring Expedition. Explorations in the Interior of the Labador Peninsula.* London, 1865.

HUBBARD, R.H. *The Development of Canadian Art.* Ottawa, 1963.

JACKSON, A.Y. *A Painter's Country.* Toronto, 1958.

KANE, PAUL. *Op. cit.*

MELLON, PAUL. *The Group of Seven.* Toronto, 1970.

MURRAY, JOAN. *The Best of the Group of Seven.* Edmonton, 1984. *The Best of Tom Thomson.* Edmonton, 1986.

O'BRIEN, MARY. *Op. cit.*

PEPPER, KATHLEEN DALY. *James Wilson Morrice.* Toronto, 1966.

REID, DENNIS. *Our Own Country Canada: Being an Account of the National Aspirations of the Principal Landscape Artists in Montreal and Toronto 1860-1890.* Ottawa, 1979.

RENDER, LORNE. *The Mountains and the Sky.* Calgary, 1974.

ROBSON, A.H. *Canadian Landscape Painters.* Toronto, 1932.

ROPER, EDWARD. *By Track and Trail through Canada.* London, 1891.

TIPPETT, MARIA and DOUGLAS COLE. *From Desolation to Splendour: Changing Perceptions of the British Columbian Landscape.* Toronto, 1977.

TOWN, HAROLD and DAVID P. SILCOX. *Tom Thomson: The Silence and the Storm.* Toronto, 1982.

WARRE, HENRY. *Sketches of North America and the Oregon Territory.* London, 1848.

WISTOW, DAVID. *Tom Thomson and the Group of Seven.* Toronto, 1982.

11. THE LITERARY IMAGINATION
At The Mermaid Inn... Op.cit.

BOURINOT, JOHN. *Our Intellectual Strength and Weakness.* Montreal, 1893.

BROWN, E.K. *On Canadian Poetry.* Toronto, 1943.

CARMAN, BLISS. *Low Tide at Grand Pré. A Book of Lyrics.* New York, 1893.

DEWART, EDWARD HARTLEY. *Selections from Canadian Poets*. Montreal, 1864.

HALIBURTON, THOMAS CHANDLER. *The Attaché; or, Sam Slick in England*. London, 1843. *The Clockmaker; or, The Sayings and Doings of Sam Slick, of Slickville*. Halifax, 1836.

JAMESON, ANNA. *Op.cit.*

KLINCK, CARL F., ed. *Literary History of Canada*. 1st ed. Toronto 1965.

LAMPMAN, ARCHIBALD. *The Poems of Archibald Lampman*. Chosen with a Memoir by Duncan Campbell Scott. Toronto, 1900. 'Two Canadian Poets: A Lecture by Archibald Lampman', delivered in Ottawa, 19 Feb. 1891. Ed. E.K. Brown, *University Of Toronto Quarterly*, July 1944.

LANDOR, WALTER SAVAGE. *Poems*, Ed. Stephen Wheeler. London, 1914.

LEACOCK, STEPHEN. *Arcadian Adventures of the Idle Rich*. London, 1914. *Sunshine Sketches of a Little Town*. London, 1912.

LIGHTHALL, WILLIAM DOUW, ed. *Songs of the Great Dominion*. London, 1889.

McCULLOCH, THOMAS. *Letters of Mephibosheth Stepsure*. Halifax, 1862.

MARSDEN, JOSHUA. *Narrative of a Mission to Nova Scotia ...* Plymouth, 1816.

MILLS, PHOEBE, *Vesper Chimes*. Halifax, 1872.

MOODIE, SUSANNA. *Letters of a Lifetime. Roughing It in the Bush. Idem.*

PRESCOTT, HENRIETTA. *Poems, Written in Newfoundland*. London, 1839.

ROBERTS, CHARLES G.D. *In Divers Tones*. Boston, 1886. *Selected Poems of Sir Charles G.D. Roberts*. Toronto, 1936. *Songs of the Common Day*. Toronto, 1893. *The Kindred of the Wild: A Book of Animal Life*. Boston, 1902.

ROBERTS, MICHAEL. *T.E. Hulme*. London, 1938.

SCOTT, DUNCAN CAMPBELL. *The Green Cloister: Later Poems*. Toronto, 1926. *The Poems of Duncan Campbell Scott*. Toronto, 1926.

SETON, ERNEST THOMPSON. *Lives of the Hunted*. New York, 1901.

SMITH, GOLDWIN. *Reminiscences. Idem.*

STEAD, ROBERT J.C. *The Empire Builders and Other Poems*. Toronto, 1908.

Index

Aberdeen, Lady, 135
Accommodation, 198
Act of Union (1840), 65
Alaska Boundary Award, 103-4
Alexander, Sir J.E., 199-200
Allison, John and Susan Glennie, 43
American Federation of Labour, 80
Americans, Canadians compared with, 112
André, Father, 149
Anglicanism, 21, 22, 60, 91
Annett, Philip, 35-6
Arnold, Matthew, 242
Art Association of Montreal, 229
Aubert de Gaspé, Philippe, 180-1

Baldwin, Robert, 60, 65, 67-8
Baldwin, Dr William Warren, 60, 61
Balfour, Katherine Jane: *see* Ellice, Katherine
Ballantyne, R.M., 145-6
Baltzly, Benjamin, 227-8, 229
Barr, Rev. Isaac Moses, 45
Barr, Robert, 247
Barr colony, 45-6
Begbie, Matthew Baillie, 192, 193
Behn, Aphra, 139
Bell-Smith, Frederic Marlett, 237
Berton, Pierre; *Vimy*, 27; *Klondike*, 56
Bickersteth, John Burgon, 27
Bidwell, Barnabas, 60
Bidwell, Marshall Spring, 60
Bierstadt, Albert, 226
Binmore, E., 132
Blake, Edward, 95, 102, 229-30
Boer War, 107
Bompas, Bishop William, 150-1
Bonnycastle, Sir Richard, 174
Bourassa, Henri, 69, 106, 107, 108, 183-4
Bourinot, John, 249
Bowser Bill, 82
Brant, Joseph, 10, 140
Briggs, William, 246
British Colonist, Victoria, 97
British Columbia, 142-3, 150-1, 191-4, 208-9, 227-8, 232, 233, 234; class in, 41-3, 49-50; joins Canada, 98-9
Broadhead, William, 240
Brock, Sir Isaac, 1-3, 6-7, 90-1
Brown, E.K., 242
Brown, George, 69, 77, 102
Burns, John, 78
Butler, William Francis, 154-6, 208
By, William, 23

Bystander, The, 99, 100

Cabet, Étienne, 75
Campbell, Wilfred, 27, 116, 235
Canada and Its Provinces, 105-6
Canada Company, 23-4
Canada First, 3, 96, 97-102, 111, 261
Canadian Club, 105
Canadian Congress of Labour, 79
Canadian Labour Congress, 79
Canadian Labour Union, 79
Canadian Literary Magazine, 24
Canadian National Railways, 206
Canadian Northern Railway, 81, 206
Canadian Pacific Railway, 78, 206, 208; encouragement of landscape painting, 229, 231
Canadian Socialist, 85
Canadian Socialist League, 85, 86
Cannington Manor, 44-5
Carman, Bliss, 110, 261, 263-4
Carr, Emily, 238
Carter, John, 79
Cartier, George-Étienne, 67, 68
Château Clique, 21, 91
Chauveau, Pierre, 177, 179, 180
Cheadle, Dr Walter Butler, 154, 201, 220
Chinese in Canada, 190-4
Christie, Robert, 1
Class, 26-56, 78; in British Columbia, 41-3, 49-50; influence of the military, 46-56; in Hudson's Bay Company, 29-31; in Lower Canada, 33; in Quebec City, 40-1; in the West, 41-6; in Upper Canada, (rural) 34-9, (towns) 31-3. *See also* Barr colony, Cannington Manor, Walhachin.
Clergy Reserves, 60, 91
Cobbett, William, 211-12
Cockburn, James Pattison, 221-2
Colborne, Sir John, 92
Coleridge, Samuel Taylor, 213
Collings, Charles John, 239
Commercial union (with the US), 104
Concomly, Chief, 145
Confederation, 11-12, 98
Confederation Poets, 261-5
Connaught, Duke of, 205
Connor, Ralph (Charles W. Gordon), 110, 114-15, 245, 247, 249, 265-6
Co-operative Commonwealth Federation (CCF), 87
Copway, George, 165-6
Cozzens, Frederick S., 49

Craig, Sir John, 5
Cran, Marion Dudley: *A Woman of Canada*, 127
Crawford, Isabella Valancy, 160-1; 'Said the Canoe', 161; *Malcolm's Katie*, 214-15
Crémazie, Octave, 180
Crowe, Joseph, 52-3
Crowfoot, 162-3
Cullen, Maurice, 235

Dalhousie, Lord, 48
Dallas, Alexander Grant, 118
Dalton, Thomas, 91
David, Laurent-Oliver, 69
Davies, Thomas, 215, 221
Davis, Robert, 37
DeCelles, A.-D., 69
de Cosmos, Amor, 2, 96-7, 99, 184, 193
De Leon, Daniel, 85
De Mille, James, 75, 110, 245
Denison, George Taylor Sr, 3, 4, 53
Denison, George Taylor Jr: and Canada First, 98, 104, 105, 106, 111
Denison, Septimus Julius Augustus, 107
Dent, John Charles, 67
Desjardins, Alphonse, 182
Detroit, 6
Dewart, Edward Hartley, 242, 244-5
Dewdney, Edward, 43
Donnelly family, 173
Doughty, Arthur, G., 106
Douglas, Amelia, 121
Douglas, Governor James, 42, 121
Doukhobors, 76, 188-90
Dryden, John, 139
Dufferin, Lady, 77-8, 151
Dumont, Gabriel, 54, 73, 74, 149, 154
Duncan, Norman, 110
Duncan, Sara Jeannette, 39, 94-5, 110, 131-2, 167, 249; *The Imperialist*, 39, 94-5, 110
Duncan, William, 76, 142-3, 150-2, 170
Dunlop, William 'Tiger', 2, 23-4, 93; *Statistical Sketches*, 24
Durham, Lord, 11, 33-4, 50-1, 64-5, 197; *Report*, 33-4, 50-1, 64, 65, 66, 99, 108-9, 175, 176, 178

Eaton, Timothy, 78
Edson, Allan, 226, 235
Elgin, Lord, 57-8, 65, 176
Ellice, Edward, 174-5, 197
Ellice, Katherine Jane (Balfour), 174-5
Elmsley, John and Mary, 32
Engels, Friedrich, 109, 111, 139
Evans, James, 146-7

Family Compact, 21, 28, 32, 39, 91, 93
Fleming, May Agnes, 110, 245

Fleming, Sandford, 118, 216, 220, 227
Foster, William A., 98, 100
Fourier, Charles, 75
Fraser, John A., 226, 231, 237
Fréchette, Louis, 180-1
French, Col. John, 54
French Canadians, 175-7; French- *v.* English-speaking Canadians, 169, 173-84; nationalism, 177-9
Frontenac, comte de, 18, 199
Frye, Northrop, 211
Fur trade, 11, 23, 145

Gapper, Mary: *see* O'Brien, Mary
Gapper, Mary, sister-in-law of Mary O'Brien, 123
Garneau, François-Xavier, 178-9
Garry, Nicholas, 120-1
George, Henry, 83, 84
Gérin-Lajoie, Antoine, 179-80
Giraud, Marcel, 73-4
Glennie, Thomas, family of, 42
Globe, Toronto, 102, 104
Goldsmith, Oliver, 212-13, 244
Gompers, Samuel, 86
Gordon, Charles W.: *see* Connor, Ralph
Grand Trunk Railway, 206
Grant, George Monro, 83, 105, 106, 118-19, 133-4, 152, 153, 191, 200, 209-10, 217, 220, 227; *Ocean to Ocean*, 118-19, 153, 191, 200, 209-10, 217
Grant, Walter Colquhoun, 42
Grey, Charles, 197
Grey, Henry, 202
Griffith, W.L., 187
Grip Limited, 239, 240
Group of Seven, 236, 238-41

Haliburton, Robert Grant, 98, 102, 111
Haliburton, Thomas Chandler, 5, 57, 94, 96, 249-7; *Sam Slick*, 57, 94, 249-54
Halifax, (in 1814) 13, 18, (in 1818-30) 20
Hall, Francis, 18-19
Hamilton Spectator, 78
Hammond, John, 235
Harmon, Daniel, 121, 144-5
Harper, J. Russell, 239
Harris, Lawren, 239-40
Hassell, John, 221
Hawthornthwaite, J.H., 86
Head, Sir Francis Bond, 22-9, 51, 61, 62, 92
Hearne, Samuel, 119, 144
Heavysege, Charles, 244, 249
Helmcken, Dr J.A.S., 42, 193
Henday, Anthony, 144
Heriot, George, 221
Hill, Joe, 81

Hind, Henry Youle, 156-8, 196-7, 216-17, 220, 225-6
Hind, William G.R., 225, 226
Hobson, J.A., 208-9
Hocquart, Gilles, 117
Hoodless, Adelaide, 134-5
Hopwood, Victor, 243-4
Horetsky, Charles, 227, 228-9
Howe, Joseph, 12, 48-9, 57, 65, 105, 205
Howells, William Dean, 110
Howison, John, 20, 122
Hudson's Bay Company, 29-30, 72, 145, 222
Hulme, T.E., 248
Hungtingdon, Father J.O.S., 83-4

Immigration, 34-9, 173, 185-95; of Chinese, 190-4; of Doukhobors, 188-90; of Europeans, 185-6; of Icelanders, 185; of Japanese, 191-2; of Mennonites, 185-6; of Sikhs, 194; of Ukrainians, 186, 188; to the US, 109-110; to the West, 42, 56, 185; to Upper Canada, 34-9, 170-2
Imperial Order Daughters of the Empire, 105
Imperialism, 95, 105-8, 110, 113
Indians, 10-11, 138-67; and fur trade, 143-6; and missionaries, 147-52; Chippewa, 142, 165; Cree, 157; cruelty of, 140-2; literature, 138, 160-2; Kane's paintings of, 158-9; Micmac, 158-9; Ojibway, 165; oral expression and writing, 162-7; Plains, 141-2, 147-8; rights, 152-3; treaties, 152-3; romantic view of, 136-40; West Coast, 142, 143, 164-5
Industrial Workers of the World, 81-82

Jackson, A.Y., 239, 240-1
Jackson, W.H., 81
Jacobi, Otto, 226
Jacques and Hay, 77
James, Henry, 110
Jameson, Anna, 37, 46-7, 61, 91-2, 116, 244; on Indians, 153-4; on the militia, 46-7; on women, 115; Winter Studies, 46-7, 61, 92, 115, 126, 153-4, 198, 213-14
Jameson, Robert, 91-2
Jaxon, Honoré J.: see Jackson, W.H.
Jefferys, C.W., 239
Johnson, Pauline, 167
Jones, Henry, 74-5
Jones, Peter, 165, 166-7

Kane, Paul, 142, 158-9, 220, 221, 223-5
Keefer, Thomas Coltrin, 204
Kelsey, Henry, 144
King, Basil, 110
King, William Lyon Mackenzie, 69

Klondike Gold Rush, 55, 56
Knights of Labour, 79, 80, 83
Komagata Maru, 194
Kropotkin, Peter, 188
Kurikka, Matti, 75-6

Labour Advocate, 82-3
Lafontaine, Louis-Hippolyte, 65, 67, 68, 179
Lalemant, Jérome, 140
Lampman, Archibald, 27-8, 234-5, 243, 245, 261, 266; 'Late November', 261-2; 'To a Millionaire', 28; 'Winter Uplands', 262
Land, the: transportation, 196-219; views of, 208-19, 224-41
Land development, 23
Langford, Edward Edwards, 42
Langton, Anne, 123, 213
Laurier, Sir Wilfrid, 94, 103-4, 106, 107, 182, 183, 194
Latham, David, 203
Leacock, Stephen, 27, 254; Arcadian Adventures, 27; Sunshine Sketches, 255
Leathes, Sonia, 136
Lepine, L.A., 84
LeSueur, W.D., 69
Levinge, R.G.A., 158
Lighthall, W.D., 243
Lindsey, Charles, 69
Lindsey, G.G.S., 69
Literature, 2-3, 28, 243-66; Aubert de Gaspé, 180-1; Barr, 247; Campbell, 27, 116, 235; Carman, 110, 261, 263-4; Connor, 110, 114-15, 245, 247, 249, 256-7; Crawford, 160-1, 214-15; Crémazie, 180; De Mille, 75, 110, 245; Dewart, 242, 244-5; Duncan, N., 110; Duncan, S.J., 39, 95, 110, 131-2, 167, 249; Fleming, 110, 245; irony, 256-7; Fréchette, 180-1; Garneau, 178-9; Gérin-Lajoie, 179-80; Goldsmith, 212-13, 244; Haliburton, 5, 57, 94, 249-54; Heavysege, 244, 249; Johnson, 167; King, 110; McClung, 131, 135, 137, 207-8; McCulloch, 250-2, 253, 256, 257; McDougall, 147-9; Machar, 27, 84; Mair, 3, 4, 160, 218-19; Montgomery, 116, 129, 131, 265; Moodie, 35, 59, 126-7, 245-6; Nelligan, 181; O'Grady, 203; Parker, 114, 245; Richardson, 2, 3, 24-5, 110, 115, 138-9, 159-60; Roberts, 88, 101, 110-11, 180, 218, 243, 257, 259-60, 261, 262-3; Sangster, 2-3, 202-3, 244; satire, 249-57; Scott, D.C., 27, 161-2, 234-5, 245, 261, 264-5; Seton, 110, 257-9; Sellar, 36; Stead, 207, 248; Stringer, 247-8; Traill, 36, 38-9, 125, 246
Literary activities, 24, 39, 110, 134

Literary Garland, 24
Lizars, Robina and Kathleen, 37
Lloyd, Rev. Exton, 45
Lorne, Marquis of, 229
Lount, Samuel, death of, 21, 66
Lowe, John, 185
Lower, A.R., 4
Lower Canada, 58, 64, 66-7, 92, 175
Loyalists, settlements of, 10

Macauley, Ann, 124
McBride, Richard, 191-2
McClung, Nellie, 131, 135, 137; *Clearing in the West*, 124-5, 127, 128, 207-8
McCulloch, Thomas, 250-2, 253, 256, 257
McDonald, Archibald, 30, 145
MacDonald, J.E.H., 239-40
Macdonald, Sir John A., 3, 77, 79, 80, 94, 102, 103, 106, 111, 191, 230, 261
McDougall, Colonel, 52
McDougall, George Millward, 147-9
McDougall, John, 147
MacFie, Rev. Matthew, 192-3
McGee, Thomas D'Arcy, 26-7, 168-9, 246-7
McGregor, Gaile, 115, 116
McGregor, John, 19-20
Machar, Agnes Maule, 27, 84
McKay, Joseph William, 30
Mackenzie, Alexander, 28, 102
Mackenzie, William Lyon, 21, 22, 58-60, 61-4, 65, 66, 68-9, 91, 92, 96, 169, 199
McLean, John, 31
MacLennan, Hugh, 176
McMillan, James, 122
MacNab, Sir Allan, 21, 204-5
Macoun, James Melville, 217
Macphail, Andrew: *The Master's Wife*, 125-6
McTavish, John George, 121
Mair, Charles, 3, 4, 97-8, 99-100, 102, 108, 160, 218, 261; 'August', 218; *Dreamland*, 3, 4; *Tecumseh*, 3, 4, 160, 218-19
Makers of Canada, 106
Manitoba Act (1870), 72
Marryat, Frederick, 112
Marsden, Joshua, 248-9, 257
Martin, Thomas Mower, 231-2
Marxism, 84, 86, 87
Mathews, Peter: death of, 21, 66
Matonabee, 119
Matisse, Henri, 231, 236
Maud, Aylmer, 188
Maugham, Somerset, 231
Mavor, James, 188, 189
Mawedopenais, 162
Maxwell, Upper Canada, 74, 75
Mercier, Honoré, 181, 183, 184
Merritt, William Hamilton, 23
Metlakalta, B.C., 76, 150-1

Methodism, 61, 92
Methodist Book and Publishing House, Toronto, 246
Métis, 11, 54, 70-4, 99, 119, 145, 149-50, 154; rebellions, 70-4, 112
Middleton, General Frederick, 51, 73
Mills, Phoebe, 244
Milne, David, 238
Milton, Viscount, 154, 201, 220
Minto, Lord, 112
Mitchell, Elizabeth: *Western Canada Before the War*, 128
Molson, John, 198
Monck, Frances (Feo), 40-1, 48, 101, 128, 201, 215
Montgomery, Lucy Maud, 116, 129, 131, 265
Montreal, (in 1814) 19, (in 1820s) 19-20
Moodie, Dunbar, 37, 59, 93
Moodie, Susanna, 20, 170, 205; class-consciousness of, 35, 93, 245; on Rebellion of 1837, 59, 66; *Roughing It in the Bush*, 35, 59, 126-7, 129, 245-6, 249
Moorsman, William, 20
Morice, Father A.G., 147
Morrice, James Wilson, 230-1, 235
Morris, Alexander, 162
Morris, Jan, 209
Morris, William, 226
Mountain, Bishop Jacob, 91
Morgan, Henry J., 97
Muir, Alexander, 107

Nanaimo, B.C., strike in, 81-2
Nation, The, 94, 101, 102
National Policy, 102-3, 111
Nationalism, 95, 96, 102, 103, 105-8, 111, 113; French-Canadian, 107-8
Nelligan, Émile, 181
Nelson, Robert, 22, 64, 65-6, 67
Nelson, Wolfred, 22, 66, 68
Nevers, Edmond de, 177-8
New Brunswick, 11-12, 13, 18
New Democratic Party (NDP), 87
Newfoundland, 6, 12, 13
North West Company, 5, 29, 163
North West Mounted Police, 53-6, 207
North West Rebellion, 51, 71, 73
Notman, William, 226, 227
Nova Scotia, 11-12, 13, 14, 15
Noyes, John Humphrey, 75

O'Brien, Lucius, 19, 232-4, 237
O'Brien, Mary, 19, 123-4, 141, 201
O'Donohue, P.J., 84
O'Grady, Standish, 203
Onderdonk, Andrew, 191
Ontario Workman, 78
Orange Order, 100, 173

Oregon Boundary Treaty, 5
Otter, William, 52
Owen, Robert, 74, 75, 80

Pacific Scandal, 102
Painting, 221-41; Carr, 238; Cockburn,
   221-2; Cullen, 235; Edson, 226, 235;
   Fraser, 226, 231, 237; Group of Seven,
   236, 238-41; Harris, 239-40; Heriot, 221;
   Hind, 225, 226; Jackson, 239, 240-1;
   Jacobi, 226; Jefferys, 239; Kane, 158-9,
   220, 221, 223-5; MacDonald, 239-40;
   Martin, 231, 232; Milne, 238; Morrice,
   230-1, 235; O'Brien, 232-4, 237;
   Rindisbacher, 138, 222; Thomson, 240-1;
   Walker, 236-7; Warre, 223; Watson,
   237-8
Palladium of Labour, 79, 82
Papineau, Louis-Joseph, 21-3, 66, 68-9, 96,
   179, 183
Parker, Gilbert, 114, 245
Parkin, George, 105
Pequis, Chief, 163
Phelps, Minnie, 132
Photography, 226-9; Notman, 226; Baltzly,
   227-8; Horetsky, 228-9
Piapot, Chief, 163
Picturesque Canada, 232-3
Pierce, Edward Michell, 44
Pilot, The, Montreal, 96
Population, ethnic mix of, 169, 172, 187
Porter, John: *Vertical Mosaic*, 28
Powell, I.W., 151
Pratt, E.J., 181
Prescott, Henrietta, 244
Prevost, Sir George, 5
Province of Canada, 65, 68, 96
Publishing, 245-7
Puttee, A.W., 84, 85, 87

Quebec (province), 13-14; French- *v.*
   English-speaking Canadians, 173-84
Quebec City, 19, 88
Queenston Heights, Battle of, 21

Racism, 108
Rae, Dr John, 145
Rebellion Losses Act, 57-8
Rebellions of 1837-8, 21, 22, 58-64, 65-6,
   69-70; in Lower Canada, 58, 64, 66-7,
   92, 175; in Upper Canada, 58-64, 65-6,
   92; results of amnesty, 66-9
Red River Rebellion, 71-2, 73, 98, 99
Red River Settlement, 11, 14, 163
Reform, 22, 57-87, 92; compared with
   revolution, 58; in Lower Canada, 64; in
   Nova Scotia, 65; in Upper Canada, 60-5;
   responsible government, 65
Regional differences, 13-15

Responsible government, 65
Revolutionary and non-r. societies
   compared, 58, 88-9
Richardson, John, 2, 24-5, 110, 159-60;
   Canadian Brothers, 2, 24, 25, 110, 138-9;
   Hardscrabble, 24, 139n.; *Maud
   Montgomerie*; 110; *Monk Knight of St John*,
   24; *Tecumseh*, 2, 3, 160; *Wacousta*, 2, 24,
   115, 138
Rideau Canal, 18, 23; strike on, 76
Riel, Louis, 71, 72, 73, 74, 99-100; in Red
   River Rebellion, 71, 72, 181; in North
   West Rebellion, 73, 181-2; response to
   death of, 181-3
Rindisbacher, Peter, 138, 222
Roberts, Captain Charles, 6
Roberts, Charles G.D., 88, 101, 110-11,
   180, 218, 243, 257, 258, 259-60, 261,
   262-3; *Kindred of the Wild*, 257; 'The
   Morning', 263; *Orion*, 261; 'Tantramar
   Revisited', 262-3; 'Watchers of the
   Swamp', 259-60
Robertson, Colin, 121-2
Robertson, John Ross, 100
Robinson, John Beverley, 21-2, 51, 61, 66,
   92, 96; description of, 93
Rolph, John, 60, 61, 68
Rose, George McLean, 247
Ross, Alexander, 70-1
Ross, Malcolm, 261
Rousseau, Jean Jacques, 139
Rowe, Arthur H., 79
Royal Canadian Mounted Police, 76; *see
   also* North West Mounted Police
Royal Canadian Navy, 80
Royal Military Academy, Woolwich, 221
Ryerson, Egerton, 21, 22, 61, 65, 66, 132,
   133
Ryerson, George, 21
Ryerson, John, 66
Ryerson, Joseph, 21

Salaberry, Charles Michel d'Irumberry de,
   5, 6, 22
Sangster, Charles, 2-3, 244; 'Brock', 2-3;
   'St Lawrence and the Saguenay', 202-3
Saunders, Marshall, 110
Schoolcraft, Henry, 153, 164
Schultz, Dr John Christian, 72, 99-100
Scott, Duncan Campbell, 27, 161-2, 234-5,
   245, 261, 264-5; 'At Gull Lake', 264-5;
   'The Forsaken', 161-2
Scott, F.R., 184
Scott, Thomas, 72, 140
Seton, Ernest Thompson, 110, 257-9; 'Red
   Ruff', 258-9
Shirreff, Patrick, 171
Selkirk, Lord, 5, 72, 121, 163
Sellar, Robert, 36

Shanadithit, Nancy, 164
Shortt, Adam, 106
Short, Elizabeth, 133
Siegfried, André, 64, 112-13, 175-6
Sifton, Clifford, 186, 187, 189-90, 229
Sikhs, 194
Simcoe, John Graves, 32, 34, 92
Simpson, Frances (Mrs George), 122
Simpson, Governor George, 30, 120-1, 122, 146, 159, 197-8
Smith, Goldwin, 33, 39, 50, 84, 94, 99, 100-1, 104, 105, 111, 152-3, 176-7; *Canada and the Canada Question*, 33, 39, 50, 104; *The Week*, 84, 100-2, 243, 261
Smith, Michael, 4
Smith, Ralph, 84
Smith, William Alexander: see de Cosmos, Amor
Social Democratic Party, 87
Socialism, 74-87; Socialist Party of Canada/B.C., 85ff.; strikes, 76; unions, 76-83; Winnipeg General Strike, 74
Socialist Party of Canada/B.C., 85, 86, 87
Sointula, B.C., 75-6
Southesk, Earl of, 154, 214, 230
Sproule, J.C., 187
Stead, Robert J.C., 207, 248; *Homesteaders*, 207
Steele, Colonel Sam, 54, 55
Stowe, Emily, 133, 134
Strachan, John, 21, 22, 32, 89-90, 91, 92, 93, 94, 170-1
Strickland, Thomas, 37
Stringer, Arthur, 247-8
Sulerzhitsky, Leapold, 188-9, 190
Sweet Grass, Chief, 162
Swiftsure, 198-9

Talbot, Edward Allen, 20
Talbot, Thomas, 23, 34
Tardival, Jules-Paul, 178
Tarte, Israel, 182
Tecumseh, 1, 2, 6, 90, 138-40, 160
Thibault, Father, 139
Thompson, David, 11, 144
Thompson, Thomas Phillips, 82-3, 86
Thomson, Tom, 240-1
Thoreau, Henry David, 89
Tolstoy, Leo, 188
Toryism, 22, 88-113
Trades and Labour Congress, 79, 80, 83, 84
Traill, Catharine Parr, 36, 38, 39, 38-9, 125, 246; *Backwoods of Canada*, 36, 38, 39; *Canadian Settler's Guide*, 123, 126, 141; *Female Emigrant's Guide*, 126
Traill, Thomas, 37

Transportation, 1, 17, 18, 23; canals, 199-200; canoe brigades, 197-8; Red River carts, 200; steamboats, 198-9, 200-2; railways, 203-8
Trollope, Anthony, 109
Trudel, François-Xavier, 182

Unions, 76-83, 86; Canadian Congress of Labour, 79; Canadian Labour Congress, 79; craft, 76-7; IWW, 81, 82; Knights of Labour, 79, 80, 83; legalization of, 79; strikes, 80, 81-2; Trades and Labour Congress, 79, 80
United States, 7-8; migrations to, 109-10; union with, 111. *See also* Americans, War of 1812
Upper Canada, 13; in 1818, 18-19, 31-3, 34-9, 58-64, 65-6, 92, 170-2

Vancouver, B.C., 208-9
Van Horne, William, 229, 230-1, 234
Victoria, Queen, influence of, 116-17
Victoria, B.C., 49-50, 97, 142, 191
Voice, The, 85, 87
Voltaire, 139

Walhachin, 44-5
Walker, Horatio, 236-7
War of 1812-14, 1-15
Warre, Henry, 223
Warren, Josiah, 75
Watson, Homer, 237-8
Week, The, 84, 100-2, 243, 261
Welland Canal, 18, 23; strikes on, 76
West, Rev. John, 120, 121
Whitton, Henry Buckingham, 77-8
Wilde, Oscar, 237
Williams, Parker, 86
Wilson, Lieut. Charles, 49-50
Wilson, Ethel: *Innocent Traveller*, 209
Wilson, William, 164
Winnipeg General Strike, 74
Women: and temperance, 135; doctors, 133; domestics, 130; earnings, 129-30, 132; *habitant*, 122; immigration to B.C., 118; Indian, 119-20; in industry, 130-1, 132; in the West, 121-3; lawyers, 134; *les filles du roi*, 117; organizations, 134-5; pioneer, 122-8; rights, 135-6; suffrage, 136-7; teachers, 131-3; upper-class, 128-9; writers, 131-2
Women's Institutes, 134-5
Woodsworth, J.S., 84, 187
Wrigley, George, 85

York (Toronto), 19, 31-3
Yukon Field Force, 56